D0207868

ARTIST AND PATRON IN
POSTWAR JAPAN

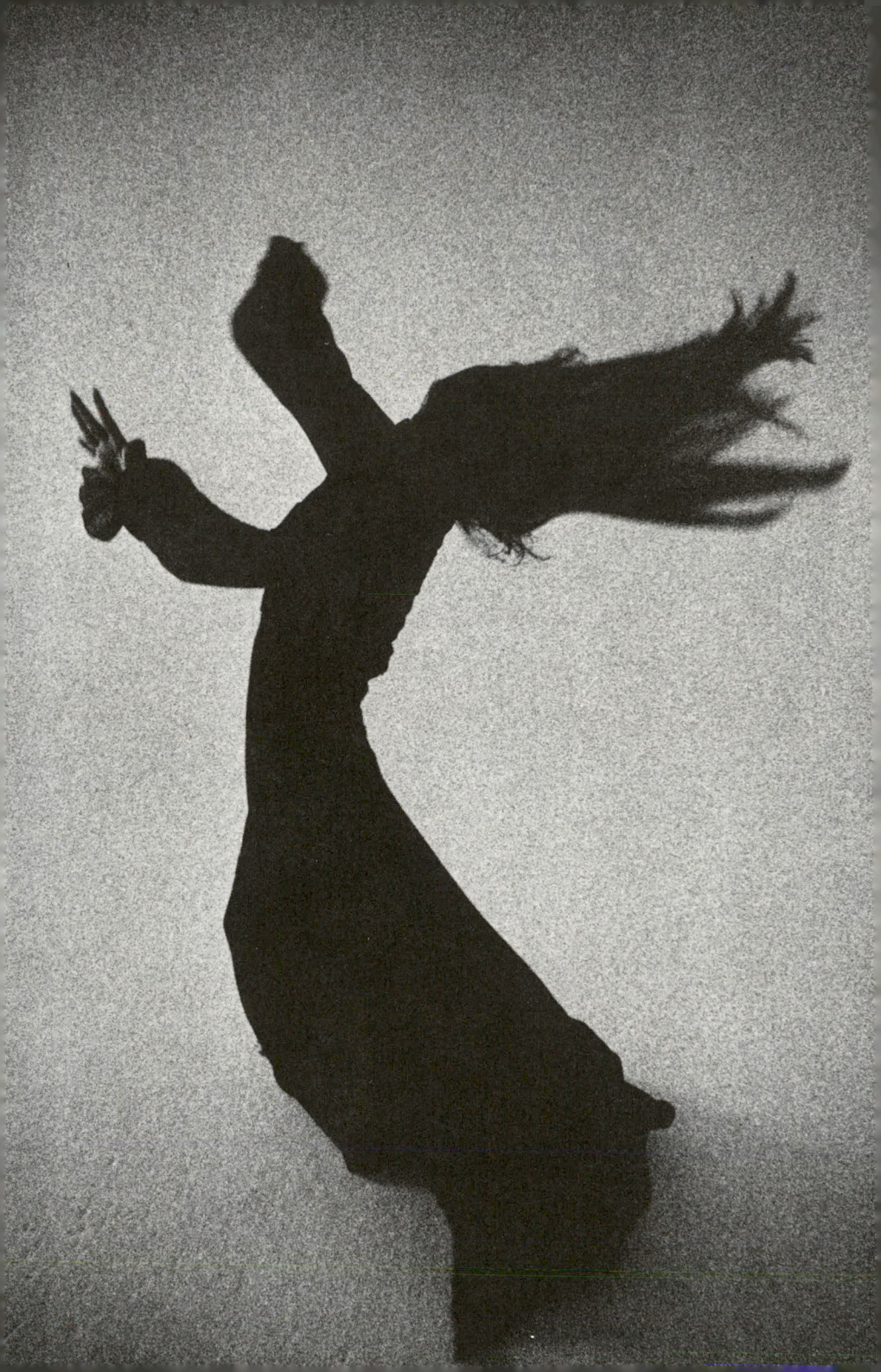

THOMAS R. H. HAVENS

Artist and Patron in Postwar Japan

Dance, Music, Theater, and
the Visual Arts, 1955-1980

PRINCETON UNIVERSITY PRESS

Copyright © 1982 by Princeton University Press
Published by Princeton University Press, 41 William Street,
Princeton, New Jersey
In the United Kingdom: Princeton University Press,
Guildford, Surrey

All Rights Reserved
Library of Congress Cataloging in Publication Data will be
found on the last printed page of this book

This book has been composed in Linotron Sabon

Clothbound editions of Princeton University Press books
are printed on acid-free paper, and binding materials are
chosen for strength and durability

Printed in the United States of America by
Princeton University Press,
Princeton, New Jersey

Frontispiece: Akiko Kanda in *Barbara*, premiere June 1980, Tokyo.
KISHIN SHINOYAMA

CONTENTS

A NOTE OF THANKS

FRESH from a twenty-four-hour flight on a piston-engine DC-6 from Los Angeles, with stops at Honolulu and Wake Island, I arrived for my first immersion in Japanese society ten days after the tumultuous demonstrations against the Japan-U.S. security treaty quieted down in June 1960. My earliest encounter with the Japanese arts came the next Tuesday morning when I met my first class of conversational English students, a sleepy-eyed group of young geisha at the Hasegawa Teahouse in Tokyo's Akasaka district. What has happened to the arts and Japanese society in the two decades since that memorable summer job is the main focus of this book, and it seems in order to express my thanks to the Princeton Club of Japan and the Ōsawa family for making my first visit so rewarding.

In preparing this introduction to the postwar social history of the arts in Japan, I have benefited from the kind help of many friends. I am especially indebted to Kawahara Hiroshi for generous hospitality during 1980-1981 when I was a visiting fellow at Waseda University. The following persons in Japan also kindly aided my studies: Akimoto Ritsuo, Isamu and Kazuko Amemiya, William Crocker, Vanessa Geiger, Gyōten Tomoo, the late Kenneth E. Heim, Ishibashi Fusako, and Tasaka Hiroshi.

For advice about my work, I am particularly grateful to James R. Brandon, Delmer M. Brown, Liza Crihfield Dalby, David G. Goodman, Marius B. Jansen, Donald Keene, Bruce H. Kirmmse, Joyce Malm, Henry DeW. Smith, II, Kent C. Smith, and Valdo H. Viglielmo. William P. Malm, Nancy R. Pettengill, and D. Eleanor Westney kindly read the entire text and offered timely advice.

Much of the information in this volume is based on interviews, mainly conducted during 1980-1981, with persons who are well informed about the arts in Japan. Without exception the individuals listed among the sources at the back of the book answered my questions with candor and courtesy, and I am grateful to them all for their cheerful cooperation in mapping an uncharted topic. I am especially indebted to Adachi Kenji, Hara Toshio, Honda Shingo, Inumaru Tadashi, Akiko Kanda, Dennis and Keiko Keene, Walter Nichols, Nobumoto Yasusada, Ōkawa Takeo, Donald Richie, Amaury Saint-Gilles, Tachikawa Ruriko, Tsuji Yutaka, Yano Tomomitsu, Yokoyama Tadashi, and Yoshii Chōzō.

The directors and staffs of the following libraries provided generous help with research materials: National Diet Library, Tokyo; Waseda University Library, including the Tsubouchi Memorial Theatre Museum; Connecticut College Library, especially Helen Aitner.

I am very grateful to R. Miriam Brokaw, William Hively, and the staff of Princeton University Press for providing their customary expert editorial and production care.

The editors of *Dance Research Journal* have given permission to reprint parts of my article, "Rebellion and Expression in Contemporary Japanese Dance," *Dance as Cultural Heritage: Selected Papers from the ADG/CORD Conference 1978, CORD Dance Research Annual XIV*, New York, Congress on Research in Dance, 1982.

Funds from the John Simon Guggenheim Memorial Foundation, the Japan Foundation, and the History Gift Fund established by an anonymous alumna of Connecticut College speeded my studies, and I am grateful to each of these sources for generous assistance.

Finally, I acknowledge the indulgence of readers in accepting a few stylistic conventions. Japanese surnames precede personal names, except in citations of most Western-language publications by Japanese authors and except for the names of a few Japanese artists, such as Seiji Ozawa, who have become well known abroad. Discursive notes appear at the foot of the page; bibliographic notes are gathered following the last chapter. Japanese-language titles of organizations mentioned in the text are listed in the index. Terms commonly employed in writing about the arts, such as "traditional," "modern," or "serious" (as in "serious music"), are used as conventions despite their lack of precision. For converting yen to U.S. dollars, one dollar is reckoned as 360 yen during 1945-1971, 300 yen during 1972-1976, 250 yen in 1977, 220 yen during 1978-1979, and 200 yen in 1980. Whenever possible, changes across time in expenditures on the arts are expressed as percentage changes in yen terms, to eliminate the effects of differing currency conversion rates. In principle, all information is current as of the 1980-1981 arts season and the Japanese fiscal year 1980, ending March 31, 1981.

Shimotakaido, June 1981

ARTIST AND PATRON IN POSTWAR JAPAN

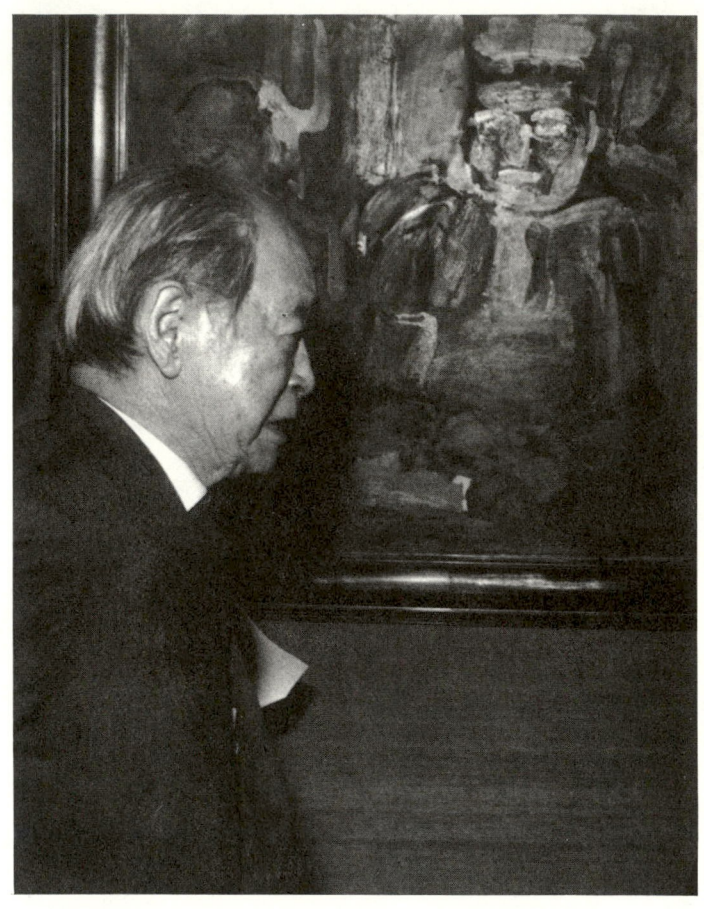

Umehara Ryūzaburō, Japan's richest painter,
attends a Ginza gallery opening in February 1980
at age 93. YOSHII GALLERIES

CHAPTER I

Art for Society's Sake

"THESE are nonsense pictures," shouted a young Tokyo artist late one afternoon in November 1980. "They are worthless junk!" With a meter-long pipe, Yamashita Kaname systematically slashed thirty-seven works by Umehara Ryūzaburō and other leading Japanese painters at the Tokyo National Museum of Modern Art; he managed to rip three million dollars' worth of oils and watercolors before he was stopped. "I want to become a famous artist," he told the security officers who seized him. "Umehara's paintings are nothing but coloring-book drawings." Why did people consider the twenty-three Umeharas he had just gashed so valuable, the attacker wondered, when his own impressionist works that had once won him a prize in Osaka were shunned in Tokyo?

The criminal pleaded guilty the next January, and curators assured the court that the damage would be repaired.[1] This Cromwellian episode raised questions about art in contemporary Japanese life that were seldom discussed during the comfortable 1960s and 1970s: Is there an accredited view of culture, maintained by an establishment of arts officials, in or out of government? What value does society place on the artist's work: the expression of beauty, the interpretation of timeless human emotions, and criticism of the surroundings? How—and how well—do the Japanese support and reward their artists?

Now so well as one might expect, according to Seiji Ozawa, the most internationally recognized Japanese artist of the 1970s: "one of the defects of Japanese society is that ordinary citizens do not feel proud of the arts and contribute to them."[2] It is true that individuals rarely make gifts directly to art institutions in Japan, nor do foundations or corporations take up

3

much of the slack. During the seventies the national government increased its appropriations to modern performing-arts groups, but by the end of the decade the subsidies for fresh works still amounted to just $5.7 million.[3] As of 1980 the official Agency for Cultural Affairs devoted 40 percent of its total budget of $200.12 million to the arts as a whole; most of the rest was used for historical preservation, protecting important cultural assets, and related programs. Prefectural and municipal bodies each made proportionately smaller provisions for the arts.

These modest but hardly insignificant figures offer only a hint of the true scope and variety of the arts in Japan today. Although direct patronage in the form of subsidies is still underdeveloped, market support for nearly every genre is very substantial. Serious music, dance, theater, and the visual arts in Japan are overwhelmingly commercial: they are mostly financed by income earned from ticket sales, advertising, recording, radio and television, the sale of products and services, and revenues from professional instruction.[a] This is equally true for the traditional performing arts, which are just as marketable as the modern genres introduced from Europe during the past century. And it is also true for the more popular forms of art.

For perhaps as long as any other nation, Japan has had a thriving popular culture. Even in so prosperous and media-saturated a society as contemporary Japan, higher culture and popular culture have not become indistinguishable; there is much vitality and satisfaction in each. Whether the nonprofit, higher-culture sector is still elitist, as it once was, seems doubtful. If elitist means achieving excellence and populist means providing access, to borrow the formula of Livingston L. Biddle, Jr., the postwar Japanese arts have almost certainly become both.[4] Now that 90 percent of the population considers

[a] Dick Netzer estimates that 85 percent of the arts sector in the United States is commercially financed. Netzer, *The Subsidized Muse: Public Support of the Arts in the United States*, New York, Cambridge University Press, 1978, p. 12.

4

itself middle class, a huge audience exists for the arts in the broadest sense—popular and higher, live and recorded, verbal and nonverbal, literary as well as plastic and performed arts. Cultural life in the form of attendance or participation in an art activity has grown more diversified and more widely diffused throughout the country during the past thirty years than at any time in Japan's history.

The pages that follow offer an introduction to the social history of the arts in postwar Japan, mainly painting, sculpture, print making, and the live performing arts, both traditional and modern. The focus is on the relatively narrow nonprofit portion of the total industry where the greatest risks, both of innovation and revival, are taken in the name of art. A great deal of interesting art lies outside this focus, but the genres treated here are useful prisms for refracting the modern experience of the arts in Japanese culture as a whole.

The aim is to show how and why the Japanese have supported the arts, especially those that are the most commercially precarious, during the period from the mid-1950s to 1980. The mid-fifties seem a useful starting point for several reasons. The economy regained its prewar level of output in 1955 and began to grow, almost without pause, at an average rate in real terms of 11 percent a year until the world oil crisis in 1973. (From 1973 to 1980 Japan continued to outperform the other main industrial economies.) The first all-new stage for modern drama, the Haiyūza, opened in Tokyo in April 1954 and initiated a new phase in Western-style theater in Japan. The contemporary era in dance dates precisely from Martha Graham's visit to Japan in November 1955, and the following year was the first major exhibit that presented Japanese artists side by side with their counterparts from abroad. The mid-1950s also mark the beginnings of the postwar arts establishment, an informal but very tangible system that has rewarded those who succeed by its rules but frustrated others, such as the painting slasher Yamashita.

This inquiry into the social nature of art is not meant to be an essay in art criticism, although interpretive remarks are sprinkled here and there. In thinking about art and life in contemporary Japan, it is worth remembering W. H. Auden's observation that the historian of society can say why Shakespeare's poetry is different from Browning's but not why it is better. Without seeking esthetic judgments, readers of history are invited to consider the place of art in postwar Japan, confident that they can "look for social meaning without soiling the face of beauty."[5]

THE COMPASS OF MIDDLE-CLASS CULTURE

If the philosopher Suzanne Langer is correct that "all art is the creation of perceptible forms expressive of human feelings,"[6] astonishingly diverse forms of expression, reflecting people's esthetic and emotional needs at various levels of taste, have appeared in Japan since World War Two. Statistics are scarce, but there is no doubt that the arts sector in the widest sense has generally flourished, although not uniformly for each of its components, during the past three decades.

The visual and performing arts as gainful occupations underwent a considerable transformation after the mid-1950s. Today there are about 30,000 professional visual artists in Japan, double the number in 1955,[b] and there are another 170,000 amateurs who produce art objects for exhibition.[7] Only a few hundred artists, at best, make a living exclusively from selling their works. Nearly all those who are considered professionals have side jobs in teaching, commercial design, advertising, or the other commercial mass media. About 1,000 sculptors currently turn out works for sale, of whom Iino Kiichi, president of the Contemporary Sculpture Center in Tokyo, considers only thirty "true professionals."[8] Many thousands of persons produce prints, but only 500 or 600 of them regard print making as their main occupation.[9] Perhaps

[b] The figure excludes 40,000 class A architects (1973). See Noboru Kawazoe, *Contemporary Japanese Architecture*, trans. by David Griffith, Tokyo, Kokusai Kōryū Kikin, 2nd ed., 1973, p. 15; Robin Boyd, *New Directions in Japanese Architecture*, New York, George Braziller, 1968, p. 31.

2,500 professionals create calligraphy and another 3,500 work at crafts. Many people in Japan, as elsewhere, use more than one medium, but most of the country's visual artists are painters—more than 20,000 of them classed as professionals—who produce for a domestic art market estimated in 1980 at $750 million.[c] About half of them paint in the modern Western style, with oils and other contemporary materials, and the other half work in the Japanese style, mainly using watercolors but also ink.[10] But the distinction between Western and Japanese styles has become one basically of artistic factions since World War Two. In theme and technique the two are often indistinguishable, and between them Japan has been producing more paintings than any other country for at least twenty years.[11]

Not even dealers are sure how many persons buy and sell art for a living in Japan, but a good guess is that there are about 1,500 art galleries in Tokyo and 2,000 in the whole country. Something like four-fifths of them are exclusively for rent, without stock on consignment or by commission, where artists can hold shows of their own and hope to catch the attention of critics as well as customers.[d] At least two-thirds of the galleries opened in the 1970s when the Japanese art market soared. Nine of every ten works sold during that decade were produced by Japanese artists.[12]

Corporate and individual collectors accounted for most of the purchases, since Japan in 1980 still had relatively few

[c] The estimate of Segi Shin'ichi, president, Joint Art Research Institute, Tokyo. This figure represents the annual volume of retail sales of oils, watercolors, graphics, sculpture, calligraphy, and other media by Japanese artists in the Tokyo market, where nearly all the high-price art in Japan is sold. Segi estimates that the value of foreign art sold in Tokyo in 1980 was another $250 million. Very little contemporary Japanese art is exported. Segi interview, December 9, 1980.

[d] The figures include commercial establishments handling works of art, excluding curios and ordinary folk-crafts, from all eras and parts of the world. The overwhelming number of nonrental galleries deal in contempoary Japanese paintings. Segi interview, December 9, 1980; Setsu Iwao interview, December 15, 1980; Watanuki Fujio interview, November 7, 1980; Yokota Shigeru interview, December 15, 1980; Yoshii Chōzō interview, October 14, 1980.

public or private art museums—especially for contemporary works. In that year there were 313 art museums of all types, almost double the number in 1967, but more than two-thirds were privately operated and usually had small collections. Only two institutions as of 1980 had holdings greater than 10,000 items, the Tokyo National Museum and the Tenri Sankōkan. Total attendance at art museums in 1974 was just under 10 million, and another 30 million visited general, scientific, and historical museums.[e] There is little doubt that the numbers who went to see standing exhibits at art museums grew somewhat during the seventies,[13] but special shows at department stores and public exhibit halls continued to attract the largest crowds, as they had in the 1950s and 1960s, especially when the theme was European art of the past century.

National census figures show that theater and dance have expanded side by side with the visual arts. Between 1955 and 1975 the combined number of actors, actresses, and dancers increased by two-thirds to 37,400—even though live drama lost 40 percent of its audience. Presumably employment as television actors and actresses, especially in advertisements, more than covered the dropoff, since there are still many more professional actors and actresses than dancers even today.[14]

Commercial theater since the war has been dominated by two large entertainment corporations, each of which also produces movies and supplies talent to radio and television. The larger of the two in aggregate revenues, Tōhō, has specialized in modern plays and musicals since the late sixties, leaving kabuki and its derivatives to Shōchiku. Thanks to Shōchiku's support, with help also from the national theater after 1966,

[e] In 1972 there were 1,821 museums of art, science, and history in the United States (Japan in 1975 had 328 in these categories). Total U.S. attendance at art museums in 1978 was estimated at 175 million. Gideon Chagy, *The New Patrons of the Arts*, New York, Harry N. Abrams, Inc., Publishers, 1972, p. 52; Karl E. Meyer, *The Art Museum: Power, Money, Ethics*, New York, William Morrow and Company, 1979, p. 59; *Time*, December 31, 1979, p. 50; Japan, Office of the Prime Minister, Bureau of Statistics, *Statistical Handbook of Japan 1980*, Tokyo, Bureau of Statistics, 1980, p. 131; Sōrifu Tōkeikyoku, *Nihon tōkei nenkan*, Tokyo, Sōrifu Tōkeikyoku, 1980, p. 614.

kabuki is once again solvent for the first time in forty years. Its success allowed Shōchiku to outearn Tōhō from the live stage in the late 1970s. Commercial theater audiences began to grow again after 1975, and Ōkōchi Takeshi, manager of Tōhō's Imperial Theater in downtown Tokyo, estimated in 1980 that paid admissions in the capital were approaching 8 million.[f] The figure for the country as a whole is at least twice this size.

Among traditional genres, bunraku puppet theater had the most parlous existence after the war. When Shōchiku could no longer prop it up, the government and NHK, the public broadcasting corporation, began subsidizing bunraku's revival together with the city and prefecture of Osaka. Today almost 100 performers belong to the bunraku association, which presents two-week programs four times a year in Tokyo, and the same in Osaka, to a total audience of about 150,000. Performances of nō theater that are open to the public attract roughly the same numbers. Kabuki, by contrast, has about 350 actors, all but fifty of them under direct or indirect contract to Shōchiku. Kabuki plays ten months a year at the Kabukiza theater in Tokyo, eight at the national theater, and shorter engagements elsewhere in Tokyo as well as in Nagoya, Kyoto, and Osaka before 1.5 million customers.[15] Its modern offshoot, shinpa, is likewise viable because of Shōchiku's entrepreneurship. Founded in 1887 and already considered a traditional art today, shinpa has about sixty-five actors and normally operates six months a year at the newly rebuilt Shinbashi Enbujō theater in Tokyo.[16]

For all its hand-crafted inefficiency, live theater is still the artistic core of drama, and in Japan the modern theatrical movement known as shingeki is the artistic core of live theater. Shingeki, which began in the first decade of this century, presents nonmusical plays, whether by Japanese or foreign play-

---

[f] The estimate includes commercial plays, musicals, kabuki, and revues. Ōkōchi Takeshi interview, November 19, 1980; Takeshi Okochi, "The Theatrical Situation in Tokyo and the Imperial Theatre," conference paper for International Box Office Managers Conference, Atlanta, January 1981, p. 6.

wrights, done in the manner of the modern Western stage. In practice all European and American drama short of the contemporary avant-garde, including Euripides and Shakespeare, is considered shingeki. With strong support from organized labor, shingeki grew robust after the war and drew large audiences to its realistic productions throughout the fifties. After being whipped by factionalism, commercialism, television, and new underground troupes in the 1960s, Japan's modern theater sought out fresh audiences in the seventies and today attracts more than 2 million customers nationwide.[g] Virtually all its plays are staged not by performers chosen through auditions but by permanent production companies, which perform for set engagements because theater space is tight and Japanese promoters shirk the indefiniteness of an open-ended run.[17] Although many avant-garde or underground productions are of the highest artistic significance in the Japanese theater world, the combined attendance at all such performances probably does not exceed 100,000 per year.[h]

Even slimmer audiences turn out for concerts of contemporary music, most of them offering works by the two or three dozen most active Japanese composers. Altogether perhaps 150 persons compose art-music in Japan today, nearly all of it in the current international idiom, but many of them write for traditional Japanese instruments as well. Tokyo is unquestionably the music capital of the country, with hundreds of concerts and recitals each month in contemporary,

[g] Shingeki companies put on straight plays that might appear on or Off-Broadway, mainly the latter. Okōchi estimates that 6.6 million persons see shingeki, musicals, and commercial dramas each year in Tokyo. About 120 of the country's 135 shingeki groups are based in the Tokyo region, even though 70 percent of the audience for shingeki is now found on the road. In 1979-1980 Broadway alone drew 8.3 million during its first forty-six weeks. Okochi, "Theatrical Situation," p. 6; *New York Times*, May 11, 1980.

[h] Kara Jūrō estimates the attendance for his well-known Red Tent Situation Theater (Jōkyō Gekijō) troupe at 15,000-20,000 per year. Satoh Makoto, leader of Theater 68/71 (also known as the Black Tent), reportedly puts the population of avant-garde theatergoers at 9,000 nationwide. Kara interview, November 10, 1980; David Goodman, "Satoh Makoto and Japanese Underground Theater," seminar paper, Japan-United States Educational Commission, Tokyo, January 30, 1981.

classical Western, and traditional Japanese music. Iwaki Hiroyuki, lifetime conductor of the NHK orchestra, thinks that "Tokyo is probably the world's biggest music city."[18] The 1975 census showed that 45 percent of the country's 65,600 professional musicians were clustered in the Tokyo region. Most of the increase in the national total (triple the 1955 figure) came about because 30,000 additional women became professional musicians during 1960-1975: by the mid-seventies one-third of all musicians were women between the ages of twenty and twenty-nine. Another 20,000 persons, many of them women, teach music in elementary and secondary schools.[19]

Tokyo is the home of eight full-scale symphony orchestras playing regular seasons for subscribers, but the number is misleading because the country as a whole supports only fifteen orchestras that can be considered professional. There are another forty off-campus amateur orchestral groups.[i] The Tokyo orchestras average three performances a week and go on the road regularly to build audiences throughout the country. Koshimura Sadanao, manager of the Japan Orchestra Association, puts the annual audience for the nation's professional orchestras at 3 million,[20] about what it was in 1970 but now more geographically spread out.

Japanese instrumentalists, especially string players, perform with major orchestras and chamber groups around the world. By one estimate, 400 Japanese musicians are currently employed in Europe and another 100 in the United States.[21] On the other hand, the number of foreign performers visiting Japan for brief engagements reached the remarkable sum of 20,000 in 1980, triple the number a decade earlier and a major worry to domestic musicians and their unions. Although many of them are jazz combos from neighboring Asian countries

---

[i] In 1975 the United States had more than ninety professional and 1,300 amateur orchestras of all types. See Aspen Institute for Humanistic Studies, *The Arts, Economics and Politics: Four National Perspectives*, New York, Aspen Institute for Humanistic Studies, 1975, p. 65; Chagy, *New Patrons*, p. 48.

playing small-town cabarets, one performance of classical Western music out of every five is now given by foreign musicians—who typically draw larger crowds, for more than twice the ticket price, than their Japanese counterparts.[22]

"The national audience for opera is gradually increasing," according to Kawachi Shōzō, the executive director of Japan's largest opera company, Nikikai. He estimates that the country's eleven main opera groups draw 100,000 persons to their performances each year, and other more informal companies and chamber operas have their own smaller audiences. Since Nikikai was formed in 1953, there has been a larger increase in the annual number of performances than in the national pool of opera-goers, which is about 10,000 for domestic performances and three times that number when a famous company visits from abroad.[23]

But orchestral, instrumental, and vocal performances of classical Western music provide a living for only a small minority of the country's professional musicians—perhaps 2,000 at most. Thousands more are employed playing popular music, both contemporary and premodern, both foreign and Japanese, and a few of them have become television and recording stars. Doubtless the single most important source of income for musicians is teaching, whether as one of the 15,000 who give lessons for the giant Yamaha and Kawai piano companies or as a home-studio instructor in traditional Japanese singing.[24] No one seems sure how many people study music in Japan, but in 1976 a majority of all elementary and junior high-school students reported they were taking after-hour lessons in one art form or another. The best estimate is that about 1.5 million people (many of them school-age children) are now studying piano and another 500,000 the violin.[25] Each year more than 350,000 pianos and 40,000 violins are manufactured in Japan, and by 1979 nearly one household in six had a piano (almost two-thirds had stereos, on which to play the products of the nation's billion-dollar-a-year record industry).[26]

Hardest of all to determine is how many persons are studying traditional Japanese music. In 1977, a typical year, there were just 215 public concerts in Tokyo of traditional instrumental music (samisen, koto, shakuhachi) or singing (kouta, hauta, nagauta). But most hōgaku, as traditional music is known, is played for private audiences, and no one knows their size. Thanks to amateur patronage from businessmen, kouta ballads are the most popular genre among pupils of hōgaku, with perhaps 600,000 to 700,000 students nationwide. Koto, with approximately half a million, is now slightly larger than samisen, and another 250,000 to 300,000 pupils are thought to be learning nagauta (long epic songs).[27] Nō is mainly studied by women for its elegant dance technique, but considerably more than 100,000 businessmen are taking lessons in nō chanting. Other traditional styles have correspondingly smaller followings. The total number who pay to study all forms of music in Japan is now greater than ever before, but it probably does not match the 6 million who are learning floral art (another 2.3 million are currently studying tea ceremony).[j]

No art form in postwar Japan has relied more greatly on teaching, or grown more vigorously as a result, than dance—so much so that Japan is now second only to the United States in numbers of professional dancers. In 1980 total audiences at public concerts, which represent only a fraction of the overall attendance, were about the same as those in America in 1965 (roughly 1 million). Altogether there are about 2,000 professional ballet artists, 4,000 professional contemporary dancers, and 50,000 or more licensed teacher/performers of classical Japanese dance. All three genres, like traditional Japanese music, folk dancing, and nō drama, hold far more private recitals than public performances. The latter happen mainly in the big cities, but the total number who see ballet, contemporary dance, and classical Japanese dance each year is very much greater if private events are included.[28]

---

[j] These are 1979 estimates, probably conservative ones since tea and flower schools customarily understate their memberships and revenues for tax purposes. *Statistical Handbook of Japan* 1980, p. 137.

13

Money to support the public concerts comes mostly from the profits of teaching dance to more than 700,000 pupils in ballet, 800,000 in contemporary dance, and 1 million in classical Japanese dance (nō, which includes dances of its own, also has well over a million students). The total dance population has nearly doubled in the past fifteen years. There are four main schools of classical dance, but teaching is so lucrative that more than 200 other artists have established themselves independently as heads of competing schools, nearly half of them in the past ten years. There are more than a dozen major studios in both ballet and contemporary dance, but in the same way as classical Japanese dance most of the instruction takes place in the teacher's home or neighborhood studio.[29] Like learning to play the piano or the koto, Japan's new middle-class families have come to consider studying dance an excellent way to cultivate refinement in their children—particularly their daughters, who form the great majority of pupils taking private lessons in every art form except kouta and perhaps nagauta, the favorites of many businessmen.

The Artist in Postwar Society

The arts have blossomed to this degree since the mid-1950s because they serve the social system, not just the artist's need for expression. They have flowered in a cultural climate buffeted by two paradoxical elements. One is the explosive diversification of artistic modes in Japan after a decade and a half of relative cultural homogeneity, 1937-1952. The other is the notable standardization of taste and leisure that took place as more and more Japanese thronged the cities, underwent uniform schooling, bought TVs and mass-market publications, and aspired to the accepted symbols of middle-class life—including the arts. Hand in hand with this "streamlining" of cultural life, as George Orwell once put it in another context, has come the Japanese government's policy of diffusing what it calls "outstanding works of higher culture" to all corners of the country.

Diversity and dissemination are praiseworthy goals, in the view of most Japanese artists, but each has inherent hazards. Diversifying since the war has often been equated with adopting the latest artistic fad from abroad, sometimes at the risk of abandoning indigenous expressions or, more simply, embracing mediocrity. And spreading any chosen set of art forms to a public already growing more standard in habits and preferences naturally alarms those who fear the uncritical absorption of an establishment view of culture. Diversity in the arts and uniformity in the social matrix are scarcely unique to either Japan or the postwar era, but they carry great cultural weight among a people already homogeneous who for more than a century have often leapt at the chance to diversify if it meant adopting new movements and styles from the West.

Without exception every major genre in the modern visual and performing arts possessed a multiformity in 1980 that hardly existed in Japan twenty-five or thirty years earlier. The reason was much more than just a matter of how much activity a wealthier public could support. The new variety of both creative works and revivals, starting in the mid-fifties, was partly a national response to wartime austerity and postwar rehabilitation.[k] But more importantly, nearly all the expressions of beauty and of sentiment that brightened the Japanese artistic landscape after the mid-fifties took place in terrain suddenly exposed, after a long period of darkness, to the

[k] A minority of critics in Japan, citing censorship early in the American occupation and restrictions on labor toward the end, believe the military authorities enforced an antidemocratic cultural policy during 1945-1952. The boom of interest in American popular culture since the mid-1950s, in one view, is a sign of "American imperialist cultural aggression" that has caused the "deterioration" of Japanese culture. Yamashita Fumio, *Atarashii seiji to bunka*, Tokyo, Shin Nihon Shuppansha, 1975, p. 17. See Hidaka Rokurō, "Sengo bunka undōshi no susume," *Iwanami kōza Nihon rekishi geppō*, 25, May 1977, p. 5; H. Paul Varley, *Japanese Culture: A Short History*, New York, Praeger Publishers, expanded ed., 1977, pp. 235-236. Roland Palsson points out the meagerness of mass culture but also a reduced fear of state manipulation of the arts in most countries after 1945. Palsson, "Cultural Policy for an Open Society," in Stephen A. Greyser, ed., *Cultural Policy and Arts Administration*, Cambridge, Mass., Harvard Summer School Institute in Arts Administration, Harvard University Press, 1973, pp. 6-30.

sunlight and the storms of art movements from abroad. Japanese painters, playwrights, composers, and choreographers were stirred by the same movements that stimulated their colleagues overseas, especially existentialism, the imbroglio over socialist realism, and the postmodern rejection of modernism that led to a brief marriage of the avant-garde visual and stage arts,[L] notably in performance art.[30] No less than artists elsewhere, the Japanese offered disparate answers to each of these worldwide currents, whether by turning to superrealism in prints and design or to its antithesis, nativist romanticism, in architecture, the underground theater, and progressive ballet. Most of all, Japanese artists during the past quarter-century have grappled ingeniously with the question of national identity in the most international age in Japanese history.[m] Even traditional Japanese music and classical dance have experimented with contemporary compositions in response to the remarkable public preoccupation, especially in the 1960s and 1970s, with what it means to be Japanese. Diversification, in brief, has meant more than a simple adaptation of foreign techniques or trends.

Standardized pastimes, on the other hand, attracted larger and larger numbers of new followers and raised questions about how the new artistic variety could expect to survive.

[L] Elements of Buddhist thought found in the plays of Mishima Yukio, Abe Kōbō, and others cannot mask their strongly existential nature. The same is true of the novels of Abe and Ōe Kenzaburō. Much Japanese contemporary dance, in which the movement rejects canons of truth and exercises free choice, is consonant with postwar existentialism. Few if any foreign artists have received more adulation than Jean-Paul Sartre and Simone de Beauvoir during their visit to Japan in the autumn of 1966. On socialist realism, cf. the many international literary meetings held in Tokyo in the 1950s and 1960s, the artistic contacts with China after 1957, and the ruckus over a convention attended by members of the Japanese P.E.N. Club in Seoul in June 1970. See *Zusetsu Nihon bunkashi taikei*, XIII, *gendai*, Tokyo, Shōgakukan, 1968, pp. 264-268; Asahi Shinbunsha, *Asahi nenkan 1967*, Tokyo, Asahi Shinbunsha, 1967, p. 717; *Asahi nenkan 1971*, p. 691.

[m] Landmarks of the debate included the security-treaty crisis of 1960, the Olympiad and the Chinese nuclear-bomb tests in 1964, the Meiji centennial in 1968, and the Japan Inc. discussions of the 1970s. See *Asahi nenkan 1966*, pp. 636-637, for a summary of views on the meaning of the postwar era.

Along with higher earnings came more free hours, especially for people employed in the urban economy. Family spending on reading, music, art lessons, and the like was nearly five times higher in 1978 than in 1965, prompting the government to claim in a white paper on leisure that the "Japanese engage in cultural activities" in their spare time, "not merely seeking release" like their counterparts in Western Europe.[31] For men, according to statistics published by the prime minister's office in 1980, the favorite cultural activities are listening to music, seeing movies, and playing musical instruments. Women prefer flower arranging, listening to music, watching films, playing instruments, and tea ceremony.[32] Using different categories, the Leisure Development Center estimated in 1980 that photography was roughly twice as popular among adults as painting, drawing, or writing prose or Chinese-style poetry, and three times as popular as writing haiku or waka verse. The leisure center calculates that virtually the same numbers of persons attend art shows as serious Western music concerts and that modern theater and kabuki are each about two-thirds as popular as art shows and concerts.[33]

As in the United States, education is more useful even than income or place of residence in predicting who will take part in the arts. The education ministry has estimated that college-educated citizens are nearly 60 percent more likely to participate than high-school graduates.[34] Seeking various artistic outlets is now routine among well-educated families, but it is less certain that other new middle-class households escape the cultural uniformity of television and comics during their leisure time. In short, there is a growing impulse toward standard cultural expression in Japan today, but not necessarily a standardization of cultural product.

Japan by 1980 had virtually completed the democratization of access to culture that began when heavy industry grew and the cities swelled during the first quarter of this century.[35] Once the province of the privileged, the arts are now available to nearly everyone, often at bargain prices. The automatic prestige they used to accord their practitioners is diminished,

17

but extra payments will assure the would-be pupil a teacher or school with more cachet. As with education after 1945, broader public participation in the arts has prompted people to find clever ways to reinforce status, by assigning higher value to certain institutions, studios, and individuals than others—preserving hierarchy and assuring equality of entree but not of attainment. The difference with arts activity, compared with education, is that pure merit is less often recognized, whereas money and length of study are correspondingly more rewarded.

The ability to confer status is only one aspect of the growing popularity of art. Getting involved with the arts helps people escape routines or fill out blank spaces, as for mothers with older children. It provides a chance to test one's identity and to fix one's values, particularly in a society where religion has lost much of its reality. The great concert halls and cultural centers built around the country during the 1970s have become the temples and shrines of the late twentieth century. Someone who performs in them, Tachikawa Ruriko of Star Dancers Ballet, predicts that "the Japanese people will more and more start seeking art and assisting it as they realize material prosperity isn't fully satisfying."[36] In this vein, what William P. Malm says about Japanese music is appropriate for all the arts:

> Japanese arts are often characterized as being able to achieve a maximum effect with a minimum of material. It is in this way that one skillful performance of one shakuhachi piece may be able to move a listener as much in five minutes as does a Mahler symphony in an hour. We must not evaluate the last thirty years of music in Japan in terms of data; it must be judged in terms of value. Every layer of music in Japan, from popular through the traditional classical, is viable and often it is beautiful. It would seem that a sensitive and musically flexible Japanese can have the best of all musical worlds in Japan today.[37]

This laudable aspiration is tempered by at least three important enigmas facing artists in present-day Japan. One is that despite all their education and participation in the arts, Japanese audiences are still dazzled by blockbuster events from abroad. Nineteen seventy-four was "the year of the spectacle," a good illustration of how crowds will turn out for famous stars. The visitors that year included the Munich opera, Maria Callas, the Greek national theater, the national French contemporary ballet, Martha Graham, the New York Philharmonic led by both Bernstein and Boulez, and the runaway celebrity of the year, *Mona Lisa*. Western culture, as the *Asahi nenkan* noted limply, "seems to have unlimited appeal." The interest continued right through 1980, when foreign art shows reached an all-time high and gave no sign of abating thereafter.

Yet however cosmopolitan city life has become, and whatever the attraction of exotic art objects,[38] a survey taken in 1980 disclosed that 64 percent of Japanese had no wish to associate with foreigners.[n] The ambivalence about foreign contact is a paradox Japanese artists have had to confront throughout the postwar period. Audiences welcome Japanese artists who have had professional experience abroad, but only up to a point; the painter or musician who emulates foreign models too closely is apt to draw criticism for abandoning native culture. For their part, many artists feel slighted when the public adulates overseas visitors and ignores Japan's own performers.

A second impasse for many artists is the problem of artistic individuality in a newly democratized country of tightly knit

[n] Total foreign visitors to Japan were 366,649 persons in 1965, 811,672 in 1975, and 1,290,000 in 1980. As of 1980, about 4 million Japanese travel abroad each year. *Nihon tōkei nenkan*, 1980, p. 275; *Japan Times*, March 10, 1981. Amano Ryōichi, executive, *Mainichi* newspapers and long-term resident of Great Britain, cautions against making too much of the poll on foreign contacts. He notes that most Japanese "are interested in Western material culture, not interpersonal contact. . . . The language barrier is the most difficult bar. Japanese feel embarrassed not to be able to communicate with foreigners, so some are shy and say they'd prefer not to associate with them." Amano interview, December 22, 1980.

19

social groups. If everyone has an equal chance, some ask, why does social standardization so often seem to snuff out one's access to an audience? Alienation from accepted social standards and preferences is by no means unique to Japan or to the postwar era, but in the 1970s it produced a new "age of introversion" reminiscent of the autobiographical novel-writing two generations earlier.[39] Artists, like other professionals in Japan, are very conscious that they lack the automatic status conferred by belonging to a governmental or corporate bureaucracy. A number of them believe that big business and the state have monopolized wealth, power, and social standing, leaving artists very little space in a tightly contested social order and damping criticism in the bargain. Many would agree with the writer Michishita Kyōko that the arts "are usually regarded more as entertainments than as serious critiques of society,"[40] a diversion for escaping the important business of governing and making money. Artists everywhere risk being mistaken as mere entertainers, but it is understandable that the great centralization of money and authority in postwar Tokyo seems menacing to many of them because of its capacity to blunt their flair, and perhaps even the individuality of their art. However democratic the society has become, stepping out of line still invites censure.

A third problem for postwar artists is their endemic preoccupation with technique at the cost of expression, especially in modern genres. The art scholar and critic Etō Shun likens contemporary Japanese painters to musicians who win international contests "because of their technical competence in classical routines." But painters and musicians often "lack a feeling, an idealistic appreciation for the spirit of the works." No doubt the engagement with technique is partly the product of caution toward the outside world. Hase Takao, managing director of the NHK orchestra, says that "Japan mastered the techniques of Western music in a hurry but is still far behind Europe in its spirit." The film maker Kurosawa Akira concurs: "it may look as if Japan is very wealthy to the outside world, and this may be true in a material sense. But it's not true in a spiritual sense."[41]

To risk the embarrassment of flawed technique or a memory lapse onstage is apparently far more fearsome to many performers than failing to capture the mood or passion of the work itself.° Still it is well not to press the attack too hard, since Japan a century ago discovered the fallacy of distinguishing sharply between technique and value. Although no art form is a truly international language, few concert-goers would deny that interpretations of Grieg or Graham by top Japanese performers are based on more than technical mastery alone.

PATRONS AND AUDIENCES

Until very recently, Japanese artists have enjoyed only modest patronage from government agencies, private corporations, or wealthy individuals. They have had to rely on market support from audiences and pupils by organizing particularistic ties with specific consumers. The principal features of patronage since the war have been the systematic cultivation of selected clienteles by arts leaders in each genre and the recent enormous increase in subsidies from the state.

A key problem for postwar artists has been the lack of a true public for their works. Every art form, traditional or modern, visual or stage, depends on private audiences to a degree unimagined in Western Europe or North America. Haryū Ichirō, an essayist on art and literature, believes that the idea of "the public" was closely identified with the Japanese state between 1890 and 1945 and that since the war Japan has had little sense of the public interest, only a set of separate private ones.[42] Relatives and friends of the performers commonly make

---

° The contemporary dancer Kei Takei, based in New York, criticizes Japanese dancers for "attempting to go very much the technical route," and the conductor Iwaki Hiroyuki notes that most Japanese speak of "performing," not "playing," their musical instruments. Takei, quoted in Cynthia Lyle, *Dancers on Dancing*, New York, Drake Publishers, Inc., 1977, p. 155; Iwaki, *Iwaki ongaku kyōshitsu*, Tokyo, Kōbunsha, 1977, pp. 10, 89.

21

up 90 percent of the turnout for opera, dance, and music concerts in both the premodern and modern styles. Most who attend one-person exhibitions are somehow connected with the artist whose work is on display. Many theater troupes force their actors and actresses to sell tickets to family or friends. Foreign artists who are anxious to appear in Japan are sometimes deceived by the large numbers studying their métier, unaware that these pupils will usually attend a performance only if their own teacher or someone else with whom they have a tangible link is on the program.[43]

The custom of painting or performing for private audiences stems from the distinctive headmaster (iemoto) system of the traditional Japanese arts. A headmaster is the leader of a fictive kin group, patterned after the premodern family, that forms around a teacher in the traditional arts and certain other pastimes. Normally an artist performs only before others trained in the same school of instruction. Today the system prevails in nō theater, kyōgen, traditional Japanese music, and classical Japanese dance, as well as crafts and skills like tea ceremony, flower arranging, incense sniffing, martial techniques, sumo wrestling, and even certain new religious organizations. Bunraku has stage names but no headmaster system; kabuki does not use the term and has no amateur students, but as a hierarchical method of controlling the art through heritable roles "in actuality it is a kind of iemoto."[44]

In the Tokugawa period there was a strong headmaster system in scholarship and painting, remnants of which can still be found in university professorships and teacher-pupil relationships in Japanese-style painting. The open-submission artists' associations, with their networks of members throughout the country, function socially if not economically like a headmaster system. Even more informal versions include the circles of pupils who gather around teachers in piano, violin, ballet, and contemporary dance; the modern theater company also bears a resemblance to the headmaster method of perpetuating an explicit artistic approach.[45]

In the traditional arts, the system transmits a pattern of

22

performance that includes both techniques and the intangible nuances of the particular school. Pupils imitate both the teacher's general bearing and specific way of executing the art, and they are forbidden to express their own interpretations until they themselves become authorized teachers. In the most extreme form, the artistic pattern is a secret not to be revealed to outsiders, although the publishing industry and television have made most of the technical feats available to anyone who is interested. But learning an art requires more than developing the skills themselves. It fosters a way of life involving unspoken understandings among the initiated, and the headmaster system best imparts the collective mood and spirit. This method maintains a premodern emphasis on the act of singing or dancing rather than the contemporary focus on the work of art itself.

Each school of interpretation has amateur students who support it economically and supply the next generation of teachers. In previous centuries pupils apprenticed themselves to teachers and became virtual members of the family, and even today a strong superior-subordinate relationship reminiscent of the feudal bond between lord and follower continues to prevail for as long as the pupil studies the art. Students are obliged to perpetuate the teacher's approach and may not switch to another school or even another instructor in the same one. For their part, teachers reward their pupils' loyalty by patronizing them.

The result is that authority is an even more important attribute than skill. The pupil who studies classical Japanese dance for six or seven years, almost regardless of talent, can be expected to take a stage name (*natori*) for a fee of $5,000 or more and enjoy the right to teach.[46] Tea schools confer tea names, and other arts grant licenses and certificates at regular intervals, not necessarily to recognize artistic achievement but to reward longevity with symbols of membership in the group. Only persons with stage names in classical Japanese dance have the right to change scripts or alter the choreography, but even so the headmaster always retains the right to expel anyone from the school for being disloyal or failing to pay periodic fees.

Although the headmaster method began among the aristocratic and warrior arts of the fifteenth century, the present system took shape during the 1780s when rich merchants aped the Tokugawa elite classes by taking up their artistic diversions in even greater numbers than before. By the mid-nineteenth century there were so many students, and the authority of headmasters had decayed so badly, that a cluster of new schools sprang up in classical Japanese dance and traditional music, especially kouta. Nō drama, on the other hand, had almost no amateur pupils before the twentieth century, even though it was not exclusively an aristocratic genre in the Edo period. After the restoration of 1868 wiped out the samurai class, many arts schools lost their chief backers and struggled along until the 1920s, when well-to-do urban families started sending their daughters for lessons in the polite accomplishments.[47]

The great middle-class engagement with the arts after World War Two converted the headmaster system into a nationwide institution with far more respectability than it had ever had in the pleasure quarters of nobles or merchants. As the tight social order relaxed the arts schools became less exclusive, and it was much easier to start a new school of classical Japanese dance or traditional music after 1945. Industrialization and higher standards of living gave middleaged women the time and money to join their daughters in taking lessons, usually in a traditional rather than modern genre. As students of many ages began paying big fees for the privileges of receiving training, playing concerts, and accepting the school's name or its certificates, the headmaster system grew far more commercial than ever before, not necessarily to the benefit of its art.[48] The same is partly true of classical Western music, ballet, and contemporary dance, but despite their growth as big businesses there is a certain amount of competition among would-be performers, whereas the headmaster system shields classical dancers and traditional musicians from direct rivalry with fellow artists by allowing them to perform only before members of the same school.

Japanese arts fans group themselves into private noncompeting clienteles, patterned after the structure of a family, which are composed of relatives, friends, classmates, and others with whom the artists have concrete bonds. The audience identifies mainly with the individual artist or performing company, not with the overall art form, in much the same way as a worker feels allegiance to a specific workplace, not a craft or profession as a whole. World-class stars manage to draw well in Japan in spite of this fragmented audience, and there is unquestionably a general public for various classes of film and literature. Still the audience for the arts has become highly specialized as new art forms and subgenres have sprouted in the last twenty-five years. The lack of a general public has made it hard for newcomers to be heard or seen, but the thousands of durable, loyal private followings have assured many other artists that they will have long-range support for developing and refining their skills.

Recognizing the role art has come to play in Japanese life, both for those who watch and those who take part, an official government task force in 1977 trumpeted "an unprecedented rise" in public expectations of the arts.[p] Like many governments elsewhere, the Japanese authorities in the 1970s found that culture was in the "public interest at home and national interest abroad."[49] They set up two main organizations to promote these interests, the cultural agency of the education ministry (1968) and the Japan Foundation (1972). The government arts subsidies, as in other countries, are "in roughly inverse proportion to the numbers of customers who actually benefit."[50] Total state spending on cultural services, according to one study, rose slightly in the seventies,[51] but there was a clamor in 1980 for much more.

Obscured by the selection of a new prime minister in July

---

[p] William J. Baumol and William G. Bowen found little evidence for similar claims in the United States in the early 1960s. Baumol and Bowen, *Performing Arts: The Economic Dilemma*, Boston, M.I.T. Press, 1968, pp. 8, 68.

of that year was a blue-ribbon study by Yamamoto Shippei and others called the *Age of Culture Report*. It recommended a 500 percent rise in the budget of the cultural agency and a series of measures to make the 1980s the age of culture. Shortly before the report was made public, the *Asahi* newspapers noted many defects in the nation's public libraries and concluded that "our country is an economic giant but a cultural dwarf."[52]

By 1980 Japan was a prosperous nation quite capable of sustaining a great deal of arts activity, but neither foundations nor the government were the main sources of support. "If you think in terms of government aid and foundation grants," notes Katō Mikio, associate managing director of International House in Tokyo, "you miss the real story about arts patronage in this country. The indirect ways of patronizing the arts are essential, but also harder to discover."[53]

One of the indirect ways is from artists themselves. Painting, playing music, dancing, and acting have been hobbies for generations among various privileged classes in Japan, activities carried on for love, not money, by those with the means to afford them or the dedication to sacrifice in order to pursue their interest.[q] Even today well-to-do Japanese pay to dance a role with an ostensibly professional ballet company or sing a part in an opera. The same amateur ideal prompts many businessmen to study traditional Japanese singing or classical dance throughout their careers.

But most important of all are the countless private audiences and small affinity-groups that turn out for particular exhibitions and performances, for reasons that almost always transcend a general interest in the art itself. Usually the impetus is a personal connection, based on social dynamics that far surpass the simple snob-appeal that impels certain Americans

---

[q] I am indebted for comments on this point to Dennis Keene, who notes that Pope may have been the first writer to earn a living and that the idea of the professional artist is quite recent in the West. Keene interview, November 29, 1980. I am also indebted for similar comments to Nobumoto Yasusada, interview, January 30, 1981.

to join the art league or the friends of music. Whatever the intention, very sizeable private expenditures on arts activities are the consequence. This highly segmented market for the arts helps to make up for the relative dearth of benefactions from wealthy individuals, private corporations, or (until recently) public programs to aid exhibitions and performances.

CHAPTER 2

A Poverty of Patrons

JAPANESE businesses spend three times as much money every day entertaining on expense accounts as they contribute to private nonprofit groups, including the arts, in a whole year. The corporate wining and dining, at $14.5 billion for the year ending March 31, 1980, was so great that it surpassed the national defense budget by $2 billion. According to the National Tax Agency, the private nonprofit sector—including schools, welfare and research groups, and arts institutions—received just $128.8 million in corporate contributions, about 2 percent more than the previous year.[1]

Business firms are the merchant-princes of contemporary Japan, now that progressive tax tables and postwar land reform have flattened the pyramid of individual incomes and pared the fortunes of rich families who helped artists before the war. As in Great Britain, the tax laws discourage companies from aiding the arts,[a] but a more basic reason for the poverty of patronage is that the idea of private philanthropy has very shallow roots in Japan.

PAST FORMS OF PRIVATE PATRONAGE

Confucianism in premodern times spoke of benefiting the common good, a doctrine that was eventually reinterpreted by utilitarians and then nationalists in the late nineteenth century. The tradition of pure philanthropy, as an abstract, idealized love of humanity, had little place in the socially fragmented feudal era or the more mobile order of the past century,

---

[a] In Great Britain the government permits tax-free corporate gifts to the arts only if the gifts are directly related to business purposes. In 1977 private concerns donated $1.8 million to the arts, less than 1 percent of total arts patronage. *New York Times*, July 2, 1978.

in which tightly structured interest groups have competed for advantage and higher status. Instead the Japanese for many centuries have patronized home-town artists and others with whom they are personally connected, but rarely the entire art form and almost never the arts as a whole. As the critic Donald Richie puts it, "Japan has had no Medicis patronizing all the arts, no Esterhazys"[2] willing to sponsor a universe of artists at their courts. Aid was intended not for the general good of unknown artists, let alone an anonymous public, but for the particular benefit of a private individual, family, or school with whom the donor shared a close personal tie, not just a love of art.

Shinto was the nurse of the arts in old Japan, but the esoteric priest Kūkai (774-835) was their tutor and Buddhism their benefactor for nearly a millennium.[3] Neither religion imparted much of a charitable tradition, whether for the arts or for social welfare. During the Tokugawa period (1603-1868) Kyoto aristocrats and regional fief lords, the latter scattered in castle towns, patronized art because it reinforced their status, adorned their ceremonies, and lent refinement and cultivation to the new warrior elite. Yet samurai sons were steered toward writing and calligraphy rather than music or sculpture. The professional painters and poets of the era were often members of families favored by generations of fief lords. At the same time other arts gave social standing and rich entertainment to many of the prosperous big-city merchants of the period.[4] For some of them, the Chinese amateur ideal, like the Western renaissance man, pointed the way to self-cultivation: the *bunjin* (person of culture) was a social type as well as an artistic style.

Government became the main benefactor of the arts after the Meiji restoration in 1868, but old aristocrats continued to protect artist-craftsmen whose forebears had long served their families. The state promoted an official architectural style and an official statuary, both derived from the West, and it created government arts institutes with exhibitions and concerts at the start of the twentieth century. A modern market system developed in both the visual and stage arts, with works for sale to anyone and performances open to the anonymous public simply for the price of admission—especially in the new theater, music, and ballet introduced from Europe shortly after 1900. By the Taishō era (1912-1926) it became possible to speak of an audience of commoners in the big cities, although older forms of patronage continued, especially in the traditional arts. People began to regard a work of art as an object separate from the act of creating it, something to be bought, valued, and displayed. But only when cultural life became fully democratic, after World War Two, did most Japanese stop thinking of art as singing, dancing, acting, or painting and start regarding the work as something to be esteemed in itself.[5]

Early in the century a few of the new industrial magnates, such as Matsukata Kōjirō and Ōhara Magosaburō, began collecting art, building museums, or aiding orchestras, and others with deeper roots in the feudal aristocracy, like the theater patron Hijikata Yoshi, also sometimes helped artists. Both prestige and pleasure seem to have impelled them. The same is true of others in the upper classes who tried to maintain the folk arts and traditional crafts, but they had a nationalist motive as well: conserving a native tradition, including so-called "creative print making," against the revolutionary art movements seeping in from abroad.[6] Private patronage before the war was scattered, mostly individual, and only rarely reached beyond painting and sculpture.

The war destroyed the aristocracy and reduced landowners and the military leadership to traces of their former influence. The manufacturing and commercial middle classes more and more dominated the country, together with the national bureaucracy. Corporate wealth soon took the place of the great private fortunes, which had been ruined by postwar inflation and egalitarian reforms. There are still many rich individuals in Japan, and some of them patronize the arts even without much tax incentive to do so. Nonetheless it is the great business concerns and their foundations, representing the new social elites, that seem the most natural fresh sources of aid for artistic activities today. Yet their gifts each year are only a fraction of their daily bills for food and drink.

BUSINESS, BUREAUCRACY, AND THE ARTS

"In the old days," says Shibazaki Shirō, director of the national theater, "rich businessmen like Yoshida Kōzaburō used to help traditional Japanese music and classical dance. Now corporation presidents are all salarymen, not individualists like those patrons before the war." Adachi Kenji, who directs the Tokyo National Museum of Modern Art and formerly headed the government's cultural agency, points out that more women than men take an interest in the arts and that the young businessmen who do like the arts have little free time early in their careers. "By the time they reach retirement, they have the leisure time but are too old for the contemporary arts, so they patronize traditional Japanese arts instead. Thus there is little pressure generated within corporations themselves for helping the arts." Hase Takao of the NHK orchestra agrees,[b] noting that doctors and engineers are the principal male fans of classical Western music; businessmen prefer the visual arts if any modern art at all.[7]

But more than a lack of time or interest explains why business is so little engaged with the arts. Ohara Shigeo of the finance ministry points out that Japanese enterprises were absorbed in reinvestment and expansion during 1955-1975 and only afterward began to contribute much to charity. Little precedent and much caution attaches to generalized philanthropy, Adachi says: "companies tend to give money to organizations directly related to their business activities. Since few firms have commercial dealings with the arts, most are reluctant to aid them."[8] Few businesses have recognized the

[b] Both Adachi and Hase find politicians little more sensitive to the arts than businessmen. Hase says even cabinet officials "dislike attending concerts" by the NHK orchestra. Adachi observes that politicians rarely go beyond "displaying art for political purposes, especially traditional Japanese paintings or crafts, in their homes or offices to impress people." Hase interview, October 14, 1980; Adachi interview, October 22, 1980.

31

direct or indirect benefits of helping artists unless there is something of tangible value involved for their employees or their profits.

Instead there is the common view that government, not private enterprise, should pay the subsidies because the arts are a national resource. Even Matsushita Kōnosuke of Panasonic, who is a major arts patron, says that "orchestras should be run on tax monies like museums and zoos, not according to individual tastes." Many people in and out of the business world respect official sponsorship and believe that it is somehow safer for public agencies to promote the arts than private companies or foundations, which might be self-interested. Ōka Norio, chairman of CBS-Sony, thinks some fellow executives use this argument as a refuge from artists who want money because they do not know how to turn down unworthy applicants. But others, he notes wryly, think "refusing to contribute is like an order of merit"[9] and take stubborn pride in saying no.

Businessmen and other wealthy people in Japan feel "no sense of social obligation or moral duty to contribute for public benefit," says Kawashima Takeyoshi, a Tokyo lawyer, "nor does prestige accrue from philanthropy." Even the "foundations in Japan are dead, insofar as the arts and cultural activities are concerned," says Katō Mikio of International House. Spending for the public welfare is often seen as the duty of the government, not the responsibility of private wealth, and the tax laws help to make sure that the authorities can control nonofficial charities rather than encourage them. The government view seems to be that anything worthy of a tax exemption should be run by the state itself, not a private institution. Tax exemptions are selfish and rob the government of revenues, shifting the burden unfairly to other citizens. Ever since the late nineteenth century, according to the scholar Tanaka Minoru, this approach has meant that "private charity depends on official policy and official favor."[10] It is small wonder that businesses have felt reluctant to help out artists, no matter how deserving.

FOUNDATIONS, COMPANIES, AND TAXES

Charitable contributions by individuals and corporations are regulated by the civil code of 1896, the trust law of 1922, and finance-ministry rules issued in 1961. Currently there are more than 16,000 private nonprofit charitable corporations functioning as foundations in Japan, most of them small and only about 2,500 of them operating on a national scale.[c] The Diet has created more than 186,000 other charitable corporations by legislation, including schools, temples, churches, and the Japan Red Cross. A separate category of "special corporations" includes NHK (1950), the national theater (1963), and the Japan Foundation (1972). The first charitable trusts, distinct from all these charitable corporations, were established in 1977.

Private foundations, like other charitable corporations, are exempt from national taxes. Businesses and other incorporated entities may write off contributions to any charitable corporation as business losses for tax purposes, up to .125 percent of their capital including reserves plus 1.25 percent of their net profit for the year. Few companies have taken advantage of even this small opportunity to help arts groups, although many use it to give to other organizations.[d] Individ-

---

[c] There are two types of charitable corporations (*kōeki hōjin*): incorporated associations (*shadan hōjin*), which numbered about 7,500 in 1975, and foundations (*zaidan hōjin*), of which there were about 8,500 in that year. They differ in how they are organized but both function effectively like foundations. See Tanaka Minoru, *Foundations in Japan: Their Legal Provisions and Tax Regulations*, Tokyo, Japan Center for International Exchange, 1975, pp. 8-13; Japan Center for International Exchange, *Philanthropy in Japan*, Tokyo, Japan Center for International Exchange, rev. ed., 1978, pp. 4-5; "*Kigyō no shakai kōken*" *shiryōshū*, 1980, Tokyo, Sanken, 1980, passim.

[d] Business aid to the arts is relatively recent in the United States, increasing more than ten times in the 1970s. Since 1935 the internal revenue code has permitted U.S. corporations to deduct up to 5 percent of taxable income for charitable contributions (in France the figure is 1 percent). Few American companies give even 1 percent, only a fraction of which goes to the arts. Corporate gifts to charity (more than $2 billion) in the U.S. exceeded foundation grants for the first time in 1979, and firms now calculate their aid to the arts at $300 million a year. Such fund-raising schemes as united arts funds and televised solicitations are untested in Japan. See Baumol and Bowen,

uals may normally deduct 25 percent of their annual personal incomes for contributions. Those who want to give funds beyond this limit must pay taxes, and they must pay capital-gains taxes on their gifts if they donate appreciated real estate, securities, or art objects to existing private foundations or arts institutions.[11] Such restrictive regulations have done little to brighten stages or fill galleries.

It is true that tax and social-security obligations in Japan were much lower during the sixties and seventies than in other major industrial states, although the burden rose sharply in 1981.[e] But very few donors have been public-spirited enough to contribute if it means paying extra taxes. The novelist Ariyoshi Sawako tried to give $50,000 from the profits of a recent best seller to aid the elderly but changed her mind when she learned it would cost her nearly another $50,000 in taxes. Since corporations often use the .125 + 1.25 formula to contribute to welfare activities like the Boy Scouts and Little League baseball, arts leaders hesitate to ask companies to make gifts when they know it will force them into higher tax payments.[12]

A bright note was sounded in 1976 when the finance ministry, acting under its own regulations of 1961, began letting other ministries give permission to certain charitable corporations to receive tax-exempt gifts beyond the normal formula, provided they are also receiving assistance from the national treasury. In the case of foundations that help artists, the permission comes from the education ministry, at first for two years but renewable after that. This allows corporations to give another .125 percent of capital and reserves plus 1.25

Performing Arts, pp. 66, 329-330, 353; Chagy, *New Patrons*, passim; Aspen Institute, *Arts*, pp. 35, 65; Meyer, *Art Museum*, pp. 31-35, 65; Robert Brustein, "Can the Show Go On?" *New York Times Magazine*, July 10, 1977, pp. 9-11, 54-59; Netzer, *Subsidized Muse*, pp. 96-107; *New York Times*, April 15, 1980 and October 26, 1980.

[e] The combined tax and social-security burden in 1980 was 31.5 percent of national income, compared with 1977 figures of 38.1 percent for the United States, 47.8 percent for Great Britain, 52.1 percent for West Germany, 53.6 percent for France, and 72.8 percent for Sweden. Finance ministry report, quoted in *Japan Times*, February 18, 1981.

percent of net profits each year without paying taxes, but the difference is that the designated foundations compete only with each other, not with the Little League, for the additional contributions. Individuals may give to these same foundations without regard to the 25 percent limit.

The purpose is to help environmental groups, associations that award scholarships, and arts organizations build up their endowments, and for some this has happened. But the system does not recognize that arts groups almost always have chronic deficits. And a Catch-22 provision is that nonprofit groups need at least $25,000 in capital before they can be recognized as foundations and receive the public aid which is prerequisite for being specially designated. "This stipulation is not necessarily bad," argues Adachi Kenji, "because it guarantees that the government assistance goes to financially stable institutions and reassures corporate contributors that their money will not be wasted." Yet Tachikawa Ruriko, who managed to raise enough funds to turn Star Dancers Ballet into a foundation in 1981, is aware how easily the regulations can be used to strengthen established groups already favored by official grants.[13] Since aid from the state is a requirement, the plan amounts to a matching-grant system, and many individuals and private businesses are reluctant to contribute knowing the taxpayers will bail out the organization if they don't.[f]

---

[f] Under the finance ministry's 1961 tax regulations, there are three classes of "designated research corporations" (*shiken kenkyū hōjin*) qualifying for the extra tax-exempt contributions. One is research organizations in the pure sciences, of which there were about ninety in 1980. A second group consists of certain social welfare foundations and all private schools and colleges, which are called *tō* (etc.) in the official term *shiken kenkyū hōjin tō*. There were about 13,000 such nonprofit groups in this category in 1980. The permission to receive tax-exempt gifts in categories one and two lasts indefinitely. The third category, also recognized since 1961 and called *tō*, consists of miscellaneous foundations. Unlike the others, they must be receiving state aid to qualify for designation, which is given for an original two-year term and renewable thereafter. Foundations that help the arts received their first designations as *tō* in 1976. In December 1980 the tax bureau of the finance ministry did not know how many foundations belonged to the third category, but its three top officials agreed that the number was smaller than either of the first two categories. Only a handful in category three aid the arts. Certain

Bureaucrats in the 1960s and 1970s were often finicky, and sometimes downright capricious, about approving new charitable corporations and designating groups to receive tax-free gifts,[14] but a number of companies and even a few individuals set up new private foundations in the seventies despite the official chill. The corporate impulse toward good works resulted less from an access of altruism than from a need to deflect public criticism that companies had hoarded resources and spoiled the environment.[15] The occasional individual benefactors of the 1970s sometimes set up their new foundations to trim inheritance taxes, but most of them were impassioned devotees, like the rich prewar patrons in Japan, who truly loved the arts. Hara Toshio, who opened a museum of contemporary art in January 1980, notes that tax laws do not make private gifts nearly so inviting as in the United States. Only the original benefaction that forms a foundation is fully tax deductible; all gifts after that are taxable as soon as they exceed the ordinary limits for corporate and personal contributions. Thus far the authorities have ignored a recommendation from the cultural agency, first proposed in 1977, to cut income taxes for individuals who give art works to public or private museums. Instead they have been monitoring the foundations more carefully than ever, to make sure they are fulfilling their nonprofit purposes.[16]

Only two Japanese foundations that were interested in cultural activities had endowments greater than $45.5 million, according to a study in 1978, and just eleven others were larger than $4.5 million. The Hōsō Bunka Kikin (Broadcast Cultural Fund), at $54.5 million, was the largest foundation aiding the arts—mainly with small grants for publications and for overseas trips by the NHK orchestra. A year later, only

special corporations created by the Diet, such as the Japan Foundation, are permanently designated as *tō* by law. Utsumi Makoto interview, November 20, 1980; Ohara Shigeo interview, November 20, 1980; Ōno Shinji interview, November 20, 1980; Ōfuku Mamoru interview, October 20, 1980; Tanaka, *Foundations*, p. 18; Kokusai Kōryū Kikin, *Kokusai Kōryū Kikin nenpō, Shōwa 54nendohan*, Tokyo, Kokusai Kōryū Kikin, 1979, p. 18; Monbushō, *Zatsubun dai26go*, Tokyo, Monbushō, 1979.

163 of the nation's 16,000 foundations reported giving charitable grants of any sort, just a few of them to help the arts. A total of 419 business firms made public-service contributions in 1979, about two dozen of which went directly to arts institutions. Several hundred companies also make small gifts for current operations each year to a few arts foundations, such as the Japan Orchestra Association.[17] There is no useful estimate of the overall sum that foundations and companies are giving to the arts each year because few of them report their grants. The corporate aid is certainly only a small percentage of the $128.8 million contributed to private nonprofit groups of all sorts by businesses in 1979. Since foundations are so few and so small, their support for the arts is likewise modest. The Japanese corporation is much more important as a consumer than as a benefactor of the arts, but even then only when it is good business to do so.

Why companies help the arts at all depends on many factors, some of them peculiar to Japan. Ōfuku Mamoru, director of the Japan Intercultural Communication Society and an adviser on cultural matters for the Teijin textile empire, points out that personal initiative is crucial: businesses will make gifts because the president is an opera fan or because the relative of someone in top management is appearing in a play. Indeed it is probably harder to avoid making contributions in Japan than elsewhere when there is a personal connection, at least for individuals and sometimes for companies too. Donald Richie says that "patrons in Japan are probably more openly venal than in any other country. They are very candid about hiring a painter not because he's good but because he's someone's cousin."[18] But the gifts are unsystematic and unrecorded in most cases. Sometimes the aid is disguised, taking the form of free publicity or cut-rate studio and office space. This kind of privatized patronage is little different from the sponsorship of particular families of artists in the feudal period.

Businesses also appreciate the public-relations tonic of being listed as a concert patron or friend of the theater, provided the audiences include potential customers. New firms trying to make names for themselves often find it useful to contribute a few hundred dollars as supporters of an orchestra series, in return for a seat or two and a place on the printed program. Poster and program advertising is bought by companies selling specific products, such as leotards to dance fans, but most arts groups regard it as a very small source of income. Still the event and the firm confer prestige on each other, and the link between them helps to legitimize both in the eyes of audiences. The most favored of all is a major art exhibition, since getting the company's name on art objects probably means more in Japan than anywhere else. As Richie explains, "works of art have magical properties; they are seen as votive objects, especially when they're brought from abroad, and sponsors hope that some of the magic will rub off."[19] Artists who know how little corporate largess reaches them no doubt wish the magic worked both ways.

MUSEUMS AND EXHIBITIONS

Private support for the arts has taken many forms in Japan, particularly in the past three decades. The assistance includes a small amount of general philanthropy and a great deal of specific patronage of particular artists through gifts, grants, commissions, awards, and employment. Private sources also aid artists through commercial entrepreneurship, such as holding concerts and exhibits, that directly benefits the sponsoring newspaper company or department store. Private organizations and individuals, not national museums or other public entities, are the chief consumers of art objects and services supplied by professionals. Philanthropist, patron, entrepreneur, customer—each has become indispensable for the postwar arts world in Japan. Entrepreneur and customer are sketched in later chapters, along with their activities in the visual arts, theater, music, and dance. The focus here is on private benefactions without commercial overtones, with examples of corporate and individual financial aid to each of the major art forms.

Wealthy patrons benefited the visual arts after World War Two most greatly by developing the private art museum as a public resource, making collections old and new widely accessible for the first time. Early in this century dozens of bureaucrats and industrialists amassed large troves of classical Japanese and Chinese art, much of the latter plundered during Japan's expansion on the continent. These new self-made men gradually took over from temples, shrines, and premodern aristocrats as the main collectors. Two of the most prominent were Nezu Kiichirō and Ōkura Kihachirō, whose superb acquisitions were later placed in museums open to the public. Among the private museums founded before the war, only the Ōhara Art Museum in Kurashiki, opened in 1930 to display the collection of Ōhara Magosaburō, contained large numbers of Western art works.

Since the early 1950s, more than a dozen important museums have been founded by private citizens, often in collaboration with the business firms they headed.[g] In each case the collectors enjoyed income-tax advantages, under Japan's revised postwar statutes, when they first formed foundations to operate the new museums.[20] They were also able to pare inheritance taxes on their estates while retaining control of the art works by dominating the foundations' boards of directors.[21] Most of the collections are divided into three types: works donated by the individual patron, those given by the company he led, and those later acquired by the museum itself. The ratio varies. Those housed in the Idemitsu Art Museum, opened in 1966 in Tokyo by the oil baron Idemitsu Sazō, were mostly purchased by the museum. The Hakone Open Air Sculpture Museum, founded in 1969 by Shikanai Nobutaka,

---

[g] In a guide published in 1978, Laurance P. Roberts lists 355 museums containing art objects in Japan, of which sixteen were founded by fourteen different patrons, all but one of them since the war. The Ōta Memorial Museum and the Hara Museum of Contemporary Art were subsequently opened to the public, both in January 1980. See *Roberts' Guide to Japanese Museums*, New York and Tokyo, Kodansha International, 1978; *Japan Foundation Newsletter*, October-November 1979, p. 8; *Bijutsu hyōron*, June 1980, p. 19.

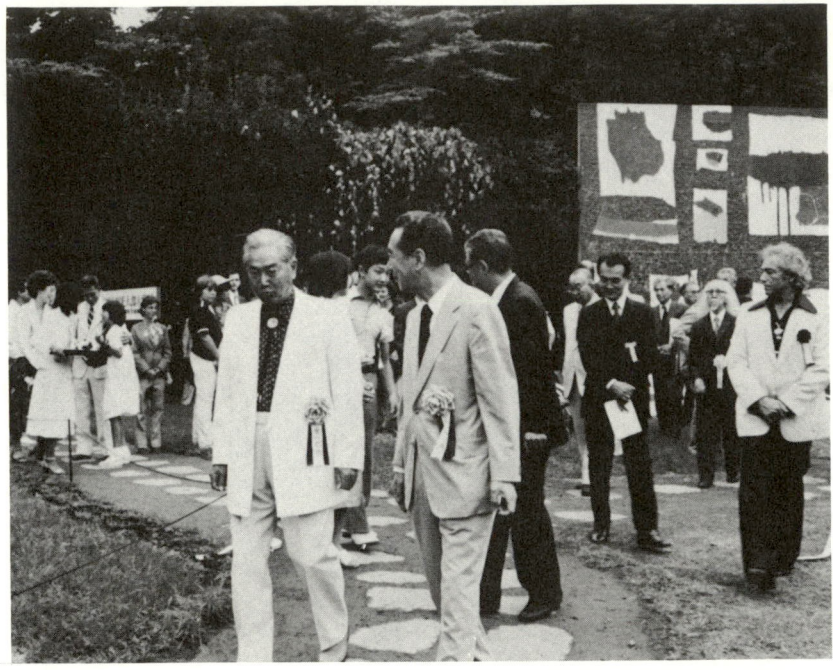

Shikanai Nobutaka, television executive and patron of the
Hakone Open Air Sculpture Museum (left), with Kawakita Michiaki,
director of the Kyoto National Museum of Modern Art, at the
opening of the first Takamura Kōtarō Grand Prize Exhibition
at Hakone in August 1980. HAKONE OPEN AIR SCULPTURE MUSEUM

includes works on loan from affiliated companies in the Fuji-
Sankei media group he heads.[22] In some cases the museums
buy art regularly, but others function mainly to preserve their
patrons' collections and acquire just a few works each year
to keep their tax-exempt status.[23]

Ishibashi Shōjirō built a fortune making tires and spent
much of it buying paintings by French impressionists and the
School of Paris—favorites to this day of Japanese gallery-
goers. In 1952 he opened the Bridgestone Museum of Art in

Tokyo, one of the first that helped make paintings available to postwar audiences. By 1977 the foundation he set up to administer the museum and its branch in Kurume had an endowment of $17.2 million. It spent $430,000 in the year ending March 31, 1977 to add to the collection and $864,000 to cover costs of running the museum not met by earned income. Today the museum is one of a handful of private facilities that can count on an annual attendance of 100,000, and it is also one of the few to help develop contemporary Japanese painting by buying the work of Japanese artists.[24]

Most of the new private museums contain art objects from earlier periods, such as the woodblock print collections at the Riccar and Ōta museums in Tokyo. The former, opened in 1972, has 6,000 works acquired by Hiraki Shinji, and the latter includes more than twice this number collected by Ōta Seizō, a life-insurance executive, and housed in a handsome new brick building opened in 1980 in Harajuku.[25] Japanese arts of earlier periods are also the strength of the Suntory Art Gallery, which was founded in 1961 and now draws 60,000 persons each year to its new location in Tokyo's Akasaka district. The permanent collection is considered very fine, but the gallery's main work is to sponsor a half-dozen special shows of premodern Japanese decorative arts each year.[26] Other patrons of premodern art are found among some of Japan's new religious sects, including the Ōmoto arts center at Kameoka and the Fuji Art Museum at Fujinomiya, established by Ikeda Daisaku of Sōka Gakkai in 1973.

Sometimes the artistic interests of corporate leaders are perpetuated by their firms long after they die. The huge Sumitomo Group opened the Sen'oku Hakkokan in Kyoto in 1970 to display 600 priceless Chinese bronzes collected on the continent by Sumitomo Kichizaemon during 1900-1925. Although the group has "no set annual level of giving for cultural activities," its trading company, the Sumitomo Corporation, has contributed funds since 1973 to theater companies, museums, and orchestras.[27] More important by far was the group's gift of the Ataka collection to the city of Osaka in March

1980, together with funds to build an annex to the municipal museum to house it. Ataka Eiichi, president of the Ataka trading company, acquired nearly 1,000 Chinese and Korean porcelains after World War Two, and Sumitomo took them over when the Ataka firm went bankrupt in 1977. The Sumitomo family had earlier given Osaka a library in 1900 and land for the municipal museum in 1921. Sumitomo believes that this new benefaction, estimated at $76 million, may be the largest corporate gift ever made to the arts in Japan.[28]

Modern and contemporary visual artists occasionally are honored by private patrons who pool contributions to erect museums housing their works. One of the most remarkable, designed by the versatile artist himself, is the Dōmoto Art Museum in Kyoto. This broad stucco building, set in the northwestern hills of the city, displays watercolors, oils, and various crafts by Dōmoto Inshō, a formidable figure in the modern Japanese art world. Smaller cities have done the same for home-town artists, usually after they die, by raising funds to preserve their works.[29] Another method that aids living painters is for museums to conduct regular programs promoting their art. The Yamatane Museum of Art was established in 1966 near Tokyo's stock market by a wealthy securities broker, Yamazaki Taneji, and now includes more than 700 paintings in the Japanese style. The curators put on special exhibits of representative watercolor artists, sponsor lectures and other programs, and confer the Yamatane prize biennially.[30]

On the whole, however, contemporary and avant-garde art has few institutional patrons and depends mainly on small individual collectors for its sustenance. Hara Toshio, who heads a timber firm, used more than $2 million of his own money to open Tokyo's first museum of contemporary art in 1980. He shows new work of Japanese artists in special exhibitions in addition to the regular displays of the museum's 200 items of postwar art from Japan and abroad. "I set up my museum," Hara says, "not to avoid inheritance taxes, since our family had already sold our valuable art to the national

42

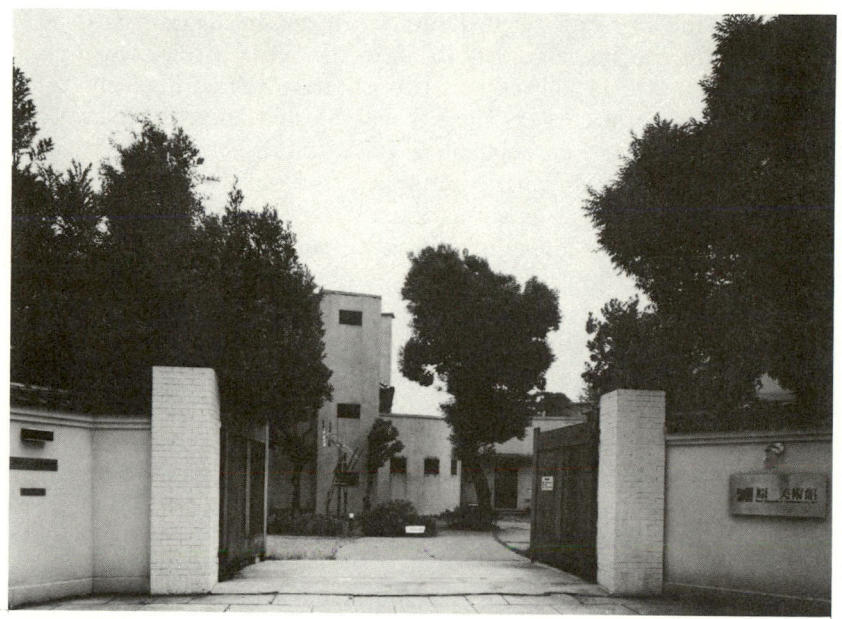

Hara Museum of Contemporary Art, opened in January 1980 by the timber executive Hara Toshio in an art-deco home at Shinagawa, Tokyo, built in the 1930s by Hara's grandfather. ANZAI SHIGEO

museum, but to promote really contemporary art. There is no other museum like it in Tokyo and only four or five others in the whole country." Hara collected most of the works in the late 1970s, "based on what I liked, not what some gallery operator told me was valuable."[31] The others that support current work include the Ōhara complex in Kurashiki, the Ikeda Museum of 20th-Century Art in Itō, and the financially crippled Nagaoka Contemporary Art Museum in Niigata prefecture.[h]

[h] The Nagaoka museum collapsed in 1980 when its chief backer, a local bank, was forced to close because of illegal loans. The collection is expected to be divided among nearby museums. Haryū Ichirō interview, November 13, 1980.

43

But the greatest private supporter of present-day artists is undoubtedly Tsutsumi Seiji, head of the Seibu enterprises in Tokyo. About a half-million persons have visited his Seibu Art Museum each year since it was opened atop the Seibu department store in September 1975 as "a museum of the people," where Tsutsumi wants the arts to relate "especially to people's lives." His aim is to make the museum a "headquarters for movements reflecting the spirit of the times" in all media, not just the visual arts, a place not only for those who love art but also "for those who love humanity."[32] Although the Isetan and Mitsukoshi department stores also call their art facilities museums, Seibu is unique in having a small permanent collection and curators to arrange the exhibits.

No one denies the related entrepreneurial advantages, but in Tsutsumi's case much more is at play. The museum has become the major locale for shows of current visual art in nearly every conceivable style, both foreign and Japanese, carefully mixed with retrospectives of twentieth-century masters like Miró, Munch, Ernst, and Henry Moore. Each year a large exhibit of floral art is also presented. Tsutsumi has encouraged concerts, lectures, poetry readings, fashion shows, and multimedia events in the museum, and an annual show called Art Today gives exposure to fresh Japanese artists. Experimental films and panel discussions take place in Seibu's Studio 200 nearby, and the Seibu theater in the Parco complex at Shibuya provides an important stage for current live drama.[33] Tsutsumi, like Hara, has a passion for art in the widest sense and has developed more forums for people to encounter avant-garde artists than any other private patron in Japan.

Corporations, on the other hand, have done a good deal since the 1950s to encourage artists through competitions and awards. A small investment in the prizes and administrative costs necessary to run a contest apparently pays better rewards to the company, especially in good publicity, than if the same sum were given as stipends to support a few artists. Painters, print makers, and sculptors respond in large numbers when a contest is announced, as much for the prestige of being selected for showing as for the exposure to new customers (selections, and even prize works, are not necessarily displayed in public). The Fuji-Sankei group started an important sculpture competition at the Hakone Open Air Sculpture Museum in 1980, choosing twenty works from 177 items submitted.[i] The Maruzen oil company has awarded art prizes since 1962, joining its competitor Shell, which began holding public art contests on designated themes in 1956.[34] Many other prizes are offered each year by the mass media, public agencies, and art associations all over the country. Yet unlike these competitions, the corporate contests are administered by businessmen who rarely know much about art, so they play safe by asking for advice from the cultural agency, especially in selecting judges. Foreign firms rely especially closely on official guidance, sometimes at the cost of perpetuating established views of art.[35]

Such insurance companies as Tōhō Life, Meiji Life, and Tokio Fire and Marine have sponsored art contests for children and exhibits of amateur art works. The latter operates a gallery, called Tokio Marine Terrace, which amateurs may borrow free of charge to display their creations for a week at a time. The Mitsubishi Group, Tokyo Gas Corporation, and Kawasaki Steel Company also run programs to encourage art appreciation in the regions they serve, which for Mitsubishi includes helping to subsidize Japanese art exhibits in the United States.[36]

One more form of private assistance to visual artists is providing them space to work. Ikeda Masao, managing director of Shin Nihon Zōkeisha, lets graphic artists, schoolteachers, and other specialists use the presses and equipment free of charge at his firm, one of the half-dozen large work-

---

[i] Prize money for the 1980 sculpture contest at Hakone, honoring Takamura Kōtarō, was $163,500, including five commissioned works by Japanese sculptors and five by foreigners. The 1980 Shell contest in contemporary painting, any style, was organized around the "pursuit of the expression of color" and paid about $10,000 in prizes. See *Japan Times*, August 10, 1980; Shell Oil Corporation, *Dai24kai Sheru bijutsushō sakuhin kōbo*, Tokyo, Shell Oil Corporation, 1980.

45

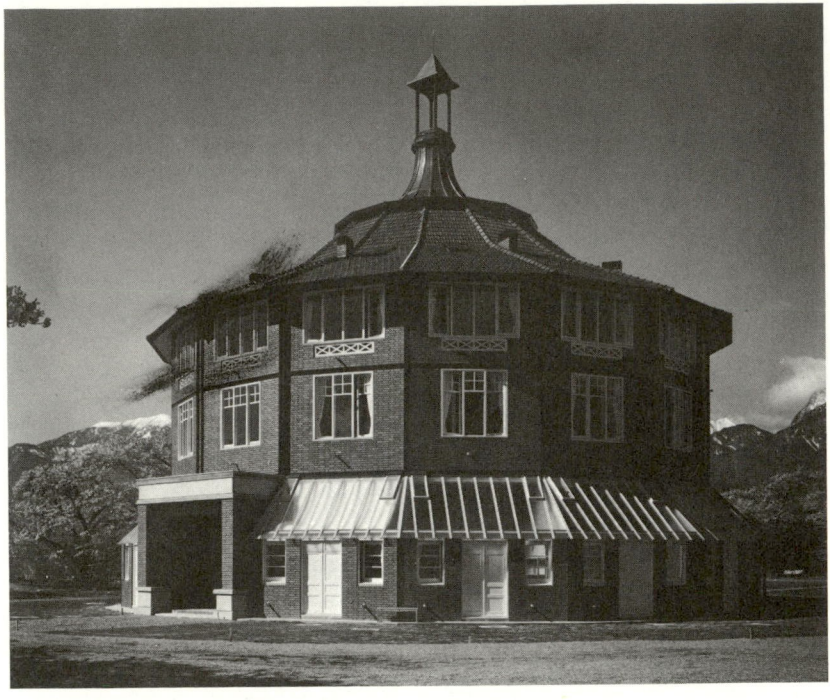

La Ruche, the main building of the Kiyoharu art colony
opened in Yamanashi prefecture in March 1981 by the
gallery operator Yoshii Chōzō. YOSHII GALLERIES

shops in Tokyo. The most ambitious philanthropy of this sort
is probably the Kiyoharu art colony, opened in 1981 near
Mount Yatsugatake in Yamanashi prefecture. Its benefactor,
the art dealer Yoshii Chōzō, hopes to emulate La Ruche in
Montparnasse, where artists from the School of Paris gathered
after World War One. He expects Kiyoharu "to become a
great culture center noted throughout the world," not only
for its artists in residence but also by means of publications,
a journal, a museum, and a library.[37]

Diversity and exposure best summarize what private patronage has done for the visual arts since the 1950s. The few

46

individuals and businesses that have made gifts at all have helped particular artists and groups in ways of their own choosing, not by a common pattern. The amount of their aid is less important than the access it has provided artists to audiences, fame, and honor—and perseverance to keep on creating.

CORPORATIONS AND ORCHESTRAS

Just as museums are the only well-endowed arts institutions in America, postwar benefactors in Japan have done more for the visual arts than for music, dance, or theater. Japanese critics are fond of citing the case of Shikanai Nobutaka, who founded the Hakone sculpture garden and the Fuji gallery in Tokyo but who is presumed to have "a poor appreciation of music"[38] because Fuji Television, of which he is chairman, canceled its broadcast contract with the Japan Philharmonic Orchestra in 1972. It is probably true that many Japanese industrialists prefer to collect paintings or sculptures because they are tangible objects that seem better investments than hearing a work of music performed. Still it is a fact that classical Western music has received much more aid from individuals and companies than either theater or dance. (Japanese court music is supported by the imperial household agency; other forms of traditional music stay solvent from fees paid by students, without recourse to major gifts from corporations.)

The best-known patron of music in the 1960s and 1970s was Edo Hideo, chairman of the Mitsui Real Estate Development Corporation and the nation's most experienced fund raiser for the arts. Edo is chairman of the board of trustees of Tōhō Gakuen University, a leading private college in music and theater, and he also heads two foundations that underwrite concerts, the Japan Performance League and the Japan Orchestra Association. His interest in music, Edo says, comes from his family rather than from a personal talent; his daughter Kyōko is a top pianist and concert organizer.

"The Japanese business world has been very late in recognizing why arts activity is important,"[39] Edo admits. He almost single-handedly raised $550,000 in early 1980 to help the performance league hold the first Tokyo World Music Contest in November of that year. The government supplied $150,000 of the total through the cultural agency. Some of the rest came by tapping firms in each industrial sector represented in the Federation of Economic Organizations (Keidanren) for "suggested shares," but Edo raised almost $200,000 by "putting a phone in my car and using it entirely to raise contributions by speaking with persons I knew well." Edo undertook the campaign because he believed that holding the contest was an appropriate "sign of the proficiency attained by Japanese musicians and because it will further encourage the level of Japanese performance."[40]

Edo's case also shows how personal ties in the business world can result in annual corporate aid to an arts organization. The Japan Orchestra Association is apparently the only foundation making arts grants in Japan that has asked big business for yearly "suggested shares" through the Keidanren network. Thanks to Edo's efforts, 199 corporations gave the association $337,000 in 1979. Another key figure is the shipbuilding tycoon Sasakawa Ryōichi, who helped bring the association an additional $492,000 from marine and automotive foundations in which he is influential. Sasakawa's interest in music centers on arts education for young people, something pioneered after World War Two by the longtime Tokyo resident Eloise Cunningham through Music For Youth programs. In the year ending March 31, 1980, the Japan Orchestra Association spent $833,000 to sponsor eighty-two concerts by Japanese orchestras, including forty-seven for youths and thirty-one more for out-of-town audiences,[j] with a total attendance of 89,000.[41] The following year the group expected it would be able to spend 30 percent more in yen terms,

[j] The youth concerts resemble in miniature the activities of Young Audiences Inc., a nonprofit group founded in the United States in 1950 to sponsor performances in schools. See Netzer, *Subsidized Muse*, pp. 137-138.

48

counting on larger gift income including $25,000 from the cultural agency. Still the level of activity it sponsors is the equivalent of only one-third of the annual budget for a typical Japanese professional orchestra, and in 1980 its subsidies were divided among twelve of them.[42]

The Japan Orchestra Association has become the biggest private patron of a performing art in Japan since it began making grants in 1973. The professed goal is to increase the number and geographic distribution of top-flight musical performances at the lowest possible prices, especially for teenagers, "to build orchestral appreciation for the future."[43] Practically all its income is from current gifts and admissions to concerts (its endowment income is only about $10,000 per year). It is a designated foundation for tax-free corporate gifts but has not yet been able to build its capital very greatly through this device. The association uses its revenue almost exclusively for sponsoring performances, although a small amount now goes for commissioning new works of contemporary music by Japanese composers.[44]

Several other private nonprofit groups hold events in classical Western music, usually acting as funnels for public funds. The Japan Performance League, which was founded in 1965 to help instrumentalists get more time on stage, is now the main noncommercial promoter of classical Western music concerts by Japanese professionals. About 1,900 musicians belong to the league, which helps them find spot jobs as well as regular employment with instrumental groups. Originally the performers financed the organization with their own dues, but today it acts mainly as a channel for government aid. The league is a designated foundation for tax-exempt corporate gifts, but its managing director, Yoshida Takayoshi, says it receives "embarrassingly little support from the business community."[45] Much smaller than the league is the Japan Performing Arts Center Foundation, a nonprofit group affiliated with the Shiki theater company that sometimes uses public money to present concerts, usually by foreigners. In effect the NHK Service Center does the same, since NHK, the government-chartered broadcaster, gets its income from subscriber fees.[k] The service center, which is technically private and nonprofit, is an impresario for all sorts of live stage events, of which the classical Western music is usually performed by visiting foreign artists.[46] Among all the foundations that sponsor music, only the orchestra association dispenses large sums originating as private patronage—and that mostly because of Edo and Sasakawa.

Several companies hold contests, festivals, and prize competitions for musicians, but the number is smaller than in the visual arts. Since 1978 Esso has run a music camp for young musicians. Mobil in 1971 began giving prizes in both classical Western and traditional Japanese music, currently awarding a total of $8,500 per year. Toshiba has taken an interest in jazz and sponsors performances by both Japanese and foreign musicians. The Hokkaido Electric Company, Tokyo Sōgō Bank, and Asahi Life Insurance Company also make small gifts to promote music each year. But Suntory probably gives the most aid to music, including a small part of the $500,000 spent each year by the Suntory Cultural Foundation, established in 1979. Each year since 1969 the distilling firm has given a music prize, currently worth $15,000, and sponsored concerts to honor the recipient. Suntory also encourages Japanese composers by buying fifty to 100 tickets each month to a concert that has at least one Japanese work on the program, distributing the tickets to the public free of charge. Truer to pattern, the firm also aids a chamber group centering on a famous cellist because a senior Suntory executive has a personal connection with the group.[47]

One other form of private music patronage is perhaps more self-interested but no less beneficial than the others: gifts from manufacturers of stereos and musical instruments. A good example is Pioneer's program of aiding seven or eight per-

---

[k] NHK collects a subscriber fee ($52.80 yearly as of 1981) from each household with a television set. About 900,000 households refuse to pay on the ground that the levy is an illegal tax. By comparison, BBC received $78 yearly as of 1981 for each color TV. See *Asahi nenkan 1980*, p. 599; *New York Times*, February 29, 1980.

formances each year by the NHK orchestra in small cities around the country. Since 1971 the Kawai piano company has run a much larger touring program for Japanese performers of classical Western music that reached more than eighty cities and towns in 1980. Kawai sponsors the Japan Chopin Society, the Japan Hugo Wolf Society, and the Tokyo Wind Orchestra, the only professional wind group in the country. Yamaha, the giant of the industry, concentrates its aid on music education.[48]

Taken as a whole, the support from private benefactors is still modest for a country that claims the world's biggest music city. Without government grants and mass-media entrepreneurship, most orchestras would starve today. Dan Ikuma, who is the leading composer of opera in Japan, believes that "music as a profession is not respected. It's terribly important to correct this low image, but extremely hard to accomplish." Part of the difficulty, as in other countries, is the lingering impression that music is a feminine occupation. Dan also agrees that businessmen "prefer visual art to music because the Japanese like what's at hand, something concrete, not abstractions. Music is too vague, and it remains unpatronized. It's seen as mere entertainment, not as a source of beauty like art objects."[49] But people have been performing Western music in Japan for just a short time compared with the long history of the visual arts, and it was only in the 1950s that the orchestra established itself as an institution with a small core of series subscribers to sustain it. Vocal and chamber groups, as well as soloists, developed their audiences in the fifties and sixties to much larger levels. Concert attendance reached a plateau in the 1970s but costs kept going up, creating a clear need for help. It takes time to develop the habit of patronage, but classical Western music is now well rooted in Japan and greater help seems likely to materialize in the 1980s.

THEATER AND DANCE

The record of private aid to both theater and dance is simpler because it is briefer. Kabuki actors have their fan clubs but the genre is commercially successful and needs no grants-in-aid. Bunraku is a ward of the state. Nō, like traditional music and classical Japanese dance, enjoys the generous revenues provided by more than a million students and needs little other patronage. The modern theater, which needs all it can find, has never been able to replace its main prewar doyen, Hijikata Yoshi. For most of the fifties and part of the sixties, modern Western-style drama, or shingeki, was too linked with labor and leftist politics to enjoy the confidence of big business. Few angels appeared to rescue precarious productions, and theater companies were almost always left to their own devices.

The most resourceful of the shingeki companies is now the largest and most nearly commercial, Shiki. It has raised a great deal of money to put on plays for children and teenagers throughout the country. Japan Life Insurance Company, known as Nissei, has aided the Shiki troupe for a long time because Shiki's leader, Asari Keita, is the son of a former top executive of Nissei. Since 1964 the company has underwritten one production each year for children in Tokyo and more recently in other cities. Through 1979, Nissei estimates that 1.5 million persons had attended 1,037 performances, all of them free of charge. Currently Shiki receives $500,000 each year from the corporation. Starting in 1979 Nissei also sponsored opera for teenagers.

No other patron has equaled Nissei's level of support for modern theater. Through the revenues of legalized bicycle racing, Sasakawa Ryōichi has arranged further grants to Shiki to subsidize plays for children. Both Kirin Beer and the Yakult dairy concern sponsored "mother and child" performances by shingeki companies in the 1970s.[50] At the same time another stage movement, shinkokugeki (literally, new national theater), enjoyed very substantial backing from Fuji Television until its debt grew so great that it went bankrupt in 1979.[L]

[L] Founded in 1962, shinkokugeki was rescued by Fuji's $56,000 in 1968 but collapsed in October 1979 with debts of $1.3 million. *Asahi nenkan 1969*, p. 724; *Asahi nenkan 1980*, p. 627.

ic than was true in
venty years earlier.
and far more likely
xpands the various
ccomplished by the
rtists would doubt-
even a single day's
account lunches.

Most imperiled of all the performing arts has been dance in the Western style, both ballet and contemporary. The top ensembles subsist on fees paid by their students and could not put on public concerts without this revenue. Individuals rarely make major gifts to dance companies or their professional federations, although the latter get a certain amount of public aid. The main patron of ballet has been Ōya Masako, who heads the International Arts Foundation and presides over its biennial world ballet contest in Osaka. For the 1980 competition the foundation looked after the traveling costs of all forty-seven pairs, representing twenty-one countries, plus one pianist for each pair. The foundation has been designated eligible for additional tax-exempt gifts from corporations, and nine of them aided the contest in 1980. But the main private contributor since the foundation was formed in the early 1970s has been the Teijin textile corporation, of which Ōya's husband was president until he died in 1980. Nonetheless the cultural agency met half the $300,000 deficit of the 1980 competition, and the Japan World Exposition Commemorative Fund, a semipublic body, paid $20,000 more. Nishina Tadashi, who is secretary vice-general of the International Arts Foundation, believes that it is "natural" that Teijin acts as the main corporate supporter. Other companies contribute because it provides "good public-relations value."[51] The foundation also sponsors a tour each year by a major foreign ballet company and aids Japanese ballet groups by buying blocks of concert tickets and distributing them to the firms that have aided it.

Japanese contemporary dancers have no big benefactor except for the cultural agency, but the Matsushita electronics and Shiraishi broadcasting interests in western Japan have become the principal sponsors of contemporary dance performances by foreign groups through the Nippon Cultural Centre, founded in 1967. Without this aid Japanese dancers and dance fans would rarely see foreign companies, whose tours always lose money in contemporary dance and often in ballet. The cultural agency helps to cover deficits for events

53

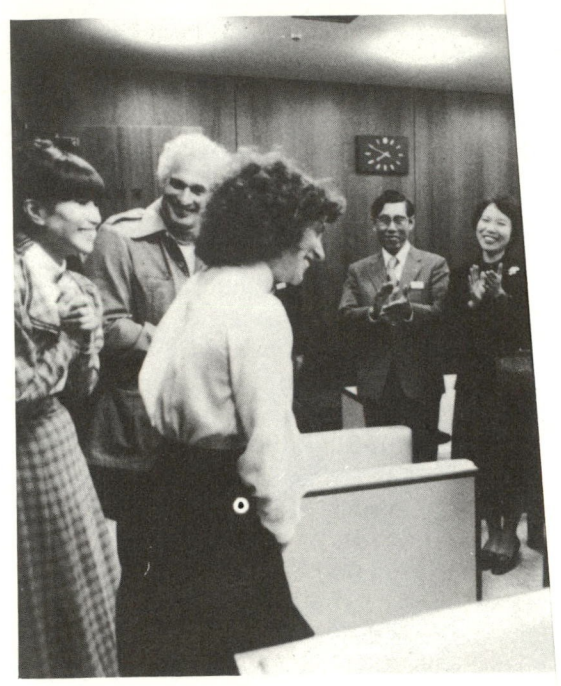

The National Theater of the Deaf, Waterford, Conr
tours Japan in 1979. In the foreground, from left:
Kuroyanagi Tetsuko, a top Japanese TV personality
sign language; David Hays and Linda Bove, leaders
Crown Prince Akihito; Prince Hitachi; and
Crown Princess Michiko. NIPPON CULTURAL CENTRE

organized by the center,^m which also send
traditional Japanese music and classical da
Although the Nippon Cultural Centre dc
annual budget, it sponsors a half-dozen n

^m The center is a designated foundation for receiving
gifts. Members of the imperial family regularly turn ou
performances. Shiraishi Hideji, its president, was form
Hideji until his father, the head of *Kyōto shinbun* and l
edged him as his natural son by a geisha.

sitive to corporate relations with the publ
the age of expansion and reinvestment tʋ
That public is now much better educated
to respond enthusiastically if business e>
arts programs beyond the levels recently a
cultural agency. For their part, Japanese a
less be cheered if companies gave them
worth of corporate spending for expense

CHAPTER 3

Arts and the State

WHEN THE Agency for Cultural Affairs announced with much éclat in September 1972 that an ancient tomb with well-preserved wall paintings had recently been uncovered at Takamatsuzaka, the Japanese public suddenly grew intrigued with archaeology and historical restoration. That same month the agency was busy getting ready for the largest autumn arts festival it had ever held, presenting new creative works by performers from all over the country. September 1972 is also when the cultural agency took over planning for the most popular art show ever seen in Japan, the *Mona Lisa* exhibit that drew 1.5 million people to the Tokyo National Museum in the spring of 1974.[a]

Preservation, innovation, and access have each been goals of national cultural policy and duties of the Agency for Cultural Affairs since it was established as a subunit of the education ministry in 1968. The law creating the cultural agency said simply that it "has responsibility for promoting and spreading culture and preserving cultural properties"[1] without a hint that creation, diffusion, and protection are often competing aims almost impossible to accomplish with a single bureau or budget. In American terms, the cultural agency was expected to be both a National Endowment for the Arts and

[a] The *Mona Lisa* show was the cultural agency's first major exhibit. The Fuji-Sankei media group turned over sponsorship to the agency in September 1972 when the French government refused to lend the painting to a private company. For many critics the show symbolized the government's absorption with famous artists, at the cost of neglecting current works. The King Tutankhamen exhibit at the Metropolitan Museum of Art, New York, during early 1979 had an attendance of 1.2 million. Adachi Kenji, *Bunkachō kotohajime*, Tokyo, Tōkyō Shoseki, 1978, pp. 38-56; Bunkachō, *Bunka gyōsei no ayumi*, Tokyo, Bunkachō, 1978, p. 271; Ebara Jun, *Nihon bijutsukai fuhai no kōzō*, Tokyo, Saimaru Shuppankai, 1978, p. 87; Enna Takio, *Chinmoku no shishatachi*, Tokyo, Shinchōsha, 1980, pp. 8-29; *New York Times*, July 30, 1979.

a National Trust for Historic Preservation, with two-thirds of its resources tied up in the latter. Other public bodies, from NHK and the Japan Foundation to prefectural and city governments, faced the same dilemmas of choosing cultural priorities but on a smaller scale. Governmental patronage of the arts in the 1960s and 1970s reached levels many times greater than the total of private gifts.

Japan resembles Great Britain in its lack of tax incentives for private giving and all of Europe in its dearth of private philanthropy for the arts. Yet unlike Europe, Japan has relied until recently on private federations and organizations of artists, not the state, to maintain and extend the arts. Fourteen of the fifteen professional orchestras, for example, are operated by independent corporations rather than directly by government entities. Most arts groups were left until the mid-1960s very much to their own devices, with little public or private help. When the official aid for artists first became sizeable about 1965, it was intended both to protect old art forms and encourage newer ones, to preserve traditional works and commission fresh ones, and to democratize cultural life by taking art to the people. Programs to attain these goals blossomed throughout the seventies, led by the cultural agency in concert with local and prefectural governments. During 1975-1980, the agency paid out a total of $152.5 million to encourage the modern arts and to spread the arts of all eras to communities from Hokkaido to Kyushu. It spent another $66.2 million on a national museum of ethnology and new theaters for nō, bunraku, popular entertainments, and the modern performing arts. Public patronage is now important in most of the Japanese arts world, however abashed performers may feel that creative activities by their groups received only $5.7 million of the cultural agency's total budget of $200.1 million for 1980.[2]

A National Policy for Culture

The Japanese government helped various arts enterprises for nearly a century before deciding on a cultural policy in the 1960s. Since everyone agreed education was essential for national wealth and power, it outranked the arts as a public priority in the 1870s and still accounted for 99 percent of the education ministry's expenditures in the 1970s (the cultural agency got the other 1 percent).[3] Museums and libraries were put under the ministry's supervision in the early Meiji period, and an official school of art was established in 1876 "to study the new realistic styles in order to make up for the short points of traditional art."[4] The state soon hired foreign instructors in painting, sculpture, music, opera, and ballet to teach the new styles from abroad. The Tokyo Academy of Music was officially founded in 1879 and the Tokyo Academy of Art eight years later. In 1949 they merged to form Tokyo University of Fine Arts, the dominant institution in arts education today.[5]

Historical preservation became another duty of the education ministry when the Diet passed the ancient shrines and temples protection law in 1897. Ten years later the ministry sponsored its first art show, known as Bunten, which continues today in private hands under the name Nitten, the largest open-entry art exhibit in the world. An Imperial Art Academy was established in 1919 to recognize outstanding achievements, and the state began awarding cultural medals in 1937, the year the art academy was broadened to take in literary and performing artists.[6] Still the arts existed before 1945 almost entirely through the efforts of private associations and troupes formed by the artists themselves, aided from time to time by generous benefactors or by commercial backing, such as kabuki and bunraku, from the Shōchiku and Tōhō enterprises.

When a cultural properties protection law was passed in 1950, the education ministry appointed a committee to give advice on how the legislation should be applied. This body, which today consists of about eighty private leaders in the traditional arts and historical preservation, has met each March for the past three decades to work out policies for cultural protection. Artistic innovation and dissemination became official responsibilities of the education authorities in 1949, but little was done to coordinate policies until a cultural office was created within the ministry in 1966. Two years later this office and the protection commission's staff were merged into the cultural agency under the leadership of Kon Hidemi, a career bureaucrat with expertise in the performing arts.[7]

The new arrangement pleased the officials who administered arts policy because the unified agency gave them more weight inside the government. Priests of the temples and shrines receiving preservation funds were happy for the same reason. The change also satisfied Satō Eisaku, the prime minister, who was then trying to consolidate bureaucratic units wherever he could. Satō knew from visiting the United States that the National Endowment for the Arts, established in 1965, had soon become popular with politicians and the public. Most importantly, the cultural agency gave arts leaders a forum in the national government, which they had been seeking since the early 1960s, and the voice to win public patronage for their organizations.[8] Politicians partial to kabuki and other traditional arts helped set up the agency, but representatives of the modern arts have been generously sprinkled on its advisory boards ever since 1968.

Some of those advisers helped prepare the basic cultural policy that year: "1. Improvement of cultural quality. 2. Spread of art and culture. 3. Protection and preservation of art and culture." Programs were needed to carry out these objectives and outside experts were brought to the agency regularly to confer with its staff, which grew to 200 by the late seventies. Since the basic policy was so brief and arid, the programs in effect became the policies.[9] The cultural agency assumed control over various arts institutions whose needs had to be taken into account in budgeting for future programs: the three national museums (regarded as a part of cultural preservation), the three—now four—national art museums (classed as cultural development), and various institutes, academies, and research units. From the start, the agency was a bureaucratic hodgepodge with diffuse duties to carry out, yet artists have rarely complained that its officials failed to consult them—only that their share of the grants has been too small.[10]

THE COSTS OF CULTURE

"Without a doubt," says Adachi Kenji, the former head of the cultural agency, "subsidies from the agency are far more important than corporate or foundation giving to the arts."[11] The cultural agency is by far the largest governmental unit at any level in Japan that aids innovation in the arts, and it is also the policy leader to which other public arts administrators turn. The national government calculates that its total expenses for "social education and culture" in the broadest sense were $477.2 million in 1980, up from just $19.8 million when the cultural agency began in 1968.[b] Of this sum the agency received $200.1 million, compared with its first budget of $13.7 million twelve years earlier. About 40 percent of each year's appropriation is now spent on the traditional and contemporary arts.

Ever since 1946 the education ministry has sponsored an autumn arts festival and since 1950 has funded the event. The first government aid given directly to arts groups came in 1959, and by the time the cultural agency was formed nine years later the education ministry was already spending $375,000 a year to subsidize new works, activities abroad, local arts organizations, and performances for young people. Still this sum was just 2.7 percent of the agency's first budget; in 1980 these same programs took up 11.6 percent of its $200.1 million budget. The cultural agency's budget as a whole grew 574 percent between 1968 and 1978 (the total national budget rose 489 percent at the same time) and went up another 19.8 percent from 1978 to 1980.[12] These figures still seem

---

[b] The figure excludes spending on schools and the promotion of science. By comparison, the budget of the National Endowment for the Arts was $154.4 million in 1980, a figure the Reagan administration proposes to cut to $98 million by 1984. *Nihon tōkei nenkan*, 1980, p. 463; Nobuya Shikaumi, *Cultural Policy in Japan*, Paris, UNESCO, 1970, p. 29; *New York Times*, January 27, 1980 and February 20, 1981.

small to artists, but it is worth noting that Japan thought of itself as a poor country until the early 1970s, ill able to afford new parks, care for the aged, and other social balm. The government probably began paying attention to artists as early as the 1960s not because they seemed more worthy than other claimants but because sponsoring the arts—especially the traditional ones—was good politics at home and good diplomacy abroad. The activity generated by the government's cash has been colorful, substantial, and sometimes almost overwhelming, especially in smaller cities that were unprepared for all the free art from Tokyo.

The main programs supported by the cultural agency have changed very little since 1968, but the government began spending much more for outreach after 1971 and new national facilities after 1975.[13] Of the three main goals outlined in 1968, preservation of all sorts took up about 70 percent of the budget until 1978, when it fell to its present 65 percent because allocations for new facilities claimed a larger share. The chief arts-related items listed under cultural preservation are subsidies for the national theater and the national museums. The theater expenses include aid to kabuki, bunraku, and the other traditional stage arts. The theater's grant leapt by 50 percent in 1975, after big losses the year before, and then rose more slowly than the agency's overall budget, to $10.6 million in 1980. Aid to the three national museums has also grown only slowly, especially allocations for new purchases. In 1980 the museums got $21.3 million from the government, down nearly 10 percent from the year before, and their acquisitions grants were frozen at $1.9 million. The total allotted to cultural preservation in 1980 was $129.1 million, an increase in yen terms of 66 percent during the previous five years. The agency's total budget rose 89 percent in the same period.

While preservation continued to gain momentum, grants to stimulate artistic creativity, nearly all of them in the modern arts, increased hardly at all during the early seventies and only 55 percent during 1975-1980, supporting the view that innovation has been losing ground in the scramble for public aid. The 1980 total of $7.1 million included $560,000 for the agency's arts festival and prizes, and another $760,000 to help artists get further training at home or abroad. The arts festival share was lower in 1980 than five years before, and the grants for further training have been effectively frozen at the same level for four years. Aid to arts organizations for commissioning new works, which started off at $56,000 in 1968, reached $2.3 million in 1975, and rose another 70 percent in yen terms to its 1980 level of $5.7 million. In the cultural agency's overall budget, no arts category grew more slowly than the program to encourage creative activity.

The third basic policy objective, treated more fully in the following chapter, involves access to the arts: schemes to spread both traditional and modern arts beyond the biggest cities, to aid national art museums, and to construct a new cultural complex in Tokyo. Part of the subsidy to the art museums also helps painters, sculptors, print makers, and other artists by providing for the purchase and exhibition of their works. In this third category the government raised its total spending on national art museums and related facilities by 71 percent in yen terms during 1975-1980 to $13.3 million. Money for acquisitions in this third program increased 79 percent, to just over $2 million in 1980, and the subvention for exhibits went up 111 percent, to $1.2 million. As in other countries, most of the aid to the museums went for stanching the chronic deficits that arose from keeping the buildings open so the public could visit.

The main outreach efforts have gone toward extending the arts to people outside the half-dozen biggest cities. This program expanded fast during 1972-1975, when Adachi Kenji served as commissioner of cultural affairs, and grew another 87 percent in yen terms between 1975 and 1980, when its allotment totaled $16.2 million. A bit more than half the annual grants for outreach were used to help prefectures and municipalities build new museums, theaters, concert halls, and cultural centers. The balance went to subsidize plays for children and teenagers, to aid touring arts festivals, and to help local arts organizations with deficits. Some of these monies ended up subsidizing big-city troupes, orchestras, and dance companies, supplementing the basic $5.7 million provided in 1980 to stimulate creative activity in the performing arts. Another portion of the outreach funds helped to support traditional performing-arts groups based in the cities. Although it is still small in relation to the cultural agency's total budget, the outreach project was the agency's most vigorous arts program in the 1970s, and it was also a magnet for private patronage, which sponsored even more events for children and high-school youths around the nation.

One more major boost to the arts in the late seventies was government aid for new national theaters and concert halls. In 1975 the cultural agency spent $130,000 for planning new facilities; by 1980 it was paying out $10.4 million to construct halls for nō, bunraku, and the modern performing arts. Even though no other arts-related component of the agency's budget grew as fast during 1975-1980 as the overall budget itself, the new theaters and concert halls, including state support for their inevitable deficits, are a major benefit to every arts group using them.

A policy is nonetheless more than programs and the funds to pay for them. The cultural agency commissioned a long-range plan in 1977, devised mainly by private experts, that picked out two familiar problems. The first was reconciling tradition with modernity. Both the premodern and contemporary arts needed further encouragement, the commission reported: "in the midst of this mixture it may be possible to see lying concealed the energy to give birth to a new culture"— a roundabout statement and a never-ending process.[14] The second difficulty was that cultural activities were still too concentrated in the big cities, despite a major push after 1971 to spread the arts to cities and towns all over the country. The agency heeded these warnings at the end of the 1970s, but its budget virtually stopped growing in 1980, and with it the chance to shore up soft spots in its programs. An irresolvable problem was that the cultural agency was the lowest priority of the government's politically weakest ministry—and grants to encourage the modern arts were perhaps the least favored program within the agency.[c] When allocations for new facilities are considered, the arts as a whole now claim a larger proportion of the cultural agency's budget than ever before, but that share is still only 40 percent of the total,[15] and just 3 percent of the total goes for commissioning creative activity.[d]

VITALIZING TRADITIONS

Today is the age of democracy for the Japanese arts of the feudal era. Courtly nō dramas, bourgeois kabuki plays, and plebian popular entertainments are now intended for everybody, and the Japanese government pays millions of dollars each year to make sure the public can attend. Perhaps the reason they are open to all, after centuries of class distinctions, is less an issue of social egalitarianism or box-office economics than a simple matter of history and value. The stratified society that produced them is safely past, and the premodern arts are valuable today not for their specific class denotations but their general worth as something both permanent in time and Japanese in location. Because they now belong to all, the traditional arts have merit both as expressions of eternal human

[c] The cultural agency is regarded as far more sympathetic to artists' needs than the finance ministry, which has virtually frozen the agency's budget through March 1982. Matsuda Tomoo, in "Nihon no ongaku bunka to dojō," *Ongaku geijutsu*, November 1980, p. 30; Yoshida Takayoshi interview, December 25, 1980.

[d] For the United States, Netzer estimates that about 17 percent of the funds paid out by the National Endowment for the Arts subsidize innovation, higher than anywhere in Europe. As for Japan, the cultural agency calculates that about 7 percent of its support for arts goes for creative activities administered by groups. In 1975 the NEA devoted about three-eighths of its budget to outreach, half to help cultural organizations, and one-eighth to preserve the cultural heritage. The categories differ in Japan, but outreach took up 20 percent of the cultural agency's arts subsidies in 1980. Preservation claimed about two-thirds of the agency's overall budget throughout the seventies. Netzer, *Subsidized Muse*, pp. 155, 160; Bunkachō, *Bunkachō yosan jimu teiyō, Shōwa 55nen*, Tokyo, Bunkachō, 1980, pp. 22-25.

dilemmas and as something distinctly Japanese. Minor differences between samurai and commoners fade in the bright light of the world arena where their great-grandchildren now play a major part. Transformed, the old arts are valued for newer, more nationalist reasons as well as for their timeless statements about the unchanging human condition. Art transcends time—but also becomes the prisoner of place.

Few countries have inherited more art worth saving, and fewer have matched what the Japanese have accomplished since World War Two in preserving their relics and artifacts. The country has become so secularized that the government is now the chief guardian of ancient temples and shrines. Protecting religious buildings and their art works is one of the major duties of the cultural agency. About 7,000 objects of art are immune to export, and more than 10,000, including buildings, are classed as important cultural properties and eligible for preservation funds. About 10 percent of the important cultural properties are considered national treasures. The forty-seven prefectures as well as municipalities have designated another 55,000 items as local cultural properties. The cultural agency also recognizes more than forty individuals and groups in the traditional performing arts as living national treasures, along with about forty-five others in traditional crafts.[16] All receive stipends to honor their achievements.

The Takamatsuzaka discoveries in 1972 helped stir public enthusiasm for historical preservation in an age of throw-away materialism, and so did the refurbishing of the great Buddha hall at Tōdaiji in Nara, a seven-year, $20 million project that ended with ceremonies in October 1980 featuring the world premiere of a new orchestral work by Dan Ikuma commissioned by the agency.[17] But the main attention of the agency is now focused on displaying old art more regularly, since many important cultural properties have never been seen in public.[18]

Bunraku and kabuki have benefited most from the state aid to traditional stage arts. Since 1966 the help has come through the national theater, a somber brown cathedral in log-cabin style overlooking the palace moat at Miyakezaka in Tokyo. The Shōchiku corporation took over bunraku from the Uemura family in 1909 and began accepting public aid in 1953 when its deficit grew large. Before World War Two the puppet theater was often regarded as just the quaint seedbed of its more important offshoot, kabuki, but partly because of prodding from foreigners in the late 1940s the government eventually decided bunraku was worth rescuing on its own merits. The state declared it a living national treasure in 1955 and excused it from taxes. Shōchiku was forced to abandon it in 1963, when the present Bunraku Association was formed with help from the education ministry, NHK, and the city and prefecture of Osaka.[19]

When the national theater opened in 1966, as a special corporation funded by the cultural agency, it provided regular bunraku and kabuki performances (four and eight times a year, respectively, as of 1980) and guaranteed the box-office shortfall. In 1970 it also began training about ten new performers a year in each dramatic form and started free summer workshops for high-school students to develop future audiences for both. Bunraku also plays in Osaka, its original home, but the national theater has been its patron and its guide in developing shorter programs that now regularly fill the 630 seats in the theater's small hall. Like commercial kabuki, bunraku has highlighted famous plays and star performers to build attendance in the past few years, but in 1981 it shuffled the schedule so that the troupe could stage complete plays, not just the most popular scenes. The national theater has given bunraku the greatest financial security it has enjoyed in a century and provided marketing expertise to maximize income and minimize the public subsidy.[e] Audiences were barely half

---

[e] Most of the bunraku puppets and script-books were burned in air raids on Osaka in 1945. The jōruri narrator and samisen accompanist, who control the tempo of the play, perform from lacquer lecterns costing $9,000 each. The high costs of production are partly met by filling the theater with audience groups put together by Sōka Gakkai and workers' drama circles. Bunraku audiences have recently grown younger, in contrast with most traditional arts, in response to the national theater's summer workshops and bunraku

67

of capacity in 1967, but by 1980 the producers managed to draw more than 90 percent of capacity for bunraku. Even so the puppet drama is a financial sponge. The theater does not disclose its subventions to each stage genre, but when it took over bunraku in 1967 the deficit was $319,000 and it is almost certainly much greater today.[20]

The theater building itself had been discussed since the turn of the century and actively planned since the Diet approved the idea in April 1958. Despite a great deal of pressure from artists in ballet, opera, and classical Western music, the committee in charge decided that the $10.8 million construction fund could not build more than two theaters, kabuki and bunraku, both of which were adaptable to other premodern art forms. Kabuki and bunraku clearly had priority, but a lack of money, not a bias against the modern genres, is why the national theater turned into the main center "to preserve, promote, and develop traditional arts"—its "paramount"[21] aim to this day.

The large theater holds 1,746 (1,651 with the kabuki walkway in place) and the small hall 630. In its first years the management filled them with outside performing groups so often that the playwright Senda Koreya dismissed it as just another "rental hall."[22] Although bunraku is still its only resident company, and that only part-time, the theater's producers have kept the halls bright in the last decade with an appealing mix of traditional arts events, while still renting them out for a number of private performances in classical Japanese dance, traditional music, and nō drama. From 1967 to 1977 the theater drew about 6 million people to see 125 different kabuki productions, fifty-three of bunraku, and scattered events in classical dance, traditional music, court music, and popular entertainments. Since then its offerings have grown ever more varied and attractive, and critics no longer complain that it is run unprofessionally—only that it costs the taxpayers too much.[23]

---

broadcasts by NHK. Takemoto Mojitayū interview, February 14, 1981; *Asahi nenkan 1971*, p. 705; Bunkachō, *Bunka gyōsei no ayumi*, pp. 83-84; *Asahi Evening News*, February 20, 1981; *Japan Times*, February 21, 1981.

Kabuki is the chief magnet, luring more than half of the theater's 650,000 customers each year. Opening the new facility has benefited both Shōchiku, which rents out its actors to the national theater, and kabuki in general. Instead of cutting into audiences at the commercial kabuki theaters, events at the new building increased overall attendance at kabuki by about a third.[24] The number of season subscribers for kabuki programs at the national theater went up steadily in the 1970s and now includes 23,000 persons, at a 20 percent discount for the series. Since the hall is 650 seats smaller than the Kabukiza theater, and only thirty to thirty-five performances of each program are offered compared with fifty at the Kabukiza, the national theater takes in considerably less revenue than would the Kabukiza for the same production.[25] Higher costs, lower income, and contract fees for the actors force the theater to run a deficit in staging kabuki, even though it has started putting on certain popular scenes and acts, not just "pure" productions of whole plays from earlier centuries, and now looks the other way when spectators carry food and drink to their seats. Kabuki also benefits from NHK broadcasts, touring arts festivals sponsored by the cultural agency, and overseas trips on behalf of the Japan Foundation, spinoffs from a support program based at the national theater.

The theater began building a third hall in December 1977, to be used by popular entertainers such as storytellers, jugglers, comedians, mime artists, and minstrels. The new structure, which cost $4.9 million, seats 300 persons and includes a library, record collection, and training facilities to perpetuate these popular arts. Skeptics warned that the essence of the mass entertainments was their confusion and vibrancy.[26] Sticking them in a hillside chapel behind the sober national theater, tucked away next to the austere supreme court building, would be like holding a beer festival in a museum. Actually the new hall has drawn well since opening in March 1979, and it helps support the commercial variety-halls for rakugo storytelling, yose vaudeville, and comic routines very much as the main theater aids Shōchiku's houses for kabuki.

The national theater is the government's flagship for the

traditional arts. When the cultural agency assumed responsibility for the theater's budget in 1968, it appropriated $1.2 million. By 1980 the subsidy was $10.6 million, an increase of 403 percent in yen terms. Currently the aid from the cultural agency amounts to about 62 percent of the theater's income.[27] The rest it earns from the box office, rentals, and auxiliary sources. By now the patronage has become a lifesaver for bunraku and an important tonic to other traditional arts that would have to put on fewer productions before smaller crowds without it.

The cultural agency decided in 1975 to build two other national facilities to house premodern art forms. One is a $28.5 million bunraku theater at Takatsu in Osaka, open in 1983, with seats for 800 and a large exhibit hall. It also has room for training new performers, since Tokyo proved to be a bad locale for learning how to recite in the required Osaka dialect. The second is a new national nō theater, open in 1982 near Sendagaya station in Tokyo. Nō and its comic accompaniment, kyōgen, were once considered snobbish aristocratic arts but have become accepted as valid parts of Japanese theater since the war. Kyōgen is easier to follow and escaped nō's elitist shadow in the 1950s and 1960s. Each has adapted well to an age of middle-class audiences, and studying nō has become a mark of refinement for women as well as men in white-collar families. Thanks to fees from more than a million pupils each year, nō has thrived without much state aid, but the new theater in Tokyo is a welcome facility in a city with only five other nō stages and a fitting monument to the world's oldest continuously practiced dramatic form.[28] Although only a minority of the cultural agency's total budget for preservation goes to the traditional arts, few theatrical performers denied by 1980 that the government was at last doing a good deal to vitalize their art.

Familiar Innovations

Creativity has been a cardinal esthetic value in Japan only in this century, mostly because of stimulus from Europe. The traditional Japanese arts rarely prized innovation for its own sake, and even today they carefully regulate who may alter a time-honored script, technique, or piece of choreography. Variations on old themes have seeped into the repertoire of every traditional art form, often burnishing their drawing power, but it is mostly their claim to continuity across historical epochs that makes them so attractive today.[29] Creativity as an absolute is a foreign idea. It had little following among Japanese artists until the postwar period. Instead, innovation has more often meant testing the limits of familiar techniques and concepts, often by bridging native and Western elements. Like other artists, Japan's postwar painters, sculptors, print makers, playwrights, composers, and choreographers have needed the past in order to rebel against it, and their creations have often revealed their debt to tradition even more clearly than their departure from it.

Still it is true that commissioning new works in the modern arts was one of the first activities of the national government when it started subsidizing artists in 1959. The main programs to help creative artists were all in place by the late 1960s and have grown very little since. It is axiomatic that foundations and governments help the visual arts less systematically than the performing arts because most visual artists work alone, outside the mantle of a troupe or company to which grants can easily be made. They are hard to find, there are too many of them to put on stipends, and there are few satisfactory organizations to administer grants on their behalf.

"It is a fact that the cultural agency mainly confines its support for the visual arts to classical Japanese art," says Inumaru Tadashi, who directed the agency from 1975 to 1980 and now heads the national theater. The government has been buying new works by contemporary artists at one-person and group exhibits since 1959 at the rate of about ten per year, a modest investment for the world's most productive art country.[f] The cultural agency sends the works on tour and then

---

[f] As of 1978 the Netherlands was spending $30 million a year in public funds to buy works by 2,000 Dutch artists. *New York Times*, December 31, 1978.

gives them to the national art museums. In another small program for contemporary art, three or four visual artists each year have been given government funds to study abroad since 1967. Distinguished older artists are eligible for election to the Japan Arts Academy, the successor to the prewar Imperial Arts Academy, which provides them a pension from the state.[30]

Mukai Kasue, who owns a Ginza art gallery, believes that the government is interested in "preserving a tradition, not creating new expressions of beauty" in art. She points out that the cultural agency sends the same functionary every time she holds a show, whether it contains sculpture, prints, oils, or watercolors, and that most of its aid goes for helping the national museums put on large exhibitions, few of which ever include living Japanese artists. Maki Jun'ichi, a painter in the Western style, agrees that the cultural agency's aid is meager but says "it is still authoritative for artists" because having your work picked for purchase confers immense prestige. The agency's own long-range planning commission recommended in 1977 that much more be done to identify and aid "hidden artists,"[31] but it left unmentioned that most flagrant deficiency: the reluctance of the national museums to sponsor Japan's artists by exhibiting or commissioning their works.

The cultural agency has helped to publicize art shows of all kinds since 1972 through a television program called *In Quest of Beauty*, now broadcast for fifteen minutes each week on twenty-four stations around the country. But some persons wonder whether the government uses television to promote an official culture, especially since a majority of the programming deals with Japanese arts, often traditional ones. A more accurate criticism is that the show slights the performing arts in favor of painting, sculpture, and crafts.[32] Also in 1972 the agency began making grants of $33,000 each to ten film makers per year to help with the costs of producing good movies. This scheme financed a number of independent art films, not just productions by the three shaky major studios (Shōchiku, Nikkatsu, and Daiei, until its collapse in 1972), which had benefited from another state program to encourage film exports during 1966-1971.[g] Since 1976 the agency has given $25,000 annually for each of five animated films produced for children's television.[33] Otherwise the cultural agency has done very little to enchance creativity in the mass media, although it runs a national film center as part of the Tokyo National Museum of Modern Art.

The live performing arts received their first public grants for new works soon after the war, in the familiar guise of an autumn arts festival. The first, patterned after those in the United States, took place in Tokyo in 1946, with a dozen volunteer performances of theater, music, and dance. Four years later the education ministry provided the first budget for the event, $14,000 for prizes and subventions. Throughout the fifties and sixties, the festival prospered in the number and quality of works performed because its awards, bearing the cachet of official approval, soon became the most prestigious in the nation. Yet as late as 1969 the government supported it with a grant of just $84,000. Then in the early seventies the cultural agency turned the festival into a major production, quadrupling its support and bringing many more participants into each of the ten divisions. In 1980 the agency's grant for the festival was $562,000, unchanged in yen terms since 1975.[34] This sum pays for about a dozen commissioned works, more than sixty-five prizes in various categories, and the excess costs of production beyond the revenues from ticket sales, program advertising, broadcast fees, and auxiliary income.

The festival as it has taken shape in the seventies is still centered in Tokyo and now includes divisions for film, radio, television, and recorded music as well as the live performing arts. Altogether about 260 productions are offered each year, a number of them several times each. Theater, music, dance, and popular entertainments are presented in three categories:

[g] The Ministry of International Trade and Industry operated a $25 million loan fund during 1966-1971 to help export Japanese films. Britain, France, and West Berlin all subsidize film making. Adachi, *Bunkachō*, p. 137; *Asahi nenkan 1967*, p. 724; *Asahi nenkan 1970*, p. 700; *Asahi nenkan 1971*, p. 700; *Asahi nenkan 1972*, p. 695; Shikaumi, *Cultural Policy*, p. 25.

(1) works commissioned by the cultural agency; (2) performances held in cooperation with the festival by companies that can coordinate their schedules (often they have received other forms of aid from the agency, for creative activity or out-of-town tours); and (3) participating performances by individuals and groups who apply to panels of judges for the privilege of competing for prizes.[h] More than 90 percent of the performances fall into this last category, but the larger instrumental, vocal, dramatic, and dance groups dominate the first two categories and often put on full-length works. During 1969-1977, according to the agency, participating entries were quite evenly divided among dance, popular entertainments, music, and theater (including nō).[35] The traditional arts, in which public competition is usually muted, have been less active in the arts festival than the modern ones. Prestige and publicity are the main incentives to the many hundreds of artists who appear each autumn, giving the cultural agency and taxpaying audiences excellent value for their $562,000. The festival, as a showcase for all the performing arts, has managed for at least a decade to balance excellence with access. Whether the same funds would yield even greater inventiveness if they were distributed directly to the artists cannot be known. But the cultural agency answers to the public, which has an interest in being entertained as well as in creativity, and the arts festival in the 1970s deftly avoided lapsing into either elitism or pandering.

Important as the festival is for bringing new art and artists to the public, the government's fellowships for further training at home and abroad do even more to elicit fresh works. The first state grant of any sort to an arts organization was for activity abroad in 1959. When the cultural agency was founded

[h] The cultural agency also selects candidates for the Order of Culture, conferred each November 3. This award frequently is made to artists. Between 1937 and 1980, 200 persons were honored, including three women. Other medals, decorations, and prizes are awarded to artists, scholars, and similar specialists for outstanding cultural achievements. Bunkachō, *Bunka gyōsei chōki sōgō keikaku ni tsuite*, Tokyo, Bunkachō, 1977, p. 26; Bunkachō, *Bunka gyōsei no ayumi*, pp. 99-101; *Japan Times*, October 25, 1980.

nine years later, it spent $121,000 annually to send Japanese artists abroad, mainly to observe and practice, but sometimes to exhibit or perform. By 1975 the outlays for foreign training reached $415,000 and then rose another 22 percent in yen terms by 1980, to $760,000.[36]

With this program the cultural agency superseded both the Tokyo American Cultural Center and the Fulbright program in exchanging performing artists between Japan and the United States.[i] The first group of Japanese artists sent abroad specifically to develop their skills consisted of four persons in 1967 (that same year the government sent 325 science and engineering students overseas). Since then the agency has picked about eighteen fellows each year for foreign training in various genres, usually for a year but, beginning in 1974, sometimes for two. More seasoned artists started receiving three-month grants in 1979. The numbers chosen in the visual arts, music, and theater (including stage design and film) have been roughly equal, slightly larger than the total for dancers.[37]

Equally useful is a newer program, started in 1977, for thirty artists a year to receive stipends for advanced training within Japan. Performing artists are especially delighted with this home-front opportunity because a long stay overseas can become counterproductive. Going abroad polishes their art and ornaments their curricula vitae, but it also ruptures the harmony of their performing groups and weakens their connections for side jobs, which they need to survive when they

---

[i] The Fulbright program exchanged performing artists from the mid-1950s until 1969. It still sends one or two persons per year each way, in crafts and visual media. The current American Centers in Japan have supplanted the earlier American Cultural Centers, which were scaled down in 1970 by the Nixon administration in prosperous countries that could henceforth support exchanges themselves. The present center in Tokyo deals primarily with issues such as trade and security, but it maintains a library, shows films, and sponsors lectures, demonstrations, and discussions by American visitors, including writers and artists. A number of other governments operate similar facilities in Japan. Sumio Kambayashi, "Modern Dance in Japan," *Impulse*, 1965, pp. 29-47; Sakuma Etsujirō interview, October 16, 1980; Walter Nichols interview, December 1, 1980; Lawrence B. Flood interview, October 22, 1980; Charles H. Walsh, Jr., interview, October 22, 1980.

return. Visual artists are more independent and less ambivalent about foreign study, having little to lose and much to gain from the chance—so much so that the cultural agency had to tell some of them in 1975 to "be prudent" about accepting advance guarantees for their works from local dealers while they were abroad on government fellowships.[38]

Neither festivals nor further training have brought new works to the stage nearly so systematically as a third major program: direct government subsidies to performing arts groups. The first grants were awarded in 1965 and totaled $12,500. After the cultural agency was formed, the aid went up from $372,000 in 1968 to $2.3 million in 1975. Five years later it was fixed at $5.7 million annually, a rise of 70 percent in yen terms.[39] In some cases the money ends up covering deficits, especially for professional orchestras, but even they are expected to use the sums to commission and perform new works by Japanese composers. As of 1980, eight regional orchestras and four more in Tokyo were receiving $100,000 to $150,000 each,[j] and the other Tokyo orchestras without separate public backing were included in the payouts starting in 1981. Certain orchestras also get various amounts to travel under the cultural agency's outreach program for children, youths, and touring arts festivals.[40] Smaller grants for performances of new instrumental works are made each year to federations of composers in both traditional Japanese and classical Western music.

At the head of the grant list each year is the Nikikai Opera Company, a reminder that art forms with the smallest audiences often get the biggest awards. Nikikai's allotment doubled between 1977 and 1980, to $500,000 per year, not merely because the group is politically ingratiated but also because at 330 members it is the largest performing arts company in Japan and a funnel for state aid to opera as a whole. The cultural agency has also supported an opera school run by

---

[j] In the United States the National Endowment for the Arts made grants in 1980 of $300,000 each to the six top American orchestras and smaller awards to 142 others, totaling $9.2 million. *New York Times*, May 21, 1980.

Nikikai. The government subsidizes opera partly to create jobs for voice majors who graduate each year from public universities (there are no dance majors at these institutions, and the state feels less obligation toward their art). Above all, opera is something a cultured country ought to have, the government believes, and it is determined to help Nikikai become a respectable company. The national subsidy covers about a sixth of Nikikai's annual budget,[41] and the group uses it to produce new operas by Japanese composers as well as works from abroad.

Ballet is another art form favored at the cultural agency. Each year it grants about $200,000 to the Japan Ballet Association, representing most of the major companies, and slightly larger sums to the Japan Ballet Council, a funnel for receiving aid formed in 1977 by four big Tokyo companies that split from the balkanized Japan Ballet Association. Each federation decides which of its member groups will get shares for staging productions of new works in both the fall and the spring. "The government would give even more money for ballet if there were more audience for it," according to Ogawa Ayako, who heads her own studio. Yet until the late 1970s ballet received far more help from the national treasury than either classical Japanese dance or contemporary dance,[42] even though both have as many students as ballet and despite the fact that creativity is the very essence of the latter.

Each year the cultural agency gives more than a quarter of its funds for creative activity to professional orchestras and about 15 percent to opera companies. Another 5 percent goes to other musical groups, including composers and performers in traditional Japanese as well as classical Western music. Dance gets about 10 percent, mostly for ballet. Theater receives most of its public funding for productions through the agency's various outreach programs, but nearly 10 percent of the budget for fostering creative activity is used each year for overseas tours by Japanese mime, puppet, and youth dramatic groups, for visiting performances by foreign companies, and exhibits, lectures, research, and publications on modern theater of all types.[43] Most of the balance goes for similar international events, publications, and off-stage services in music and dance, but a part of it helps to pay for three or four art shows at home and abroad each year. The creative-activity budget is a catchall for aiding arts organizations of many sorts, some of them amateur and most of them in modern genres. Only a slight majority of its funds are used for live productions by professional performing groups.

Nearly everyone agrees that the cultural agency is more adept at preserving and providing access to the arts than at stimulating them to innovate. Adachi Kenji admits that the agency has been "very inadequate" in respecting the autonomy of individual artists and their groups. Part of the difficulty, as Ohara Shigeo of the finance ministry points out, is a universal bureaucratic preference for making grants to federations of artists rather than to individuals, letting the arts organizations themselves decide which applicants are worthy.[44] In the Japanese case it is customary to give something to every responsible federation that applies, shirking judgments about their relative merits. Visual artists suffer the most, since they are shut out from the creativity grants to arts institutions, which in 1980 took up $5.7 million of the cultural agency's $7.1 million budget for artistic innovation.

Faced with a static budget after years of steady growth, the agency's officials worked out stiffer guidelines in 1980 that helped them begin to choose qualitatively among groups seeking help. Orchestras, which drained much of the money for creative activity in the seventies, henceforth had to meet certain size requirements and look for more local funding. Performing groups receiving national funds through their professional federations were now required to be nonprofit corporations and submit minimum performance budgets.[45] But the agency also decided to keep on dividing the money among the arts federations, rather than reach esthetic judgments of its own. The government's policy of caution, with its preference for such familiar encouragements to innovation as festivals, study fellowships, and grants to reliable arts organizations, is so well established that a big jump in the budget will be needed before the cultural agency can gamble on creativity where it is often concentrated—among individuals and the avant-garde. Even without tombs at Takamatsuzaka or mobs at the *Mona Lisa*, the agency is so diverted by its many tasks that invention in the arts is still more praised than patronized.

CHAPTER 4

Arts to the People

PAINTING, sculpture, and most arts of the stage were monopolies of urban elites in Japan, as in renaissance Italy, starting with the fifteenth century and continuing until modern times. Crafts and popular entertainments thrived at the same time in smaller towns and villages. When heavy industrialization drew millions of new workers to the cities after 1900, the urban arts, in both traditional and modern garb, began to spread downward socially and outward geographically until they became the standard forms of artistic expression for most of the population a half-century later. Yet painters and performers congregated more and more in the capital for its wealth, its audiences, and its stimulating new ideas. Like Paris or London, Tokyo came to govern cultural life so overwhelmingly that the authorities in 1949 started to strew the arts to the 80 percent of the people outside the capital region. The explicit aim was to create a real public where almost nothing but private audiences existed. The result was more traveling by metropolitan performing groups, more activity by local arts organizations, and more deference to Tokyo's tastes and policies.

THE ARTS OUT-OF-TOWN

Outreach programs run by the government have brought exhibits, concerts, and productions to every prefecture and nearly every community in the country, involving artists in both traditional and modern genres. As of 1980, the cultural agency each year spent $962,000 on live performances for children, $1.8 million on productions for high-school students, and $2.2 million for touring arts festivals and exhibitions.[a] Some of the performances took place in big cities but most were deliberately held in smaller centers. The agency also distributed $1.1 million to local sponsors to help cover deficits for performing arts events of their own, and it granted prefectures and municipalities another $10.1 million for erecting and maintaining local arts facilities. Outreach has been a pillar of the government's policy of promoting a wider access to the arts ever since the first grants were made in 1957. The allocations were still only $138,000 when the cultural agency began in 1968, but they jumped to $5.8 million by 1975, mostly because the state began helping localities build new arts centers in the early seventies. The 1980 figure for outreach, $16.2 million, was up 87 percent in yen terms from five years earlier.[1] Although practically every citizen can watch films and television shows on the arts, the government clearly believes that seeing exhibitions and attending live performances are experiences worth making available to everyone—in the case of students, at little or no charge.

The first postwar art shows sent on tour by the government were held in 1949, and the best works from prefectural exhibits were brought to Tokyo for display and prize competition starting in 1961. Six years later the cultural agency also began to hold traveling shows of works by Japanese artists that had won prizes in the annual exhibits of the top art associations. This program has been matched since 1977 by regional showings of modern and contemporary Japanese art recently bought for national or prefectural art museums by the cultural agency. In 1980 the exhibits also included foreign works acquired by the agency. The government is prodding prefectural and city museums to organize shows of their own, build their collections, and help local artists.[2] Many of the new public museums around the country are still exhibition

---

[a] Prefectures also help to subsidize these three programs. In the year ending March 31, 1979, they contributed about $500,000. They also spent $2.1 million for arts festivals of their own. Unlike the cultural agency's festivals, the prefectural ones usually include visual arts. Bunkachō, *Chihō bunka gyōsei jōkyō chōsa hōkokusho*, Tokyo, Bunkachō, 1980, p. 11.

galleries, built by national, prefectural, and local grants but with few curators or art works of their own. Until these institutions can sink roots, traveling shows from the cultural agency will have to help fill the walls.

A mixture of moral uplift and practical economics has suffused the touring arts programs for teenagers since they began with twenty-five performances in 1967. With an earnestness reminiscent of the rural self-help movements directed from Tokyo after the Russo-Japanese War and during the depression, cultural officials have taken pains to involve high-school pupils with the live performing arts. The presumption is that encounters with expressions of beauty are ethically instructive, especially for pupils whose school curriculums are weak in the arts. Road performances are also useful ways to support stage artists, and they help to cultivate fresh audiences for the future.[3]

Touring arts programs now provide eighty performances for teenagers each year, about a third of them in traditional genres and the rest split among modern drama, Western orchestral music, ballet, and opera. Like their peers in the big cities, the 90,000 teenagers in the audiences each year seem to prefer the modern arts over kabuki, nō, bunraku, classical Japanese dance, or traditional music by about three to one.[4] Since attendance in most genres is very much an age-group phenomenon, it is easy to imagine that the three-to-one ratio will shift significantly as these young people grow older. Meanwhile the performances for high-school students help administrators of the modern arts with their perennial problem: catching audiences when they are still young, since so many are women who will drift away once they have families and then choose traditional performances when they return to the theater or concert hall.

The cultural agency also gives money through the forty-seven prefectural school boards so that student performers can hold arts festivals of their own. Since 1966 the government has helped children's theater troupes play all over the country, and a formal program of touring demonstrations and performances of opera, music, ballet, and modern drama for children aged 6-13 began in 1974. More than eighty of these mass events are held every year, each drawing about 1,000 boys and girls. Such throngs make it hard for children to have any informal contact with the performers, although this is one of the aims of the program.[5]

The biggest of the agency's out-of-town performing programs is the most diffuse and probably the most artistically satisfying: the touring arts festivals that have been held every year since 1971 to put on traditional and contemporary performing arts "in every nook and cranny of the country."[6] Tickets to the 170 performances each year cost about a third of what they would if there were no subsidy, and attendance averages about 1,000 per show despite a number of poorly attended bunraku, nō, and popular entertainment events in smaller theaters. Although the audiences are older than in the high-school series, the share of performances of traditional genres is the same, about a third.[7]

The touring festival tries to reach every prefecture outside Tokyo and the Kyoto-Osaka-Kobe axis, in a brief spring section for the modern arts and a more elaborate autumn section that includes supplemental performances in several prefectures each year. Contemporary dance and Broadway musicals have recently joined nine other genres on the program. Kabuki, musicals, modern drama, and ballet make up about two-thirds of the fare in the fall; the spring is devoted mostly to orchestras. In the agency's various outreach programs, music is best represented in those for youth and children and ballet most common in the touring festivals.[b] Modern theater troupes are active, and well received, in all three.[8]

What the out-of-town tours give to Japan's shingeki companies is a chance not just to stage extra performances but

---

[b] Shimada Hiroshi, executive managing director of the Japan Ballet Association, notes that "our association has been especially active in trying to tie Tokyo ballet activity with local areas, and we have had the most success in attracting funds from the cultural agency to support performances for people outside metropolitan areas." Shimada interview, December 6, 1980.

also to build a whole new clientele while on the road. Each year the cultural agency allocates $45,000 to the council of shingeki companies, which picks six or seven of its member groups to put on one production each before teenaged audiences, for a total of 100 performances. Comparably smaller grants back about sixty performances of plays and musicals in the touring arts festival, and shingeki companies also accept funds to perform for children's audiences. Youth and children's drama groups, which usually lack shingeki's other sources of revenue, receive even more generous subsidies to appear in outreach performances. The shingeki companies have drawn private support for their young people's shows, but they have also come back on their own to schools and other civic facilities to put on plays that more than pay their way. These new initiatives are an economic necessity for shingeki, since attendance in Tokyo is shrinking, and the cultural agency is understandably happy that its outreach programs have helped the companies and new audiences find each other.[9]

The touring programs of the seventies succeeded royally in exposing out-of-town audiences to metropolitan artists, but the 330 performances sponsored each year by the cultural agency, drawing about 350,000 people, represent only a fraction of the local arts activity that occurs. Since 1977 the agency has helped municipalities put on their own exhibits and productions, both amateur and professional, with flat grants (typically $10,000 each to about seventy cities) and special subsidies. These payouts reached $1.1 million in 1980,[10] but most of the arts events that take place in cities and towns are locally financed, often commercially.

The costliest element by far among the government's agenda for extending the arts has been aid for building community museums and arts centers. No artifact better expresses the transformation of nonmetropolitan Japan in the 1970s than the regional cultural center now found in any medium-sized city. Many are monuments to architectural ingenuity; a few are sterile victims of bureaucratic banality. Two of the most striking are the Chiba Prefectural Art Museum, a multiform red brick structure with a variety of exhibition possibilities in its open interior, and the Kitakyūshū City Art Museum, a blocky piece of contemporary gingerbread designed by Isozaki Arata.

As the economy matured and the largest cities stopped growing so fast in the 1970s, prefectural capitals and other smaller centers began sharing more evenly in national commerce, manufacturing, and education. Local leaders, as Kimura Hideo points out, "built cultural centers partly to show how wealthy they've become and partly to show the influence of prefectural and city officials over cultural affairs."[11] The result was that the number of public art museums and performing-arts centers doubled during the seventies, partly inspired by aid from Tokyo but mostly by local pride.

Japan has had municipal art museums since 1926, when Tokyo opened its metropolitan gallery, but few others were built until well after World War Two. Certain prefectures and communities erected museums in the 1960s, usually to house temporary shows of local artists, but more than half of the eighty-four municipal and prefectural art museums operating in 1980 had been open less than a decade. Another eighteen prefectural art museums are expected to be ready or under construction by 1985.[12] Although a number of the new buildings own very little art and mainly display local amateurs, at least thirty-five of them, as of 1978, supported contemporary Japanese artists through purchases, exhibits, educational programs, and publications. One prefecture, Hiroshima, has formed a private foundation to endow acquisitions, and a half-dozen others use tax monies to buy art. Sometimes the new works are exorbitantly expensive foreign paintings, such as Yamanashi's purchase of Millet's *The Sower* in 1977 or a Miró that cost Fukuoka almost $1.3 million the following year. More typically the local museums acquire art by committee, a safe, conservative approach that often follows the lead of the national museums or the recommendations of the Fuji Gallery and other Tokyo institutions. Traveling shows sent around by the cultural agency and private art associations, together with special exhibits put on by local art groups, are the main events in most of the new public museums.[13]

The biggest construction boom has come in the form of multipurpose performing-arts centers, of which the paragon remains Tokyo's splendid Metropolitan Festival Hall, opened in 1961. The education ministry began helping local governments put up theaters and concert halls in 1967, and by 1980 the national aid to local public museums and cultural complexes, including construction and maintenance, reached $10.1 million per year. When the cultural agency began operating in 1968, there were 233 public centers in Japan with theaters or concert halls holding at least 500 people. By 1979 the number had grown to 509,[14] and more have opened since.[c]

The annual investment in building, administering, and maintaining prefectural and municipal arts facilities reached $277.8 million in the year ending March 31, 1979, the latest for which there are figures. Even more remarkable than the sum itself is that cities, towns, and villages paid out $131.1 million of the total and prefectures another $140.3 million, each from their own tax revenues.[15] For the decade as a whole, prefectures spent an estimated $300 million to put up new theaters, concert halls, and art museums and many tens of millions more to administer and maintain them.[16] Figures for municipal outlays during the same period are scarce, but it is unlikely that they were more than two-thirds the amount spent by prefectures.[d] The cultural agency, for its part, subsidized

[c] The centers have 586 halls with 610,683 seats altogether. Ninety of them are large concert halls holding 1,500 or more. Their total revenues in the year ending March 31, 1979 were $206.6 million, of which 75 percent were paid by public subsidies. Earned income included rentals (19 percent), auxiliary enterprises (4 percent), and box-office receipts from events sponsored by the halls (2 percent). Much of the rental activity is by commercial promoters presenting both classical Western and popular music. Bunkachō, *Chihō*, pp. 119-123; Bunkachō, *Bunka gyōsei no ayumi*, pp. 134-135.

[d] During a comparable period in the United States, 1962-1969, 173 arts centers and theaters were completed, virtually all of them noncommercial, and another 179 were in design or under construction. In 1969 the U.S. was investing more than $200 million per year in physical plant for the performing arts. Public funds are rarely used in Japan for renovating older facilities, whereas they are an important item in America's efforts at upgrading arts

new construction and maintenance of local arts facilities with about $35 million during the 1970s.[17] Even though the agency spent more of its outreach money for buildings than performances or exhibits, the new museums and cultural centers were erected overwhelmingly with local funds. The seventies were unquestionably the decade of public construction in nearly every region of Japan. Perhaps it is appropriate that a millionaire contractor with a fondness for the arts, Tanaka Kakuei, was elected prime minister in 1972.

As recently as 1968 only six prefectural governments had arts councils or other units to manage their cultural programs. Eight years later every prefecture had set up a bureau or agency to administer arts policies, partly to clear the track for aid from Tokyo. More and more the prefectures are subsidizing events managed by the local cultural centers themselves, helped along by $1.1 million each year from the national cultural agency.[18] As of 1978 they sank $17.1 million each year into visual-arts activities at public museums and performing-arts events of all types undertaken by their cultural centers. About half of the money went for performances, including productions of popular music. Another 17 percent was spent on art purchases and exhibitions, and the rest was used for a multitude of local projects. Municipal subsidies were perhaps half this amount. Altogether government at every level invested at least $17.9 million in direct payments to promote the visual arts, theater, dance, and serious music in public museums, cultural centers, and school auditoriums in 1978.[e]

---

facilities. Martin Mayer, *Bricks, Mortar and the Performing Arts*, New York, The Twentieth Century Fund, 1970, p. 1.

[e] The calculation includes prefectural expenses of about $8.6 million for visual and performing-arts events, exclusive of popular music; municipal payments of roughly half this amount; aid from the cultural agency of $1.1 million to local sponsors; and cultural-agency payments of $3.9 million for youth, children's, and touring arts-festival events. Aichi prefecture spends the most on the arts (including popular events), $11.7 million in 1978, and Okinawa the least, $67,000. The New York State Council on the Arts is the largest in the U.S., with a $33.3 million budget in 1979-1980. Bunkachō, *Chihō*, pp. 11-12; Bunkachō, *Bunkachō yosan*, pp. 22-25; Bunkachō, *Bunka gyōsei no ayumi*, p. 125; *New York Times*, December 23, 1979. An interesting case study is Nakanishi Saburō, "Chihō bunka gyōsei—Shigaken no baai," in Bunkachō, *Nihon bunka kōza*, III, Tokyo, Gyōsei, 1979, pp. 169-199.

No other prefecture has complemented the cultural agency so successfully in spreading the arts as Tokyo—appropriately so, since the city is home to far more artists than any other. Tokyo operates thirty-seven centers for the performing arts in various neighborhoods and a metropolitan art museum in Ueno Park.[19] Altogether it spends more than $7 million a year to operate these facilities and another $3.5 million to subsidize the metropolitan symphony orchestra, the nation's most costly arts festival, and many other events held under its imprimatur.[f] The city is also constructing a new public playhouse due to open in 1986. No other prefecture spends more to operate cultural facilities or promote arts events—partly because none has an art museum and a performing-arts center within ninety minutes' commute for 23 million people.

The metropolitan orchestra has the special duty of playing for school and community groups, often at no charge, in addition to its regular subscription series. The city government pays $2.4 million of the orchestra's $3.3 million annual budget, in effect supporting outreach to citizens of all ages. The metropolitan art museum, reopened in September 1975 in a handsome $13.3 million red brick building between Ueno zoo and the Tokyo National Museum, contains about 2,000 prints and oils by contemporary Japanese artists. But it has also become the world's most active rental gallery, hiring out one or more of its four main exhibit halls to about 200 artists' associations each year, whose displays of new works by their members draw about 2 million visitors. The rental fees are kept so low that the metropolitan government ends up paying more than three-quarters of the $2.4 million it takes to run the museum each year.[20] In this way the Tokyo taxpayers have become the chief angels backing exhibits of new works by visual artists in Japan.

Iwaki Hiroyuki, who has conducted the NHK orchestra on five continents, considers the Tokyo Metropolitan Festival

---

[f] New York City spent $23.8 million on cultural institutions and services in 1980, nearly all of it to keep buildings running. *New York Times*, May 13, 1980; Bunkachō, *Chihō*, pp. 13-14, 33.

Hall "unsurpassed" as a concert hall. This stunning cultural center, built in 1958-1961 for $4.5 million, includes an auditorium seating 2,300 and a recital hall holding 660.[21] Each year the city pays about $700,000 to cover the deficit in its $1.4 million budget. The losses are this big because Tokyo tries to keep events within the reach of as many performing groups as it can.[g] About 800,000 persons a year attend productions there, nearly 90 percent of which are classical Western music and the rest ballet and contemporary dance.[22] From the moment it opened, the festival hall replaced the Hibiya public hall, a venerable prewar barn, as the principal musical venue in Tokyo, and only its unaccountable policy of remaining dark on Sundays keeps it from giving people the widest possible access to music and dance.

The city began its yearly arts festival in 1968 "to make outstanding arts available to as many Tokyoites as possible at modest cost." Discount tickets are sold to about 100 performances in the modern arts and another twenty events in nō, traditional music, classical Japanese dance, and popular entertainments. Seats to orchestra concerts that usually cost twenty dollars are sold for five, and students get into many performances free of charge. The combined attendance at all the events is about 110,000 each year. Many of the modern-arts performances are children's theater and modern drama (in 1981, three shingeki companies each put on one Shakespeare play for a total of thirty-four performances). Music is relatively underrepresented, presumably because Tokyo sponsors its own orchestra throughout the year. The city spent $710,000 to subsidize the 1981 festival, covering 40 percent

[g] The basic full-day rental fee for the large hall was $1,490 in 1980, about a third of the going rate at acoustically inferior commercial halls of the same size in Tokyo. NHK Hall, also built with public monies, quoted a daily rate of $8,750 in 1980, and the Koma Stadium in Shinjuku, owned by Tōhō, asked $12,500. Few groups actually pay such fees since the halls are usually rented to organizations affiliated with NHK or Tōhō, respectively. Tōkyō Bunka Kaikan, *Yōran 1979*, Tokyo, Tōkyō Bunka Kaikan, 1979, pp. 23-25, 29; Yajima Kazuo interview, October 16, 1980; Komatsu Takeshi interview, October 20, 1980; Ogawa Ayako interview, November 21, 1980.

89

of the total budget and its whole deficit. The rest of the revenue came from the box office and $7,500 in broadcast fees from NHK.[23]

Unlike the national government's autumn festival, which cost the cultural agency $562,000 in 1980, in the Tokyo festival there are no prizes and no participating performances by groups not receiving aid. The city follows the national agency's practice of distributing payments to eleven different federations of artists, letting them choose which members should perform. In a few cases, such as contemporary dance, the federations use the grants to commission new works, but the festival is better known for staging old favorites like Shakespeare, Beethoven's *Fate* symphony, and *Swan Lake*. The result is that many creative artists feel snubbed by their own city. As the playwright Senda Koreya once put it, the authorities have no "intention of protecting the arts in a long-ranged way. They want the money to go directly back to the citizens, the taxpayers."[24] Although the national cultural agency usually gets better marks for encouraging new works, the $710,000 Tokyo spends each year on its festival is welcome aid to the performers who receive it, however weary they may be of playing Ophelia or the *Fifth*.

MODERN HOUSES FOR CONTEMPORARY ARTS

Since access means drawing the public to metropolitan arts institutions as well as sending the arts around to the people, the Japanese government began very slowly in the 1970s to transform the national art museums from reliquaries of the past into living expressions of the contemporary imagination. The authorities also finally honored their pledge, first made in 1959 when plans for the national theater had to be trimmed, to house the modern performing arts suitably. A superb site for a new cultural center in Tokyo was chosen just west of Shinjuku, design competitions were held in 1981, and the new complex was scheduled to open in 1986. By then the cultural agency hopes to be promoting all the arts with the same skill and impact that the national theater has brought to the traditional ones.

Japan's first national museum was founded in Tokyo in 1871, and two more were soon added in Kyoto and Nara. No more were built until after World War Two. In 1952 a national museum for modern art opened in Tokyo, with a branch in Kyoto starting in 1963 that was turned into the Kyoto National Museum of Modern Art four years later. The National Museum of Western Art, designed by Le Corbusier and donated by the French government, opened in 1959 at Ueno in Tokyo to display works from the collection of sculpture and French impressionist paintings assembled by the Japanese patron Matsukata Kōjirō.[h] A fourth institution, the National Museum of International Art, began in 1977 on the site of the Osaka exposition of 1970, specializing on the interaction of Japanese and foreign art. These four museums and related facilities received $13.3 million in government aid in 1980, almost unchanged in yen terms since the international museum was added in 1977, and their grants for acquisitions have been frozen since 1979 at about $2 million per year.[i]

The keystone of the four is the Tokyo modern museum, which is now housed in a $3.5 million building contributed by Ishibashi Shōjirō, the tire manufacturer and patron of the

[h] Matsukata bought the works during 1920-1923. Originally they numbered 1,000, but many of those brought to Japan before the war were scattered. The 371 remaining in France under the Nazis were returned to Japan by the French government under the terms of the San Francisco peace treaty of 1951. *Asahi nenkan 1960*, pp. 451-452; Bunkachō, *Bunka gyōsei no ayumi*, pp. 13-14; Michiaki Kawakita, *Modern Currents in Japanese Art*, trans. by Charles S. Terry, New York and Tokyo, Weatherhill/Heibonsha, 1974, p. 154.

[i] The Tokyo National Museum of Modern Art owns more than 3,000 prints, sculptures, and paintings in Japanese and Western styles by top Japanese artists from Meiji until recent decades. Its National Film Center and crafts annex are important repositories for their genres. The Kyoto National Museum of Modern Art has more than 700 paintings, prints, and sketches as well as an excellent collection of crafts. The National Museum of Western Art now contains about 600 works, twice the holdings of the new National Museum of International Art in Osaka. Adachi, *Bunkachō*, pp. 93-95; Bunkachō, *Bunka gyōsei no ayumi*, pp. 115, 118; Bunkachō, *Bunkachō yosan*, pp. 22-25.

Bridgestone museum. This new facility, opened in 1969, runs on an annual budget of $4 million to operate the main building, the crafts annex, and the National Film Center. The museum can afford to spend only $500,000 a year for new works, even though it is the nation's leading depository of modern art.[j] The problem for artists today is that "Japan has no official museum of contemporary art," according to the scholar and critic Etō Shun. The national museums date modern art not from an Armory Show but from a show of arms: it begins with the restoration of 1868 and ends soon after World War Two. Only four living artists, all very elderly, were represented at the Tokyo modern museum as of 1980, nor has that institution yet recognized architecture or design. When the national art museums buy new works, they take the cautious consensual approach favored by their prefectural and municipal avatars, picking established, noncontroversial artists even if it sometimes means buying less than their best output. When a living artist is chosen, he or she is often expected to donate the work because it is a privilege to appear in a public museum—prompting the sculptor Itō Takamichi to complain that artists have to "sacrifice on behalf of society" rather than "being supported by it."[25]

Until very recently, every time the Tokyo modern museum put on a special exhibit of supposedly contemporary art, irreverent artists would dismiss it as "art yesterday."[26] The curators used to shrink from displaying living artists, even

[j] Attendance runs about 400,000 per year at the main museum and crafts annex and another 100,000 annually at the film center at Kyōbashi. The four national art museums draw 1.5 to 2 million visitors a year, depending on special exhibits. Attendance at the three national general museums is a bit above 2 million a year. The Tokyo National Museum held 84,858 items in 1977, about two-thirds of them swords, other metallic objects, and archaeological artifacts. The Kyoto National Museum's holdings were 3,052 items and Nara's 1,392. Each is a top-rank collection of premodern art. Bunkachō, *Bunka gyōsei no ayumi*, pp. 75, 116-117, 209, 212; *Asahi nenkan 1970*, p. 711; *Asahi nenkan 1971*, p. 700; Adachi, *Bunkachō*, pp. 232-237; National Museum of Modern Art, Tokyo, *National Museum of Modern Art, Tokyo*, Tokyo, National Museum of Modern Art, Tokyo, 1978; Tōkyō Kokuritsu Kindai Bijutsukan, *Tōkyō Kokuritsu Kindai Bijutsukan yōran*, Tokyo, Tōkyō Kokuritsu Kindai Bijutsukan, 1977, pp. 89-90.

such familiar ones as Robert Rauschenberg, unless the show was a safe retrospective rather than a selection of recent works that might stir a ruckus. At the end of the seventies the museum began to overcome its preoccupation with famous names and brought in some very representative special shows of current European art and crafts. New works by contemporary Japanese were usually presented side by side with the foreign ones. The international art museum in Osaka has also tried to show present-day works from Japan as well as abroad. Gradually the national art museums are starting to support younger artists through exhibits,[27] if not yet very many acquisitions.[k] Yet a great deal still has to be done to get the public looking at current Japanese works before the national art museums can stop seeming to perpetuate an approved art that appears dated to many artists today.

Keeping up with new compositions in the performing arts will be much easier when the $100 million national cultural center opens near Shinjuku in 1986. The plan includes a concert hall for orchestras and choruses and three theaters, a large one for opera, ballet, and modern dance, a medium-sized one for modern drama, and a small one for solos, recitals, and ensembles. And like the national theater, the new center will contain archives, rehearsal space, meeting rooms, and a study center for the stage arts.[L] Inumaru Tadashi believes that both

[k] The National Museum of Western Art was embarrassed by its purchase of three works, supposedly by Derain, Dufy, and Modigliani, that turned out to be fakes. The paintings were acquired in 1964-1965, discussed at a Diet committee meeting in February 1966, and finally admitted to be reproductions in September 1971. *Asahi nenkan 1967*, p. 739; *Asahi nenkan 1972*, p. 706.

[L] Like the National Theatre of Britain, which opened its three halls during 1976-1977 on the south bank of the Thames and now costs $2 million a year to run, the cultural center will have required nearly thirty years from initial approval to completion. The 1981 estimate of the building costs alone is $100 million. Planning, land acquisition, design, equipment, and administration will drive the total much higher before it is fully operating. By comparison, Lincoln Center in New York opened its eight halls between 1962 and 1970 at a total cost of $186 million; the Kennedy Center in Washington was built with $43 million in federal funds; the French government spent $200 million on the Pompidou Center of Art and Culture. NHK Hall, the largest concert auditorium in Tokyo, with 4,000 seats, opened in 1973 at a the new cultural center and the national theater, which he heads, would benefit if they were jointly administered, because "it might make the traditional arts open to new ideas, and having modern arts people become more familiar with the classical Japanese artists might be good for the modern artists, too."[28] Hard as it is to mix the two artistically, it is even trickier organizationally. What keeps contemporary and classical dancers apart, for instance, is often group factionalism, not a clash of interpretive styles. Inumaru is doubtless right that premodern and contemporary artists have much to teach each other, but it will take great cleverness to bridge the five kilometers between the national theater facing the feudal palace moat and the new arts center near ultramodern Shinjuku.

Arts Over the Air and Overseas

To people living in Japan since the 1950s, the most noticeable public patron of the arts has been neither the cultural agency nor the city of Tokyo but NHK. To residents of foreign countries, the most visible sponsor of the Japanese arts abroad has been the Japan Foundation since it began in 1972. These two independent, nonprofit public corporations, along with a few other government-authorized organizations and international agencies, enrich the arts with cash and give them a following far beyond the audiences who can attend Japanese galleries, theaters, or concert halls.

Even though it collects subscriber fees from 28 million households, NHK is a consumer service, not a private business, and feels satisfied to break even each year.[m] Its support

---

total cost of $11.1 million. The concert hall in the new Tokyo complex will seat about 2,300 and the theaters approximately 1,850, 900, and 650. *New York Times*, November 26, 1978 and December 31, 1978; Mayer, *Bricks*, pp. 15-17; Brustein, "Can the Show Go On?" p. 56; Bunkachō, *Bunka gyōsei no ayumi*, p. 120; *Asahi nenkan 1974*, p. 710.

m Because of higher fees in 1980, NHK had a surplus of $37 million in a total budget of $1.4 billion, after losses as high as $96.3 million (1979) for several years in the late 1970s. Masui Keiji, ed., *Dēta ongaku Nippon*, Tokyo, Min'on Ongaku Shiryōkan, 1980, p. 135; *Asahi nenkan 1981*, p. 567; *Asahi nenkan 1980*, p. 599; Nihon Engeki Kyōkai, *Engeki nenkan '80*, Tokyo, Nihon Engeki Kyōkai, 1980, p. 49.

for the arts is stacked in favor of music, which benefits both from payments for live performances and through broadcasts on FM and television. The corporation grants about $1.5 million a year to cover the deficit of the NHK Symphony Orchestra, a world-class orchestra founded in 1926. It also spends at least that much each year on weekly television concerts of semiclassical music by the Tokyo Philharmonic Orchestra.[29] Instrumentalists and vocalists receive small honoraria for appearing live, and fees are also paid when NHK does an occasional TV special—usually featuring a visiting foreign group or a Japanese opera production. Through the orchestras it aids, NHK encourages other sponsors to commission Japanese composers, who are also hired directly to produce music for television programs. The NHK Service Center, NHK Hall, and Hōsō Bunka Kikin (Broadcast Cultural Fund), are technically independent cognates[30] that back musical enterprises of many kinds, including nonprofit activities in traditional Japanese and classical Western music.

Broadcasting is NHK's chief means of engaging the public with serious music, but sometimes it plays more than the audience wants to hear. Few networks anywhere survey their listeners' tastes more frequently than NHK, and all its data show that the public at large prefers Western classical music to traditional Japanese music but that popular music has a much wider following than both. Even those who actually listen to NHK-FM favor light music, film music, and popular singers over classical Western and traditional Japanese music, which together account for much more than half the music programming.[n] NHK-FM for many years has tried to devote at least nine of its eighteen broadcast hours each day to serious music and commentary. Classical Western music apparently

[n] An NHK survey of listeners in 1978 rated popular songs at 38.9 percent, film music 32.2, classical Western music 26.8, contemporary serious music 6.6, and traditional Japanese music 3.4. Teenagers form the largest following for contemporary serious music. Masui, ed., *Dēta*, p. 172; for other NHK surveys, see pp. 90, 148, 165, 169. NHK undoubtedly overplays classical Western music in relation to audience preferences, but other types of music are readily available on the radio dial, whereas NHK-FM has a near-monopoly of classical Western musical broadcasts. See Masui, ed., *Dēta*, p. 136.

lost a bit of its popularity in the mid-seventies, but there were few changes in the broadcast schedules, and NHK added four regional outlets in 1979 with the explicit understanding that they would transmit classical Western music.[31]

Television programming came under greater pressure than radio to cut back on musical broadcasts in the seventies when air time grew scarcer and audiences for music stagnated. For twelve years NHK showed its own orchestra weekly on the heavily watched general network, but in April 1976 it was replaced by a news show. To compensate, *TV Concert* was added to the NHK educational system on Tuesday evenings, but it drew few viewers in prime time. The Saturday evening *Music Plaza* performances by the Tokyo Philharmonic have been more popular because of better scheduling and, one suspects, the lighter fare. The educational network does a number of specials each year, ranging from documentaries on old Japanese musical instruments and ballet performances to music competitions and visiting foreign orchestras, usually when their tours are sponsored by the service center. Among the commercial stations TBS and TV Asahi (formerly NET) have been active in broadcasting music programs, but their audiences too have been limited. When NHK surveyed 3,000 viewers in 1976, only 236 had ever watched *Music Plaza* (their average age was forty-nine). On the other hand, although *TV Concert* draws a rating of only 0.5, this still means it is seen by half a million persons,[32] which is almost the number of seats in all the cultural centers in the country.

NHK and the privately owned TV stations fill some of the dead hours on Sunday mornings with excellent programs on the visual arts. For many years NHK has put on *Sunday Art Museum* for sixty minutes, including commentary by a critic or scholar about an individual artist as well as a rundown on major exhibitions around the country. Takasugi Tsuneo, who plans the contents, says he deliberately tries to treat different media, eras, and countries—to the consternation of contemporary Japanese artists, whose turn comes infrequently. Once or twice a year the general NHK network does a weekend special on an art topic and reaches a much wider audience. TV Asahi has also helped to publicize current art movements with its Sunday morning art report.[33]

The public broadcasting corporation has telecast plays quite regularly over its educational network in the last two decades, including kabuki and bunraku, for which it pays small fees to the national theater. It also puts on full-length productions of familiar modern plays, such as *A Streetcar Named Desire* and *Death of a Salesman*, soon after shingeki companies stage them live. In November 1980 NHK imported the thirty-seven plays in BBC's complete Shakespeare series, hired shingeki actors and actresses to dub them, and began showing one each month. Like its commercial competitors, NHK further supports drama by using talent from the major entertainment corporations, Tōhō and Shōchiku, or from the shingeki groups to put on serious plays for television. In the late seventies, NHK's reputation for underpaying artists was indirectly confirmed when it and the commercial stations resorted more and more to subcontracting fresh plays to independent producers, who kept their own costs low by offering even skimpier wages.[34]

NHK engages in many other cultural activities that intersect the arts, but it is a very different enterprise from its closest analogue, BBC. Although its revenues are less than half NHK's, BBC spent more than a sixth of its entire budget on the arts during the mid-seventies and as recently as 1980 was paying out $13 million a year to operate eleven orchestras. (BBC was also $200 million in debt that year and has since pared its support for music, whereas NHK was $37 million in the black in 1980.)[35] Although NHK's direct payments to artists and arts groups are only a few million dollars a year, the corporation is an important entrepreneur and invaluable publicist for all the arts. The prestige it imparts, if not the money, helps to rescue the most precarious art forms from obscurity.

The stature conferred by government patronage has also given lustre and lucre to Japanese artists who appear abroad. In the 1950s the foreign ministry, like those in many countries, began to send traditional performing-arts groups overseas as instruments of cultural diplomacy. This policy not only gave foreign audiences the unique art forms they wanted to see (who needs to watch a Japanese Willy Loman?), but it also presented the mystery and stateliness of nō, the quiet repose of koto music, and the colorful make-believe of kabuki, qualities the government was glad to project as emblems of Japan. Still, as recently as 1970 the foreign ministry was spending just $1 million a year on international cultural activity of all sorts, much but not all of it to send artists abroad and bring foreign ones to Japan.[36]

When the Japan Foundation was created in 1972 with an endowment from the national treasury of $13.9 million, it inherited many tasks of international arts exchange from the foreign ministry and quickly invented others of its own. The foundation's main purpose was to make foreign nations more aware of Japan by promoting its culture abroad.[37] Thanks to annual public supplements of about $5 million and a ninefold growth in its endowment, the Japan Foundation by the end of the seventies had developed programs costing $16.7 million per year to aid language teaching, research, study, publication, and international conferences, as well as arts activity in Japan and abroad. Of this sum, $3.4 million went for art exhibits and live events in the performing arts. Part of the $7.6 million paid for the exchange of individuals supported artists as well. Although the Japan Foundation is still small by international standards,° it has cooperated closely with the cultural agency and foreign ministry to send a great many traditional and

---

° As of 1976, the foundation's budget for administration and for its programs was $12.7 million (for the year ending March 31, 1980, the figure was $24.9 million, an increase of 31 percent in yen terms). By comparison, three West German foundations, DAAD, the Humboldt Foundation, and the Goethe Institute together had budgets 6.8 times the Japan Foundation's for 1976; the Alliance Française had a budget 7.5 times greater; and the British Council's was 7.7 times larger. The Japan Foundation's endowment was worth $225 million in 1980. Budget figures in the text are for the year ending March 31, 1980. Kimura Eiji, "Nihon no geijutsu josei wa kokkakei ka minkankei ka," *Ongaku geijutsu*, November 1980, p. 52; Kokusai Kōryū Kikin, *Kokusai Kōryū Kikin Nenpō, Shōwa 54nendohan*, pp. 9-18. I am grateful for comments on these points to Kimura Eiji, interview, December 8, 1980, and Frances Blakemore, interview, December 27, 1980.

contemporary Japanese artists all over the world, and it has stretched the horizons of audiences at home by inviting foreign performers and exhibits.

Quite apart from breathing fresh artistic air, going abroad is often very profitable to Japanese artists, particularly in the visual arts, because they can charge higher prices to their private pupils or the collectors of their works after they return. By the late seventies the Japan Foundation was helping contemporary visual artists take part in four or five international shows each year, as well as organizing a dozen exhibits of Japanese art for travel abroad and partly funding a half-dozen others annually. (Having your painting selected is the next best thing to going in person, although many of the artists represented have been dead for centuries.) The foundation also sponsored half a dozen performing-arts groups each year on tours overseas, ranging from kabuki to the Takarazuka revue, and it aided three times that number with smaller grants. A modest allocation was also made for assisting foreign exhibits and performances in Japan.[38] Most arresting of all, perhaps, were multimedia spectacles such as the *Japan Today* program of contemporary arts,[p] held in 1979 in New York and other cities to the gratification of audiences, artists, and sponsors alike.

Artists also benefited for a time from the efforts of the Japan Art Festival Foundation to introduce contemporary Japanese paintings, prints, and sculpture abroad. This organization was founded in 1964 with funds from the government's bicycle and powerboat races, controlled by Sasakawa Ryōichi. Its many shows in Europe and America often seemed more commercial than cultural, and when the foundation ran up huge losses its work was absorbed by the Japan Foundation in 1976. The following year another public fund, the Japan-United States Friendship Commission, began making grants for binational exchanges that currently include $300,000 each

---

[p] *Japan Today* was supported also by the National Endowment for the Humanities, National Endowment for the Arts, Matsushita Electric Corporation, and the Japan-United States Friendship Commission. *New York Times*, April 15, 1979.

year for the arts. The commission manages a U.S. government trust of $36 million in yen and dollars accruing from repayments by the Japanese government for former American facilities in Okinawa and other assistance after 1945. Its programs help to support the exchange of five creative artists from each country per year, experimentation with traditional Japanese musical and theatrical forms, and shows and tours by professional performing groups in each country. The commission has helped to introduce contemporary American art works and the National Theater of the Deaf to Japan, as well as aiding return visits by the Alvin Ailey and Paul Taylor dance companies.[39] Thus far its programs have been weakest in music.

International activity in the arts also attracted $200,000 annually in the late seventies from the Japan World Exposition Commemorative Fund, which the Diet set up in 1971 from the proceeds of the world exposition held in Osaka the year before. By 1980 its endowment was worth $77.5 million, permitting grants of $2.9 million for a great variety of projects in cultural exchange, academic cooperation, and other international ventures. The fund assists both amateur and professional groups by subsidizing international piano and ballet competitions and the annual Osaka International Festival of music at the old fairgrounds. Like the Japan Foundation and the UNESCO Asian Cultural Centre in Tokyo, the commemorative fund has also supported a number of events that involve Japanese artists with their colleagues from other Asian countries.[40] Even the embassies or cultural ministries of foreign countries will often aid a performance, exhibit, or conference in Japan if it includes artists from their nations. Japanese promoters regard the Soviet government as an especially soft touch.

PUBLIC MONEY AND OFFICIAL CULTURE

Japan began the 1980s spending about $3 per capita in public funds each year on aid to the visual and performing arts.[q] Even when the rise of the yen is ignored, the per capita figure climbed rapidly in the 1970s, mainly because of very heavy payments for new art museums and cultural centers outside the biggest cities. International comparisons are risky because of changing currency rates, separate accounting practices, and differing tax concessions in lieu of direct subsidies, but it is generally believed that Great Britain spent nearly $4 per capita in public monies on the arts in 1975-1976, about three times as much as the United States if tax preferences are disregarded. France in 1975 paid about $3 per capita in public funds, and West Germany, including all levels of government, several times that amount.[r] Once far behind, Japan in 1980 was catching up fast—its modern history in cameo.

Public patronage of the arts in Japan was mostly a dream before the mid-sixties but a fact by 1980. When so much governmental cash flooded the financially parched world of the arts, some persons feared that an official view of culture would soon begin to sprout. Through its practice of letting arts federations decide how to allocate grants to their members, the cultural agency has erased most of the fears that it would try to control the arts by playing favorites or selecting

[q] The population of Japan in 1980 was 117 million. The per capita figure includes both aid to nonprofit professional activity and assistance to amateur groups in the arts. Direct aid from Japanese public sources consisted of $80.1 million spent by the cultural agency (1980), prefectural payments of $140.3 million (1979), municipal outlays of $131.1 million (1979), NHK payments estimated at $5 million (1980), Japan Foundation aid, including the exchange of artists, estimated at $4.4 million (1979), and Japan World Exposition Commemorative Fund grants of $200,000 (1980). The prefectural and municipal aid figures unavoidably include several million dollars for popular music and folk entertainments. Additional direct aid from governmental sources included $300,000 (1980) from the Japan-United States Friendship Commission and an undetermined amount from foreign governments.

[r] The *New York Times*, June 19, 1980, reported that West German governments in 1979 subsidized theater, opera, and ballet at the level of $18 per capita. Figures in the text are drawn from Netzer, *Subsidized Muse*, pp. 51-52. See Thomas G. Moore, *The Economics of the American Theater*, Durham, Duke University Press, 1968, p. 112; Meyer, *Art Museum*, pp. 60-65; Yoshimasa Kurabayashi, *Measurement of Output in Public Supported Services for the International Comparison: A Case of Cultural Activities*, Tokyo, Institute of Economic Research, Hitotsubashi University, 1980, p. 19.

specific works for production. It is probably true that as soon as state support grows large enough to be divided among a number of arts organizations, the threat of official manipulation pales.[41] But the more subtle danger is that the federations will reward their most well-established members, not necessarily those with something to say artistically—and avant-garde companies outside the federations are often excluded entirely from the public largess. Handy as it may be to make the federations take responsibility for allocating the grants, there is also the familiar risk that they will use the funds not to encourage the most dynamic of their constituents but to prop up the feeblest, taking away the pain until the patients forget they are ill.

Bureaucratism is the enemy of artists no less than other professionals, and the cultural agency insists on detailed grant proposals, with interminable forms to be filled out, no less strictly than prefectural and municipal authorities. Bureaucratism is also a matter of attitudes. The authorities unquestionably agree on a definition of accredited Western culture that begins with Bach and ends with the School of Paris, but it is not clear how much they officially impose this outlook, or how much they need to, since artists and citizens seem to share it so widely already. The repertoire that visiting foreign artists can present is sharply restricted by which "approved" works their Japanese hosts think audiences will turn out for.[42] But perhaps the public's preoccupation with famous names and fashionable artists is as responsible as bureaucratism for the annual cacophony of Beethoven's *Ninth*.

Blandness and caution are also menaces to any art form, and in Japan they are most common among public officials at the prefectural and local levels. Partly this is because the arts are a new and relatively unfamiliar responsibility for civil servants. Ever since the Meiji era, and especially since the American-inspired reforms after World War Two, prefectural and municipal officials have poured their efforts into education rather than other kinds of cultural activity, and even today they approach the arts with more enthusiasm than experience. Understandably they look to the cultural agency for guidance, intensifying the possibility that a single approved version of the arts will be subsidized. The agency has tried to get local areas to preserve folk arts,[43] but much more of its effort is exerted on outreach programs that inevitably present a set of established metropolitan artistic expressions. Many who attend outreach events remain untouched by the experience, but the great weight of official prestige borne by a state-supported exhibit or performance means that any activity sponsored by the cultural agency is almost always presumed to be worthwhile. Politics, like fashion, is a poor but all too common substitute for esthetics in reaching judgments about art.

Less ambiguous or exceptionable is the government's attempt to export official culture of a more nativist stripe, especially once the Japan Foundation began operating in 1972. Like every major state, Japan has used art in the nation's service as a supplement to its ordinary diplomacy, sometimes provoking cries of cultural imperialism in parts of Southeast Asia. Transported abroad, kabuki and kyōgen are no longer just artistic expressions but also become symbols of the Japanese people and their civilization. As art for nation's sake, they set aside their historical class denotations and their current association with middleaged theater parties to become visual and aural tokens of the country as a whole. A cultural-agency planning report has noted that "active international cultural exchange is needed, but it would be difficult to say that our country now has a fully developed system to deal with this."[44] Art may be useful to governments that patronize it, but the Japanese authorities happily seem aware that it cannot be asked to surrender its essential character as art.

Perhaps the greatest peril of all to the arts in Japan is indifference. Adachi Kenji says:

> There is not really an official view of culture in Japan, but there are officials' views. In general, the arts are not greatly favored by the political or economic establishments. Those

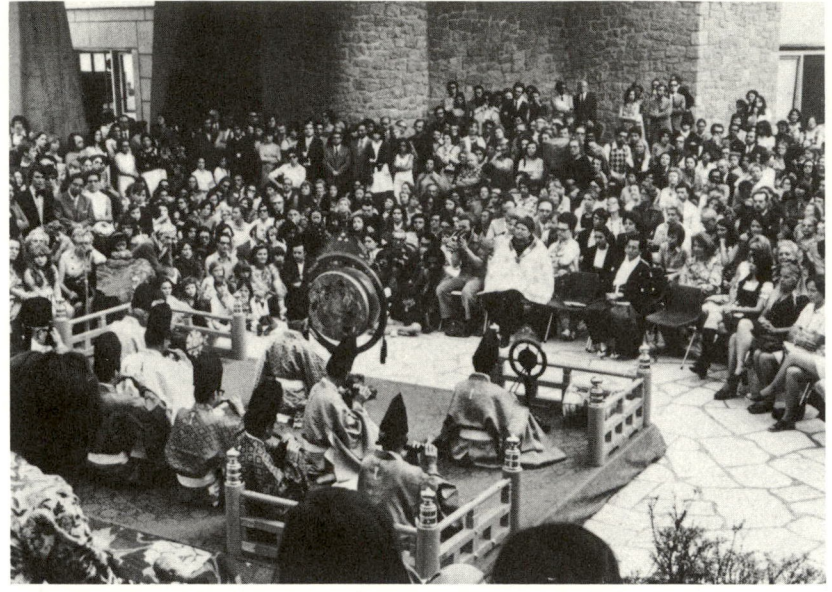

A gagaku troupe performs at UNESCO headquarters at Paris
in 1973 as a part of Japanese cultural diplomacy overseas.
NIPPON CULTURAL CENTRE

that are favored tend to be traditional arts. If a politician
or a businessman has an interest in a contemporary genre,
it is usually in the fine arts, not the performing arts. These
attitudes are rather discouraging to the performing artists,
especially to contemporary creative artists, who see the establishment as heedless, perhaps even opposed, to their art.[45]

Adachi probably understates the tyranny of accredited culture
because that culture is taken so much for granted in Japan.
But there is little question that nothing is more oppressive to
artists than to be ignored. By now public patronage has almost
removed any likelihood that they will be, by getting their art
to the people.

104

CHAPTER 5

The Visual Arts: Show and Sell

"STAR artists sell well, popular art sells well, but good art doesn't." This flinty epithet sums up life today for Japan's 30,000 professionals in the visual arts, according to the contemporary print maker Honda Shingo, who drives a pickup truck to gather old newspapers for recycling because he cannot make a living from his art.[a] Yet each year more than 10,000 students of Western-style art apply for the fifty spaces in the entering class at Tokyo University of Fine Arts, five times as many as in 1970. Most who are not admitted end up at one of the fifty other universities with art programs, which collectively turn out 30,000 majors each year to swamp the market for their skills.[1]

The allure of being an artist was at its zenith in Japan in 1980, even though a few of the young graduates will ever become popular, sell well, and earn enough to live from their art alone. Some of them come from prosperous families and choose art, rather than economics or English, because they lack the ambitious career goals of their parents' generation. Most of the others are seeking training because art has finally become a valid profession in Japan. Because full-time jobs are scarce, nearly all of the annual flood of new talent end up in teaching, commercial art, or other endeavors, producing works when time allows. When they are ready to show their art, most either submit works to the annual open-application exhibits held by the major artists' associations or hire a commercial gallery for a few days to hold their own one-person

[a] Honda Shingo interview, December 15, 1980. Like ink paintings of an earlier age, his compositions have little to do with form, Honda says: "white space is the real thing; color is the assistant." Quoted in Margaret K. Johnson and Dale K. Hilton, *Japanese Prints Today: Tradition with Innovation*, Tokyo, Shufu no Tomosha, 1980, p. 190.

shows. The exhibits at art associations, the displays at dealers' galleries, and the special shows of foreign and classical Japanese works at museums and department stores form a perpetually rotating triangle of art events that collectively give pleasure to lay audiences, inspiration to other artists, and often profit to the sponsors. The result is that art thrives while the artist survives—true too of other times and places, but by distinctive mechanisms in the case of postwar Japan.

MODERNISM AND POSTMODERNISM

Modern art in Japan has not meant a revolt against an established academicism but the creation of one where little formalism existed. Ever since the government brought Antonio Fontanesi from Italy to teach painting in 1876, all styles and movements of the contemporary West were automatically considered modern, well before modernism as a movement existed in Europe. Also modern was the updated version of Japanese painting known as Nihonga, once it began in the late nineteenth century. Western and Japanese styles were jointly emplaced in the government art college by 1900, the official art exhibition after 1907, and the Imperial Art Academy starting in 1919. The post-impressionists and the School of Paris were received not as rebels but as part of the orthodoxy from Europe that entered Japan during 1875-1925.[2] This became the accredited art, in oils and watercolors as well as sculpture, against which insurgents have struggled since the 1950s. For them, perhaps even more than for Japanese artists a half-century earlier, the question of modernism has been filled with resonances of national identity as well as established rigidities about what constitutes valid art.

Japanese art since 1900 has been irrepressibly vital and awesomely productive. The turmoil of conflicting ideas and movements, both native and foreign, has been central for its development, and so has the tedious litany of artists' societies that sustained the visual arts before the war, when there were few other supporters. But what divided the major associations after World War Two was not schools of thought or artistic sensibilities so much as customs, personalities, and group factionalism. And what separated artists even more than the styles or art groups to which they nominally adhered was usually the conflict between generations. The gradual rejection of established modernism after the 1950s took place in Western-style as well as Japanese-style painting, in Kyoto as well as Tokyo, in every artistic medium, until "the differences of content among the associations grew fewer, and as they changed the only remaining differences were generational" together with "personal struggles and conflict among cliques."[3]

Yokoyama Taikan was the major prewar figure in modern Japanese-style painting, which has preferred watercolors, ink painting, the color black, and materials such as silk and gold or silver leaf to the oils used in Western-style painting. As a student of the scholar and philosopher Okakura Tenshin, Yokoyama became the moving spirit in the Japan Art Academy (Nihon Bijutsuin), a private association whose annual exhibits are still a key outlet for Japanese-style painters. A year after World War Two ended, the official government art show reemerged as Nitten, a second important forum for Japanese-style paintings. A third organization, the New Works Association (Shinseisaku Kyōkai, founded in 1951), contained the most fresh faces and helped to bring Nihonga much closer to Western-style painting. The new group attacked the academic and elitist character of most Japanese-style painters and sought "creativity in Japanese painting based on cosmopolitanism."[4] Nihonga were now sold in frames as well as in hanging scrolls; many were huge works, to be displayed in exhibition halls and not just the alcoves of living rooms. Colors were often brighter, artists such as Hashimoto Meiji and Sugiyama Yasushi used frankly European techniques, and painters turned to abstractionism almost as often as those using oils. The postmodern love of decoration and nativist romanticism was ideally suited to Nihonga, which one critic notes has never lost its "traditional Japanese sense and concept of beauty"[5]

107

amid the rivalries of art associations and conflicts between generations.

Yokoyama's counterparts among prewar painters in the Western style were Umehara Ryūzaburō and Yasui Sōtarō, who helped to join the styles of Renoir and the post-impressionists with Japanese painting. They broke with the government's art show in 1914 and founded the Second Division Society (Nikakai), which is still a major force among oil painters. The Independent Art Association (Dokuritsu Bijutsu Kyōkai) was the first of many new groups formed in the thirties to introduce contemporary European art. This process was interrupted during World War Two but speeded up as soon as the war ended, a time when Fauvism understandably appealed to the art world because of its existential rebirth of freedom and its rejection of received authority. From there it was an easy step in the mid-fifties to action painting, with its lack of rules and concentration on the act of creating the work—a further rebuff to the canons of modern oil painting and the Japanese preoccupation with technique. Imai Toshimitsu, Dōmoto Hisao, and others living in Paris helped to break the new ground.[6]

From 1954 to 1957, the Concrete (Gutai) Group, pupils of the Osaka painter Yoshihara Jirō, developed an art of chaos and chance, much like contemporary music at the same time. Their comic happenings and bizarre footprint-paintings foreshadowed the Neo-Dadaist "events" of the 1960s and other outbursts against the terse formalism of official modern art. Saitō Yoshishige helped lead abstractionists of various sorts via the Nikakai, a rare exception to most of the established associations, which favored representational art in the fifties and sixties. In the process oils and watercolors became almost indistinguishable.

Every important postwar school of world art had its following in Japan, including superrealism, the artist as architect of temporary environments, and the nostalgic eclecticism found in the seventies elsewhere.[7] Still the conventional doctrines about how to paint in oils and watercolors remain very entrenched, even though restless artists used some of the newer elements of European modernism, along with 1970s post-modernism, to resist the weight of institutionalized modern art, which to the Japanese establishment meant nearly everything European from pointillism to Picasso. As long as art education and the art associations remain so academic, the battle will drag on.

The same is true for sculpture, which mainly produced religious works until Meiji and then mostly official statuary down to 1945. Sculpture as an art form entered from France after 1900. Ogiwara Morie's *Kneeling Nude* (1910), done in the Rodin manner, set the tone for Japan's small colony of creative sculptors for the next forty years. Not until the 1950s did European abstract motifs find their parallels among Japanese artists who were familiar with Picasso and Brancusi, such as Tsuji Shindō, Nagare Masayuki, and the Neo-Dadaist Miki Tomio. The Contemporary Sculpture Group (Shūdan Gendai Chōkoku), founded in 1960, mixed local artifacts such as castle walls and tomb figurines with new materials from abroad. Japan absorbed all the main themes of international sculpture in the 1960s and 1970s, but expressionism and abstract art evoked as well the strongly nativist feeling found in many other postmodern works in Japan, not just in sculpture. From Azuma Kenjirō to Sekine Nobuo, colors, materials, and forms seemed intensely handcrafted from the Japanese environment. As Iino Kiichi puts it, "Japan is a country of mountains surrounded by water, with a distinct nature of its own, and the best sculpture reflects this distinctiveness rather than mimicking some general international style."[8] Yet for all the inventiveness of the past two decades, much Japanese sculpture still pursues form, especially the human body, rather than the organization of space, and Rodin has not yet been unseated from the pedestal of orthodoxy.

Public sculpture lagged far behind the remarkable new architecture that appeared as Japan rebuilt its cities after the war. With so little academicism to overcome, Japanese architects soon established functionalism as their dogma in the

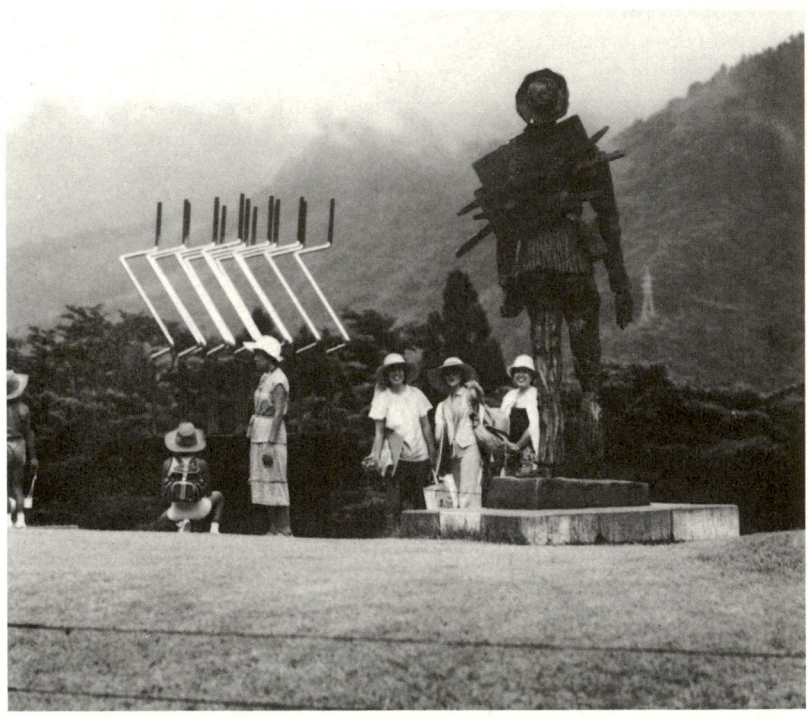

Visitors admire a work by Ossip Zadkine at the Hakone
Open Air Sculpture Museum, first opened to the public
in August 1969. HAKONE OPEN AIR SCULPTURE MUSEUM

1950s. Tange Kenzō became the doyen of modern design in
Japan, but in the mid-1970s postmodern architects such as
Isozaki Arata began to reject his massive forms in favor of
ornamentation, neoclassicism, and a more modest scale. Few
of the buildings in any style contained much sculpture in their
lobbies or courtyards. Many "office buildings of the 1970s
are handsome in exterior design," says Hara Toshio, "but
there is nothing inside them."[9] One early effort at placing
sculpture in public places was the installation of small bronze

works in Tokyo subway stations in the 1950s. "The important thing about sculpture since the war," Iino believes, "is that artists are trying to create dialogue with ordinary people, especially in public, where sculpture is not monumental but on the same level and same size as ordinary citizens."[10] Businesses do buy art, both large works and small ones, but they usually tuck them away in the boardroom or reception lounge for important visitors. The custom of spending a certain percentage of the construction costs on sculpture or other art is almost unknown in private building, although Kanagawa prefecture began requiring it for public projects in 1977 and Hokkaido followed suit in 1980.[11] Perhaps these steps will help to overcome the fact that "so many of the sculptures produced in Japan these days stay right in the studio."[12]

So do many of the works of print makers, even though Japan for centuries has been as innovative in the graphic arts as any nation. The prewar pioneers of the modern print included Onchi Kōshirō, Hiratsuka Un'ichi, and the Creative Print (Sōsaku Hanga) movement, in which the artist designed and executed the work personally. Woodblocks in various traditional, folk-craft, and radically new styles remained the favorite process through the 1950s, but then Japanese artists began using a full spectrum of materials and techniques, including etchings, lithographs, and silkscreens, often in very imaginative combinations. Conceptual symbols and more recently ultrarealism have made Japanese works seem familiar to viewers abroad. Yet Margaret K. Johnson, a Tokyo print maker, points out that contemporary graphic art has a definite sense of place: "Japanese print makers are filled with excitement from the media and the action of life in Japan."[13] Whatever their debt to international styles, a number of the most inventive print artists, like many painters and sculptors, now express a romantic link to their surroundings and often a fondness for ornamentation, as well as a nostalgia for other eras. Since Japanese collectors have shown such low esteem for their works, few print makers would disagree with Honda that good art doesn't sell—a fact that has daunted almost none of them from producing still more of it.

NITTEN: "A SYMBOL OF JAPAN"

Nowhere is the outpouring of fresh art works in Japan more visible than at the annual shows of the various art associations held in municipal galleries in some of the largest cities. More than 200 of these groups, including almost all the major ones, accept entries from the public as well as from their own members, giving any artist a chance to exhibit under the temporary umbrella of a responsible art organization. All but a handful hold their exhibitions at the Tokyo metropolitan art museum, and often elsewhere too. Calligraphy and Western-style painting dominate the contents: about a third of the groups specialize in showing calligraphy, a few others are confined to crafts, prints, sculpture, or Japanese-style paintings, and nearly all the rest concentrate on mounting either general exhibitions of various media or else oils alone. The most socially prestigious, artistically conservative, and financially rewarding annual show is the spectacle held in Tokyo each November called Nitten.

"Nitten is truly a symbol of Japan," says Maki Jun'ichi, who has shown his oils at its exhibitions. "Out-of-town museums and collectors expect it to set standards. Once you're elected a member, that's your passport to being a truly professional artist. Only then can you sell your work at prices high enough that you can hope to make a living entirely from painting. Also, to succeed in Nitten, you need the patronage of your old teacher and other artists senior to you. All of these are typical of the society as a whole."[14] Nitten, which means Japan Art Exhibition (Nihon Bijutsu Tenrankai), holds top rank not merely because it is the oldest of all the group shows but also because it was the official art display of the national government for half a century and still awards prizes from the prime minister each year.

Nitten began in 1907 as the education ministry exhibit, or

Bunten, and with various changes of name it was sponsored until 1958 by either the ministry or the Imperial Arts Academy (known since 1947 as the Japan Arts Academy).[15] Artists had long complained, and still do today, that Nitten perpetuated a dated formalism and paid no heed to new art. After a very unusual episode of political intervention by a Diet member in 1957,[b] Nitten reorganized the following year as a private corporation, promising to "carry out democratic management" and "develop fresh and healthy art among the people, without lapsing into eccentricities or triteness."[16] The same kind of discontent was rife in many other art associations. By the late sixties art students were organizing protests against Nitten, which reconstituted itself again in March 1969 and now draws unprecedented numbers of submissions and great crowds each year.

Since Nitten is so highly regarded by out-of-town curators and collectors, it is not surprising that nearly three times as many persons see its annual exhibits on tour as in Tokyo. The total attendance was more than 800,000 in 1965-1966, before reorganization reduced the size of the show. It did not reach this level again until ten years later, when 903,996 spectators gave Nitten the largest patronage in its history—three-fourths of them outside the capital.[17] Admissions paid by the public, typically $2.75 per person in 1979, earned Nitten an estimated $1,763,000 that year. Application fees from artists who submitted works brought in another $211,000, and dues from the 480 elected members yielded $65,000. According to Narita Kyōichi, the business manager of Nitten, the organization has almost no endowment or gift income, earns very little

[b] At a July 1957 meeting of the culture and education committee of the lower house of the Diet, Rep. Takatsu Masamichi attacked the nepotism and narrowness of Nitten, demanding to know why the painter Umehara Ryūzaburō had resigned from its parent organization the month before. *Zusetsu*, p. 344; *Asahi nenkan 1958*, p. 471; *Asahi nenkan 1959*, p. 478. On the earlier history of Nitten, see Kyōto Daigaku Bungakubu Kokushi Kenkyūshitsu, *Nihon kindaishi jiten*, Tokyo, Tōyō Keizai Shinpōsha, 1958, p. 482; Nihon Geijutsuin, *Nihon Geijutsuinshi*, Tokyo, Nihon Geijutsuin, 1963, pp. 1-4; Takeda Michitarō, *Nihon kindai bijutsushi*, Tokyo, Kondō Shuppansha, 1969, pp. 146-147; Bunkachō, *Bunka gyōsei no ayumi*, p. 13.

from the sale of works or catalogs at its shows, and receives aid from the government's cultural agency only for publishing its official history.[18] In effect Nitten, like other art associations, is financed by the artists themselves and the audiences who come to see their works.

Anyone may submit one work made within the past five years to each of the five divisions of Nitten: Japanese-style painting, Western-style painting, sculpture, crafts, and calligraphy. The work must not have been shown in public before, and the artist must pay an application fee (thirty dollars in 1980) for each item submitted. A jury of members in each division decides which ones will be exhibited. To be elected to Nitten, an artist must first be selected to show for several years, then invited to show, and finally be made a full member. Scholars and critics are kept off the juries, according to Narita, "to avoid a confusion of roles, since they are also involved in publicizing art events and thus, to some degree, in influencing the value of works of art."[19] Many artists who do not belong to Nitten suspect the motive has much more to do with protecting the organization's view of acceptable art, although it is also true that members may serve only once as jurors.[20]

Showing at Nitten is so glamorous and the number of artists working in Japan is now so great that 1980 was the most competitive year in its history. Submissions reached 8,825, nearly double the figure for 1960, when the show was about the same size. One-fifth of the total were selected for display, but it was much harder to be chosen if you were a calligrapher or painted with oils than if you produced watercolors, crafts, or especially sculpture (55 percent of the last category were picked, including dozens of classical academic nudes).[21] The numbers changed from year to year, but the proportions of works entered and selected in each of the five divisions varied only slightly throughout the 1960s and 1970s. Perhaps because they were the most competitive media, calligraphy and Western-style painting always had more new artists being shown each year than the others, but the show as a whole never presented more than 20 percent who were fresh faces and averaged about 15 percent during the 1970s.[c]

Even though there are roughly as many Nihonga artists as oil painters active in Japan, the latter compete much more sharply for the honor of showing at an art association's exhibit. The group shows have always set the standards for modern art in Japan, and Western-style painting has been its most representative medium. To be validated as a successful oil painter, you are expected to have your work approved by a jury of fellow artists and displayed in public. Nitten gives the best sheen of all because it carried the certification of officialdom for fifty years.[d]

Another reason why three times as many Western-style painters as Nihonga artists submit their work to Nitten is that the teacher-pupil relationship remains much stronger among Japanese-style painters. Young artists stay in touch with their teachers longer and derive more status from the connection than is usually true for Western-style painters. Nihonga is organized in a more familial, hierarchical mode that protracts the apprenticeship and discourages competition with the pu-

[c] The data for the 1980-1981 exhibit, expressed as numbers of works submitted/numbers selected/numbers of new artists represented: Total: 8,825/1,769/242; Japanese-style painting: 750/235/27; Western-style painting: 2,141/339/53; Sculpture: 312/173/21; Crafts: 1,145/443/45; and Calligraphy: 4,477/579/96. Nitten, *Daijūnikai Nitten sakuhinshū*, Tokyo, Nitten, 1980, pp. 224, 228. The percentage of submissions accepted was 32 percent in 1960, 41 in 1965, 23 in 1970, 20 in 1975, and 20 in 1980. The percentage of new artists was 14 percent in 1960, 20 in 1965, 11 in 1970, 15 in 1975, and 14 in 1980. Nitten, *Nitten benran*, Tokyo, Nitten, 1979, pp. 50-51; Nitten, *Nitten yōran Shōwa 54nendo*, Tokyo, Nitten, 1980, p. 44.

[d] Tokyo University of Fine Arts, the authorized academy of modern art, plays a similar role. Seven times as many applicants seek admission each year in oils as in watercolors, but there are fifty places for them and twenty for the latter. Entrance examinations are similar to those at other national universities. Candidates who pass the examinations then take simple tests in studio skills. No portfolio is required. "Your personality is as important as your previous art training for getting in," says the painter and photographer Anzai Shigeo. Anzai interview, October 27, 1980; Asian Cultural Centre for UNESCO, *Report on Traditional Forms of Culture in Japan*, Tokyo, Asian Cultural Centre for UNESCO, 1975, p. 12.

pils of rival teachers. Nihonga artists also rely more on their teachers to introduce them to commercial galleries. Established painters sometimes accept a dealer's commission and farm out the actual work to their pupils, "exactly like the artisans under an Italian Renaissance master."[22] It is common to keep on studying with the same teacher long after graduation and to make appropriate payments in the summer and at New Year's as well as to pay a monthly tuition. For the Japanese-style painters, Nitten and the other art-association exhibits are desirable adornments, but they are much less essential than for Western-style painters who work in the approved academic modes.

Even oil painters are discouraged from switching teachers, no matter how much it might advance their art. They usually bring holiday gifts to their teacher as well, although the link is a good deal weaker than for Japanese-style painters. Instead the art-association exhibit is the chief route to authentication. To improve chances of being accepted, the oil painter will often approach a senior figure in Nitten, perhaps even a juror if an introduction can be arranged, for an informal preview and suggestions for slight changes in hue or composition before the completed work is submitted. No honorarium is paid for this intercession, but the elder painter can expect to receive generous carfare for the studio visit and suitable season's greetings from the younger artist. No one seems quite sure how much these efforts help, but informal previews are so well established that everyone thinks they must make a difference.[23]

Another reason why "Nitten has a high reputation among artists," says the critic Haryū Ichirō, "is that it costs them less to show there than to rent a gallery. It also gives them access to the conservative art market"[24] for their typically representational, post-impressionist works. Most of the items displayed at Nitten are sold directly by the artist to regional art museums and out-of-town collectors, who will pay much more if the artist won a prize. Most of those who submit works, especially oils, are school or college art teachers in prefectures beyond the biggest cities who lack connections with commercial dealers. "Nitten has almost nothing to do with the Tokyo art market,"[25] says its leading student, Segi Shin'ichi, and few corporations buy their art there. Instead, many of the works are sold to relatives or pupils of the artists back in their home communities, as well as to local business and professional people. Just as showing in New York inflates the price a painter can charge back in Tokyo, so exhibiting in Tokyo at an art-association show enriches local artists all over the country. As Haryū puts it, "Japanese collectors buy art according to the fame of the artist, as a status symbol, not because of their interest in the work of art itself"[26]—and no event yields more cash or cachet than Nitten.

Print artists have no home in the mixed-media exhibits held by the leading art organizations. Instead they submit their new works for the spring show of the Japan Print Association, which probably displays more creativity each year than any other major group. But the print-association exhibit has far less standing than Nitten among artists or the public. The competition is much more tame, partly because there are fewer print makers, and just 1,869 persons paid to attend its two-week exhibit at the Tokyo metropolitan museum in April 1980.[e] Being chosen to show is a feather for any artist, as is true for the yearly exhibition of the College Women's Association of Japan, but there are few if any informal previews before works are submitted to either organization. As striking as much of its fresh art is, even the Japan Print Association imposes conservative standards to some extent because artists

[e] For the 1980 exhibit, 106 of 273 applicants were accepted, in addition to works by 101 full members and sixty-eight junior members. Total attendance in Tokyo was 9,549, of whom 1,869 paid. Selections from the show were later sent on tour. Nihon Hanga Kyōkai, *Dai48kai Nihon Hanga Kyōkaiten*, Tokyo, Nihon Hanga Kyōkai, 1980. For information on the print association, Ikeda Masao interview, November 26, 1980; Haryū interview, November 13, 1980; Yoneda Minoru interview, November 26, 1980; Honda interview, December 15, 1980. For information on the exhibit of the College Women's Association of Japan, Margaret K. Johnson interview, November 12, 1980; Blakemore interview, December 27, 1980.

are expected to turn in three prints in the same style developed earlier in their careers.

To critics of the art establishment in Japan, Nitten is only the most outrageous example of a bad institution. "Like the Salon de Mai," says Hara Toshio, "Nitten once played a useful role," but now it is ossified and does little for art.[27] All the formal art organizations, even the relatively open-minded print association, are often accused of discouraging new talent and frowning on innovations in technique or conception. Many artists think they are compromising their professionalism if they submit to the discipline of an art association.[28] The price for dissenting is often isolation, driving the individual who will not join a group show into the grasp of the commercial galleries.

MARKETING ART

Japan has had art dealers since at least 1910 and rental galleries since Kinokuniya bookstore began leasing its wall space for exhibits in 1936. From then until the mid-sixties the art business was genteel and quietly profitable. Then an enormous boom took place starting in 1965 and is still in progress. By 1972 rich purchasers had driven prices so high that perhaps two billion dollars' worth of art, 90 percent of it domestic,[29] changed hands that year. Not only did the gallery system suddenly commercialize, but it also expanded very rapidly because so many more persons were producing art for sale. As submissions to the art-association shows kept on rising in the seventies, more and more artists chose instead to rent galleries for their own one-person or small-group displays. The number of galleries in Tokyo, where three-quarters of the country's dealers and 90 percent of sales are concentrated, rose from 133 in 1965 to about 1,500 in 1980.[30] Roughly 300 of them are regular galleries with works in stock and the rest are strictly for hire.

Segi Shin'ichi, who heads the main research institute on the economics of the visual arts in Japan, estimates that only 300 top Japanese artists, virtually all of them painters, manage to participate in the Tokyo art market. Its sales in 1980 were about $750 million for Japanese works and another $250 million for imports, half the inflated 1972 figure but well above the slump induced by yen revaluation, oil embargoes, and higher consumer prices in 1973-1975. The favored 300, who represent 1 percent of all professional visual artists in the country, are almost evenly divided between oil and watercolor painters. Nearly all that they produce is representational, much of it sentimental, and almost none of it worth very much outside the hothouse of the Japanese market.

Like many others in business, art dealers have been clubby and closed to outsiders for many years in Japan—so much so that open auctions are still rare.[f] When Christie's contrived to hold a sale in Tokyo of art worth $5.1 million in 1981, its director for East Asian ceramics, Sir John Figgess, noted drily that "there should be a self-sustaining market here, as there is elsewhere."[31] The American collector John Powers points out that auctions seem too risky to most Japanese purchasers, who prefer the safety of working with dealers because they will take back what they have sold.[32] Instead, a half-dozen associations of dealers have been active, both with exchanging works by Japanese artists and with importing European art, particularly after currency laws were relaxed in 1963. More than 900,000 art objects from abroad entered Japan during 1962-1971, according to the finance ministry, nearly all of them paintings and prints imported by dealers rather than by museums or individuals. A few rich Japanese acquired notoriety at auctions abroad in the early seventies by buying expensive Renoirs as well as racehorses, but most of the imports

---

[f] Partly because of the legal restrictions on auctions, Seibu department stores signed an agreement with Sotheby's in the 1970s that allowed Seibu customers to bid at its auctions abroad. *Time*, December 31, 1979, p. 54; Etō Shun interview, December 25, 1980; Segi interview, December 9, 1980. See Segi Shin'ichi, *Shakai no naka no bijutsu*, Tokyo, Tōkyō Shoseki, 1978, pp. 123-130; Haryū Ichirō, *Sengo bijutsu seisuishi*, Tokyo, Tōkyō Shoseki, 1979, pp. 127-132, 141-142; *Asahi nenkan 1970*, p. 711; *Asahi nenkan 1971*, p. 711.

in the 1960s and 1970s were recent works by French or British painters that sold for a few hundred dollars. More than 100,000 foreign art works are now bought each year in Japan at a total value in yen terms not far below the record set in 1973, just before the overall Tokyo art market contracted.[g]

Greater by far have been the sales of domestic works in the past two decades. Japanese prices rose in step with the world art market in the early 1970s, when investors everywhere were looking for immunity from inflation. Then sales abroad climbed another 30 percent for top-rank art during the oil crisis of 1973-1974, but the Tokyo market for domestic art shriveled by 50 to 80 percent during the same period because dealers were overbought and relied too much on old customers rather than cultivating new ones. Many proud or stubborn artists refused to cut their prices, out of fear for their reputations, and it took several years for the galleries to work off the backlog. By the late seventies the demand for the best-known Japanese artists was once again strong, raising the total value of sales of works produced in Japan to about $750 million in 1980. Oils and watercolors claimed about 40 percent each; the rest was split among prints, sculpture, drawings, art-crafts, and other contemporary works.[33]

Where did people put nearly a million foreign and Japanese art objects each year, and who were the purchasers? Business offices, banks, trading companies, stores, hospitals, airports, schools, and public buildings of every sort by 1980 seemed bare if they did not have paintings by current Japanese artists trained in the approved academic styles. Hotels, restaurants, coffee shops, and bars routinely displayed works of art that might seem out of keeping with the rest of their decor if the setting were abroad. The nation's 30 million households were

---

[g] Japanese dealers import eight paintings for every print and eighty for every sculpture. Although most are contemporary works by little-known painters, the *Mainichi* estimated in 1978 that there were at least 300 Utrillos, Dufys, and Picassos in Japanese collections, along with 200 Renoirs, 100 Monets, and thirty each by Cézanne and Van Gogh. Very few are considered first-rate. Segi, *Shakai*, pp. 161-170, 199-209; Yoshii interview, October 14, 1980; *Asahi nenkan 1964*, pp. 649-650; Haryū, *Sengo*, p. 133.

probably the greatest consumers, numerically if not in yen value, especially now that so many people lived in apartments and other Western-style homes that invited adornment.

But more than blank walls impelled Japan's middle class to buy art. "Until recently," says Jitsukawa Nobuhiro, who directs a gallery, "ordinary people have regarded art as something for museums or aristocrats." The elite custom of displaying art turned into a fashion among millions of status-conscious citizens after the war, who learned through the schools and the media that showing off objects of beauty implied refinement and social standing.[34] By the 1970s, when so many people had so much more money than before, consumers were eager to buy works that resembled the accredited art seen in loan shows from abroad and the exhibits of the posh art associations. Other families with whom they competed for status did the same. Those who benefited the most were the few painters with big names and the dealers who handled their works.

Many persons believe that speculators were responsible for the ballooning prices of Japanese art works in the early seventies, and even today the Joint Art Research Institute estimates that 90 percent of the art in yen value is purchased by investors rather than collectors.[35] Medical doctors,[h] securities dealers, real-estate officials, and financiers are the leading individual buyers, according to the institute, but most of them know art rather poorly and meekly follow a dealer's advice. High price becomes a canon of taste to those with more cash than connoisseurship, and inexpensive works such as prints are scorned as "cheap," and thus unworthy. "Unlike New

---

[h] Doctors and dentists are permitted to deduct up to 72 percent of their income from fees under the national social-insurance system, "in lieu of actual necessary expenses" for running their hospitals and clinics, for income tax purposes. It is customary for patients to pay untaxed honoraria to physicians in addition to amounts covered by insurance. For these reasons doctors have the reputation of being rich, and some have acquired large art collections. Japan, Ministry of Finance, Tax Bureau, *An Outline of Japanese Taxes, 1979*, Tokyo, Ministry of Finance, 1979, p. 31; Kawashima Takeyoshi interview, November 27, 1980.

121

York," says Segi, "it's a dealer's market, not a buyer's."[36] Sometimes the purchaser leaves the work on deposit with the gallery, to be sold like a stock certificate when it appreciates. Many speculators in the seventies were looking for quick profits that did not materialize, but at least the investors are cushioned by the dealer's guarantee to buy back any work at the original price. As it turned out, galleries usually made more money by holding onto paintings until their value rose than by engaging in the frantic buying and selling that peaked in 1972.

The painters who blossomed most brightly in this hothouse are scarcely known in the world market: Umehara Ryūzaburō, Oka Shikanosuke, Itō Shinsui, and another dozen or more who commanded at least $10,000 per work.[i] "Many Japanese artists paint to sell, not to express ideas," says Mukai Kasue, because they know there will be a buyer for whatever they turn out. The critic Amaury Saint-Gilles says of such purchasers, "no one ever looks with their eyes at the art, only at the price." Values go even higher once painters die and cross the bar beyond all market fluctuations or controversies. Paintings are often priced by the gō, a unit of square measure the size of a post card, and investors are sometimes more concerned with the dimensions of a work than with its content. Japanese collectors and speculators alike came to the art market only recently and are still reluctant to take chances on unfamiliar names. The same is true for corporations, which buy art through their cultural departments as an investment. Shimanaka Fumio, an exhibit planner for the largest gallery in Japan, typically selects a number of works and takes them to a company on approval. Eventually the firm buys one or

---

[i] Izeki Masaaki, an art critic who heads the exhibit section of the Japan Foundation, thinks a reason why Japanese contemporary painting has little value abroad, apart from works by Leonard Foujita and a few other expatriates, is that it has had very little international exposure. It is not clear why Japanese graphic artists have been so much more active in biennales and other world competitions, unless one accepts Hara Toshio's flat judgment that "Japanese painting has little international value because most of it is so bad." Izeki interview, December 12, 1980; Hara interview, October 28, 1980.

two and returns the rest, confident that it can always recoup the investment by selling back to the dealer what it purchases.[37] In this way the gallery system reinforces caution on the part of its customers and helps to maintain the artificially high prices claimed by the favored 300.

French painters and their Japanese disciples are the most popular among purchasers because the Barbizon school, the impressionists, the post-impressionists, and then the School of Paris dominated European painting when Japan was first exposed to Western art. Impressionism and its literary cousin, naturalism, happened to appeal to artists when they were introduced to Japan because they focused on the loneliness and sensory perceptions of the individual at a time of rapid industrialization and personal alienation. But this alone does not explain why the impressionists hold such an attraction for the public today. Instead it is a question of stages in Japan's cultural history. Like Victorian armchairs and antimacassars, impressionism was taken in and made a part of the culture in almost frozen form, its popularity enduring much longer in Japan than in France. A special show of contemporary art draws 30,000 to 50,000 at a major museum in Tokyo; if it were a show of impressionists, ten times this number would appear. Collectors and gallery-goers are both "very fashion-conscious," Segi explains, "recognizing famous names and schools without having very strong educations in art."[38]

Art is bought like other fashionable items in Japan. People seem willing to pay inflated prices, whether investing, giving gifts, or adding to their own collections, because of the status the objects confer. The intricate web of social obligations requires that status be continually recognized and reconfirmed, driving the prices for emblems that fulfill this need well past their objective worth as it might be independently judged. Art is often costly far beyond its value outside the culture or even beyond the artist's need to make a living. Both Nitten and the gallery system are hothouses of inflated prices, warmed by the nexus of status and social obligation that art helps to reinforce.

123

The artist who has no interest in the art associations and no teacher to make introductions to a regular dealer can try to crack the market by having a one-person show of ten or twenty fresh works in a rental gallery. Even complete unknowns can hold their own shows, paying $150 to $250 per day for a one-room Tokyo gallery plus the costs of posters, an opening, sometimes a catalog, and the obligatory picture post cards bearing a few words of greeting from a teacher or critic, for which the artist pays an honorarium. Although relatives and friends feel obliged to buy something, the main point is to capture the attention of critics from the newspapers and art journals, in the hope that a regular gallery will pick up the artist's work on consignment. Out-of-town painters sometimes have fan clubs from their home towns who travel to Tokyo for the show and support them by purchasing works on display, but most one-person exhibits are considered a success if even a quarter of the items are bought. The artist who cannot make contact with a regular gallery takes the unsold works home and hopes that collectors who saw the show or read of it will get in touch directly. At the very least the event embellishes the artist's curriculum vitae. Many of them hold rental shows, which are almost never retrospective, several times a year—they are far more active than their counterparts in New York.[39]

If a regular gallery invites the artist to stage a one-person exhibition, there is no rental or publicity charge but the house takes its cut of whatever is sold. Most galleries keep 40 percent of the sale price, which is almost always set by the artist, either for works on consignment or for those at one-person displays. Occasionally a dealer will commission a painting or an edition of a print, paying the artist when it is delivered. A show at a regular gallery gives the artist access to its list of customers, which averages about 800 names in Tokyo but goes as high as 3,000 at Yoshii Galleries. None will disclose its list. Artists themselves keep careful mailing lists of past and potential customers, often about 500 names in length. Most galleries calculate that 10 percent of their purchasers do the bulk of the buying and that virtually everyone who appears at a one-person exhibit, whether by invitation or not, is there just to look. The traffic in a regular gallery doubles when there is a special show, to 100 per day at Yoshii and 150 at the colossus of the trade, Tokyo Central Art Gallery, on the site of the former Queen Bee cabaret in Ginza.[40]

As with the art associations, a hierarchy of galleries affects how much artists can charge for their works. Nichidō is usually considered the most aggressive and perhaps the most important of all the dealers. An artist who shows at Nantenshi can jack up prices, even if the wall space is only rented from what is normally a regular gallery. Any Ginza dealer, rental or not, adds polish to an artist's record. Regular galleries usually stock the full range of media in which their artists work, but few of the relationships are formalized with contracts, and artists try to get more exposure by spreading their output among several dealers. Even small galleries, with just an owner, a part-time helper, and a small inventory, are considered "very stable and profitable," according to Shimanaka, because their costs are low and many customers prefer works that have been squirreled away in the storage closet of an out-of-the-way gallery, somehow finding them rare because few others have laid eyes on them.[41]

Critics, hugely powerful in the Japanese art market, are a main reason why there is such "a great lack of open criticism in the art world," according to Kawashima Takeyoshi. It is almost universally believed that newspaper critics are the worst offenders, since most of them are reporters rather than specialists on art. Certain critics survey the upcoming shows and plan the space on the page to be given to each, including photographs, depending on the honoraria they can expect to receive from the artist or gallery.[42] Five hundred dollars is considered usual for a favorable review (Paris prices are said to be double this amount, with New York somewhere in between). It costs artists as much as $2,500 to have photo essays on their work appear in one of the monthly trade journals, and they also pay stiff fees for listings in the *Art Yearbook*, where they may set whatever prices they wish for their works—typically two or three times their actual value.[j]

Kimura Yōichi, editor of the independent art review *Bijutsu techō*, quickly adds that "true critics don't take money." There are about seventy critics in a position to affect artists' careers in Tokyo, perhaps ten of them persons whose words are taken very seriously. By no means do they all accept payments. Galleries write off the fees to those who do as publicity expenses and add them to the prices they charge customers. Kimura tells of receiving a handsomely decorated cake as a souvenir from a dealer as he left after attending an opening. "When I looked in the box, I discovered an envelope with money in it. I left the money where it was, wrapped it up again, and returned the box, cake and all." With this system in effect, it is small wonder that writers rarely say anything critical. They have an interest in perpetuating the impressionist orthodoxy that keeps art prices mushrooming, and without their attention artists cannot expect to become known.[43] There is nothing illegal or unusual about the payoffs; they are the grease that keeps the hinge of true criticism remarkably silent.

Prints are a special case because regular galleries often find them too inexpensive to handle and because print makers rely somewhat more on the world market to establish their reputations. Many of them turn out gigantic works, ill-suited to Japanese houses, because they hope to win awards at international biennales. A few graphic artists sell their output through dealers abroad, and more of them work with galleries patronized by foreigners in Japan. Yōseidō Gallery and the Contemporary Print Center are two leaders among the 100 or so dealers handling more than a token number of prints. Wa-

---

[j] Segi Shin'ichi believes that fees paid to Tokyo critics are lower than in other art capitals because the gallery system is currently a seller's market and trade journals provide a means of publicity for pay. The main *gyōkaishi*, as the journals are known, are *Shin bijutsu shinbun, Art Graph, Art Vision*, and *Gekkan bijutsu*. The art annual, *Bijutsu nenkan*, lists about half the country's 30,000 professional artists. Segi interview, December 9, 1980; Amaury Saint-Gilles interview, December 6, 1980; Kimura Eiji interview, December 8, 1980; Kimura Yōichi interview, December 12, 1980.

126

tanabe Fujio, president of the print center, points out that the clientele for graphics of all kinds is much wider than for oils or watercolors because the average cost is just fifty dollars— much lower than for fresh works of comparable quality by American artists. Prices stay low not only because there are so many print makers producing so many prints but also, as Margaret Johnson says, because "the Japanese still have a grudge against the print as an art form."[44]

So many impediments keep artists from selling very well in Japan that it is perhaps perplexing that such large numbers of them keep on creating new works. Both of the major vehicles to renown, the art-association exhibits and the gallery system, are clannish and conservative. Only a dozen dealers specialize in truly contemporary art, but even the most devoted among them rarely commission fresh works. Regular galleries are mainly interested in vying with one another to handle expensive foreign art and the works of the 300 Japanese with established reputations. Dealers import a great deal but have done little to develop sales abroad for Japanese artists. Renting a gallery is costly and the result fleeting, critics are both cautious and elusive, and there is not much of a general public for art—just a set of private clienteles carefully developed by galleries among their business connections and by artists among their friends and relatives. Museums have exercised very little leadership in promoting current works, and auctions are still foreclosed as a channel to new customers. And even if there were more outlets for selling art, most art objects are too large and overpriced for ordinary purchasers, who enjoy few tax incentives to collect art or to patronize other collections through gifts. Nor has the government done very much directly to encourage visual artists, either as benefactor or as customer.

Worst of all are the conventional expectations most Japanese seem to hold for art. "Everyone assumes that you will specialize in one art form and stick with it," says the abstract painter and print maker Kamiya Shin. "It's very hard to change your style or medium—people expect consistency. Like other adults, artists are supposed to be labeled as a follower of a

127

particular style or group for their whole careers." Although many Nihonga students now rebel against painting precisely like their teachers, they like all other artists are expected to settle on a style, establish an identity, and cling to it.[45] Japanese purchasers want art to look like something and to be in the approved mode—the human figures of Rodin, the French painting of 1875-1925, or the modern Japanese watercolor style developed under European tutelage during those same years. The value they place on art, and their willingness to buy it, are determined mostly by social factors unconnected with esthetics, such as fame, fashion, and costliness. Very few people buy art simply because they like it.

Becoming an artist is neither prestigious nor profitable in Japan today, but tens of thousands of young persons have tried to succeed at it in the 1970s as an alternative to jobs in trade, manufacturing, or government that might have attracted them a decade or two earlier. In the more open society of the postwar period, there were no longer many guild restrictions to control entry into the profession, and art lessons in school or with a neighborhood teacher prompted many students to continue at a university or art academy. There the teachers usually encouraged rather than criticized their efforts, especially at private institutions that depended on tuition from huge numbers of students. Once they became the pupils of established teachers, they could hope to make a go of it not because they were good but because they belonged. Students learned to presume on the indulgence of their mentors, so that nowhere along the way was much criticism proffered, judgment entered, or bad art called bad.

When they graduated and swarmed the job market, students usually had to settle for teaching posts in elementary or secondary schools or else take positions in commercial art. Others made a living by teaching private pupils, usually young children, in their own studios or neighborhood centers, charging twenty-five dollars or so per month for weekly lessons. (Private instruction was generally a more important source of income for dancers and musicians than for visual artists.) Still others, like the truck driver Honda, took whatever work they could find and devoted any spare time that remained to their art.

"Japanese artists have a great sense of pride," says Johnson, "a very real self-respect." They consider themselves art professionals first and often will not talk about their side jobs, even if they work full time at them. Nor do they readily complain about the sacrifices they make to produce their art. Many have had to move two hours or more outside central Tokyo, since artists need space and the capital offers so little. Their costs for paper, brushes, pigments, and other materials and equipment are so high that print makers often cannot afford to produce an entire edition at once. Women artists usually have to take side jobs in occupations considered appropriate for their gender, which often means waitressing or being a bar hostess. Their works are welcome at the art-association shows because of the submission fees they pay, according to the painter Takikawa Yoshiko, but women find it hard to be taken seriously by critics or regular galleries.[46]

Both men and women artists make sacrifices because of their professional dedication and sense of dignity. Some specialists think that their persistence will soon start paying more rewards. Jitsukawa Nobuhiro believes that collectors in the 1980s will include "many more ordinary people who buy art for its own sake, something valuable to have in their own homes." Etō Shun agrees, comparing the situation for Japanese artists in the 1980s with that in Europe and America in the 1950s: "they are on the edge of a real breakthrough."[47] True as these forecasts may prove to be, the visual arts have thrived in the postwar period, as they did long before then, mainly because artists love their vocation and are willing to patronize it themselves.

GLAMOROUS ART SHOWS AND THEIR ENTREPRENEURS

So great is the power of advertising and the media, and so strong the universal human temptation to see the latest marvel, that several million persons turn out for the two dozen or more major exhibitions of foreign and classical Japanese art held in museums and other large galleries throughout the country each year. Art from abroad accounts for at least two-thirds of these special shows and three-fourths of the audiences. Ever since World War Two, the leading newspaper companies have been the most important organizers and sponsors of top-grade foreign art displays. Their only real rivals at undertaking flossy shows during the 1950s and 1960s were the large department stores, but finally in the seventies the national general museums and national art museums also became active in putting together major exhibits. Without the newspapers and department stores, the art on view in Japan would have been vastly more insular and far less inspiring to artists and lay audiences. Without the art shows to draw customers, the newspaper companies and department stores reckon that their sales could not have grown so rapidly as they did. Art, especially foreign art, turned out to be increasingly good for business, and more of it was on show in 1980 than ever before.[k]

The first exhibit of French art held in Japan took place in 1912, but very few other displays of any form of foreign art were held until after 1945. Starting about the turn of the century, the rival dailies, *Asahi* and *Mainichi*, sponsored musical events along with expositions, sports tournaments, and excursions for the frank purpose of building their circulations. Railway companies were the other main corporate entrepreneurs of cultural activities before the war, and it was natural that their affiliated department stores replaced them in this role when the age of middle-class commerce bloomed starting in the 1950s.[48]

Immediately after the war Japan was kept in cultural as well as economic and diplomatic isolation by the occupying authorities. Frances Blakemore and others developed excellent exhibits of American arts, but there was little cultural initiative

[k] Time Inc. and Control Data Corporation each announced in July 1979 that it would begin to sponsor art shows at major museums. *New York Times*, July 19, 1979.

from government, business, or higher education during the late forties and early fifties. "Japan was in a cocoon after the war," says Sakazaki Tarō, director of cultural affairs for *Asahi*: "citizens could not travel abroad, and foreign culture had to be brought in so that Japan could once again catch up with the West, as in Meiji." With their string of correspondents around the world, the papers were in a good position "to raise the human level of the Japanese people," according to Chiba Kihei of *Yomiuri*, by brightening their pages with cultural columns after several postwar years of crime and disaster stories. *Mainichi* too "felt an obligation as an opinion leader to restore the level of culture in our country and show that art is for the common people," notes Yamamoto Noriyuki, art director for the paper.[49]

The newspapers also knew that sponsoring art and music would improve their images and confer a respectability they had not previously enjoyed. Cultural events seemed an ideal way to cultivate new readers among the well-educated. But the most important reason, as Amano Ryōichi readily points out, was "to increase the circulation of the newspaper." The postwar vacuum in cultural leadership provided the occasion for newspaper companies to promote foreign arts events, but without their leavening effect on profits the publishers would not have continued to sponsor cultural activities out of a spirit of philanthropy alone. As entrepreneurs rather than benefactors, the newspapers have not always recovered their direct investments in the events they stage, but they have found that the overall corporate benefits of promoting culture outweigh the costs.[50]

Yomiuri and *Mainichi* took turns sponsoring the most impressive art shows during the late forties and early fifties, a time when *Asahi* concentrated on musical events and the national museums were too poor to undertake big exhibits of their own. In 1949 *Yomiuri* also began the annual Japan Independent show for domestic artists, which finally gave out tempestuously in 1964. *Mainichi* held an international contemporary-art exhibit and a show of contemporary Japanese

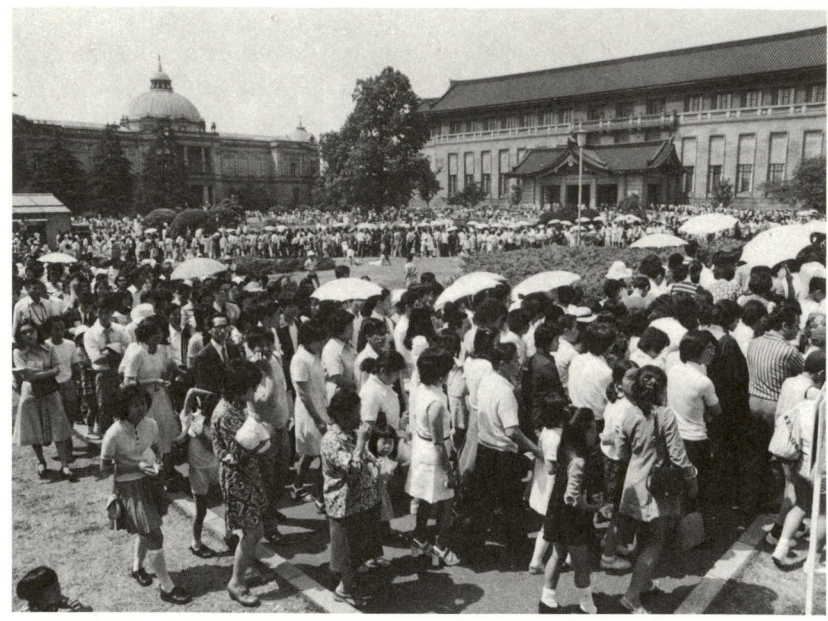

Some of the 1.5 million spectators who saw the *Mona Lisa* exhibit at the Tokyo National Museum in the spring of 1974. YOMIURI SHINBUNSHA

art in alternate years, starting in 1952 and continuing today. The three rivals still bicker over which was the first block-buster display of foreign art, but most who saw it say the Louvre show of 1954-1955, sponsored by *Asahi*, inaugurated the age of colossal art exhibits in Japan. It was the largest and costliest show ever held in Japan to that time, with 365 items of French art from the middle ages to 1840. Altogether it drew 1.1 million persons in Tokyo, Kyoto, and Fukuoka, the nation's first million-person exhibit and still the twelfth largest ever in Tokyo.[51]

For the next twenty years the newspapers, and to a lesser degree the department stores, sponsored nearly all the mass-appeal art shows from overseas and a number of classical

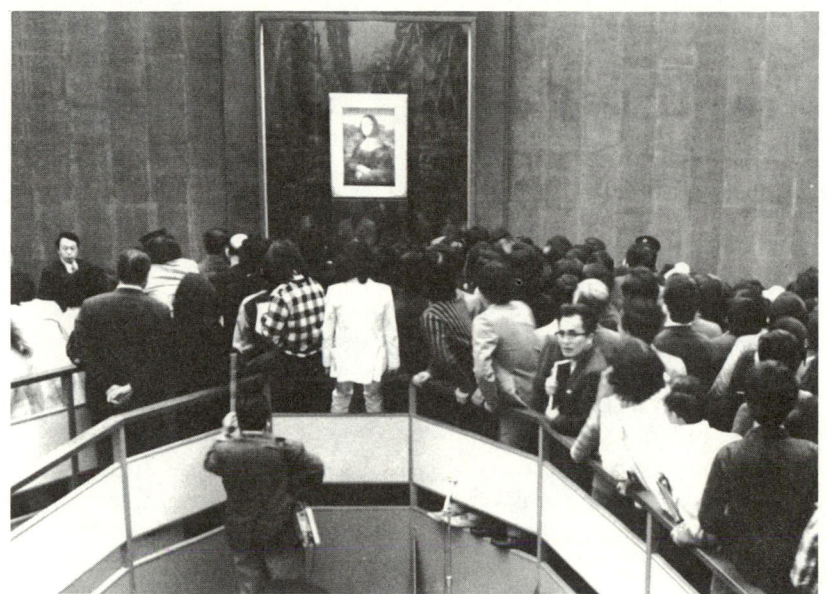

Crowds viewing *Mona Lisa* inside a special building constructed for the exhibition at the Tokyo National Museum.
YOMIURI SHINBUNSHA

Japanese exhibits as well. Their resources were so great, and those of public institutions so meager, that the national museums undertook only thirty special exhibitions of foreign art on their own between 1947 and 1967. All the others were backed by newspapers or other outside agencies. Then during 1968-1978 these same museums sponsored or cosponsored seventy-seven foreign art shows,[52] and ever since the *Mona Lisa* extravaganza in 1974 the cultural agency and national museums have ranked with the newspapers and department stores as the main promoters of full-scale exhibitions.

The acme of spectacular foreign-art displays came in the early 1960s, when four of the five biggest shows ever held in Japan took place. They included a second Louvre exhibit in

133

1961-1962, ancient Egyptian art in 1963, the *Venus de Milo* to celebrate the Olympiad in 1964, and a King Tutankhamen show the following year that in Tokyo outdrew the 1979 King Tut exhibit in New York. All were held in national museums and all were sponsored by *Asahi*, which was then the leader in the vicious circulation battles among the three largest dailies. Much of the success *Asahi* had in staging huge art events stemmed from its colorful cultural director, Enna Takio, who importuned Malraux to lend *Venus* and Nasser the King Tut masks.[L] Backed by President Murayama and the paper's other owners, Enna functioned as the unofficial cultural minister of Japan at a time when there was no formal one.

"Our mission was to import foreign culture," says Enna, "because the government was busy rebuilding the country and had no time to devote to it." His successor as cultural director for *Asahi*, Tsuji Yutaka, took office just as the government's national cultural agency was beginning in 1968. He held a more modest view of the role of the press: "I believed that cultural activity abroad should be carried out by diplomats, not by private newspaper companies, but this outlook took a long time to gain favor." Amano Ryōichi, who directed *Mainichi*'s cultural projects in 1971-1973, believes that "we were promoting international understanding" by holding exhibits of art from abroad. Enna agrees completely but Tsuji demurs: "I found that there could be no true mutual under-

---

[L] The King Tut show was made smoother when *Asahi* raised $1.1 million to rescue Egyptian cultural monuments from the rising waters behind the Aswan dam. "Mr. Nasser was very happy after the show with its success," Enna says. Enna interview, December 11, 1980. The King Tut show, second to *Mona Lisa* as Tokyo's largest in attendance, drew 1.3 million persons in that city in six weeks, compared with 1.2 million in three months at the Metropolitan Museum of Art in New York in 1979 for a somewhat different show. Asano Shōichirō, "Asahi no tenrankai," *Asahijin*, August 1980, p. 85; *New York Times*, July 30, 1979. Overall the 1965 show drew 2.9 million persons in Tokyo, Kyoto, and Fukuoka, the largest for any art exhibit ever held in Japan. The top five art shows in Tokyo: *Mona Lisa* (1974), 1,505,239; King Tut (1965), 1,297,718; *Venus de Milo* (1964), 831,198; the second Louvre exhibit (1961), 722,082; and the ancient Egypt show (1963), 632,543. Asano, "Asahi," p. 85. See Enna, *Chinmoku*, pp. 30-61, 104-139; *Asahi nenkan 1962*, p. 619; *Asahi nenkan 1963*, p. 664; *Asahi nenkan 1964*, p. 648; *Asahi nenkan 1966*, p. 695.

standing, only misunderstanding. Still, cultural exchanges can help to build good will among countries. It is a failing of current Japanese cultural policy that the government expects other countries to understand Japanese culture as we see it, rather than letting them accept it as they see fit."[53] Perhaps the heart of the matter is not understanding or the lack of it but a simpler truth: art is eternal, but it has different meanings in different places.

By the late 1960s it was becoming much harder to come up with bombshell exhibits. After the large *Asahi* shows early in the decade, no newspaper company managed to put on a display drawing more than 500,000 in Tokyo until *Yomiuri*'s Renoir show and *Mainichi*'s Goya exhibit, both in 1971. One reason, says Sakazaki of *Asahi*, is that Japanese began traveling abroad and no longer needed to stand among the throngs at special exhibits back home in order to see foreign art. Another factor is that more and more works from overseas were being shown in Japan after the mid-sixties, fragmenting the audiences. A third reason is that "by the seventies nearly every genre of really famous art had already been exhibited in Japan, the novelty had worn off, audiences were exhausted, and people were growing more selective."[54] Doubtless the newspaper companies were not unhappy, as Tsuji delicately puts it, "to be relieved in the early seventies by the cultural agency and the Japan Foundation of much of the heavy responsibility they had previously borne for sponsoring cultural activities."[m]

But the press in no sense abandoned the arts. *Yomiuri* took

---

[m] Enna says that "there was never a shred of competition between the cultural agency and the newspapers. Mr. Kon and I always collaborated fully." He adds that "the agency and the national museums learned from us how to present major shows, and by the seventies they were ready to do an excellent job." Enna interview, December 11, 1980. *Asahi*'s cultural activities were trimmed somewhat in 1976 after a long battle over many issues between the Murayama family, which owns about 35 percent of the stock, and the Ueno family (20 percent) in alliance with the paper's senior staff. Much of Tsuji's staff dispersed to positions with General Arts Corporation and the Nippon Cultural Centre, and Tsuji himself moved over to a top post with Asahi Broadcasting Corporation. *New York Times*, March 19, 1978; Tsuji Yutaka interview, December 8, 1980.

over from *Asahi* as the most aggressive promoter of foreign cultural events in the seventies, as a part of its successful campaign to become number one in sales. Of the eighteen largest shows ever held in Tokyo before 1980, *Asahi* sponsored seven and *Yomiuri* six—but five of *Yomiuri*'s six took place in the seventies, compared with two for its competitor.[n] As befits the tone of its pages, *Yomiuri* has a reputation for backing more events with mass appeal and promoting them more shrilly than the other publishers, but rivals could scarcely quarrel with its lineup of Picasso, Utrillo, Renoir, and Degas between 1975 and 1980—or with the tonic these masters provided to its circulation.[55]

Despite the great attention the media gave to their own displays of foreign art, a dozen or more special exhibitions of premodern Japanese works also steadily drew crowds each year starting in the mid-fifties. The national general museums put most of their slender budgets for exhibits during the fifties and sixties into shows of national treasures and other rare objects not usually seen in public. Newspapers and department stores have also promoted classical Japanese art. *Asahi*, for example, put on an exhibit of Buddhist works that was seen by more than a million people in five cities during 1980, marking the restoration of the great Buddha hall at Tōdaiji in Nara. But few if any other displays of Japanese classics have drawn this well: special shows of premodern Japanese works accounted for just five of the eighty-three most popular exhibitions in Tokyo during 1954-1979.[56] Newspapers usually backed one or two displays on classical Japanese themes each year but preferred to organize shows with the widest mass appeal, which in 1980 still meant French painting just as much as it did when the first Louvre exhibit was held in 1954.

To promote sales, each of the top three dailies sponsors

---

[n] Of the top eighty-three shows during 1954-1979, *Yomiuri* sponsored twenty-three, *Asahi* twenty, *Mainichi* twelve, *Nikkei* twelve, *Tokyo shinbun* four, *Sankei* one, and museums or department stores the other eleven. Asano, "Asahi," pp. 84-85.

several hundred events a year including sports,° chess tournaments, charity-fund drives, scientific and technical displays, and photography contests. Along with the high-school baseball championships that two of them conduct, the papers are proudest of their activities in the visual and performing arts and devote more staff to them than to any of their other promotions. *Asahi* presents between thirty and forty art shows a year, most of them small in scale and many of them backed by one of its four regional offices rather than the whole enterprise. In a number of cases the paper cosponsors by lending its name and publicity but no cash. *Asahi* also puts on about twenty musical events each year, by Japanese and foreigners, in both serious and popular music. *Yomiuri* tries to do one major art show a year with at least 100 works, plus a dozen or so at small museums or department-store galleries. Its musical promotions are down to two or three a year, now that commercial impresarios have found Western classical music generally profitable, but *Yomiuri* also sponsors a major symphony orchestra. *Mainichi* does three or four big productions annually, most of them special art shows, as well as holding its regular exhibits of contemporary and international art in alternating years. It also runs a respected music contest, gives film prizes, and operates the largest calligraphy exhibit in the world. Even virtual bankruptcy in 1977 did not deter *Mainichi* from continuing its cultural events: "if we gave them up," says Amano, "*Yomiuri* would quickly take them over."[57]

A full-scale special exhibit costs at least $1 million to produce and can go as high as the $3.5 million *Asahi* spent in direct outlays for its Tōdaiji show in 1980. Exclusive of free advertising in their own publications and staff salaries in their cultural planning departments, the newspaper companies usually break even each year on their arts events taken as a whole.

° *Asahi* "has nearly always preferred to sponsor amateur sports," Sakazaki Tarō says, ideally with a cosponsor such as the November 1980 Tokyo women's marathon that was financed by Shiseidō—perhaps the first time a women's running event was sponsored by a cosmetics firm. Sakazaki interview, December 24, 1980.

For several years in the 1960s, *Asahi* ran a deficit of about $840,000 on cultural events with a total budget of $4 million, but the paper sloughed off its worst money-losers to the cultural agency or the city of Tokyo and it now sponsors cultural activity with a total budget of $15.5 million each year without losing money.[58] *Mainichi*'s finances were so parlous in the 1970s that cultural promotions "always had to make a profit" to offset other activities on which the paper took a loss. In 1980 its arts events were worth $10 million, double the level a decade earlier in yen terms.[59] *Yomiuri*'s budget for cultural activities, excluding its orchestra, was $11.5 million in 1979, with a $1.5 million deficit.[60] Including smaller investments by other daily newspapers that promote events of their own, the press currently sponsors art exhibits and performing-arts productions at a level of $45 to $50 million a year.

The idea for an art exhibit often originates in the newspaper's cultural department, although sometimes a department store, museum, or other outside agency approaches the paper with a theme. Either way, every major show is approved by top management before the newspaper's name can be used as sponsor or cosponsor. The Tokyo National Museum is in such demand for big exhibits that it must be reserved at least three years in advance. At one time the newspapers used their own staff or hired consultants to plan the contents of some of their shows, with predictably sloppy scholarship, slapdash catalogs, and bad art scattered in with good.[61] Since the mid-sixties, much closer consultation has taken place between sponsors and the museum professionals, who now have charge of research, displays, and publications. When special exhibits are held at department stores without curatorial personnel, the old abuses are more apt to persist. As for the shows of foreign art seen in Japan since 1954, only a few have been touring exhibits organized abroad. Nearly all have been planned and executed entirely by Japanese sponsors for exhibition only in Japan, a mammoth labor typically involving several years' preparation and many trips overseas to borrow the works from collections in various countries.[62] The displays that result tend to be very large, often assembled with ingenious legwork from obscure locations, and sometimes very uneven in quality.

Each newspaper company tries to have a show of French impressionists every few years, but now that most of the famous themes have been treated the planners are giving more attention to African and Southeast Asian art, as well as further displays of Chinese and Korean classics. The permanent collections in Japanese museums are still so weak on Western art, and the turnover of young people in the big cities, the largest part of the viewing public, is so rapid that sponsors are also bringing back works by artists who have drawn well before. "A really big show puts the prestige of the whole paper on the line, not just the cultural department," notes Amano. "We set up an organizing committee with the prime minister and foreign minister on it. We bring in a member of the imperial family to cut the ribbon."[63] Often the newspapers distribute 20,000 to 30,000 free tickets to their shows, about 10 percent of which end up being used.[64] But the papers agree there is no way to measure the impact on sales, even though they all think it is positive. As Amano says, "it is impossible to tell what effect, if any, a big exhibit has on circulation, but it gives the reader a positive cultural image of the newspaper."[65]

By the early 1980s each of the top three dailies predicted that its cultural role would dwindle as public agencies, commercial producers, and television stations took over more and more promotions. "The newspapers barely earn a profit," says Sakazaki, "whereas the earnings of the TV stations are fabulous. We have always refused to pay fees when we borrow art from museums abroad, but the TV stations go so far as to use foreign galleries to rent works for their shows."[66] To a considerable degree, however, the question of sponsorship is merely an issue of which division within a single media-conglomerate does the promoting, since all the major papers have tie-ups with television stations.[p] So long as the cultural

[p] The close tie-ups are *Yomiuri*-NTV and *Sankei*-Fuji TV. *Asahi*-ABC grew stronger in 1980 as *Asahi* bought back its affiliate's stock. *Mainichi* has loose

139

agency's allocations remain static and the exhibition budgets of the national museums stay frozen, sponsorship from the mass media, whether print or electronic, will almost certainly help Japan maintain one of the busiest exhibit schedules in the world.

More and more frequently in the late seventies the newspaper companies cosponsored special art shows with the leading department stores without investing funds. The partnership became more important to the stores when the cultural agency banned the display of national treasures and important cultural properties in department-store galleries after a bad fire in a large Kumamoto store in November 1973. Before then the department stores had displayed a great deal of classical Japanese art, since such shows were usually more compact than the huge affairs held in the national museums. Once they lost the prestige of showing valuable old art, the stores were eager to cooperate with newspapers because of the validating effect they provided. Working with a newspaper also assured publicity for the exhibit.[67]

Japanese department stores have long sold works of art, like any other commodity, and frequently take in more than $500,000 on a lot of 700 contemporary Japanese oils and watercolors. Most of them handled only foreign art before the 1970s, usually obscure contemporary representational painters from France, but when the market for domestic art swelled they began selling the conventionalized domestic styles to customers who knew the store better than the art. Since the 1950s several dozen major department stores have also put on special exhibits of works not for sale, mainly foreign art. The motives, according to Katase Keisuke of Isetan, were the same as for newspapers: to increase sales by attracting new customers and to educate the public about art.[68]

Collectively the Tokyo department stores outearn their counterparts in any other city and are usually considered more

ties with TBS and NHK in cultural matters. *Nikkei* has a link with TV Tokyo, the weakest of the stations in the capital. Amano interview, December 22, 1980; *Asahi nenkan 1981*, pp. 568-569.

swank than any except possibly those in London. Chiba Kihei, who plans art exhibits for *Yomiuri*, considers Mitsukoshi, Isetan, Takashimaya, and Seibu in that order the most "active" stores for art events, but the implication is that they are also the most desirable. Mitsukoshi's status apparently derives from being the oldest department store, since many Tokyo residents prefer both the merchandise and the art at Isetan's main store in Shinjuku. Several dozen others around the country sponsored comparable exhibits during the 1960s and 1970s, either on their own responsibility or with the blessing (but rarely cash) of newspapers, embassies, or other agencies. During 1954-1979, nineteen of the fifty largest art exhibits in Tokyo took place at department stores, and these large shows were almost always mounted with the cooperation of a newspaper company and occasionally with its financial support as well.[69]

Three of Tokyo's biggest stores, Isetan, Mitsukoshi, and Seibu, have renamed their art galleries "museums" since 1975, but the name change has not won them an exemption from the ukase against showing important cultural properties and national treasures. All of them write off their operating expenses as public-relations costs and staff them with personnel from their advertising or public-information departments. Only Seibu has a small permanent collection and curators to plan its exhibits. Isetan and most other department stores rotate their ordinary displays, which average forty works of art, almost weekly. Major shows rarely last more than two weeks in a department store because many who attend them are regular store customers. Both Isetan and Seibu count on drawing at least 1 percent of the 300,000 persons who shop in their stores on Sundays and holidays to the top-floor museums to see the current exhibit. Weekday crowds are about half this size, but a blockbuster like Isetan's Renoir show in 1979 attracts more than 10,000 per day. Even more than the newspapers, the department stores must plan their exhibits with the preferences of their patrons in mind—young women in their twenties and thirties with money to spend on the building's other floors before they leave. Store exhibits are too brief, except for a few at Seibu, to draw well enough to rank among the very largest held in Tokyo, but in the late seventies it became common to send them on tour to prefectural and municipal museums where they were seen by very large audiences.[70]

Seibu observes the wishes of its poet-patron, Tsutsumi Seiji, by confining its shows almost entirely to contemporary art. Most other stores put on forty-five or fifty exhibits a year, but Seibu does only fifteen. Both Seibu and the other top stores calculate their total yearly attendance for art shows at about 450,000 to 500,000, but Seibu undertakes far more of its events without outside sponsorship than any of the others. The reason is simple, says Kaneko Kikuo, head of the museum's planning department: "the Seibu museum is so well established that it generates its own publicity and does not need help from newspaper companies." The museum sustains an annual loss of $300,000, a remarkably small sum in light of its many enterprises in theater, film, poetry, and the avant-garde. "Anyway we think of the deficit as advertising expenses," Kaneko explains, "and consider it very cheap. Holding the shows casts a certain subtle image on the goods we sell. Our emphasis on contemporary art helps establish a very contemporary image in the minds of the modern young women who shop here. There is no doubt the art museum brings in customers."[71] There is also no question that only Seibu among the major department stores acts as benefactor as well as entrepreneur for present-day Japanese artists.

DESPITE tepid support from public agencies, the visual arts were probably more accessible to Japanese in the postwar period than any other art form. For a few hundred yen anyone could see a special exhibit in a museum or department store sponsored by an art association, newspaper, or the museum or store itself. Private museums opened their regular collections to the public at nominal fees, and by 1980 more than

1,000 shows at commercial galleries were available each week free of charge.

It is not surprising that the new throngs of viewers bestowed stardom on the relatively few schools, styles, and artists with familiar names. Modern painting is just a century old in Japan, and its broad appeal is much more recent. Lacking any real contact with art before the 1950s, people naturally looked to established institutions to certify acceptable art. The Japanese are neither the only star-struck nation on earth nor alone in expecting tutelage from official academies, art associations, and museums. Still the cultural setting for art in the postwar period was distinctive. As always, new ideas and movements from abroad had to contend with Japan's geographic isolation and relatively homogeneous culture. Education, urban living, and the mass media probably standardized social expectations more thoroughly in Japan than anywhere else, inhibiting people from learning to judge critically or buy art simply because they liked it.

The postwar democratization of access was much more complete for the public than for artists. The idea of the painter as professional rather than hobbyist was scarcely known before the war and took a long time to sink roots thereafter. Nitten and the other art associations carefully regulated how many newcomers were selected for display each year by enforcing established standards of acceptable art. The commercial market turned into a pyramid of many hues, with only a lucky few at the apex famous enough to prosper from their art. Newspapers promoted contemporary artists through prizes, contests, and exhibits, but they spent far more on foreign art displays that stimulated rather than remunerated Japanese artists. Although anyone could enter an art-association competition or rent a gallery to hold a one-person show, the Japanese art world remained a vertical mosaic in 1980, carefully constructed to reward accredited forms of art that were dictated more by fashion and by the prestige of Nitten, newspapers, and the School of Paris than by definitions of beauty or simple personal taste.

CHAPTER 6

Theater: Playing Safe

POLISH AND profit are the hallmarks of Shiki, Japan's largest modern theater company. Shiki divides its actors and actresses each year into eight sales teams and sends them around to corporations to sell tickets. "Banks and hospitals are especially good customers," says Aoi Yōji, who occasionally helps to direct productions, "because they both employ lots of people from Shiki's chosen market—women between graduation from high school and marriage."[1] By handing out theater tickets to their employees, the banks and hospitals build good will in these poorly paying occupations. By filling the seats with young women, Shiki perpetuates the essentially private audience it has cultivated over the past twenty years.

Shiki is probably the only $7.5 million production company anywhere that forces its stage talent to doff the periwig and take up the salesbook. For a group that performs 600 times a year before 300,000 customers still to use its players this way is a mark of how long the ignoble social station assigned to acting has endured in Japan. Only since World War Two has theater fully established itself as an art, not just entertainment, and become a profession rather than merely an avocation. In 1945 there were only three modern drama groups and no acting schools in Japan. Today at least 4.5 million playgoers turn out each year to watch professionals perform artistic dramas of every genre from Broadway musicals in plush auditoriums to guerrilla theater in canvas tents.[2] Yet to a considerable degree the players themselves still support their own art, whether selling tickets to bankers or sewing costumes for *Candide.*

Realism and Its Limits

The modern drama movement began in the earliest years of this century as an earnest effort to replace Japan's traditional theater of entertainment with contemporary plays derived from the European stage that contained symbolic meaning. By 1900 most of Shakespeare had been translated, but in the next decade the infant shingeki (modern theater) companies found the naturalistic acting and realistic settings of Ibsen especially congenial with their struggle against the past. But the greatest influence came from Russia, particularly after the October revolution of 1917. The pathbreaking Tsukiji Little Theater in Tokyo, opened in 1924 by the patron Hijikata Yoshi and his director Osanai Kaoru, somehow managed to put on 114 plays during its stormy five-year life. Eighty-nine of them came from abroad, more from the Soviet Union than any other country. Chekhov, Tolstoy, and Gorky were special favorites.[3]

Dramatic realism prompted by the spread of industry and city living became the main doctrine of Japan's modern playwrights for the next thirty years. Many of them, such as Kubo Sakae, dealt with contemporary crises through socialist realism; others like Kishida Kunio preferred the medium of psychological realism that had been developed earlier in the fiction of Natsume Sōseki. In the early 1930s the modern theater movement fell into tiresome struggles between its proletarian wing and the police censors, who feared baleful influences from Moscow. Yet the essence of shingeki was its modernness rather than foreignness, engrossed as it was with personal and social changes that were happening within Japan.[4] In any event, traditional genres such as kabuki and storytelling were still enthroned, and the modern theater remained a tiny avantgarde until after the war.

Aided by the repeal of censorship and support from the labor unions, shingeki blossomed as a main artistic force during 1945-1955. By the mid-fifties the number of companies had grown from three to twenty, and a successful play might attract 20,000 customers compared with 3,000 before the war. Starting with an all-star production of *The Cherry Orchard* in 1946, plays and techniques from Soviet Russia were once again in vogue and remained so until American playwrights and the theories of Brecht grew popular in the mid-1950s. By then about half the productions by shingeki companies were foreign works and the other half Japanese plays, a proportion that has remained stable ever since.[5]

Socialist realism found its postwar expression among playwrights such as Kinoshita Junji. Devoted though he has been to Marxist views of history, Kinoshita has also taken up folk legends and other richly nativist themes in his plays, and his *Twilight Crane* (*Yūzuru*, 1949) has been produced in many forms as often as any Japanese work since the war. The humanist Fukuda Tsuneari approached reality through Christian commentary in *Typhoon Kitty* (*Kitty Taifū*, 1950) and in his fresh translations of Shakespeare. Others such as Katō Michio, Tanaka Chikao, and the Marxist apostate Miyoshi Jūrō worked out a theater of realism based on early Japanese literature and themes from kyōgen and kabuki. All these playwrights were turning out new works in the late 1940s and early 1950s, when experimental plays by Japanese authors would probably not have survived without help from the big newspapers and especially the labor unions.[6]

New dramas from abroad helped to cement psychological realism as the keystone of shingeki in the mid-fifties. Williams and Miller were the successors to Ibsen and Chekhov; skillful productions of *A Streetcar Named Desire* and *Death of a Salesman* filled out the spectrum of realist orthodoxy that still draws large crowds whenever a revival is offered. But the Japanese playwriting that was going on at the same time was never so derivative as Western-style painting in relation to its foreign paradigm. Language was part of the reason. Moreover without an official academy of modern theater, authors had more room to flout the received conventions and experiment

146

freely. All of shingeki was innovative in relation to the huge bulk of traditional Japanese theater and could not afford to insist on a uniform means of dramatic expression. Competition from movies and television reminded producers that the box office tolerated neither ossification nor endless dispute about pure versus ideological plays.[7]

No art form was more conflicted by the tense demonstrations in 1960 against the Japan-United States mutual security treaty than shingeki, whose activists hoped the protests would begin a new age in the Japanese theater. Instead it ended an old one. While some partisans took their crusade abroad in an epic trip to China that autumn, the modern drama movement soon began a flight from realism that continues today. As with postmodernism in the visual arts, the reasons were more generational than ideological. Already in the late fifties younger playwrights like Mishima Yukio and Abe Kōbō had abandoned the notion that drama had to be written to Western standards.[8] During the next decades a few authors stepped outside the established production companies to try open-ended runs when stages for them could be found. Many shingeki companies ruptured in the early 1960s over quarrels that their older leaders could no longer compose.

By 1966 the new Nissei and national theaters and the refurbished Imperial Theater made larger plays possible, and shingeki tours grew more common when prefectural and municipal cultural centers started opening around the country. The Bungakuza troupe took Morimoto Kaoru's *A Woman's Life* (*Onna no isshō*, 1945) to eighty-two cities in 1968-1969 and set a new record for consecutive performances with 597. Some companies even began adapting kabuki scripts for the modern stage, while kabuki actors occasionally appeared in shingeki pieces. Exactly a year before his death, Mishima produced his own kabuki play at the national theater in November 1969, at the sumptuous cost of $225,000—a mark of how commercial, diversified, and removed from conventional realism the modern theater had become.[9]

147

Other young opponents of realist drama and the system for producing it began an underground "little theater" movement in the mid-sixties, partly in reply to the anti-dramas of Ionesco and Beckett but mainly as a romantic hunt for meaning in Japan's commoner tradition. Their aim was not to restore the prewar era but to resurrect fragments of it in order to build a more meaningful present. They revolted, like the avant-garde everywhere, against the established institutions that defined modern theater—"the archaeology of art," as Martin Friedman puts it—even though their main targets, the shingeki companies, were barely twenty years old.[10] The underground groups were much affected by the pop art of Yokoo Tadanori, who used the ash can of everyday items from the early twentieth century in his nostalgic compositions. From Kara Jūrō's mock kabuki under a red tent, aping the pariah beggars' theater of Edo riverbeds, to Suzuki Tadashi's *Trojan Women* with its traditional stage techniques, the avant-garde rediscovered literary elements in its use of language and usually pursued issues of personal as well as political identity.[11] All the underground playwrights scoffed at realism for its dated focus on exploitation and alienation in the dark ages of heavy factory labor. Now Japan lived amid material comforts and technical wizardry, but the individual had little purpose. The customs and artifacts of ordinary commoners in the 1920s were a good place for these progressive avant-garde dramatists to look for meaning, but most of them were too tentative and cynical to define it very clearly.

Yet realism and the shingeki companies remained the backbone of modern theater in the 1970s, joined by a wave of foreign troupes on tour and the greater popularity of translated Broadway musicals at the end of the decade. Shingeki remained very intellectual, as Yamazaki Masakazu has observed, in spite of dissent from breakaway playwrights and the younger generation underground. The Mingei company stuck by the pure socialist realism of the Moscow school, the Haiyūza group continued producing Ibsen and Brecht, and even the quasi-commercial Shiki company faithfully staged the early postwar French plays for which it had become famous in the fifties.[12]

The great variety and vitality of theater in the 1970s were reinforced when kabuki showed renewed drawing power and foreign companies continued to visit, although many of them lost money if they did not come from London. Walter Nichols, president of the Azabu Artists agency in Tokyo, points out that language problems usually kept foreign troupes' productions from becoming hits in Japan and that cautious playgoers turned out only for established names. Members of the Royal Shakespeare Theatre Company visited several times in the seventies and attracted large crowds, but the American Conservatory Theater had more trouble finding fans for Agee and O'Neill. The Royal Shakespeare company's tours in 1970 and 1972 inspired Japanese producers to forget shingeki's early distaste for Elizabethan drama. Instead Japanese casts put on six different Shakespeare plays in 1972, including three separate productions of *Hamlet*. All eleven of his comedies were presented by Japanese troupes in 1975-1976, the first big cracks in shingeki's inveterate reluctance to show humor on the stage. Even *Waiting for Godot*, who never arrives, proved rewarding when the comedy finally reached Kinokuniya Hall in 1980, twenty-seven years after it was first produced in Paris.[13]

Like the postmoderns in dance and the visual arts, Japan's young avant-garde troupes assaulted conventional dramaturgy during 1965-1980 without incurring much reproach from artists even younger than themselves. "Things are in a bit of a lull," says one of them, the director-playwright Aoi Yōji. "I respect what Mr. Kara is doing with the Situation Theater but I find myself somewhere between the new anti-shingeki troupes and the new-new groups of younger directors who haven't yet really emerged." While kabuki and Broadway musicals go on entertaining, shingeki and the underground groups variously address or ridicule reality—leaving the sharpest edges of innovation to artists like Aoi who stage plays in Buddhist temples too small to warrant sending the performers out to sell tickets to bankers.[14]

Houses and Audience Associations

Japan may have had as many theater buildings for serious drama before World War Two as any country, long before the cultural agency and local authorities began building the out-of-town centers where so many shingeki productions now take place. It also had a huge number of professional companies that went on the road to perform. The spread of radio and the movies, especially in the 1930s, cut into the audience for local live drama and turned many of the houses into cinemas. New rail lines let playgoers see first-rate productions in the cities in place of minor-league offerings back home. Then wartime mobilization wiped out road shows and aerial bombing during the last nine months of the conflict turned many structures in the cities to rubble.

Japan entered the postwar period with just a handful of urban theaters usable for live drama and few audiences of regular theater patrons. Air raids had destroyed 40 percent of Osaka and 50 percent of Tokyo, leaving only the Osaka Kabukiza and a half-dozen large halls in the capital available after the surrender. Then the occupying army took over one of the big Tokyo buildings and several smaller theaters, so that very few stages for commercial or modern dramas were left. *Mainichi* soon opened a multipurpose hall in Tokyo suitable for plays, as did Mitsukoshi in late 1946, and eventually other newspapers and department stores followed suit. The Shinbashi Enbujō (1948) and Kabukiza (1951) reopened for traditional dramas, backed by Shōchiku's entrepreneurship, and several other new or rebuilt commercial theaters had opened in Osaka and Nagoya by the early 1950s. But in 1952 Mitsukoshi suddenly barred shingeki from its hall because of political activities in the corridors during performances, robbing modern drama of its most important stage until the Actors' Theater opened in April 1954 at Roppongi in Tokyo, the first all-new house for contemporary plays in the postwar period.[15]

A few public auditoriums were put up in the big cities during the fifties, but shingeki companies often had to rent department-store halls dating from the 1930s and other unsatisfactory locations. When they performed out-of-town, it was often in public gymnasiums and community centers. In the early sixties five of the biggest Tokyo department stores closed their auditoriums to expand the sales area, a blow to musicians as well as actors and actresses only partly redressed when Mitsukoshi opened a new theater in 1974. Five large houses holding 1,500 or more were completed in Tokyo, Nagoya, and Osaka between 1963 and 1967, all except the national theater for commercial productions. Heartened that the Actors' Theater had paid off its debt within seven years, other shingeki groups and real-estate investors opened small halls holding just a few hundred customers, and coffee shops and restaurant theaters for just a few dozen patrons also sprang up in the sixties.

Prefectural and municipal officials began building facilities for live drama in the 1960s and put up many more of them in the next decade. Part of the impetus, especially in the sixties, came from local amateur troupes who needed stages and from audience associations that arranged shows for their members when big-city companies came on tour.[16] The new public theaters helped to transform fifteen or twenty of the largest shingeki and children's-theater groups into truly national companies, just when a fresh set of houses was opening in Tokyo to provide better space in the city where most of them were based. The 478-seat Seibu Theater began operating in 1973 and came up with new ways to cosponsor current plays with the production companies. Iwanami and Mitsukoshi both opened their new theaters in 1974, joined by halls suitable for shingeki in Takarazuka in 1978 and Osaka in 1980.[17] The 360-seat Hakuhinkan Hall in Ginza was completed in 1978, the same year Shōchiku unveiled its Sunshine Theater on the site of the old Sugamo prison near Ikebukuro in Tokyo. An important auditorium for underground theater opened in 1979 in a movie house nearby. Perhaps it is fitting that the most recent building for modern drama as of 1980 was a reincar-

151

nation of the first, the brand-new Actors' Theater in Roppongi.[a]

Including public and commercial halls as well as the facilities operated by production companies, Tokyo now has about
100 theaters where plays can be performed. Three houses stage
kabuki and a half-dozen do nō, including a 100-seat theater
opened in 1973 in Ginza and the Suidōbashi Nōgakudō, rebuilt in 1978. Eight specialize in storytelling and other popular
entertainments, while two others mostly offer revues. Currently there are just fifteen theaters in Tokyo that regularly
present modern plays and musicals. All other productions of
contemporary drama take place in the city's sixty-seven rental
halls, where dance, music, and other events are also held, or
else in coffee shops, bars, and restaurants. Twelve of the 100
theaters are larger than 2,000 seats and another eighteen hold
between 1,000 and 2,000 persons. Nearly all these facilities
are too big for serious plays. Tokyo has very few houses
containing 1,000 to 1,200 seats, considered the ideal size on
Broadway.[18]

Every dramatic genre in Japan short of the avant-garde has
relied since the war on audience associations of one sort or
another to help produce spectators to fill its theaters. The
most important by far for shingeki has been the workers'
drama organization known as Rōen (Kinrōsha Engeki Kyōgikai), which now provides its members tickets to leading
plays each month at a 20 to 30 percent discount. Today the
Rōen branches around the country are second only to schools
in supplying customers for professional modern drama, and
collectively they account for a quarter of the 2 million persons
who attend shingeki productions each year. Without Rōen's
support when there were no other audiences, many young

---

[a] The Haiyūza Theater earns about 30 percent of its income from the
Haiyūza company, a close affiliate that rents the house for some of its Tokyo
productions. Other revenues come from rentals to competing shingeki companies, nontheatrical groups, and conferences. Offices, restaurants, and bars
in the building bring in additional income. "We expect to produce more of
our own productions here starting in 1981," says its manager, Kurabayashi
Seiichirō. Kurabayashi interview, November 11, 1980.

theater companies would not have survived the late forties and early fifties, nor could shingeki groups have developed road tours in the 1950s so early or so successfully as they did. Although Rōen is now smaller than at its peak in 1969, it often provides the critical margin that lets a company break even for the year.[19]

Most Rōen branches in the fifties charged their members a monthly fee of twenty-eight cents in return for six performances a year; dues were higher for Rōen units that held events more frequently. In return, the typical theater-appreciation society offered discounts as large as 50 percent to anyone who agreed to see one play a month in the big cities or six to nine a year in the smaller communities. It hired a hall, acted as promoter, and guaranteed a visiting shingeki company a full house for its one-night stand. Members of the Tokyo Rōen usually received instead an exclusive performance of a work then in production, at cut-rate prices. Since the performing company covered its daily costs in the 1950s with a house just 60 percent filled, it could offer the play at 40 percent off if Rōen assured a sellout.[20]

Rōen's slogan since it began in 1948 has been "good cheap theater for everyone,"[21] but from the start it has been closely linked with the labor movement and the leftist political parties. Since socialist realism and proletarian theater were so integral to modern drama before the war,[b] it is natural that labor and the parties promoted amateur plays in the country's workplaces and mobilized audiences for professional shingeki productions in the late forties. At its height in the 1950s, the workplace theater movement included more than 1,500 groups in offices and factories, a time when roughly the same number of amateur dramatic societies unconnected with the workers' theater were performing in towns and villages all over Japan.[22]

[b] The Japan Proletarian Theater League (Purotto), founded in December 1928, set up 220 theater circles among laborers and others, mainly in Tokyo, during 1929-1931. At its peak, this antecedent of Rōen had 3,425 members (January 1932). Tickets to left-wing plays cost about a fifth of the usual charge at the Tsukiji Little Theater in 1924-1929. Abe Bun'yū and Sugai Yukio, eds., *Rōen undō*, Tokyo, Miraisha, 1970, pp. 12-15.

These various groups were the basis for audience organizations formed locally in the fifties throughout the country, some affiliated with Rōen and many not.

Local Rōen organizations remained autonomous even after a national council was formed in 1963, and they usually chose realist dramas by mainline shingeki companies that were compatible with Rōen's origins in politics and the labor movement. But even in the ideologically straightened fifties, high-quality theater took precedence over doctrine, the more so for audience organizations unrelated to Rōen. To lure as many members as possible, the Rōen units stressed that theirs was an association of workers and not just laborers, as did the related but much larger music-audience group Rōon. By the late 1950s more than 40,000 persons belonged to local Rōen chapters and at least that many more were members of independent audience circles, based on community amateur companies, that likewise promoted shingeki. Rōen has never sponsored productions of traditional Japanese theater, nor did the independent audience associations do so very often before all but the biggest of them folded in the 1960s.[23]

The Tokyo Rōen was founded in 1955 by the politically activist National Cultural Conference and soon quarreled over which plays should be chosen and who should pick. After the riots against the security treaty in 1960, Rōen units all over the country began debating how pure or popular their plays should be, how much voice members should have in selecting them, and whether workers should still be the main target. As the middle class grew larger, Rōen added more white-collar members and increasingly demanded good theater without political messages. Still the organization prospered. More than 300 performances for Rōen members, often exclusive shows, were being given by shingeki companies in the early sixties, allowing a well-established troupe such as Mingei to do half its season on the road. At its most flourishing the movement sponsored nearly 1,000 performances for 133,000 members in 1969, before dipping to a plateau of about 900 events and 110,000 members during the 1970s.[24]

The Japanese drama world was not unique in its preference for audience organizations—Rōen's model was the people's theater (Volksbühne) of Weimar Germany—but when their grip began to weaken in the early seventies the shingeki companies had to compensate by developing school performances and other road shows. The main reasons Rōen lost members after 1969 were commercialism and consumerism. Dynamic theaters like Nissei and the Imperial in Tokyo and Chūnichi in Nagoya started putting on modern dramas for profit, without relying much on production companies and even less on Rōen. Musicals grew popular and successful in the late seventies, to the dismay of most shingeki groups except Shiki, which staged a number of them. Rōen was slow about tapping this new interest, even though its members ranked commercial productions of *West Side Story, Fiddler on the Roof,* and *Man of La Mancha* among their top seven favorites in 1976.[25]

Watching serious modern drama required an intensity that not all audiences could sustain, says Tanaka Mitsuru of the Yokohama Theater Research Institute, especially when easier fare was available. Not only were there more musicals and other lighter commercial productions in the 1970s, but also the cultural agency, local public bodies, and other audience associations were offering their own programs in direct competition with Rōen. Television and professional sports gave consumers even more choice, and the greater privatization and formlessness of spare-time activity among young people made them think twice about buying a Rōen ticket a month in advance for a night on the town with the group. At the same time theater patrons were impatient with the monotony of Rōen's selections, tired of its inner bickering, and put off by its fossilized structure, according to Abe Bun'yū, who manages its Tokyo headquarters. Many of them now wanted to choose plays for themselves and attend when and where they pleased, adds Yamabe Yoshihide of the National Cultural Conference, even if it meant surrendering their discounts. And by the 1970s organized labor had less command over the leisure activities of workers, who grew steadily more middle class and less tractable.[26] A weighty political theater from hardcore shingeki companies dating back to the forties no longer appealed very much, even to the middleaged majority of Rōen's membership.

Rōen in the 1970s finally faced the fact that office workers and other salaried employees were the ones "who can afford to pay the admission, who have the time to spend in the theatre . . . thinking they're going to get some culture," according to Senda Koreya of the Haiyūza company. These white-collar playgoers wanted more panache and less politics, and the Tokyo and Osaka Rōen branches responded more quickly because they were losing members faster than the outlying units.[c] The fare was at last broader by 1980, membership was reasonably steady at a ten-dollar monthly fee, and the eighty-two Rōen chapters gave discounts on events to more than 110,000 members. No longer was Rōen powerful enough to fill a house very often for one set evening of a production, except in smaller locations with few other entertainments. Instead, like the other audience organizations it bought up blocks of seats for several dates of a run and offered members a choice.[27]

Rōen for all its partisanship played both angel and shepherd to the shingeki companies, rescuing a number of them in the late forties and guiding them to new out-of-town audiences in the 1950s and 1960s. The other main audience organizations have either been local in scope or more concerned with musical attractions than noncommercial theater. The music audience association called Onkyō, founded by employers to answer Rōon, fit poorly with the leftist bent of postwar shingeki, and in any case it was weak outside Tokyo and Osaka. Min'on and its far smaller affiliate Min'en, the Democratic Musical and Theatrical associations sponsored by Sōka Gak-

---

[c] Senda added that "if you ask the members, as is done in Tokyo, to vote for what they want to see, the results always indicate very clearly that what they want to see are famous plays with famous stars." Senda interview, *Concerned Theatre Japan*, summer 1970, pp. 72-73.

kai, had greater organizational strength than Onkyō but little more role in drumming up audiences for shingeki.

Theatergoers who disliked the political or religious proclivities of Rōen and Sōka Gakkai often joined local audience organizations like the Tokyo Citizens' Theater (Tomin Gekijō), which started in the late 1940s. The citizens' theater was founded by the city government to promote traditional and contemporary theater as well as other performing arts, but after 1958 it operated as an independent entity financed by the membership. It offered reduced-rate tickets to ten plays a year in a sampler of genres. Beginning in 1955 it also arranged a separate shingeki season series, which gradually grew from five to twelve performances a year by 1964, when 5,000 persons belonged. Other special seasons were offered in kabuki, music, and film. The overall membership climbed to 37,000 in 1958, fell back a bit in the early sixties, and is currently steady at about 30,000. The modern-drama series dropped off to 2,000 members by 1976, for the same reasons of commercialization and diversity that buffeted Rōen in the seventies, but shingeki companies as well as producers of kabuki and other commercial plays are grateful for the ten performances it now supports through block ticket purchases for each of its three theater series. Sometimes the Tokyo Citizens' Theater still marshals enough customers to buy an exclusive presentation of a current shingeki production. Those who belong to the organization are older, less overwhelmingly female, and more interested in drama education than is true for the other audience groups, and the membership has little turnover despite changing fashions on the stage.[28]

Many young playgoers now find it distasteful to join a drama circle of any sort, but the audience organizations still supply nearly a third of the national attendance at shingeki plays and almost 10 percent of the clientele at commercial theater, including kabuki.[29] Shingeki companies maneuver extensively to have a forthcoming production listed with Rōen or another group, and they plan their offerings with members' preferences at least partly in mind. Even when audience organizations were indispensable for the survival of modern drama performances, they never truly wagged the production companies, if only because playwrights and directors held views about politics and art that were at least as doctrinaire as Rōen's. More decisive than ideology has been the organizational power provided by the audience groups, guaranteeing the companies a steady attendance and transforming shingeki from an infant and "faithful island off the coast of European drama"[30] into a genuinely national theater.

Enterprising Companies

Contemporary theater in Japan has no investors to back plays, no independent producers to stage them, no agents to represent actors and actresses, no open auditions to assign roles, and no long runs for smash hits or short ones for flops. The heart of shingeki is the production company, a finely graded hierarchy of all the people needed for a play from author, director, and business manager to actors and actresses, stagehands, and service personnel. The director is the key figure, a sharp departure from kabuki. Many playwrights who are permanent members of shingeki companies end up doubling as director so they can retain control of the production. "The contemporary theater troupe is like a modified family,"[31] says Inumaru Tadashi of the national theater, offering status and security but demanding loyalty and obedience.

Production companies have staged modern drama professionally in Japan ever since it was introduced from Europe right after 1900. Like their rivals in kabuki, shingeki groups have almost always performed year-round and, when appearing in their home cities, changed the plays once a month. In some ways the production troupes seem like enormous resident stock companies, but most of them do not break for the summer and many tour out-of-town for several months a year. More than 130 members belong to Haiyūza, the stodgiest of the three main Tokyo companies. About 80 percent of them are actors and actresses, and the rest are technical and

158

managerial staff. Mingei, the purest devotee of realism, and Bungakuza, the most nearly commercial of the three, are both almost twice this size if apprentices are included. The biggest of all is Shiki, which started a decade after the others by offering existentialist plays from France, rather than progressive theater, and later grew very profitable through the enterprise of its leader, Asari Keita. About twenty mainline shingeki companies offer full seasons and tour the country each year, and another 115 smaller professional or quasi-professional groups perform regularly.[32]

Even though 10 percent of them make a profit, Japan's contemporary theater companies are considered noncommercial because they are organized according to economic principles different from big businesses like Tōhō and Shōchiku. Shingeki groups can afford to be so much larger than resident companies abroad because they pay only a pittance and employ much of their talent only part-time. Most have five pay grades for actors and actresses, guaranteeing them a minuscule salary based on 100 performances a year whether they actually appear on stage or not. Only a fifth of the players act often enough to exceed the guarantee and earn extra money. Bonuses and benefits are minimal. Most performers have to take side jobs, especially in television dramas and commercials, but only with the company's blessing and an agreement to turn over 30 percent or more of their outside earnings to its treasury.[33] Still the members identify so closely with their group that it would be unthinkable to switch to another. The only recourse for dissidents is to form a brand-new company. Shingeki troupes are both economic entities for producing plays and moral communities of people devoted to art—and their chief director's approach to it. Group solidarity and esprit are the company's most precious assets, and the most quickly lost of all its virtues.

During the 1970s each of the three main Tokyo companies put on between seven and ten plays a year, some of them only for the road, and performed 300 to 400 times a year. Some of the works were fresh productions and a few were premieres, but many others were revivals. The basic season for each company's regular Tokyo subscribers, audience-organization patrons, and individual playgoers consisted of five or six productions, running two weeks each at the longest. Even when special performances for children, schools, and arts festivals in the capital are included, shingeki's audience in Tokyo slipped by nearly a third between 1965 and 1980. By one count, the average number of performances for plays put on in Tokyo by the nine top companies fell from 14.9 in 1965 to 10.5 in 1976, and it is even lower today. Houses customarily held 300 to 500 spectators and were rarely more than two-thirds full, unless the bill was Shakespeare or *Streetcar*. Only Shiki could count on drawing 10,000 or more to each of its five regular productions.[34] With tickets a standard fifteen dollars in 1980, shingeki was no longer a bargain compared with the array of entertainments constantly available in Tokyo, and it also faced most of the plagues that weakened Rōen in the 1970s: commercialization, uncommitted consumers, and an image of earnestness in a supposedly mellower age.

Despite fissures between generations and major defections in the seventies, each of the three big companies energetically uncovered new out-of-town markets in schools and new local cultural centers big enough to make up for the dropoff in Tokyo. Rōen was the major instrument for drawing shingeki out of the capital in the fifties and sixties, but a decade later the school circuit became even more useful for building crowds. Only a dozen of the largest companies systematically developed road tours, none more successfully than Shiki, which hired away Abe Yoshitada to clone the immensely effective network he had built for Bungakuza. By 1970 half of all shingeki performances and a majority of the customers were already on the road; ten years later more than 60 percent of performances and 70 percent of the audiences were found there, mainly because the companies filled huge school auditoriums with pupils, at bargain rates. Usually the shingeki group assumed the modest financial risk itself, but sometimes school principals added subsidies to their standard encouragements that every student make sure to attend. Out-of-town is also where companies took their big hits when the fixed run in Tokyo ended, until they could be rebooked for short spells in different theaters back in the city.[35]

Kurabayashi Seiichirō, manager of Haiyūza's new Actors' Theater and the most knowledgeable student of shingeki audiences, estimates that more than half the box-office income for modern drama is now generated on the road, even though tickets are cheaper there. In order of importance, children's and high-school performances, Rōen events, and plays supported by public agencies for children, teenagers, and touring arts festivals are the main ways the leading companies muster crowds outside of Tokyo.[d] So great is the attendance on the road, Kurabayashi says, that the average audience for a performance by one of the top groups is nearly 1,000 persons, despite the weak showing during the basic season in Tokyo.[36]

The initiatives with new audiences on the road forced shingeki companies to restrict their already cramped repertoires to familiar plays put on by famous stars, especially ones whom students had seen on television. The fare also had to be deemed suitable for the women who attended, mostly young unmarried ones, since they comprised 60 percent of the audiences in Tokyo and 70 percent elsewhere by the end of the seventies.[37] Companies that were barely alive in 1950 and conscientiously pursuing their own stage idioms in 1960 had become substantial businesses with a far-flung but reliable clientele by 1980, often no longer able to innovate or give their younger playwrights even an atelier production.

As shingeki grew more artistically cautious and commercially enterprising, some of the younger members accused the companies of embracing capitalism in the business office while

---

[d] "Most school performances are undertaken by the companies themselves," Kurabayashi says. "Aid from the cultural agency and prefectural governments is a very small proportion of the total school theater activity by professional companies." About fifteen companies put on 1,500 performances for high-school students and another 3,000 for younger children, in schools and community cultural centers, each year. Kurabayashi interview, November 11, 1980.

161

professing socialism on stage. A more pertinent criticism was that the companies were growing bureaucratized and losing their sense of common endeavor, especially when stars were off filming series for television months at a time and could not join road tours.[38] Some actors left in the early seventies to form new companies, an inevitable and often healthy process. Others resigned to go into commercial theater or entered it directly after acting school without joining a shingeki group at all.

Rōen scolded several troupes for becoming too profit-minded and briefly boycotted Haiyūza, but the company producers recognized the axiom that costs in the live theater rise much faster than the consumer price index, even with no unions in Japan to enforce Equity wages. By one estimate, production expenses tripled between 1960 and 1970, then more than doubled again during the next ten years,[e] rising 48 percent faster than the overall cost of living in Tokyo during the same two decades. Faced with these figures, the shingeki groups began refusing to take costly chances on new or experimental plays. Instead they turned to well-heeled theaters such as Seibu, Mitsukoshi, and Kinokuniya Hall to cosponsor more and more productions from the canon: Williams, Miller, Inge, and sometimes Brecht.[39]

The regular audiences for these presentations as of 1980 were young, as they have always been for shingeki, with the 20-25 age group the single largest. They were better educated and more often white-collar than playgoers right after the war, like the nation as a whole, and at least as transient as the unmarried office-worker population in any large city. School

---

[e] Kurabayashi puts the cost of an average production at \$5,555 in 1960, \$12,500 in 1965, \$16,666 in 1970, \$30,000 in 1975, and \$67,500 in 1980 at prevailing rates of exchange. In current yen terms, on an index with 1960 as 100, this represents a rise to 300 in 1970 and 625 by 1980. The Tokyo consumer index rose from 100 in 1960 to 176 in 1970 and 422 in 1980. Kurabayashi Seiichirō, "Zuisōteki ni sengo shingeki o kangaeru," part 3, *Teatoro*, May 1979, p. 110; *Asahi nenkan 1981 bekkan*, p. 356. See Gekidan Shiki, *Gekidan Shiki sōritsu 25shūnen kinen*, Tokyo, Gekidan Shiki, 1978, pp. 25-26.

performances helped the companies recruit future audiences, but the problem of replacing theatergoers who quit work to rear families and no longer attended very often remained endemic.[40]

Audience organizations such as the Yokohama Citizens' Theater reported that their clientele for modern drama was a bit older and more settled than the playgoers who subscribed to a company's season in Tokyo or simply appeared for a particular play. About 40 percent of the Yokohama group in 1976 were in their twenties, but another 35 percent were over forty. Three-fourths were employed, mainly in office work, education, and, for men, technical fields. Sales, commerce, manufacturing, and the professions were underrepresented, except for medicine. More than three-quarters of the crowds at events sponsored by the Yokohama Citizens' Theater were women, compared with about 60 percent in Tokyo.[41]

Kurabayashi believes that the audience organizations prove that serious contemporary drama appeals to persons of many ages and that the biggest attendance problem facing the companies is that "of social conditions for seeing the theater"—a lack of patterned attendance after age twenty-five among former fans who do not belong to an audience group. Aoi Yōji, who saw thirty-seven plays during a Herculean three-and-one-half-week trip to New York in 1980, is less sure that Japanese audiences will ever show the enthusiasm he found on Broadway: "when a house is full, it is very full, but it is very quiet" compared with New York, and "the atmosphere of the theatre is formal and studious, like that of a lecture or a library."[42] No doubt the soberness of the medium itself makes patrons behave with almost churchly decorousness.

The box office currently brings in about 50 to 60 percent of a major company's income each year and even more for smaller groups. The overall budgets of the three big troupes tripled in yen terms during the seventies, reaching about $4 million in 1980 for Haiyūza and $5 million for Bungakuza and Mingei. Shiki, the giant of the lot, reported a $7.5 million budget the same year.[43] These companies and four or five others earn a profit—in Shiki's case a substantial one—and the remaining shingeki groups rely on sacrifices by their members to break even for the year.

For the biggest companies, Rōen and the other audience organizations supply a sizeable minority of ticket sales, especially on the road, and each of the shingeki groups also has a patrons' circle (*tomo no kai*) composed of season subscribers who account for 10 to 20 percent of the attendance in Tokyo.[44] Although the earliest production companies long before World War Two had patrons' circles under various names, the first modern subscription series was offered by Haiyūza in 1968. In 1980 Mingei had the largest circle, with more than 5,000 subscribers, and another fifteen main companies had 1,000 to 4,000 each. Subscribers received a 20 or 25 percent discount by agreeing to see the entire five- or six-play season but were not expected to pay dues or otherwise contribute to the company ("we're independent," Kurabayashi says with pride).[f]

A few seats for the basic Tokyo performances are sold through the twenty outlets of Playguide, a commercial ticket agency whose greatest value to shingeki is conferring importance on a production by handling its tickets. Another source of audiences is friends and relatives of the players, whether or not they buy a season's subscription. Everyone else at a regular Tokyo performance is an ordinary theatergoer who has either reserved a ticket by phone or simply dropped in.[45]

Now and then a company still puts on an exclusive performance of a play in production if the Tokyo Citizens' Theater, Rōen, or other audience group can fill the house. Corporations also sometimes commission theater parties for their customers and employees, although usually they choose kabuki or a modern commercial play. Bungakuza, a smoothly managed enterprise, each August offers about twenty performances of a single production in the national theater's large hall for customers of the Seibu department store, apparently

---

[f] Patrons' circles have many names and resemble supporters' clubs (*kōenkai*) maintained by many politicians. Patrons' circles are also found in nō theater. Steve Comee interview, October 8, 1980.

the only such tie-up between a store and a shingeki company in Tokyo.[46]

Since out-of-town audiences now account for 70 percent of shingeki's annual attendance, several companies have built circles of patrons in key cities on the road to supplement the school circuit, regional Rōen units, and events sponsored by the cultural agency, local governments, or sometimes private corporations (the latter mainly aid performances for children). Shiki has formed the biggest network of out-of-town supporters, who help out with costumes, lodging, and other local arrangements as well as drumming up sales. Since 1970 the company has planned its tours by working closely with Onkyō, the employers' audience organization, and with Nippon Steel Corporation, the Japan Medical Association, and other groups with which Asari Keita is connected.[47]

Apart from what it earns for performing, a major company has two big sources of revenue: its acting school and the "company tax" it collects from actors and actresses who work part-time in movies, radio, and television. All the big shingeki groups except Haiyūza operate two- or three-year acting schools that charge tuition and entrance-examination fees as stiff as those at the private universities. About 1,000 students apply each year to Bungakuza's school, even though there is no assurance that any of the fifty who are accepted will be allowed to join the company after they graduate. Smaller companies offer just a one-year curriculum because they need the new talent for their productions, in effect finishing the training after admitting them to the company and starting them on salary.[g]

The "company tax," or *gekidanzei*, is even more critical for

[g] Shiki's school, founded in 1956, became independent of the company in 1967. Since 1970 both have been administered by the parent corporation, General Arts. Haiyūza's acting school began in 1949 but dissolved in 1967 when Senda Koreya began teaching at Tōhō Gakuen University, whose theater graduates still do well in the company's admission tests. *Gekidan Shiki*, p. 27; Ozaki Hirotsugu, "Shingeki II," in Tsugami Tadashi et al., eds., *Engekiron kōza*, 1, *engekishi*, *Nihonhen*, Kyoto, Sekibunsha, 1976, pp. 178-179; Machida Yutaka interview, October 29, 1980; Don Kenny interview, October 8, 1980; Aoi Yōji interview, October 30, 1980; Kurabayashi interview, November 11, 1980.

the yearly budget and in some cases exceeds the group's income from the box office, according to Inumaru Tadashi. Every top company has a handful of stars who make as much as $100,000 a year in film and broadcasting while on loan from the group. Although Haiyūza takes only 20 percent of the actor's or actress's outside earnings, according to Kurabayashi, other theater people commonly refer to the "30 percent tax" even when it runs as high as 40 or 50 percent. Without this cash, Senda Koreya has said, the Haiyūza would never have survived: "I'll tell you how I built the Actor's Theatre. I acted in twenty-nine movies in two years. I wasn't the only one." Imperative as these earnings are, companies find it hard to keep plays in repertory with their best talent so frequently absent, and there are inevitable jealousies over disparaties in income, which are greater in theater than in any other performing art.[48]

With such diverse forms of revenue and fewer than a quarter of its performances held during the company's basic season, when art is at its peak but audiences are most fickle, shingeki depends very little on the good will of theater critics and is far less risky than the producer system in other countries. "Plays don't flop in Japan," says the kyōgen actor and theater specialist Don Kenny. "How can they? The company's there, the patrons' circle is there, the acting school is there, and there's also big money on the road."[49] Under the company system with its set-term engagements, a miserable production has to be carried along for a few weeks at most. Just as there are no real flops, there are also very few smash hits. But the object is not necessarily profit, and the shingeki company for all its rigidity has been the one indispensable vehicle for advancing contemporary theater in postwar Japan.

Whatever creativity the company system sacrificed because of its elephantine size, hierarchical command, or capitalistic enterprise was appropriated after the mid-1960s by the underground theater movement. The dozen or so most important avant-garde troupes attracted no more than 5 percent of shingeki's 2 million attendance during the seventies, but they were meaningful both because they spurned dramatic realism and because they tried to redefine the theater group primarily as a social rather than an economic unit. To some degree shingeki and avant-garde companies both had to serve economic as well as social purposes, but the underground groups purposely minimized the auxiliary trappings that were better for business than art: movie and broadcast work, acting schools, performances for commercial groups, and other profit-making promotions.[50] They had no common dogma for opposing realism, any more than the shingeki companies themselves expressed a single approach to reality on the stage, but the avant-garde troupes unanimously rejected the production company as an institution.

Underground groups today perform in portable tents, basement coffee shops, campus auditoriums, temples and shrines, and the open air. They pay each member from director to stagehand an identical wage of ten or twenty dollars per performance and nothing at all during the long off-season. Kara Jūrō's Situation Theater, or Jōkyō Gekijō,[h] puts on two of his plays each year about twenty times each, drawing most of its 15,000 customers from university men and women in Tokyo despite an active road schedule. Kara, who was arrested in 1969 for pitching his red tent in a park near Shinjuku without a permit, has twenty-five members in his troupe and now pays the national railway corporation $100 per day so that they can perform in a pitted lot near Ryōgoku station in Tokyo. Kara's nostalgic plays resemble a poor-people's vaudeville that parodies postwar culture for playgoers in jeans and sweatshirts seated on old straw mats. The Situation Theater has no subscriber series or patrons' circle because, Kara says, "I'd begin to worry if audiences were too friendly" and came out of habit or fashion instead of interest in what was happening on the dirt stage. Tickets to avant-garde plays cost a standard

---

[h] "I am not an existentialist," Kara says, "but I chose the name after studying Sartre's emphasis on human situations in his plays." Kara interview, November 10, 1980.

nine dollars in 1980, enough in Kara's case to cover almost the entire $150,000 yearly budget of the red-tent company.[51]

Suzuki Tadashi's Waseda Shōgekijō, Satoh Makoto's black-tent group, and the quasi-underground Tenjō Sajiki company led by Terayama Shūji operate on equally slender resources, although Terayama has compromised with the shingeki system enough to pay his actors and actresses on a graded scale. But the result is hardly different: the basic wage for a six-performance tour in Kyoto during 1980 was fifty dollars, out of which the players had to pay their bus fares, and the director and stars earned little more. Satoh's group routinely pays fifteen dollars for a Tokyo performance and twenty dollars out-of-town.[52]

The underground theater is now so well established in Japan that a ten-volume *Collected Works of Kara Jūrō* is being issued by a Tokyo publisher. Although it may no longer merit the label avant-garde, the movement is still financially precarious and relentlessly scornful of the shingeki company system. What is true of shingeki for all its flaws is even truer of the hand-to-mouth underground groups, as the scholar David G. Goodman notes: "the contemporary theater is one of the few places where Japanese can speculate publicly and openly on ultimate, eschatological issues. Actors and actresses are willing to pay to do this."[53]

PLAYS FOR PROFIT

"When you think about entrepreneurs of the performing arts," says Nagai Michio, the former minister of education, "you think of Tōhō and Shōchiku. Between them they are responsible for probably 50 percent of the live productions in Japan."[54] Tōhō and Shōchiku are the two leviathans of commercial theater, staging plays for profit and drawing at least half the total national attendance at public performances by professionals in the live performing arts. Each of the two corporations earns most of its income from movies and television, but their stage plays and revues were bringing in a combined total of about $110 million a year by the end of the 1970s—ten times the estimated box-office income of shingeki and the underground troupes. A big proportion of the 16 million fans who pay to watch plays in a commercial theater each year attend Tōhō or Shōchiku productions, and millions more see independent commercial performances in restaurants, bars, and clubs.[i] A good deal of what is offered on Tōhō's and Shōchiku's stages is pure entertainment outside the bounds of Broadway, on or off, but much of it is legitimate art ranging from kabuki and its spinoffs to New York musicals in translation.

Shōchiku, Tōhō, and many other organizations put on kabuki before World War Two, and Shōchiku has monopolized it commercially only since 1975. In that year Tōhō abandoned kabuki not because its productions were unattractive but because musicals were becoming even more profitable. After many years of instability, kabuki turned into a moneymaker in the late seventies and now accounts for three-fifths of Shōchiku's $60 million earnings each year from the stage. About 1.5 million people see kabuki in Shōchiku houses or the national theater each year, and many times that number watch taped, direct-broadcast, and studio performances on television. More recent genres derived from kabuki, such as shinpa and shinkigeki comedies, attract somewhat under a million customers and earn Shōchiku a sizeable minority of its yearly revenues from producing plays.[55]

Kabuki revived soon after the war and by 1952 was packing the theaters almost as regularly as it does today. When au-

---

[i] There is no reliable way to calculate the total national audience for professional live performing arts each year because data are sketchy and many of the performances are given for private audiences. (See chapter one for estimates of the attendance at events open to the public.) The figures in this paragraph are drawn from the sources cited in chapter one and *Asahi nenkan 1981*, p. 594. The financial connection between the film studios and the New York stage grew strong in the 1970s, although the organizing principle differed from the production companies that Tōhō and Shōchiku have effectively become. Movie companies have replaced the record companies of the 1950s and the music publishers of the 1960s as Broadway's major corporate investors. *New York Times*, July 15, 1979.

diences began to slip later in the 1950s, the producers more and more turned kabuki into a spectacle of great flair and bravura, developing new scripts by contemporary playwrights that had just enough classical overlay to seem authentic. They also began selecting gaudy "verdant programs" containing the most popular acts and scenes from older works, usually a historical play, a dance number, and a drama of manners. The idea was to present safe, pleasant shows that would rake in profits. The difficulty with such frank commercialism was that the genre became stereotyped and only the star actors who drew throngs got to perform.

By the 1960s the top stars were being overworked, and still are today, with television assignments and almost daily stage appearances for long hours at a time, without much vacation. Critics often brushed aside the star system in the seventies as "a public-relations phenomenon, not a genuine artistic development,"[56] but without young magnets such as Ichikawa Ennosuke and Bandō Tamasaburō, Shōchiku could not have lured youthful audiences back to kabuki in the late seventies. Even the national theater has taken to featuring the popular stars it borrows from Shōchiku in showy programs that dismay purists. Kabuki roles are inherited and actors start as small children, but no wealthy patrons support them individually as was the case in the nineteenth century. Instead Shōchiku has helped organize fan clubs for the actors like the ones that formed in Tokyo and Osaka before World War Two. Such is the magic of television that the clubs are now even stronger outside the largest cities. Tamasaburō's fan club had the most well-known president, Ōhira Masayoshi, until the premier's sudden death in 1980.[57]

The Tokyo Kabukiza is the showcase for kabuki, which is now so profitable that Shōchiku holds 500 performances there each year. About 80 percent of the seats are filled at the daily matinee and evening programs when kabuki is playing, but Ōkawa Takeo, Shōchiku's chief producer, puts the paid attendance at 70 percent because the corporation distributes so many free tickets to vendors and clients of its other enterprises.

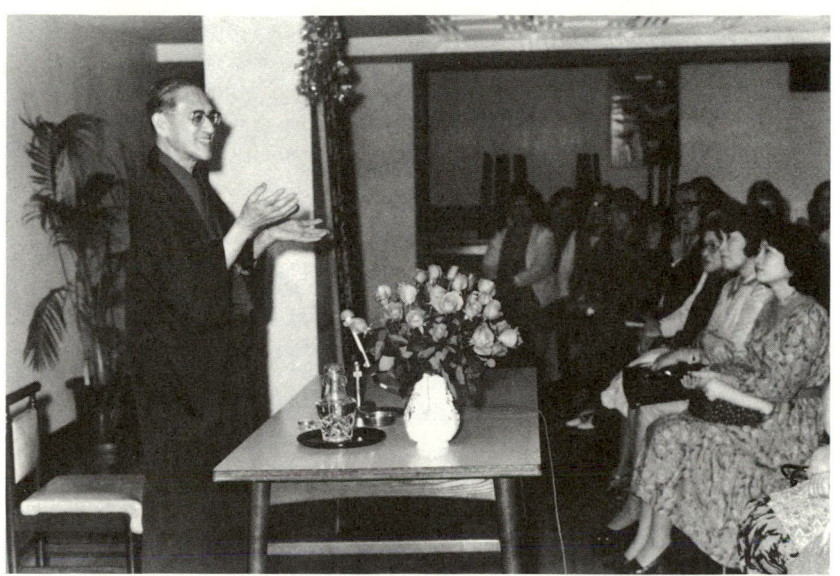

The kabuki actor Kataoka Nizaemon meets members of the patrons' circle at the Kabukiza theater in Tokyo.
SHOCHIKU CO., LTD.

More than 750,000 persons see kabuki while it is showing at the Kabukiza each year, and another 150,000 watch performances of related genres during the two months kabuki is not offered. About 200 meters away, the newly rebuilt Shinbashi Enbujō also stages kabuki, shinpa, and other commercial productions for Shōchiku, and kabuki programs are likewise offered in the corporation's theaters in Nagoya, Kyoto, and Osaka.[58]

Shōchiku's producers sit down with representatives of various theaters each summer to decide the next year's rotation of actors, since the corporation controls all but fifty of the country's 350 performers. Kabuki actors are rented out to the national theater and other commercial theaters as well as appearing in Shōchiku's own productions. The famous ones are

171

expected to do demonstrations for their fan clubs around the country and join the stage musicians three or four times a year for public-relations sessions with the Kabukiza patrons' circle. This group, the Phoenix Club, consists of 2,000 season subscribers who pay regular ticket prices but get free programs, the choicest seats, and a chance to learn from the performers the inside tricks of makeup, gestures, and instrumentation.[59]

Audience organizations are a more important source of customers, especially the Tokyo Citizens' Theater, the employers' musical organization Onkyō, and to a lesser degree the Sōka Gakkai affiliate Min'on. As with most shingeki events today, the audience groups buy up blocks of seats for several dates picked by the Kabukiza and let their members select which performance of a given production to see. Large department stores such as Takashimaya in Yokohama produce 750 to 800 customers a month for kabuki, and electronics manufacturers often buy tickets for their dealers to use as promotional giveaways with their retail customers. Associations of merchants along busy neighborhood streets sometimes organize outings at the Kabukiza for themselves as well as the shoppers who patronize their stores. Travel agencies regularly include a kabuki show as a part of their package tours for out-of-town visitors. Women's associations are especially lucrative because kabuki is so popular among middleaged housewives. Corporations also like to hold theater parties for their employees when an anniversary of the company's founding is celebrated. Each of these organizations gets discounts for its bulk purchases, and Ōkawa estimates that groups of all kinds account for half the attendance each month at the Kabukiza.[60]

They are even more important at Tōhō's Imperial Theater, the flagship of its seven live stages, which collectively earn the corporation about $50 million in revenues each year. Tōhō concentrated more and more during the 1970s on modern plays and musicals from abroad, after many decades of presenting kabuki, popular entertainments, revues, and variety shows, some of which are still in performance. Since the mid-

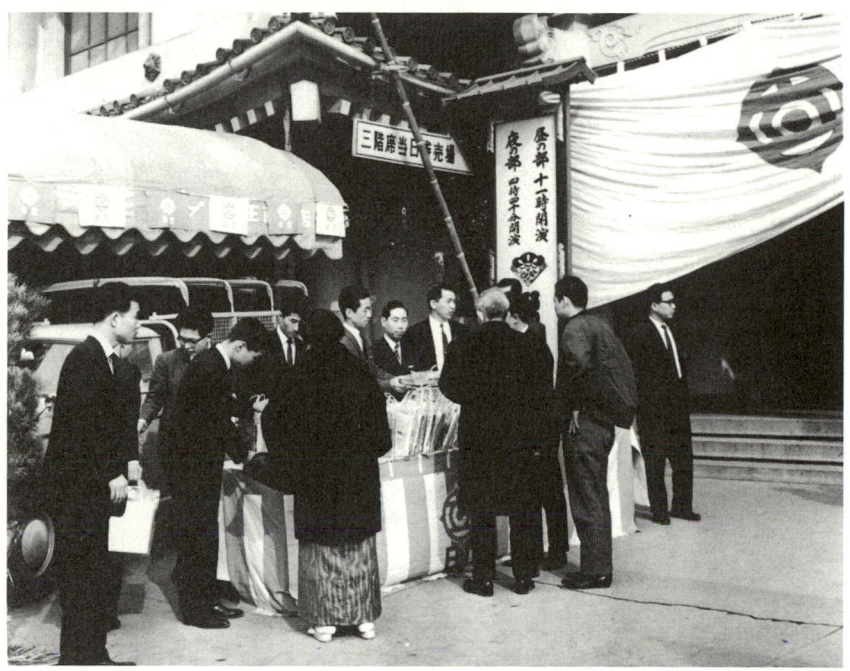

A theater party organized by the Hitachi electrical-goods
firm receives box lunches and souvenirs before
a performance at the Kabukiza in Tokyo. SHOCHIKU CO., LTD.

seventies the staple at the Imperial Theater has been the "home
drama," a delicate euphemism for soap operas based on such
popular television programs as *Katsu Kaishū* (a nineteenth-
century statesman) and *Wind and Clouds and Rainbows*. The
other big attraction has been the musical from Broadway, a
genre that Tōhō first produced with an all-Japanese cast performing *My Fair Lady* in 1963 but developed into a commercial success only in the late seventies.[61]

Like most Japanese theater organizations, Tōhō usually
changes plays once a month whether they bomb or soar. Hits
are restaged many months later when space can be found. Its

173

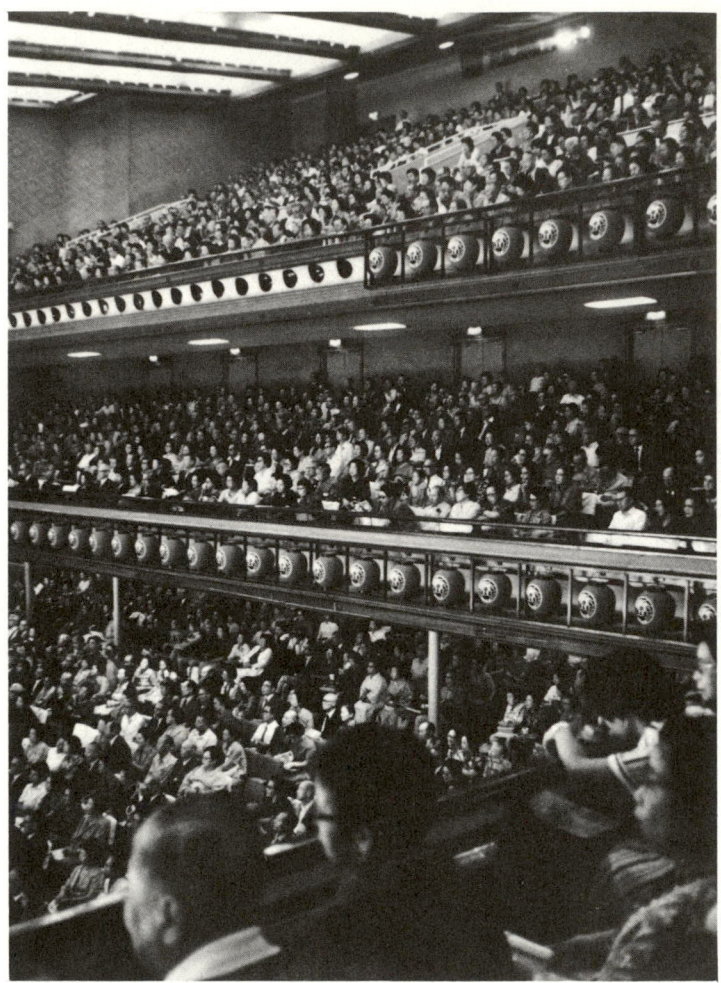

Audience watching a play at the Kabukiza in Tokyo.
SHOCHIKU CO., LTD.

longest run has been a revival of *Fiddler on the Roof*, which played 103 times during April, May, and June 1980 at the Imperial Theater and drew 99 percent of capacity at a thirty-five dollars top. *Man of La Mancha* and *The King and I* also attracted large crowds in 1980, but so did the home dramas during their six months on the bill. The theater also sometimes offers Shakespeare or books a popular entertainer for a month of recitals. Its productions are put on by actors and actresses under contract to Tōhō, usually with exclusive agreements that guarantee a yearly minimum from television, films, and the stage but forbid outside work. Like the rest of the Japanese drama world, there are no unions in commercial theater.[j] Ōkōchi Takeshi, manager of the Imperial, declares that "Tōhō does not have a theater company," but he smilingly admits that he has twenty producers and a lucrative drama school in the basement, making it plain that Tōhō is a production company in all but name.[62]

The Imperial Theater, at 1,900 seats, is smaller than the Kabukiza and puts on 500 performances a year compared with 600 for its rival. But the Imperial has a higher rate of sales, mostly because of the boom in musicals. About 80 percent of those who attend commercial theater as a whole are women, says Kurahashi Takeshi, director of the Tsubouchi Memorial Theater Museum at Waseda University, "who are fans of home drama from TV on a group outing with their friends to the theater."[63] At the Imperial, according to Ōkōchi, the figure is closer to 90 percent for musicals and 95 for soap operas.[k] Nearly the entire matinee audience are women between the ages of forty and sixty; evening performances draw

[j] Musicians in the Imperial Theater's pit orchestra belong to the Japan Musicians' Union.

[k] A study for the League of New York Theaters and Producers, completed in 1980, showed that 51 percent of Broadway playgoers were women, 42 percent college educated, and 55 percent under age thirty-five. Persons with household incomes over $25,000 were 41 percent of the sample. Baumol and Bowen found American audiences for all the performing arts in the early sixties remarkably similar in profile. *New York Times*, March 16, 1980; Baumol and Bowen, *Performing Arts*, p. 84.

more heavily on unmarried women on their way home from work.[64]

Audience organizations and department-store mailing lists turn out 10 percent of the attendance at musicals and home dramas at the Imperial, with Min'on, Onkyō, and the preferred customers of the Takashimaya store at Nihonbashi accounting for more than Rōen or the Tokyo Citizens' Theater. Each has a contract with the Imperial and many other theaters, giving an average discount of 30 percent off regular prices. The management restricts the dates, times, and numbers of tickets distributed to the audience groups. It also employs eight salespeople to sell blocks of 100 or more seats to other group customers at cut rates, typically companies organizing outings for their employees or promotions by Matsushita or Hitachi to improve retail sales. Like the Kabukiza, Tōhō also sells tickets to large women's associations for performances at the Imperial Theater, and even the agricultural cooperatives sometimes buy seats when their members come to Tokyo on excursions. Corporate groups account for nearly half of each audience, and their reservations are accepted before the tickets go on general sale.[65]

Advance purchases through Playguide are small but useful for publicity, as with shingeki. The leftover tickets are returned to the theater the night before the performance.[L] Reservations with the box office by telephone amount to 15 percent of the attendance. Walk-up purchases ahead of time run another 15 percent, and tickets sold the day of the event usually take up about 10 percent.[66] By boosting its sales to target groups, Tōhō plays safe and practically assures that no production will fail.[m] But to make a profit, the theater relies on the general

[L] Japan has no computerized ticketing system or credit-card scheme comparable to Ticketron or Chargit, apparently because runs are brief and credit purchases are often restricted.

[m] Tōhō also operated such theaters for live performances as the Takarazuka group for dance and opera, the Tōhō Engeijō for the more traditional popular entertainments, and the Nichigeki Gekijō and Nichigeki Music Hall for stage and nude shows until the landmark building at Yūrakuchō in Tokyo was removed in 1981. It also operated such profitable facilities as the Shinjuku

public—a well-defined one of middleaged housewives and young working women—and takes proportionately greater risks than shingeki, with its many private audiences.

After years of spotty success, musicals are at last popular, and more of them are in prospect henceforth. Like the operas of an earlier century, musicals are hard to follow in the original and even harder to translate into idiomatic Japanese that works well onstage. But most theater people agree that young audiences are more familiar with Western music now than a decade or two ago, and there are good actors and actresses available to perform Broadway musicals.[67] Tokyo is still considered a better market than the road—true of every modern performing art when it was first introduced from abroad.

In common with nearly every playhouse in Japan, the Imperial Theater has an early curtain for evening performances, usually six o'clock, so customers can leave work in time to be in their seats, catch a bite to eat in the basement restaurants during the forty-five minute intermission, and leave the theater by nine to be home by ten or ten-thirty. So many people commute such vast distances in Tokyo that going home from work and coming back into town for an eight-thirty performance is out of the question.

When the large and stylish Nissei Theater opened in 1963, its owners tried to become Tōhō's and Shōchiku's first real competitors in commercial legitimate theater by introducing a producer system for modern straight shows and musicals. They hired some of the leading shingeki directors to supervise open auditions and put on performances that might profit the backers—usually the parent Nissei life insurance firm itself. The dynamo of Shiki, Asari Keita, and the novelist Ishihara Shintarō got the venture started, but by 1965 it was clear the experiment had failed. The directors soon left in a huff, calling

---

Koma Stadium, a theater with twice-daily performances by famous Tōhō singers or actors and actresses who present both dramas and musical reviews to overwhelmingly female audiences. Shōchiku profited from similar enterprises, including its Engeijō for popular entertainments and Kokusai Gekijō for revues and other stage shows, both at Asakusa in Tokyo. Ogawa interview, November 21, 1980.

the Nissei Theater nothing but "an enormous advertisement for their company."[68] The shingeki companies were hostile to its commercial threat, and they discouraged their players from trying out. Nissei was a latecomer to staging plays, and often it was regarded as a predator trying to seize a few stars so it could make contracts with audience organizations. Open casting turned out to be a charade, because public competition is anathema to most Japanese artists and the bulk of the roles were already meted out in advance. The life-insurance executives grew tired of bailing out unsuccessful productions, and in 1967 the theater was turned into a rental hall used mainly by the shingeki groups that a few years earlier had called it "the agent of monopoly capitalism."[69]

Nissei also put on Broadway musicals performed by visiting foreign companies in 1963-1964, as well as Peking opera and the Comédie Française the following season. But soon it turned the management of such attractions over to commercial impresarios on a rental basis because not even Eliza Doolittle or the *Bourgeois Gentilhomme* could rescue the theater from debt. Through Asari's thick ties to the insurance corporation (his father was once an officer), Shiki became the principal tenant in the late 1960s and remains so today. Starting in 1970 the management also began renting the house to Tōhō and Shōchiku for two months each year, putting further distance between itself and the mainline shingeki groups. In the seventies Asari helped the theater retain a modified producer system, powered by Nissei life-insurance money channeled through General Arts and its subsidiary, Shiki. He held auditions among actors and actresses who had defected from the drama companies early in the decade, and he contracted with famous television stars for the leads. Most of the parts still went to Shiki members. The Japanese production of *Chorus Line* (1979) had the closest thing to open auditions of any commercial play in the seventies, and the cast ended up with the most non-Shiki performers ever in an Asari production.[70]

"THERE is no incipient movement toward Broadway methods of production" despite the successful musicals at the end of the 1970s, according to Don Kenny, "because the Japanese theater couldn't stand it."[71] From giants such as Tōhō and Shōchiku to cottage troupes like the Situation Theater and Satoh's black tent, Japanese performers need some form of production company to supply a sense of shared purpose and provide a shell for nurturing their art. There is little place in Japanese society for out-of-work actors and actresses trying to latch onto a part while waiting on tables or living on welfare. There is equally little room for individual playwrights or directors without contacts with some form of production group, a film maker, or a television studio. All of them tend to congregate in small clusters because they need one another until they can become established, and usually long after.

Performers and their business managers also recognize that they need well-defined, stable audiences, preferably in groups that can be counted on to appear regularly. Almost like fashion designers or specialty magazines, Japanese theater companies and commercial producers have developed an intricate set of carefully targeted markets that complement rather than overlap, avoiding much direct competition. These delineated clienteles reflect the expectations of different age groups of each sex, a bow to the obvious truth that middleaged suburban housewives are no more likely to appear at Kara's red tent than are male university students at a soap opera.

Still it is a worry to company producers that going to the theater is not widely accepted by men between the ages of twenty-five and sixty. Well-educated men, the most probable would-be customers for all the live performing arts, apparently find artistic outlets through their places of employment or pursue other art forms, such as writing and painting, at home. It is also not customary for married couples to go out together for the evening.

But the issue of locating new audiences is larger than this. Even when school performances and amateur plays are taken into account, the number of Japanese who attend the theater is very widely thought to be small by international standards. Ōkōchi Takeshi believes many persons are reluctant to shed their patterned reserve and involve themselves with a live event on the stage—especially a verbal one—with the degree of engagement that all but the simplest entertainments require. "The Japanese prefer leisure-time activities in which they can remain passive," he says, "and they love to go sightseeing, watch TV, or attend an art show"[72] rather than take in something that demands a more active form of participation. Although many boisterous audiences can be found in more popular entertainments, there is little doubt that a strong sense of propriety and decorum, carefully developed among children at all levels of society, inhibits spontaneous involvement with the theater and makes many who do attend feel they must sit stone-still in almost prayerful silence.

CHAPTER 7

Music: Cultivated Clienteles

"JAPAN MADE a great effort right after the war to become a 'cultured country.' People thought almost no sacrifice was too great to educate their children in a refined manner. It became socially respectable to learn a musical instrument, especially for young women."[1] This is how Tsunematsu Yukitoshi, vice president of the Japan Musicians' Union, explains the gargantuan growth and remarkable feminization of the Japanese musical world since 1945. Until the early twentieth century, most who practiced applied music or the other polite accomplishments were men, and the substance of their art was entertainment. Only after World War Two did it become fully acceptable for middle-class women to study arts previously linked with sensual pleasure. Their aim was not merely to discover how to create beauty through sound; they also hoped to acquire a degree of refinement and a measure of self-mastery.

As more and more pupils jammed studios to learn traditional Japanese or classical Western music, their lessons began to focus on performance and to play down leisure-time diversion. Technique became the cardinal precept; enjoyment became an afterthought in the pell-mell to polish endless études and offer flawless recitals. Because music after the war was seen as a performing and interpreting art, not one that innovated, millions of new students dutifully learned to emulate classical routines and muffle their imaginations. Yet despite the regimented training that postwar pupils have undergone, "Japanese composers are very active and quite original," says Ichiyanagi Toshi, one of the most inventive of all. "The creative composers here just now are really creative."[2] Pleasure, performance, and innovation were three of the main motifs

181

as music turned into a genuine art practiced by professionals whose occupation became so reputable that nearly 45,000 people, two-thirds of them women, joined it during 1955-1975.

FUSIONS AND CROSSOVERS

In Japan, perhaps more than any other musically sophisticated country, "the mechanisms of publicity, concerts, contests and funding give the illusion of a full, consonant culture" received from nineteenth-century Europe. Correspondingly, they discouraged new compositions, as Edward Rothstein has said of modern music in general. Narrative music from the age of European democracy, with novel-like tales of events played by orchestras in large concert halls, appeals to middle-class audiences in Japan far more than the terse tonal abstractions of modern compositions. "Like everywhere else," says the poet-critic Akiyama Kuniharu, "the audiences for contemporary serious music in Japan are limited. But there is a great deal of activity." A dozen or more contemporary music festivals, two dozen programs devoted to individual composers, and at least that many group premieres are held each year. Nearly 400 fresh works of serious Western-style music, as well as large numbers of contemporary Japanese-style compositions, are presented in concert every year, and Japanese artists also turn out hundreds of scores for plays, films, radio, and television.[3] Many of the thirty or so most active composers have transcended the technical limits of both traditional Western instruments and their classical Japanese counterparts by writing works that fuse in some fashion the themes, structure, or instrumentation of the two very distinct musical cultures. Others have written thoroughly contemporary works that acknowledge how separate Japanese music is from its Western equivalent.

The government made classical Western music the norm when it founded the Tokyo Academy of Music in 1879, but for almost 100 years the state did very little to encourage

182

composers. A few rich music lovers like Konoe Hidemaro, Ōhara Magosaburō, Ōkura Kishichirō, and Tokugawa Yorisada commissioned new works and sponsored concerts before the war. The New Composers' Federation, founded in 1930, broke fresh ground for modern music in Japan, but most composers continued to write in either the French or the central European mode. Yamada Kōsaku, Taki Rentarō, and Nobutoki Kiyoshi were the most accomplished of the tiny band of prewar artists who composed classical Western music.[4]

The Experimental Workshop, opened in 1949, launched a flotilla of multimedia inventions lasting into the 1970s, most of them works that recognized but did not mimic parallel developments abroad. Foreigners began drawing on traditional Japanese music almost before Japanese composers in the fifties started transcribing court music and folk tunes for Western instruments. Takemitsu Tōru's *Requiem for Strings* (1957) and Mayuzumi Toshirō's *Nirvana Symphony* (1958) were among the most successful creations in this vein. John Cage visited Osaka in 1962 to introduce his ideas about musical indeterminacy, the main theme of avant-garde composing in Japan during the sixties. His leading proponent, Ichiyanagi Toshi, wrote works based on chance operations and live voice-sounds such as *Extended Voices* (1966) and *Tokyo 1969*. Cage was received with much more reserve when he returned with the Merce Cunningham dance company in 1976,[5] but the avant-garde remains a major force in Japanese composing even though Ichiyanagi and his New Directions group have moved well past their art of abandon.

Beyond the crossover between traditional sounds and Western instruments in the fifties and the pure experimentation that peaked in the sixties was a newer, more nativist fusion of contemporary international music with traditional Japanese instrumentation, beginning about 1965. Takemitsu's *November Steps*, first performed in 1967 in New York, was one of many works showing his deftness at writing for the Japanese lute and flute as well as for Western ensembles. "I must not be trapped by traditional instruments any more than by all other kinds," he said in the early 1970s. His goal was "to make a living order that combines the fundamentally different musical phenomena of the West and Japan"[6]—a task he compared in 1981 to "mapping out a garden" whose elements seem to change as the observer shifts perspectives while walking through it. Now that "there is no longer one central tradition"[7] in art-music, Takemitsu and a number of other composers seem to believe that any country can produce valid works drawing freely on both domestic and foreign idioms, so long as they retain coherence as compositions and an integrity of spirit—a quality almost inevitably linked with the artist's national identity.

Like the underground playwrights and the postmodern dancers and painters of the 1970s, composers such as Akutagawa Yasushi, Mamiya Michio, and Hayashi Hikaru related their music to contemporary Japanese life by using native themes unconnected with movements or techniques from abroad. Some critics found them "a bit conceited" for showing so little regard for current composing in other countries.[8] The combination of Japanese and Western instruments as well as ideas made it hard to distinguish between the two traditions in many of the newest works, according to the musicologist Koizumi Fumio, but whenever contemporary composers used premodern Japanese elements or techniques "usually the result sounded more traditional than modern."[9] Both as avant-garde experimentation and as a free-form fusing of Western ingredients with native sounds, contemporary music by the end of the seventies had traveled far beyond the Austro-Germanic mode favored for so long at the official academy in Ueno Park.

Private patronage of composers evaporated after the war along with the great fortunes that once had made it possible, and very few of the 150 professionals who write serious music in Japan today have never had to teach to earn a living. Takemitsu is a rare exception, but only because he has done scores for seventy-three movies and now writes to augment his income from composing. During the golden age of Japanese cinema in the 1950s, there were far more opportunities to prepare film music than today, but radio and television have taken up the slack. Few artists have qualms about working for the mass media, Takemitsu points out, because "composers for films in Japan have a much greater freedom than Western film composers," and even the avant-garde leader Ichiyanagi writes soundtracks "when I find a director who is interested in serious music."[10]

No one is quite sure how much is spent each year to commission new works, but Ichiyanagi finds that "the situation is quite favorable in Japan compared with other countries." The cultural agency, prefectural governments, NHK, and the Japan Orchestra Association all earmark part of their aid to symphonies for commissioning fresh works. The New Japan Philharmonic has been the leading sponsor of new compositions among the professional orchestras, but nearly all of them play contemporary Japanese works almost beyond the capacity of audiences to pay attention. Choral societies, opera companies, the national theater, and the Japan Olympic Committee also commission works from time to time. Official ceremonies requiring new commemorative music usually include premieres by relatively safe, noncontroversial composers like Dan Ikuma, who says that his "music doesn't touch on electronic processes, chance operations, or other avant-garde techniques, so I may be criticized for being a little unprogressive." Although royalties are modest and few universities employ composers to teach general-education courses, Ichiyanagi believes he and his colleagues are "freer artistically" than composers in Europe, where "so many are indirectly employed by the state."[11] Their creativity seems to be invigorated by independence from both Hollywood and the government—a tonic for any art.

Another noticeable group of composers are the two dozen or so who write contemporary hōgaku, or Japanese-style music. Miyagi Michio was the founding father of this movement, which grew prominent after 1958 when the Hōgaku Yonin no Kai flute ensemble was formed to play very simple, modern

185

music written for traditional Japanese instruments. Composers were encouraged in the 1960s both by the "shakuhachi boom," a wave of interest in the Japanese flute helped along by John Cage and others abroad, and by the new eagerness of Western-style composers to use native instruments to perform their works. Much of what contemporary hōgaku writers produced was a spare, frugal reworking of old Japanese folk melodies, eventually in the context of a total theater including popular entertainments and classical dance.[12]

The workers' musical organization Rōon supported concerts of contemporary hōgaku starting in 1959, on the sturdy premise that "classical Western music is something different from our folk harmonies . . . something remote from the common people and the workers."[13] Support from Rōon helped the new compositions find audiences far broader than the private groups that usually gathered to hear conventional songs performed according to the customs of particular schools of instruction. The Japan Music Group, formed in 1964, became the most productive source of new hōgaku songs. But soon it was turning out works almost indistinguishable from contemporary Western-style music, and the movement crested in the early 1970s. Partly its energies were absorbed by the more nativist compositions written for Japanese instruments in the seventies, but for the most part hōgaku artists had reached a technical plateau with their pure, simple instrumentation. Regular performances of the genre continued throughout the 1970s, even when much of the hōgaku offered at the autumn arts festival turned traditional once again after 1975.[14]

Like Western-style composers, those who write contemporary hōgaku have to teach to make ends meet. Now that notation is widely used for learning Japanese-style music, composers earn at least small royalites when it is published, and a few of them profit from writing scores for movies and television dramas. The biggest claim on their time comes from students, who usually insist on training in contemporary hōgaku not merely because it is simple to master but also because it is usually played by ensembles, creating far more job possibilities than is true for traditional Japanese music. As the ethnomusicologist Kishibe Shigeo puts it, "contemporary hōgaku is really what keeps traditional Japanese music alive"[15]— and teaching is what keeps most Japanese and Western-style musicians solvent.

PAYING TO PLAY

"Japanese parents encourage their children to take lessons of some kind because learning an art form helps train you spiritually," says the businessman-librettist Nobumoto Yasusada. More than half the nation's families now send their school-age children to after-hour classes in some skill or art, most commonly calligraphy, music, or dance. Part of the motive is to ape Western middle-class manners, or at least to keep up with the people next door, by instilling refinement and furbishing the prospects for a good marriage, especially for daughters.[16] But an equally weighty aim is to build character by teaching children to master their minds, spirits, and emotions. Boys sometimes seek self-cultivation through martial skills or other regimens, but for most children the weekly piano drill or brushwork lesson is part of the routine of learning to be a grown-up.

Japanese often refer to teaching the traditional arts as the "cultivation" or "training" industry (*shūgyō*), a mark of the ethical as well as esthetic purposes of taking lessons. It amuses many older performers that almost half the parents who send their children for training in a performing art choose traditional Japanese music or classical dance, genres that just a generation ago were still too closely associated with the pleasure districts to offer much spiritual instruction.[17] Learning the koto or Japanese dance is now a thoroughly respectable pastime and a worthy means to self-cultivation for millions of middle-class students who have no experience, or even interest, in the world of the professional entertainer.

Musical education in the public schools has little to do with the postwar boom in studying hōgaku, since classical Western

187

music has been the norm for a century and still dominates the curriculum. So strong was the Germanic bias of accredited musical culture that hōgaku musicians had to go to the Diet before winning their fight to be included in Tokyo University of Fine Arts when it opened in 1949. Although hōgaku is now heard in junior high-school music classes,[18] musical education at every level still has far more Chopin than shakuhachi. This scantiness, together with what many parents believe is a lack of moral education in the schools, sends thousands of children to private teachers each year to begin lessons in hōgaku that often continue for a lifetime.[a]

A slight majority of the 2 million or so who were studying traditional Japanese music at the end of the seventies were instrumentalists, since singing requires a good voice and takes a long time to learn. Koto replaced samisen as the most popular instrument during the 1970s, even though a stage-quality koto now costs about $2,500, several times the price of a good samisen or shakuhachi. Pupils of all ages pay between fifty and seventy-five dollars a month for weekly lessons lasting twenty minutes from teachers who usually have forty students or so. Normally the teacher is a certified instructor in one of the various schools that exist for each instrumental and vocal genre (in the case of koto there are just two). Pupils are expected to perform at a yearly recital, paying the teacher about $250 per song for the privilege of appearing in public as his or her student. If the composition is a work of contemporary hōgaku performed by an ensemble, the players divide the cost of the $250 honorarium. Ostracism still prevails in hōgaku, as in all the traditional arts: instructors refuse to accept a pupil who has already studied with someone else, although they have less leverage over dropouts who fail to turn up for the recital because of the stiff fee required.[19]

Teachers, in turn, are supposed to appear periodically at

[a] Dan Ikuma, Honda Shingo, and many other artists speak of a "rebound effect": Japan takes a renewed interest in its traditional arts (e.g. shakuhachi, ukiyoe) because of their popularity abroad. Dan interview, December 23, 1980; Honda interview, December 15, 1980.

recitals sponsored by the musician who trained them or sometimes by the headmaster of their particular school. During the late autumn and spring seasons, there are two or three such events every day in Tokyo alone. The attendance on these occasions is just as private as at the student recitals, consisting entirely of families and friends of the performers and other musicians of the same school. Members of the audience often leave an envelope with cash at the lobby, marked for the acquaintance whose number they have come to hear. The head teacher and other instrumentalists customarily remain on stage for the whole recital, accompanying each musician in turn during the single song he or she gets to play. The entire program consists of forty or more works and often takes six hours to complete. The performer pays the head teacher $500 as an honorarium for the chance to appear, and smaller sums go to the other accompanists and for sharing the rent of the concert hall. A recital of nagauta (long epic songs) can cost the singer twice as much as one for koto, because of the large numbers of accompanists required—a key factor in the declining popularity of this genre.

The expenses of the yearly recital are like dues the hōgaku instructor pays to retain certification and the right to teach ordinary pupils, whose tuitions and stage fees keep the whole vertically arranged recital system upright. Middle-class families have become the main financial props of hōgaku and the major reason why the top-ranking teachers have grown rich during the past twenty years, but it is less clear that their patronage has done much to advance the art of music itself. Hōgaku performers rarely attend recitals by rival schools and almost never hone their talents through open competitions. The most outstanding musicians sometimes put on public concerts, which nearly always lose money because rentals, costumes, and accompanists are so costly and the public for such events is so small. But well over 90 percent of all hōgaku performances are private,[20] held before audiences with a financial stake in the recital system and little basis or enthusiasm for criticism.

Although females of nearly every age make up the great majority of hōgaku pupils, businessmen have long made traditional singing their favorite artistic diversion and currently outnumber women among students of kouta. Many thousands of them pay fifty dollars a month to learn the art of singing because it is a useful skill for company drinking parties and official occasions, including corporate entertaining with geishas. "People feel more at ease if you dance and sing as well as converse at geisha houses," according to Nobumoto. "It's good for building human relationships that otherwise couldn't occur in the business world."[21] Like everyone else studying a traditional genre, businessmen are expected to appear in recitals each year, with appropriate payments on all sides, and normally they continue taking lessons throughout their corporate careers.

Still "it is very important to remember that businessmen regard kouta as a hobby," Nobumoto adds, "not just as a business formality."[22] By supporting it for pleasure as well as profit, company executives stick closer to the original earthy flavor of the traditional performing arts, before middle-class families and the government's cultural diplomacy turned them into rarefied esthetic exemplars. Whatever the motives that prompt people to study the traditional arts, hōgaku now thrives side by side with Western music as an "equally logical but different"[23] system of expressing beauty through sound, still patronized almost entirely by the players themselves.

"Hardly anyone studies hōgaku these days to become a professional," Dan Ikuma points out, whereas 10,000 Western music majors a year graduate from Japan's colleges and universities, three times as many as in 1965 despite very little growth in the market for their talents. Nearly nine-tenths of them are women. About 2 percent of the graduates in 1979 found jobs as performers, and most of the rest who did not leave the field entirely took full- or part-time positions teaching in schools, private studios, or on their own, often moonlighting in unrelated work.[24] Like most visual artists, dancers, and theater people, Japan's Western music professionals are proud of their art and sacrifice a good deal to pursue it. (Hō-gaku teachers are equally proud but less impecunious, since so many are married women with other sources of household income.)

Nearly 2.5 million pupils study some form of applied Western music today, the majority of them dutifully coping with keyboard exercises for much the same reasons of snobbery and self-cultivation as their peers who are learning hōgaku. One good index of how the clientele has grown is that in 1960 only one household out of fifty had a piano, compared with one out of six today. Nihon Gakki, the maker of Yamaha, claimed first place among the world's piano manufacturers in 1969, fifteen years after it opened a network of teaching studios that today includes 9,500 locations in Japan and 230 overseas. Most other instruments have likewise grown more popular in the past two decades, a time when the market for recorded classical Western music mushroomed to its present level of $50 million a year.[25]

Unlike students of traditional Japanese music, many children begin playing Western instruments in school before starting private lessons on the side, and very few of them continue the training past their teens. The fees paid to teachers are much less standardized than in hōgaku, ranging from fifteen dollars a month to the neighborhood teacher for a weekly half-hour lesson on the violin or piano for small children to forty dollars or more per one-hour session with a prestigious instructor for more accomplished pupils. On the whole Western music lessons cost a bit more than hōgaku classes, but the overall outlay is lower because student recitals seldom require honoraria to the teacher, only an assessment to share the costs of renting an auditorium. But the hierarchy of recitals still tyrannizes teachers, if not their pupils, since they are often expected to perform at events sponsored by the musician with whom they trained, paying a sizeable fee for the honor, and they usually have to sell a block of tickets to students and friends when their former teacher appears in a public concert.[26]

191

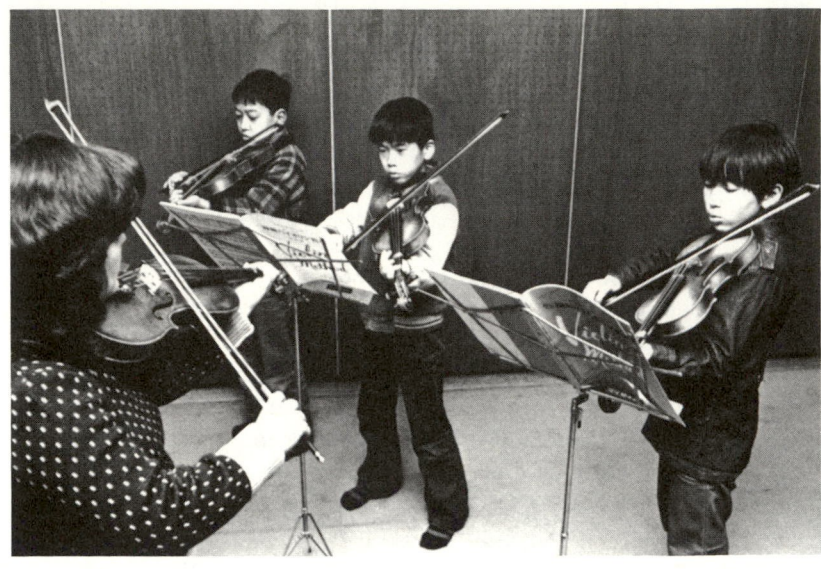

Studious children with numbed fingers practice their violins
in an unheated wintertime classroom. MIN'ON

Performance is the chief focus of music training, whether
for private amateur recitals in hōgaku or public professional
appearances in classical Western music. The goal for the would-
be professional is to win acceptance, very much like the top
300 in the visual arts: "either you're accepted as an artist or
you're not, and the Japanese arts world helps perpetuate the
mystique," says Lawrence B. Flood of the American Center
in Tokyo. "Even the younger artists trying to win recognition
accept the rules and perpetuate the myth of acceptability."
For concert musicians this means technical proficiency in performance, and almost the entire apparatus of music instruction is weighted toward appearing on the stage. The most
famous exception is Suzuki Shin'ichi's "mother-tongue method"
of teaching violin to small children by having them play side
by side with their mothers.[27]

192

To become a successful performer and win recognition, the aspiring Western-style musician submits to a discipline scarcely less costly or confining than the headmaster system of hōgaku. "Big bosses still dominate the top levels of musical training in Japan," says Iwaki Hiroyuki. "They form a kind of mafia and take large amounts of money under the table." Promising high-school-age pupils pay substantial fees to study privately with the leading teachers in their communities, who are often graduates of Tokyo University of Fine Arts or private colleges such as Tōhō Gakuen, Kunitachi, or Musashino. Periodically a professor from one of these institutions makes flying visits to former students now teaching all over the country and gives twenty-minute lessons to their ablest young pupils, most of whom will soon be seeking entrance to the university. The professor receives several hundred dollars from each pupil for one of these lessons, Iwaki estimates, and an even larger honorarium at the time of university admission.[28]

The private colleges also often collect contributions from students when they are admitted, although on a much smaller scale than most private medical and dental schools.[b] Throughout their college careers, students continue to make periodic cash gifts to the professor as well as to their former teachers back in their home communities, adding up to several thousand dollars across four years. Tsunematsu Yukitoshi of the Japan Musicians' Union estimates that, from age five to twenty-three, it costs $80,000 or more for lessons, instruments, equipment, and fees to become a concert violinist.[29] It is no wonder "the poor learn the cello,"[30] an unglamorous instrument re-

[b] The education ministry informally allows private colleges and universities to accept up to $50,000 in contributions at the time of admission. On February 4, 1981, President Nagaki Daizo of Kitasato University announced that his institution would return "excessive" contributions received in 1979 and 1980 from new students averaging $55,000 beyond the permissible limit. Altogether the university accepted $16.3 million in off-the-book gifts from 190 students in 1979 and 1980, in addition to $12.7 million in declared contributions. Although admission to top art and music colleges is severely competitive, it is not thought that these institutions receive "excessive" donations. See *Japan Times*, February 5, 1981.

quiring no such schedule of hidden payments to smooth the route to acceptance.

Since the student's own teachers serve as examiners for both entrance and graduation, little objective appraisal takes place just when it is most needed—exactly as with the visual arts. The test comes later, on the public stage, but to get there in the first place it helps to be the former student of a famous professor. In this respect training in Western music combines the open competition typical of oil painting with the teacher-pupil connection found in Nihonga. What the training system does for raising the level of music in Japan is uncertain, according to Dan, who asks rhetorically, "why do so many people study Western music? Fashion?" Iwaki concedes that teacher-pupil relationships are very tight in Europe as well, but "the system as a whole is much more open there." He believes the Japanese music establishment should be teaching fewer well-to-do dabblers and that "talented students need more channels to get ahead." All too many of them are forced to seek their training in places like Vienna, where two-thirds of the foreign students are Japanese because a musical education is cheaper there than in Tokyo.[31]

The 4.5 million persons who study voice or instruments are the financial base for the pyramid of performance in the Japanese musical world. Their yearly fees for instruction and recitals undoubtedly surpass by far the total income from all public professional concerts of serious music each year.[c] Except for businessmen singing kouta at company parties, it is hard to tell how much pleasure or musical innovation ensues from all the effort to climb the pyramid, but there is little

[c] Tsunematsu puts the total budgets (not earnings) for events by foreign musicians at $50 million per year, perhaps half of which is for classical music. The combined budgets of the fifteen professional orchestras and eleven main opera companies amount to about $55 million a year. Revenues from all other live professional performances of serious music are estimated at well under $50 million annually. Tsunematsu Yukitoshi, "Ongakuka shōgai no sōkessan," *Ongaku geijutsu*, May 1979, p. 45; Bunkachō, *Bunka gyōsei no ayumi*, p. 77; Okōchi interview, November 19, 1980; Koshimura Sadanao interview, November 5, 1980. See chapter one for details on Japanese orchestras and opera groups.

question that very few of the millions who pay to play ever win acceptance. Still the effort is presumably worthwhile if it affords the learner greater self-mastery.

MUSIC AND IDEOLOGY

Group singing has cheered people's spirits and reinforced the dogmas of clerics and rulers for many centuries, but in Japan the chorus is a modern institution introduced from Europe in the late nineteenth century and little used for ideological purposes until after World War Two.[32] In the early postwar years various labor groups, new religious sects, and employers' federations established huge choruses for workers and believers all over the country because they found that group singing served doctrinal as well as recreational aims. In the 1950s and early sixties several of the choral movements turned into audience associations for the appreciation of music—mainly classical Western music at first, later traditional Japanese works as well as jazz, folk, rock, and other popular genres. The musical audience organizations mixed art and ideology at least as thickly as the theater audience groups, but they also buttressed serious Western music and helped circulate it throughout the country at a time when there were few other sponsors. The most important was also the earliest, the workers' musical association Rōon (Kinrōsha Ongaku Kyōgikai), founded in 1949.[d]

Rōon traces its ancestry to the Japan Proletarian Music League, an illicit prewar group modeled after the Barcelona Workers' Music Council that had been founded at the suggestion of Pablo Casals in 1926. The more immediate inspiration was the workers' choral movement led by the singer

[d] Iwaki found audience-organization customers attentive when he conducted before them in the 1960s, noting that they all started and ceased applauding at once, as though on cue. Iwaki Hiroyuki, "Kokuhakuteki chōshūron," *Chūō kōron*, October 1970, p. 221. Alvin Toffler discusses commercial audience associations such as Community Concerts Inc. and Civic Concerts Inc. in *The Culture Consumers: A Study of Art and Affluence in America*, Baltimore, Penguin Books, 1965, pp. 135-136.

Seki Akiko and known as Utagoe, which originated with a May Day concert in 1946 and fanned out to many parts of the country after the American occupation authorities banned a general strike called for February 1, 1947.[33] Rōon was born in this same atmosphere of labor ferment and political dissent, and it too encouraged choral singing among the workplace units that quickly spread after the first Rōon chapter was founded in Osaka in 1949 by the composer and future Diet member Sudō Gorō. From the start Rōon's main activity was presenting "good music for many people at cheap prices," which in practice meant sponsoring concerts of classical Western music for fees as low as fourteen cents. Although its bylaws spoke of "increasing members' esthetic sensitivity and cultural refinement through good music," the organization also made it plain that "Rōon acts in solidarity with many specialists and with other progressive, democratic movements to accomplish its objectives,"[34] political as well as artistic.

Unlike the companion theater group Rōen, the music association invited overseas artists to Japan and during the 1950s became the major sponsor of foreign classical-music concerts, many of them by performers from the Soviet Union and East European countries. The first popular-music program for members occurred in 1953, but for most of the decade the Western classics and modern Soviet compositions were staples, mainly performed by Japanese artists for whom the Rōon circuit was a godsend.

When the national council of Rōon chapters was established in 1955, the movement's combined membership was already 120,000. Five years later it had soared to nearly 390,000, and by 1965 the total number who belonged to the 190 Rōon branches reached 633,000, the all-time peak.[35] Then the membership began to disappear very fast in the late sixties, sinking to just 170,000 by 1972. At first the leadership blamed the defections on "organized opposition in the form of reactionary thought" and "interference from management" through the employers' music association Onkyō.[36] But soon it became obvious that there was more competition from commercial impresarios as well as rival audience groups and that music fans wanted to hear performers from the United States whom Rōon had deliberately passed over. The idea of a set season selected for members by their branch leaders lost its appeal, as in the case of Rōen, when a greater variety of musical and other activities became available.[37] Stereos, television, and the general embourgeoisement of labor also took their toll.

Rōon's answer was to separate music somewhat more from politics and to bend with the tide of commercialism that swept across Japanese stages in the seventies. It began purchasing blocks of tickets for Broadway musicals in 1969, added summer camping and winter skiing trips, and offered discounts on movie tickets, records, audio equipment, and music lessons to keep up with its competitor Onkyō. For a time the membership perked up, rising to 211,000 in 1974, but since then it has withered to the current figure of 160,000.[38] Yet the group never abandoned its antiwar activities, and its choruses have gone on singing even though there are fewer voices to fill them.

Today Rōon offers its members more than 500 events throughout the country each year, nearly all of them groups of seats at regular performances rather than exclusive engagements for Rōon alone. As recently as 1970 the number of productions it sponsored was much smaller, but at that time a single program would often be repeated 150 or 200 times for members all over the country. Today almost two-thirds of the events are some form of popular music, and traditional Japanese music is now heard as often as classical Western compositions. But there is still room for six of Tokyo's professional orchestras to tour as Rōon's guests, and out-of-town symphonies are invited to appear each year on its schedule as well. The organization also still supports nearly 200 appearances each year by classical musicians from abroad, mainly the socialist countries. By guaranteeing a full or partly full house for another 250 performances a year by Japanese artists on the road, Rōon continues to help find customers for classical Western music, as it has for more than a quarter-century.[39]

Rōon's main rival in the biggest cities has been the Music Cultural Association (Ongaku Bunka Kyōkai), founded by big business in 1955 and known to everyone as Onkyō. Its 8,764 corporate sponsors are a who's who of the same business world which otherwise patronizes the arts so parsimoniously, arousing the well-founded suspicion that their motive is more than a love of music alone. This gigantic audience association, which exceeded a million members in 1980, started off with almost the same slogan as Rōon's, "good music for workers cheaply," and professed to have "no political connections or bias at all," according to Fujiwara Tamon, head of its Tokyo organization.[40] Although Onkyō may not have "favored any particular ideology,"[41] it was very frank about admitting that it was designed for "enterprise defense" against "excessively powerful ideological movements" in its plants. At the tenth general convention in 1973, the national Onkyō council approved a membership drive "to offset the new positive cultural maneuvers of the left-wing forces"—that is, Rōon's rightward swing toward commercialism.[42]

In this spirit of ill-disguised scorn for Rōon and its political backer, the Japan Communist Party, Onkyō built a hugely successful apparatus in Tokyo and Osaka that today offers the members of its fifty-nine chapters large discounts to nearly 6,000 events each year in music, theater, film, and recreation of many sorts. Of the 1,000 musical performances, most are popular and only a minority are in classical Western music—often by foreigners—and almost none are hōgaku. Since so much Onkyō activity is based in the largest cities, its support for serious music is more geographically concentrated than Rōon's, and its audiences are no larger. Still Japanese orchestras, ensembles, and soloists welcome its members wherever they appear, and Onkyō has become a chief booking agent for high-quality musicians from abroad during the 1970s.[43]

Onkyō began in Osaka in 1955 and from the beginning

invited workers in its sponsoring companies to form choruses, because group singing was a good way to overcome the fact that "many young people have lost their ideals and continue to be restless." Aided by the Federation of Economic Organizations and the labor ministry, Onkyō has held a national choral festival for its members each year since 1958, and in 1971 it began training leaders to organize musical activities in factories and offices. Music was clearly a useful management tool for improving labor relations, and without this function it is not likely that businesses would have set up a cut-rate ticket scheme simply as a fringe benefit. Classical Western musicians have been the incidental but very willing beneficiaries of a program to thwart their old friend Rōon, and for every Rōon customer lost in the seventies Japanese orchestras have probably gained an Onkyō member in the audience.[44]

Onkyō became more popular while most other audience groups shriveled in the 1970s because it catered skillfully to the tastes of its main market, young clerical workers in business offices (60 percent of its members today are women and 80 percent are persons under age twenty-six).[45] It is the most commercial of the audience groups and has no ties of ideology or sentiment to any art form to keep it from responding to shifting audience tastes. Onkyō is a smoothly run, well-financed operation with public-relations skills that appeal to the rapidly changing young clientele it serves. Today it is virtually a cut-rate commercial ticket agency sponsored by employers who never had much interest in music and no longer fear Rōon, but who would be loath to face the outcry from their employees, the orchestras, and the theaters if they abandoned Onkyō.

Closer to Rōon in both structure and impact on serious music has been the Democratic Music Association (Minshu Ongaku Kyōkai), an audience group usually known as Min'on sponsored by the lay Buddhist organization Sōka Gakkai. Huge bands and enormous choruses have been part of Sōka Gakkai's program of moral uplift through group participation

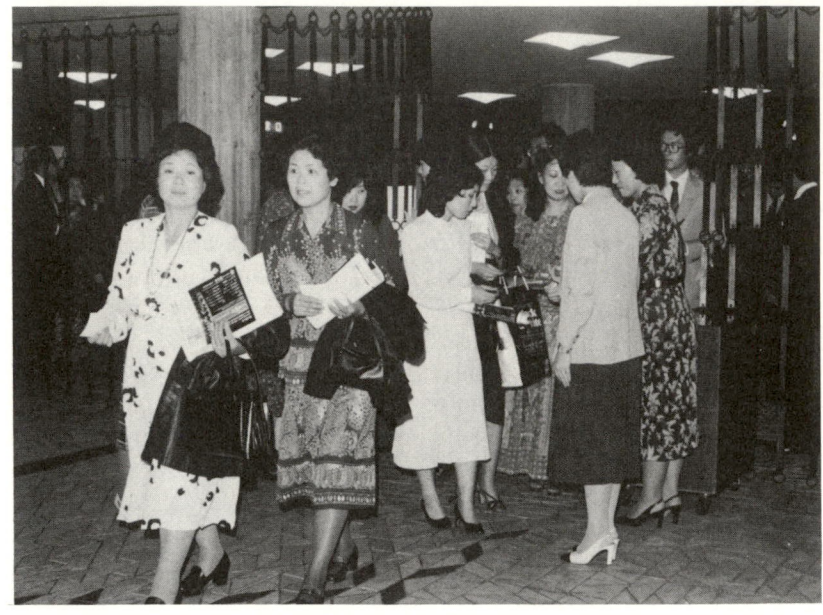

Members of the Min'on audience association arriving for a
concert at Tokyo Metropolitan Festival Hall. MIN'ON

since the early 1950s, and classical Western music was included when Min'on was established in 1963. Its stated aim was to spread the classics among the public and elevate the quality of popular music. From the start Min'on was linked to politics as well as religion, through Sōka Gakkai's Clean Government Party (Kōmeitō). Thanks to the awesome power of Sōka Gakkai, Min'on built its membership to more than 2 million by the end of the seventies and promoted a greater range of serious musical events than any of the other audience associations.[46]

Although Rōon naturally feared the newcomer when it started, the two have ended up sharing many of the same artists from abroad, since their programming is so similar. Min'on also runs a national music contest every year, rotating it among vocal performances, chamber music, and conducting, and since 1969 the group has sponsored a contemporary music festival, now held annually, for which it commissions new works. It supports Japanese orchestras in three main ways. Like the other audience associations, Min'on buys up blocks of tickets at a discount so that members can attend regular performances or fills the house for an exclusive engagement, both in the orchestra's home city and on the road. It has also sponsored more than 1,250 school performances by symphonies, ensembles, and soloists since the early 1970s. The third way it aids orchestras is to hold nearly three dozen "citizens' concerts" in Tokyo each year and others in big cities around the country.[47] The group also acts as underwriter for extravaganzas from overseas too costly for ordinary impresarios or nonprofit sponsors, such as the lavish tour of the Vienna State Opera in October 1980.

Commercialization overtook Min'on in the seventies no less than other audience groups, and today the vast majority of its events are films, commercial theater, traditional storytelling, and popular music, including premodern folk singing. Its membership fees and ticket prices are the same as for the other organizations, but Min'on offers its members a far smaller choice of events and leaves recreational activity to other Sōka Gakkai units. Most who belong· are Sōka Gakkai followers, and like Rōon members they represent a wider range of age groups than Onkyō. Although Min'on picks many middlebrow selections and sponsors relatively few serious music programs, it turns out large crowds to hear the performers lucky enough to appear on its schedule.[48] In the 1970s it became a force more or less equal to Rōon and Onkyō in drumming up audiences for classical Western music, and its network of local chapters and school concerts now makes Min'on as important as Rōon in turning the orchestras into truly national institutions.

Nothing helped to democratize the postwar performing arts quite so much as the audience association. The alliance between artists and audience organizations was entirely natural, prompted both by general social structure and specific historical circumstance. In Japan, the performing arts and society at large are strongly oriented toward tangible groups, and audiences are highly suitable entities to organize. Once they were freed from military censorship, the arts needed new customers just when many Japanese were looking for cheap entertainment. Forming an audience association made sense economically for performer and spectator alike, and it gave people a group activity to join with their friends. It also provided orchestras with carefully cultivated clients who could be counted on to appear regularly for concerts. And the audience organizations also served the religious and political purposes of their sponsors in the fractious ideological climate of the first two postwar decades.

When the interests of performers, customers, and organizers converged, the result was a much wider access to live performances and a far broader base of support for the arts among Japan's new middle class than ever before. Although their collective impact on serious music and live theater is smaller now than ten years ago, audience associations will almost certainly endure for as long as the performing arts need customers and customers need cheap seats.

Making Musical Ends Meet

"There are too many orchestras in Tokyo," says Koshimura Sadanao, manager of the Japan Orchestra Association, "playing too many concerts in houses with empty seats and paying their musicians wages that are far too low." Yet aside from the NHK symphony, Japan's professional orchestras average just ten performances a year for their regular series subscribers and the general public, each of them a single playing of a different program. Since the national audience has been static for more than a decade at about 3 million and surprisingly few customers appear for their basic seasons,[49] the country's fifteen orchestras have had to create an elaborate meshwork of private audiences much like those of the shingeki companies. The eleven main opera groups have also spent a great deal of time on the road searching for new fans. Even so, both the orchestras and the opera companies have had to depend increasingly on grants and subsidies to balance their budgets, the more so because they all face talented competition from foreign musicians.

Orchestras are the cynosures of public attention and the centerpieces of the classical Western musical establishment in Japan, but their concerts add up to fewer than a quarter of all the professional performances of serious Western music each year for which admission is charged. For every symphony appearance there is a piano recital, an instrumental perform-ance by a soloist or chamber group, and a vocal music event in the country's 550 concert halls. Nearly 40 percent of these occasions are sponsored by the musicians themselves, without other backing of any sort. About a fifth of the performances nationwide, and nearly a third in Tokyo, are given by visiting artists from abroad. Throughout the seventies there were somewhat more than 1,000 professional concerts charging admission each year in Tokyo and several times that number in the country as a whole. Amateur activity by university and community groups was even more frequent. Including spon-sored performances in schools, parks, prisons, hospitals, old people's homes, and local cultural centers, the professional orchestras played about 2,200 concerts a year—only a tenth of them for their regular subscribers and walk-in customers.[50]

Because so few of the symphonies have well-defined audi-ences in their home cities, their music directors are very sen-sitive to box-office tastes that are already sharply limited to famous works by baroque and romantic composers. Still there was a Bruckner boom in the mid-1960s and a run on Fauré in 1969. To celebrate the 200th anniversary of Beethoven's birth, 2,200 Japanese musicians played all 140 of his works in 1970, predictably ending with a full-scale performance of the *Ninth* in the Budōkan a week before Christmas.[e] Seven

---

[e] The most frequently played Beethoven works in the six Kinki prefectures during 1904-1976 were symphony no. 5 (*Fate*), symphony no. 9 (*Choral*),

years later the 150th anniversary of his death received almost as much attention, true also of Schubert a season later.[51]

Although it is not quite obligatory to build every program around a Beethoven symphony, two studies from the Osaka-Kyoto-Kobe region show that his orchestral music was played more often in the early seventies than any other composer's, followed by Mozart, J. S. Bach, Tchaikovsky, and Brahms.[52] There is no reason to think that the situation has changed since. Now that orchestras have to travel so much to find new audiences, there is little time to rehearse any but the most standard numbers, and their repertoires, like those of the shingeki companies, are further confined because out-of-town fans expect to hear famous works. There is scant margin for innovation, and contemporary Japanese composers suffer most.

The top-ranking NHK symphony was founded in 1926, but the orchestra is essentially a postwar institution in Japan, born and reared in the intense competition among broadcasting companies and later sustained by civic pride. Asahi Broadcasting took over the Konoe orchestra, founded in 1951, and renamed it the ABC symphony in 1956, the same year that the Fuji Bunka Hōsō station established the Japan Philharmonic. *Yomiuri* and its broadcasting affiliates founded the Yomiuri Japan symphony in 1962, the country's only all-male orchestra because "there weren't well-qualified women musicians available," according to the man responsible for the policy, Yoshida Takayoshi.[53] Today it still has no women, an anomaly among major world orchestras.

Like radio symphonies that flourished in other countries during the 1930s and 1940s, Japan's broadcast orchestras had to diversify when television and high-fidelity equipment changed people's entertainment habits. The ABC symphony did not survive the transition, disbanding in 1961, and the old Tōhō orchestra, which became the Tokyo symphony in 1951 when it was bought by Tokyo Broadcasting, collapsed in 1964 after

and the *Appassionata, Kreutzer*, and *Moonlight* sonatas. Ōsaka Ongaku Daigaku, *Nishi Nihon ongaku bunka shiryō '78*, Osaka, Ōsaka Ongaku Daigaku, 1978, p. 29.

the station cut off its funding and the group's managing director, Hashimoto Kanzaburō, drowned himself in a canal. The present Tokyo symphony orchestra is a reorganized version of the defunct group.

The Japan Philharmonic has struggled to hang on ever since it suffered tedious labor problems and lost its contract with Fuji in March 1972. The heaviest blow came the following summer, when its nonunion musicians split off to form the New Japan Philharmonic, and expensive litigation over the broadcast contract dragged on into the 1980s. The Tokyo Philharmonic, founded in 1948, is viable mainly because NHK pays it $1.5 million or more each year to put on forty-eight concerts, but it too has had to cultivate new clienteles in the past few years.[54] Six of the eight current orchestras in Tokyo and at least one other elsewhere trace their origins to the broadcast media, but all of them have long since broken their dependence on the airwaves and found new live audiences throughout the country.

Most of the other orchestras, starting with the Gunma symphony in 1945, were established by civic groups backed by funds from city and prefectural governments, which usually let them use public concert facilities at cheap rates when they played at home. In return most of them have regularly played public-service concerts in schools and community centers. In the past ten years these orchestras too have broadened their audiences by going on tour,[55] and like most of the Tokyo groups they have come to depend on subsidies from the cultural agency to wash away red ink.

Japanese orchestras in 1972 earned 76 percent of their income at the box office or through season subscriptions, according to Kurabayashi Yoshimasa, who heads the main research project on the economics of the performing arts in Japan. (The comparable figure for American symphonies that year was 45 percent.)[56] Today the proportion of earned income is presumably lower, since expenses have risen much faster than income from a constant audience base. Public and private grants of all kinds, which Kurabayashi puts at 24 percent of income in 1972, are now correspondingly more important for keeping orchestras from default.[f]

Every symphony has a patrons' circle of season subscribers, but they account for an even smaller fraction of the year's revenue than is true for similar circles in shingeki. Only the NHK orchestra, which offers three different series of ten performances and plays each program twice, earns as much as a third of its annual income of $7.5 million from regular patrons. But even this superb symphony lost about 3,000 of its 18,000 subscribers during the seventies and now draws barely 2,000 customers per concert to its mammoth hall holding twice that number.[57] The Osaka Philharmonic, which counts Matsushita, Kansai Electric, and four media companies among its patrons, derives 16 percent of its $2 million yearly revenue from the patrons' circle. More typical is the scrappy Tokyo Philharmonic, whose 950 subscribers produce about $150,000 a year, 6 percent of the orchestra's $2.7 million income. Like subscriber circles in shingeki, the orchestra patrons' groups "produce very little corporate or individual giving beyond the basic cut-rate ticket prices they are paying when they buy the series," according to Matsuki Shōgo, secretary-general of the Tokyo Philharmonic. Each time the NHK symphony plays one of its sixty regular subscription concerts, it sells fewer than fifty seats to individuals who want to hear that single performance. More representative is the Tokyo Philharmonic, which counts on 850 such customers per concert at each of its ten subscription offerings and tailors its programs to make sure they appear.[58]

[f] Data are too fragile to allow an exact calculation, but the following estimates seem prudent. The combined budgets of Japan's fifteen professional orchestras totaled about $37.5 million in 1980. Known grants and subsidies, mainly from public sources, were $6.2 million; estimated grants and subsidies, also mostly from public sources, were another $4.5 million. Beyond this $10.7 million total were unknown amounts from *Yomiuri* to its orchestra, from the NHK Service Center, from spot broadcast contracts, and from opera and ballet services. The box office and season subscriptions cannot exceed 70 percent of orchestras' combined income today; the true figure may be closer to 55 percent. These estimates are based on data given in chapters two through four.

206

Aid from the cultural agency is a slightly more important source of revenue than patrons' circles for most symphonies. In 1980 the agency granted an average of $135,000 to twelve orchestras for creative activity and this much again in some cases for sponsored performances on the road. The total payments by prefectural and municipal governments are somewhat larger than the support from the cultural agency, but they are very unevenly distributed since nearly two-thirds go to a single orchestra, the Tokyo Metropolitan. Foundations, corporations, and private individuals provide even less than the patrons' circles. Nearly all the rest of the orchestras' revenues come from a patchwork of sources peculiar to each group, ranging from the NHK symphony's huge subsidy of $1.5 million from NHK to smaller items such as broadcast contracts, performances for ballet and opera, and out-of-town concerts sponsored by audience organizations.[g] Very few Japanese orchestras earn much from recording contracts. And with traveling costs for 100 musicians and their instruments so intimidating, the symphonies have been more reluctant than the shingeki companies to risk road performances on their own, without local sponsors. Yet out-of-town concerts claim at least a quarter of the average orchestra's schedule and produce nearly a third of its annual attendance.[59]

Regional symphonies supported in part by public agencies are often more imaginative than the ferociously competitive Tokyo eight. The Sapporo orchestra, which celebrated its twentieth anniversary in 1981, has done an all-Takemitsu program that drew specialists from Tokyo. The Kyushu orchestra, one of the newest professional groups, is another of the most daring and active. The Gunma symphony, from its

[g] Matsuki Shōgo lists the variety of audiences for the Tokyo Philharmonic in 1979: NHK broadcast work (48 performances); ballet, including the Kiev and Bolshoi companies (21); opera (16); a Kyushu tour sponsored by local governments (16); Rōon (12); cultural-agency touring arts festivals (10); regular subscription concerts in Tokyo (10); concerts for the Japan Orchestra Association (10); cultural-agency youth performances (3); Min'on (3); other local public agencies (3); and miscellaneous (8). Matsuki interview, October 14, 1980.

origins in 1945 with eight performers in Takasaki, has become a strong group musically with a weak financial base that was further softened in 1980 when the cultural agency tightened its rules for aid. The Osaka Philharmonic, like most regional orchestras, gets slightly more than a quarter of its income from national, prefectural, and city governments and plays a large number of public-service concerts in return. The busiest performer of free events is undoubtedly the Tokyo Metropolitan symphony, which receives almost two-thirds of its revenue from the city and each year plays eighty school concerts as well as other community events without admission charges.[60]

All the orchestras spend 70 to 75 percent of their budgets on personnel, about evenly split between conductors and soloists on the one hand and musicians on the other, and the rest on administration, rehearsal space, hall rentals, travel, upkeep on instruments, sheet music, and the like. The budgets of most orchestras swelled by 50 percent or more between 1975 and 1980, forcing them to play away from home more often and offer programs appealing to the fashions of youth more than the tastes of purists. The Tokyo Philharmonic, for example, put on concerts in 1980 with the venerable jazz performer Watanabe Sadao to draw more young people.[61] Still there is little sign that the general audience for classical Western music is growing, only that it is decentralizing.

Starting wtih the Yomiuri Japan symphony in 1970, eight professional orchestras formed unions and now belong to the Japan Musicians' Union (Nihon Ensōka Kyōkai), a 3,000-member association of classical Western music performers founded in early 1972 right after strikes hobbled three Tokyo orchestras at the height of the Christmas season. Although the JMU has not succeeded in enforcing a uniform wage among the unionized orchestras, it has lobbied successfully with management on minimum numbers of performances, contract rights, broadcast opportunities, and fringe benefits. It has also battled the government to no avail over the concert admission tax and the union's attempt to restrict the admission of foreign performers. "Japan has no closed shops yet," says Tsunematsu Yukitoshi, "but we're working on it." He admits that it is difficult to organize performers who see themselves as individual artists, not workers, especially when there are far more players than there are jobs.[62] Under the circumstances, there is no reason to think that unions have featherbedded or otherwise driven the costs of running an orchestra unnaturally high.

The JMU does what it can to find full- or part-time jobs for its members, and it also spends about $20,000 a year from the dues it collects to sponsor several dozen live performances at the Seibu department store and the small Hibiya concert hall. Many musicians, whether employed by the orchestras or elsewhere, also make money with temporary chamber groups formed for specific occasions, supplementing the four regular chamber ensembles currently active in Tokyo and two others in the Osaka area. Orchestra members sometimes earn extra fees by soloing with amateur groups, performing in ensembles for small ballet or opera productions not requiring a full pit orchestra, or serving as accompanists for recitals of all sorts.[63] Again, the big money is in piano and violin, and the poor indeed play cello.

Given the overwhelming power of the media and the Japanese fondness for star performers, it is small wonder that orchestra managers resorted to hiring famous guest conductors once again in the late 1970s, as they had fifteen years earlier. Briefly, in 1970, only one of the symphonies had a regular music director from abroad, but a decade later foreigners acted as regular or guest conductors for nearly all the professional orchestras. "In this age of jets," says Hase Takao, managing director of the NHK symphony, "there is no need for a permanent conductor"—although he readily admits he tried to entice Herbert von Karajan from Berlin for that position because he is the world's best-known conductor to Japanese audiences. Musicians generally say they prefer the familiarity of a regular music director who can develop a style, but they too have a stake in drawing crowds, and for the same reason they usually bear in silence the recent proliferation of foreign soloists in the key vocal and instrumental parts.[64]

Most of the crowds who appear for concerts by Japanese orchestras are clearly defined by the sponsor or occasion: a Rōon or Min'on audience, a school performance paid for by the cultural agency or by a corporation interested in moral uplift, or an arts-festival program for a prefectural education board. The most fickle audiences are those for the basic subscription series in the orchestra's home city. Less is known of symphony audiences than of modern drama fans, but the ones who attend the basic season seem to be young (the peak is in the early twenties), well educated, and "very reserved," according to Iwaki Hiroyuki. NHK subscribers, who are atypical, were 60 percent male in a 1977 survey. Most music administrators say the average customer at a regular Tokyo performance is a young unmarried woman.[65]

But a composite portrait of the average audience is somewhat beside the point. Exactly like shingeki, the symphonies have tried to cut their risks by paring the regular season to the core and developing as many discrete, dependable clienteles around the country as possible. Music critics, who are much freer with their opinions than art critics because there is no artificial pricing system to protect,[66] have little bearing on an orchestra's ability to draw customers. Most programs are given only once in the same location, very few concerts are easily available to the general public, and most who attend are there with a group or for a specific purpose, not because they have made a critical artistic choice. By maximizing reliable audiences and minimizing caprice, Japan's orchestras have managed to make ends meet in spite of a stagnant market for their product.

The prospects for foreign musicians in Japan became less certain in 1980 as well, after a decade of rich artistic activity by visiting performers and great profits for their commercial backers. Soon after the war the mass media promoted concert tours by world-class artists, and by the late 1950s Japan was a regular part of the international circuit for classical Western musicians. The Philadelphia Orchestra, Boston Symphony Orchestra, and New York Philharmonic all appeared in Japan not long after the war, but European performers were invited far more frequently because agents in the 1950s found that many music fans believed "if it's European, it can't be bad."[67] The Osaka International Festival in 1958, backed by *Asahi*, was the first of many gatherings of the world's best musicians that have continued almost without pause ever since. When jet aircraft went into service across the Pacific in 1959 and Japanese foreign-exchange rules were eased four years later, the stream of visitors speeded up. Commercial impresarios began booking the safest attractions with the biggest names, leaving esthetically pleasing but financially risky events such as opera to nonprofit sponsors. The foreign musicians found Japanese audiences appreciative and often returned a few years later for further engagements.

The justice ministry and the Japan Musicians' Union concur that the number of foreign performers in all genres who visited for brief engagements tripled during the seventies to about 20,000 a year. More than half came from North America and Europe, mainly classical rather than popular artists.[68] Three-fourths of all concerts by classical musicians from abroad occurred in halls holding 1,500 or more, where commercial agencies invariably booked their prize attractions: the orchestra from overseas or the Bolshoi ballet. Newspaper companies and local government agencies continued to sponsor soloists and chamber groups from abroad during the 1970s, while audience associations backed events of all sizes by foreigners.[69] Colleges and universities, a major part of the concert route in other countries, scheduled very few events because their auditoriums were usually too small and they were often located in large cities with ample facilities off-campus.

Seven impresarios were especially aggressive in developing markets for foreign classical-music events in the 1970s, managing nearly three-quarters of all the commercially sponsored performances by classical Western artists from abroad.[h] Others

[h] Most agents also handle jazz and pops musicians from abroad. The two largest commotions of the seventies were caused by the Bay City Rollers in December 1976 ("the greatest fuss since the Beatles visited in 1966") and

acted as agents in selling foreign attractions to both these promoters and nonprofit sponsors, audience associations, and government agencies. By the end of the decade, about twenty overseas orchestras a year were touring the country, with tickets surpassing $100 a seat for the ne plus ultra to Japanese music fans, Karajan and the Berlin Philharmonic.[70]

Commercialization overtook the serious music world in the 1970s as completely as it transformed theater and the visual arts. Japanese promoters used the hype of the record world and the gloss of slick public relations to boost foreign orchestras on the strength of their stars. When impresarios brought in the New York Philharmonic or the Philadelphia Orchestra, they wisely arranged to have Leonard Bernstein or Eugene Ormandy conduct. Walter Nichols of Azabu Artists sees the 1980s as "a watershed for foreign attractions in Japan. I doubt the economy can continue to stand these high prices. The market is saturated, there are too many events competing for a limited audience, and no American attractions sell any more except the top-top events with true star appeal."[71] No doubt the flood of foreign performers has cut into audiences for Japanese musicians in the biggest cities, and market pressures may well trim the flow from abroad in the eighties. Still it is hard to imagine that Japan will cease to be a forum where the world's very finest music is heard.

Rocketing ticket prices and famous stars became equally commonplace in Japanese opera during the 1970s. Ever since the Rome national company visited in 1951, foreign operas toured the largest cities, backed by NHK, audience groups, newspaper companies, and their home governments as well as the cultural agency after 1968. Characteristic of how much Japan's 30,000 opera fans were willing to pay for a prestigious event was the October 1980 tour by the Vienna State Opera, with top ticket prices of $145. Min'on, which sponsored the visit together with *Asahi*, accepted the entire risk and tried to disarm critics by announcing in advance that it "expects a

---

Bob Dylan in early 1978, the latter drawing 150,000 fans to eleven concerts. *Asahi nenkan 1977*, p. 722. See *Asahi nenkan 1979*, p. 622.

huge deficit" which it would cover with "reserves accumulated over the past years." Still it seemed extravagant when Min'on took a $1.5 million loss on the engagement, the total budget for which was an astounding $8.5 million.[72]

Costs are a worry as well to the eleven main domestic opera companies, especially since their tickets sell for only a fourth of the prices commanded by foreign groups visiting Japan. The peak decade for opera activity was 1955-1965, a time when audience organizations replaced newspapers as the chief backers of performances by Japanese groups. Since 1965 public agencies, nonprofit sponsors, and the companies themselves have taken over as the main promoters.[73] Increasingly the opera groups have had to concentrate their resources, giving fewer but more lavish productions compared with ten or twenty years ago.

None of Japan's opera companies is full-time or strictly professional, even though the biggest, Nikikai, has an annual budget as large as a typical professional orchestra ($2.9 million in 1979). About thirty of its 330 members are singers paid by the performance, and the rest are amateur dancers, chorus members, technical personnel, students at its school, and managers.[i] Apart from the students, most are music teachers or persons in other professions who love opera. Nikikai's basic season in Tokyo consists of five productions a year, each performed four or five times, for an audience of 1,500 subscribers and 2,500 to 3,000 others for each work staged. Audience organizations do not purchase tickets for its events. Nikikai also puts on about twenty-five out-of-town performances a year, two-thirds of them underwritten by the cultural agency and the rest by the Bicycle Promotion Association.

Even though the government deliberately aids Japanese operas so they can develop a creditable level of performance, Nikikai earns more than 70 percent of its income from the box office and relies somewhat less than most orchestras on

[i] Kawachi Shōzō, executive director of Nikikai, says "it is not true that singers have to pay for their roles" despite numerous undocumented assertions to the contrary. Kawachi interview, December 3, 1980.

grants and subsidies. Smaller companies such as Fujiwara, Osaka Kansai, and Kansai Nikikai are even more part-time, often hiring Nikikai singers for their productions, and several of them specialize in certain forms of opera to avoid overlapping with Nikikai's emphasis on German and Austrian works.[74] Although Nikikai's well-to-do audiences in Tokyo pay prices well above the average for operas put on by Japanese performers, all the companies subsist primarily on the unpaid participation of the great majority of their members—the true patrons of the art.

JAPANESE arts leaders have labeled the 1980s "the age of culture," hoping for a public commitment to fulfill the efforts toward becoming a cultivated country begun by millions of private families soon after the war. Art-music became democratized during the postwar period because middle-class parents wanted their children to improve themselves through learning traditional Japanese or Western instruments and audience organizations wanted to put high-quality performances within the reach of nearly everyone, both financially and geographically. In most respects Japan is as musically sophisticated today as any nation, with a wide array of living genres that provide enjoyment and satisfaction at all social levels. Although formal music education leaves something to be desired, most Japanese schoolchildren are the envy of fellow students abroad because of their versatility with instruments and skill at reading music, often acquired from after-hour lessons.

Creativity managed to thrive despite methods of training that stressed technical accomplishments and encouraged performing careers with glamorous orchestras or operas. Many musicians, especially pianists and string players, grew so accomplished that they found jobs with the world's leading symphonies and chamber groups. Audiences grew more diverse and less easily mobilized by membership associations in the 1970s, when more commercial attractions competed for their attention, and the star system assured that the same social éclat accrued from attending a prominent concert as from studying an approved instrument. Although there sometimes seemed to be more performances than audiences to hear them, the glut of aspiring musicians in the 1970s was no greater than the deluge of would-be professionals in theater, dance, or the visual arts. Those who patronized the myriad musical events presumably drew pleasure from the experience, even though attending the orchestra still carried overtones of the same earnest self-cultivation that parents forced on their children at the keyboard or music stand.

CHAPTER 8

Dance: Contemporary Classics

HUNDREDS OF proud parents and fidgety children pack the municipal concert hall on a late spring afternoon almost anywhere in Japan to watch their daughters and sisters dance in the yearly recital of the local ballet school. Powerful speakers pour forth the familiar Tchaikovsky themes as the ten-year-old in her white tutu runs onstage to dance Odette or Odile from *Swan Lake* with a guest prince from a major Tokyo ballet company. The audience claps politely after the three- or four-minute pas de deux, the child is smothered in praise and gardenias, and the parents shell out fifty dollars to photographers and even more to the videotape team that records the event, complete with music and dubbed voice-over, for the family archive. While the exhausted young ballerina is led off to change, another of the 100 or more pupils has come onstage to do her routine with the tireless prince charming, who leaves town on the late train to begin rehearsing for another recital a few days later in a nearby city.[1]

Each child appearing in the spring recital pays the teacher $150 to $250 for the privilege, either in cash or by selling twenty to thirty tickets at $7.50 each (most families buy their allotment and give them away to friends and relations). They also pay about thirty-five dollars a month for twice-a-week lessons throughout the year, and extra money is needed for costumes and pointe shoes (at least a pair a month at twenty dollars per pair). Since Tokyo danseurs are much in demand out-of-town, a guest artist can make as much as $1,500 for an afternoon's work as the male lead at a local recital. By keeping rehearsals down to a single day before the event, a superstar like Nishi Yūichi of Shimotakaido in Tokyo can do ten recitals a month when he is not dancing with the Maki Asami Ballet Company.

After the day's expenses are met, the ballet school ends up clearing $10,000 to $15,000, which is used to subsidize the next public concert by its affiliated company. Unlike traditional Japanese music instructors, the head of the school does not have to share the proceeds with his or her former teachers. In varying degrees, student recitals supply the critical margin by which not only ballet but also contemporary and classical Japanese dance survive as art forms today. Middle-class families have become the economic backbone for all three main types of dance-art by sending 2 million of their children each year for lessons predictably geared toward technical mastery and stage performance. Dance subsisted before World War Two mainly on the patronage of the entertainment quarters. Today teaching provides the overwhelming bulk of its income and the main subsidies for stage performances in each genre.

CLASSICS AND POSTMODERNS

Like the other arts derived from Europe, Western-style dance entered Japan during the Meiji period—but just barely. In 1912, the last year of Meiji, the new Tokyo Imperial Theater brought the Italian ballet master Giovanni V. Rossi from London to teach both conventional balletic technique and the principles for modern creative ballet. Japanese audiences instantly turned ballet into a classic tradition, oblivious to the fact that it had seemed too frivolous, and perhaps too leggy, to be seen by proper young ladies in Europe during most of the nineteenth century. In his four years in Japan Rossi trained the generation that pioneered Western dance before World War Two.[2] As in Europe and America, ballet was the parent of the prewar modern dance movement, and the two remained closely identified until the 1930s as cognate insurgents against the indigenous dance heritage.

Even though it was taken in as a fixed orthodoxy from Europe, Western dance was as consciously iconoclastic as shingeki because to win acceptance it too had to surmount a weighty native tradition. The classical dance of Tokugawa kabuki stemmed from the stylized movements of fifteenth-century nō actors and ultimately from kagura-shrine dancing at the dawn of Japanese history. As the scholar Gunji Masakatsu points out, Western ballet movement was radiant and extensive, the arms stretched high, the body on pointe, leaping and pirouetting as though breaking free from the earth's shackles, whereas the classical Japanese dance against which Rossi and his followers rebelled was compacted and intensive, with arm gestures moving toward the body's center, hips close to the ground, and feet in contact with the floor, portraying a world of reality, not daydreams. Western dance showed the beauty of youth, but Japanese dance often treated the beauty of age. Ballet also asked its pupils to learn steps that could eventually be combined into any number of works, whereas classical Japanese dance taught complete pieces one at a time.[3] Rossi and his pupils introduced an art radical in techniques of movement, esthetic ideals, and teaching methods. The first public performance of the new idiom staged entirely by Japanese artists took place in June 1916, when the pioneer choreographer Ishii Baku used ideas from creative ballet to produce a dance-poem inspired by William Butler Yeats.

The dance-poem is also how another Rossi protégé, Itō Michio, made a name when his sensuous solos established him as a major choreographer in American during the 1920s and 1930s. Ishii, Itō, and others such as Eguchi Takaya and his wife Miya Misako studied abroad after World War One and eventually brought home dance styles heavy with expressionism from the Denishawn school in Los Angeles or Mary Wigman's institute in Germany. Another group went to Europe during the same period to master more conventional ballet styles. Still another style found its way to Japan when the classical ballerina Anna Pavlova drew throngs to the Imperial Theater in September 1920 and returned with her exiled sister in 1922 to teach the Russian balletic tradition.

Ballet had a certain following in the late twenties and early thirties, but modern dance offered regular concerts of new pieces each spring and fall and attracted full houses twice a month to Hibiya public hall in the early 1930s. The landmark work was Ishii's *Light and Dark* (*Meian*), an interpretation of the moody egoism and foreboding alienation in Natsume Sōseki's last novel.[4] Perhaps more than any other composition, this number helped to make Western-style dance a decisively Japanese form of expression. When Eguchi demonstrated Wigman's businesslike neue Tanz in 1934, audiences began to distinguish between ballet and modern dance, a separation that became much clearer after World War Two.

Ballet grew so popular in the biggest cities during 1945-1955 that it became practically synonymous with Western dance. The idea of a dance-play, already familiar from kabuki, appealed strongly to audiences in this period of cultural desiccation because of its fantasies of beautiful maidens and handsome swains. Students who tried ballet found it congenial because it trained them to execute stereotyped movements like arabesques, much as classical Japanese dance insisted on following set techniques. In the mid-1950s ballet became a disarmingly gentle weapon of cultural diplomacy in the cold war, bringing the Bolshoi, Leningrad, and New York City ballets for tours that stimulated Japanese dancers to form fresh companies of their own. Since audiences soon showed their preference for the most familiar classics, they were little disturbed by the narrowness of the Bolshoi's repertoire (today just thirty-two works, all but four of them Russian, mainly post-1917) and much dazzled by its effortless sentimentality.[5]

The torrent of ballet visitors, promoted by newspapers, audience associations, other nonprofit sponsors, and later the cultural agency and commercial impresarios as well as foreign governments, induced the new Japanese companies to specialize in either the contemporary mode of Robbins and Balanchine or the European classics—mainly the latter. Ever since Komaki Masahide first presented the complete *Swan Lake* in 1949, Japanese ballet fans have jammed the theaters for such standard romances as *Giselle*, the *Nutcracker*, and *Sleeping Beauty*.[6] Each of the three biggest Japanese companies has found a distinctive style and offered much fresh choreography of its own, but the classics are still the basis of their programs.

The Matsuyama troupe, formed in 1948, is the best-established ballet company in Japan and the only one that has tried to create a regular season. Its original works show the impress of contemporary Chinese theater—the group is sometimes called the red women's brigade—but classical routines are still its mainstays. Another group, the Maki Asami company, put on enormously ambitious performances of old and new works, through the skill of the dancer Tachibana Akiko, immediately after it was founded in 1963. Within three years it had lost nearly $50,000 on its productions, many of which brought in guest stars from the Soviet Union and East Europe, but the group kept on dancing thanks to the revenues from its huge ballet school. The Tchaikovsky Memorial Tokyo Ballet Company, which started in 1964, is the most businesslike of the Japanese ballet groups and the only one that has never used foreigners in the lead roles. But it has imported many Soviet coaches to help with productions, as well as choreographers from France, Cuba, and elsewhere. The troupe has sponsored tours by various ballets from abroad, and its own repertoire is by far the most classical of all the Japanese companies. It has also had the most success abroad.[7]

Postwar ballet has nonetheless been far more than a copy of the European or New York stage. Although neo-romantic nativism was even stronger among avant-garde contemporary dancers, various ballet choreographers in the late sixties and seventies wrote fresh pieces that drew on historical traditions in the Japanese arts. From the start the Maki Asami company attempted new works based on early Japanese literary themes, as did the Matsuyama group in numbers such as *Gion matsuri* (1963). Five years later Mishima Yukio showed his extraordinary versatility with *Miranda*, a ballet by leading Japanese dancers to honor the Meiji centennial. Many of the new works left more blank spaces on the stage and in the story than Western ballets, an ellipticality that some critics found appropriately Japanese. Undoubtedly the most inventive of the

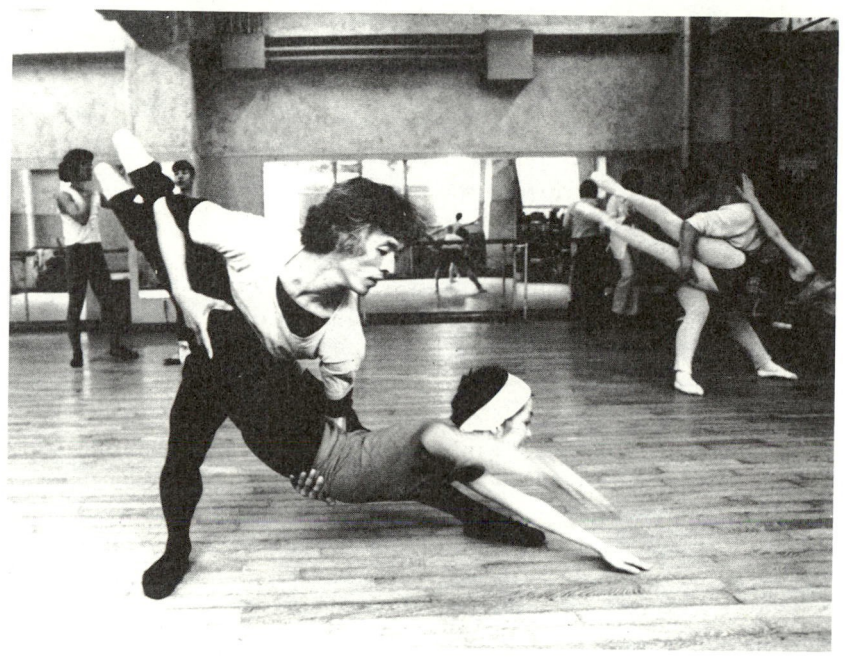

Kataoka Michito (danseur) and Murabayashi Miyuki rehearsing for a company performance by Star Dancers Ballet, Tokyo.
STAR DANCERS BALLET

companies was Star Dancers Ballet, founded by the prima ballerina Tachikawa Ruriko in 1964 and much influenced by the choreography of Anthony Tudor. The group put on ninety foreign and domestic works during 1964-1979 that emphasized ballet as theater, not "museum pieces" or "athletic meets," and built a loyal following "without subsidy, special favor or Swan Lake."[8]

But "official ballet culture, with its heavy Russian and classical European emphasis," makes it very difficult to keep contemporary works in the repertoire, says Kasuya Tatsuo, who directs his own company. The choreographer who wants to create a new production faces higher costs because the music

221

must be commissioned, more time is needed to rehearse the new steps, and little outside money is available to support fresh works. Most new creations are performed and then junked, since Japanese ballet fans seem to prefer *Coppélia* to Kasuya or any other contemporary artist.[9] Although superb danseurs like Hori Noboru now appear in stunning new compositions, the world-class prima Morishita Yōko of the Matsuyama company best symbolizes Japanese ballet today. This exquisite ballerina, who weighs just thirty-eight kilograms, has probably danced more classical roles than any other artist anywhere. From the moment she won a gold medal at the Varna competition in 1974, Morishita has been the one Japanese ballet performer of unquestioned distinction because of her flawless appearances on three continents as Swanhilda, Giselle, the Firebird, and, inevitably, Odette-Odile in *Swan Lake*.[10]

Visiting foreign artists also inspired a vast amount of activity among Japanese performers of contemporary dance after the war, and the results were artistically far more adventurous, if no better rewarded financially, than the efforts of most of the ballet groups. Right after the surrender in 1945, dancers trained abroad during the 1920s and 1930s returned to the stage, and they soon set aside solos and duets in favor of performances by ensembles and full companies. But contemporary dance was fully revitalized only in the mid-fifties, partly because of a brief tour in November 1955 by the Martha Graham Dance Company. Her style immediately took on the status of canonical doctrine among contemporary dancers, and even today the classic lyrical tradition of Graham at her peak looms over much of the fresh choreography. During the next decade practically every important contemporary-dance group from America performed in Japan, and more and more Japanese went to New York for training, a few of them with government scholarships starting in 1964.[11] Several ended up dancing with the Graham company, the Alvin Ailey group, and other top-line New York troupes. By the mid-sixties Japan was America's one serious rival as a center of contemporary

222

dance—true also of jazz, the only other uniquely American art form.

Japan's most creative performers discovered that contemporary dance offered clusters of visual impressions rather than the simpler clarity of ballet, and they found that these complex and often intermittent images appealed strongly in a society where communication without words was much favored. Choreographers chose their themes from all of life and nature, rather than limiting themselves to the religious or aristocratic subjects portrayed in other dance genres. Many of their compositions conveyed the existential texture of daily life in a complicated urban world, one that choreographers neither idealized nor condemned but simply tried to present as it was.

Although the borders between dance genres do not easily submit to definition, three layers of contemporary dance have developed during the quarter-century since Graham first appeared in Japan: classical modern dance in the Humphrey-Graham tradition (modan dansu); postmodern or vanguard dance influenced by Trisha Brown, Simone Forti, and Lonny David Gordon (gendai or zen'ei buyō); and gendai or ankoku butō, an even more avant-garde dance theater of nativist nostalgia paralleling the underground playwrights who perform in tents.[12] In the 1960s much of the new Japanese choreography was still openly derivative, but by 1975 there was little question that artists in each layer were grappling with problems of present-day life in a thoroughly Japanese way, not through some bland mid-Pacific style.

No Japanese dancer has shown a greater array of themes through movement than Akiko Kanda, who is Graham's best-known pupil in Japan. "I find it hard to talk systematically about dance," Kanda has admitted. "I hardly ever consciously think about what dancing is, what dance means to me." The unifying thread of her diverse choreography since the late sixties has been the transformation of woman, past and present, young and old, both Japanese and foreign. Kanda has ransacked the legends of early Japanese drama for themes she often portrays to music from the accordion, chansons, the

Chinese fiddle, or Gershwin. She has also put on physically demanding solos based on the life of Marie Antoinette (*Conciérgerie*, 1974) and the loves of a young woman (*Barbara*, 1980)[13] that show her greater control of detail and wider range of styles than any other performer active during the 1970s in Japan.

Atsugi Bonjin was the most representative postmodern choreographer during the same period, inasmuch as his trilogy of *Kamu, Haku,* and *Hana wa kurenai* (1969-1970) denied the dance dictum that something has to be expressed. His performers stopped time with Polaroid camera shots and ran laps around a gym floor to show that movement was all that counted and that their dance of exhaustion had no higher purpose than the physical self. In *Retsukigo* (two parts, 1975) he rehabilitated the body, which had disappeared inside a huge transparent vinyl pillow two years earlier in *Vanish*. His occasional partner Watanabe Gen went a step further in *Utopia* (1977), which emphasized freedom for all humanity. Watanabe's utopia was one not of fantasy but of dissonant abandon, in which each performer set aside existing conventions of movement and danced entirely in accord with his or her physical capabilities.[14]

Two other vanguard choreographers developed the ideas of rebellion and personal freedom even further in the 1970s. Tanegashima Yukiko approached her art through "situationalism" or "circumstantialism" (*jōkyōron*) in works such as *Pianissimo* (1973), which put the dancers through seventy minutes of vigorous, almost driven movement without values or meaning apart from the reality of the flesh. Hanayagi Suzushi, who performs classical Japanese dances each year in New York, also puts on experimental farces in Osaka that spoof *Swan Lake* without creating any alternative meaning. All that she and her company reveal are certain events at a certain time with particular people, through movement that is much less beautiful but much more tangible than Kanda's classic modern dance. Like Atsugi, Watanabe, and Tanegashima, Suzushi comes very close to "that creative freedom which finds ultimate expression in being a law unto one's self."[15]

The artist who took the postmodern concentration on the body to its limits in the 1970s was the ankoku butō leader Hijikata Tatsumi, whose Asbestos Theater in Shinjuku is famous "for bizarre dances best described as neo-baroque theater."[16] The op artist Yokoo Tadanori has had as great an effect on Hijikata as on the underground playwrights, prompting the choreographer to find significance in the detritus of everyday life early in the twentieth century because contemporary society is so barren and meaningless. Hijikata is almost as polemical about Kanda's flowing modern dances as he is about ballet. He takes the body as it is, dealing with the world as it exists, rather than remolding human movements to explore literary legends or outright fantasies. *Hitogata* (1976), with Ashikawa Yōko as the lead dancer, showed Hijikata's belief that movement is the most concrete, definite, and pivotal aspect of the body, an absolute found in each individual's body, immune to idealism or human will.[17] It simply exists by itself, beyond Graham's and Kanda's fusion of mental and physical activity, side by side with Atsugi's and Suzushi's denial of any purpose beyond movement itself.

In 1965 the themes of most contemporary compositions were very clear: happiness, sorrow, anger, jealousy.[18] Then the postmodern artists and avant-garde followers of Hijikata's so-called dance of darkness began to offer works that were more puckish, uncommitted, and indistinct. Their emphasis on the situation or circumstance, and their ambivalence about it, seemed very well tuned to the nonabsolute, concrete quality of most Japanese social thinking after the war. The tangible matrix of daily interaction with other people marked out the limits within which choreographers defined the individual dealing with the realities of contemporary society. Nearly all the dancers from Kanda to Hijikata have reacted against the formalism of ballet and rejected the weight of past art or ideas about destiny. Choice and freedom are the hallmarks of the movement shown on their stages. Thus far few younger choreographers have surfaced to explore layers different from these various antiexpressionists who have made Tokyo as exciting as any city outside New York for contemporary dancers.

Classical Japanese dance after the war slowly began to convert from a salon art to one also seen in the public concert hall. Just as contemporary dancers began using kabuki themes in the mid-1960s, classical Japanese choreographers started to write new works for ensembles as well as soloists, in feeble imitation of a corps de ballet. The Tōyoko department store in Tokyo began sponsoring an annual festival of new pieces for classical Japanese dance in 1968, and both the cultural agency and the Tokyo city authorities have given money each year to encourage creativity. Such leading contemporary-dance personalities as Fukuda Ippei, Shōji Hiroshi, and Orita Katsuko began working with classical Japanese choreographers in the early 1970s,[19] but the results fell short of a formal movement comparable to contemporary hōgaku.

Several artists in the Hanayagi school of classical Japanese dance borrowed from contemporary-dance choreography to offer highly abstract works in the mid-1970s, including Hanayagi Shigeka and Hanayagi Teruna. The latter hired one of the favorite stages of contemporary dancers, the Jean Jean theater in a church grotto in Shibuya, to produce "underground" Japanese-style dance that succeeded artistically and played to full houses in 1975-1976. Hanayagi Chiyo adapted the Graham method to teach basic movements before starting students on complete dances, a shocking challenge to the hoary custom of transmitting a dance tradition intact.[20]

Gradually the number of public concerts in classical Japanese dance increased, helped along by NHK programming that showed ten times more performances of the genre than of ballet or contemporary dance. Most of the public productions by the end of the seventies were sponsored by government agencies, either through grants for creative activity or through arts festivals, but far more performances, as before, took the form of private recitals for audiences connected in some tangible way with the artists who appeared.[21] As with traditional Japanese music and the other dance forms, teaching remained the bedrock of classical Japanese dancing, and its proceeds were so lucrative that all but the most devoted performers had little incentive to improvise or display their talents in public.

HONORING THE HEADMASTER

Shortly before individual returns are due each year the Japanese authorities publicize a few sensational cases of income-tax evasion. In January 1981 the police raided the home of Ikenobō Sen'ei, headmaster of Japan's largest school of floral art, and discovered a safe containing $600,000 in the floor of his living-room alcove beneath a vase of fresh flowers. Ikenobō was accused of failing to report this income over the previous five years, received as honoraria from students when he sponsored displays of their skill. "Because they can deliver a large number of votes at election time by dragooning their myriad pupils,"[22] flower teachers can usually count on politicians to keep the tax inspectors at bay, but in this case the apparent abuse was too large to cover up.

Shocking as the disclosure was, Ikenobō was by no means the wealthiest headmaster of an artistic school. The income he reported for 1979 was $381,000, compared with $1.3 million for Sen Sōshitsu, head of the Urasenke tea school. By comparison, Oh Sadaharu, the all-time home-run king, declared $833,000 in income for 1979, and the wealthiest practitioner of a Western-derived art, the oil painter Umehara Ryūzaburō, reported $773,000. None was among the top 100 incomes for the year.[23]

The headmaster system in nearly all the traditional Japanese arts has prospered since World War Two because of new patronage from millions of middle-class families. Among schools of the performing arts, none have grown richer than the various branches of classical Japanese dance, which is quite possibly the world's most expensive art form to learn. By now the headmaster system, with its spiderweb of teacher-pupil relationships spread all over the country, is largely independent of the pleasure districts where it began centuries ago, and it is easily the largest source of support for the most popular genre of dance-art in the country, classical Japanese dance.

The market for lessons of every sort ballooned during 1955-1965 because of economic prosperity and the postwar baby boom. Studying dance or Debussy not only trained children spiritually and provided them with a talent, Inumaru Tadashi points out, but it also "gave persons of all ages a circle to join, a group centering on the teacher."[24] Many people liked having a teacher to depend on for instruction and moral support, someone they could take direction from and talk about afterward with their friends. (Not just doctors and dentists but even barbers and hairdressers are called "teacher" by their assistants.) Being a good wife and wise mother, the prewar formula, was redefined to mean mastering the skills of beauty and acquiring an air of cultivated refinement. By the 1970s it was customary for families to spend fifty dollars a month or more for some combination of after-school tutoring and arts training for each child in elementary and junior high school—perhaps math lessons twice a week and ballet two other afternoons. The clientele for lessons stopped growing by 1980, some arts administrators think,[25] probably because of declining birthrates rather than any doubts about the personal or social advantages of learning an art form.

Studying either classical Japanese dancing or the dances of nō theater means submitting to the discipline of the headmaster system for as long as the pupil continues to take lessons—often for many decades. Only men appeared on the nō stage in the Tokugawa era, but since the early twentieth century women have studied as amateurs and now form the majority of pupils, especially for nō dancing (men prefer to learn chanting). Today well over a million students pay fifty dollars or more per month to study with a licensed teacher in one of the five schools of nō, and they must also fork over an honorarium to the teacher to appear at the annual recital. Students receive certificates rather than stage names, and the school strictly regulates who may become "specialists," or full-time professional actors. Specialists teach three times a week for just three months a year, enough to cover the deficits from their public performances and make a tidy living besides.[26]

The million or so students of classical Japanese dance are dispersed among more than 200 schools, each with its own headmaster. The Fujima, Hanayagi, Wakayagi, and Bandō schools are the largest. Most of the others have been founded in the past twenty years by breakaway teachers "since anyone can take on the title headmaster and found an independent school," says Hinoshita Yoshimitsu, business manager of the Japan Classical Dance Association. "Its success depends entirely on whether it draws students," ten of whom form the bare minimum that a one-teacher school needs to survive. Usually pupils pay a private teacher about ten dollars per lesson for five or six individual or small-group sessions a month, although NHK and the newspapers run large courses in classical Japanese dance for half this price.[27] The big money changes hands, as in nō and traditional Japanese music, at the time of the yearly recital.

Both amateur students and professional teachers with stage names are expected to perform in private recitals and pay extravagantly for the privilege. Since most professional instructors do not have enough pupils to fill a program, they often sponsor joint recitals with other teachers in the same school of dance. The student ordinarily pays the teacher an honorarium of $300 to $500 or is forced to sell the equivalent in tickets to the event.[28] A portion of the fee is passed along to the headmaster. Each pupil appears in a brief number and quickly retires backstage to receive well-wishers, who come and go freely in the audience while the day-long program is underway. The same kinds of invited audiences that appear for ballet or hōgaku recitals fill the auditorium, except that there is a greater age range among the friends and relatives attending because performers go on studying for most of their lives.

Gaudier by far are the yearly recitals by the teachers themselves, who perform for the headmaster or the senior teachers who originally trained them. A professional with a stage name (*natori*) in classical Japanese dance spends nearly $10,000 to put on a single ten- or fifteen-minute number, and most recitals offer about two dozen such works. If it is a duet, the performers divide the costs. The headmaster or senior teacher receives at least a third of this amount as an honorarium and can earn $75,000 or more for a single recital, of which several are held every day by various schools during the busiest seasons. Dancers with stage names are willing to pay the headmaster such sums because they need to keep the right to teach, realizing too that part of their allure to amateur pupils comes from bearing the school's name.[29]

Among all the Japanese performing arts, a full-scale recital of classical dance is unsurpassed for its opulence, but the atmosphere is one of subdued elegance rather than parvenu ostentation. A woman performer pays huge sums to rent a luxurious kimono of silk brocade, and she offers generous tips to the dressing-room assistant, the wig arranger, and the stage second who hands her a fan and helps her into zori. Each of the dancers shares in the rental of the hall and pays additional fees for sets, screens, and the runner who trots across the stage pulling the traditional orange, green, and black striped curtain. The half-dozen singers and samisen accompanists receive about $100 apiece from the recitalists for each number.[30]

The dancer sometimes also has to bear the costs of printing invitations for family and friends, ordering box lunches for them, purchasing their tickets, and perhaps giving them souvenirs in the well-known wrapping of a chic department store. As in the case of hōgaku recitals, guests often leave cash contributions for the performers at the lobby, where it is not rare for a tax inspector to be lurking discreetly.[31] Since many of those who are invited are amateur pupils of the dancer who is appearing, their fees sustain the recital system thrice over: through monthly tuitions, honoraria when they themselves perform, and gifts at the teacher's recital.[a]

[a] A widely publicized episode symbolized the large sums contributed by audiences when Onoe Shōroku, a kabuki actor who was then the head of

To prepare for her performance at the Fujimorikai concert in December 1980, the professional dancer Fujima Tsurutarō had to practice her fifteen-minute number for two months. "I rehearsed for this performance six times each month with my teacher," who picked the selection and collected sizeable tuition payments for supervising the practice sessions. Tsurutarō's yearly kimono bills are about $5,000, and she has a side job as a Ginza entertainer to support her art. When the relatively new Segawa school held a Valentine's Day recital at the national theater in 1981, it hired a top bunraku narrator, Takemoto Mojitayū, and a leading samisen artist, Nozawa Katsuhei, to accompany part of the six-hour-long program. Like most such events, the setting was quietly ornate, with dancers in vivid scarlet and gold kimono and black high-lacquer clogs against a backdrop of conventionalized simplicity. The well-heeled audience included many elderly men and geisha from the Shinbashi-Tsukiji district of Tokyo, where a number of the performers worked.[32]

Although the headmaster system has long since escaped the demimonde, training dancers to entertain at geisha houses remains a source of prestige for the dance schools, despite the fact that most geisha end up performing only for undemanding and uncritical audiences of graying businessmen and politicians who patronize their establishments. In light of the rivalry geisha face from sleek Ginza bar hostesses and sophisticated entertainers in Roppongi clubs, many persons have predicted their demise. But Liza Crihfield Dalby, the ranking scholar of the subject, estimates that there were still 17,000 registered geisha in the mid-seventies, and others believe the number may be even greater now. All of them study some form of classical Japanese dance, although few advance to the point of taking stage names. Even those who do so do not necessarily

the Fujima school of classical Japanese dance, sponsored a major recital. A large barrel-like drum was placed at the front of the theater and Shōroku had to jump into it more than once to trample down the envelopes thick with 10,000-yen notes donated by the audience. Onoe Tatsunosuke, whose dance name is Fujima Kan'emon, has succeeded Shōroku as head of the school. Kishibe Shigeo interview, January 26, 1981; Kawashima interview, November 27, 1980; Nobumoto interview, January 30, 1981.

teach, since having a stage name is a status more than a function. As Kawashima Takeyoshi puts it, "the name *natori* is highly respected, but people are relatively uninterested in artists' individual skills."[33]

Nearly everyone agrees that the headmaster system thwarts competition and preserves a way of life and art that is not subject to objective critical standards. Most performers in a traditional art seem to believe that "it's beautiful because it's ours, not ours because it's beautiful." In this sense the traditional arts resemble the Tokyo art market, in which large sums of money likewise maintain an artificial hierarchy with internalized standards of artistic value. Like vanity publishing or shows by Sunday painters, such a system does little to improve the state of the art because it is very hard to learn anything from people who never disagree with you.

Still, for all its defects, the headmaster system has protected the traditional arts when few other supporters were available. Many Japanese seem to think the regimen needs to be made simpler and less expensive, but Katō Mikio of International House points out that headmasters "are not exploitative, because the Japanese people willingly pay their money" to keep the system intact.[34] As long as studying an art fulfills so many social as well as esthetic needs, the traditional arts are likely to stay firmly perched on the financial rock of the Japanese middle class.

FROM STUDIO TO STAGE

"There really are no professional ballet companies in Japan, despite their claims," says Ogawa Ayako, who directs her own group, "since the dancers usually are not paid for their performances. Even the male leads make most of their money from out-of-town student recitals, not from dancing with the company, and many of the ballerinas have to pay if they want to perform."[35] What is undeniably true of ballet is equally the case for contemporary dance, whose companies are weaker and audiences slimmer. Japanese ballet artists and contemporary dancers are professional teachers who depend on revenues from middle-class pupils to finance the public concerts of their art. Their companies are invariably part-time enterprises without independent existences. In most cases the dance academy is the main body and its performing company an appendage that could not survive on its own.

Although ballet lacks a headmaster system, it like the other arts in Japan is a closed world full of subjective teacher-pupil affinities, bitter rivalries among schools, and cloying encouragements to all but the most inept learners. Yet at least it enforces standards through open competitions for students of real talent and through the demands of public performance, unlike the airtight universe of classical Japanese dance. The future ballerina usually starts with the neighborhood instructor, paying thirty-five dollars a month for two ninety-minute lessons each week and $150 or more to perform in the annual recital. Parents are rarely able to judge the teacher's qualifications and prefer having their daughters study with the other neighborhood children, although there is no absolute bar to switching studios if it seems warranted.[36]

"There are too many ballet teachers in Japan," according to Nishina Tadashi, an executive of the principal private foundation aiding the genre. "Instead of perfecting their art to only a partial level and then turning to teaching, ballet dancers should pursue it further." Shimada Hiroshi of the Japan Ballet Association notes that anyone can take classes for a few months at a well-known ballet academy and then hang out a shingle to teach privately. Both men agree that there is a thirst for learning ballet and that performing by itself provides no livelihood for dancers, but they despair at the lack of professional controls or uniform standards, especially in comparison with classical Japanese dance.[37] Even so, the average ballet or contemporary-dance teacher has at least seventy-five pupils, three times the figure for classical dance, and 30 percent in a recent survey reported teaching more than 150.[38] Such numbers alone make it very difficult to enforce professional discipline, no matter how well trained the instructor.

The biggest and most prestigious teaching enterprises are the commercial academies operated by major ballet companies. The Tchaikovsky Memorial Tokyo Ballet Company, the Maki Asami group, and the Matsuyama company all run tightly organized and extremely efficient schools with more than 500 pupils from early childhood on up. The largest is the Hōmura Tomoi Ballet Academy in Osaka, with 2,000 students. All of them charge fees comparable to those of individual neighborhood teachers for younger pupils and proportionately more for students who need additional hours as they mature. The bulk of those studying ballet are children, and most who learn contemporary dance are young women. The total number of persons who have studied one or the other now exceeds the figure for classical Japanese dance, but because pupils of the latter go on taking lessons for decades, the numbers studying it at any given moment are somewhat greater (about a million, versus 700,000 for ballet and 800,000 for contemporary dance).[39]

What students learn at ballet school reflects the czar-like grip of the classics. "Only in Japan," says Hattori Chieko, president of the Japan Ballet Association, "do ballet companies put on the full *Swan Lake*, and only here do the academies force children to learn the unfamiliar as well as the most famous scenes." Since training for everyone is pointed toward performance, *Swan Lake* has become the Nitten or *Ninth* of the ballet world. Hattori adds that "no one ever stops to ask whether the children perform it well. What counts is that you have danced *Swan Lake*, not how well. In other countries dancers quit if they have no talent, but in Japan no one wants to criticize, so dancers go along without really competing very severely."[40] With so few artistic controls, almost anyone can appear onstage by belonging to the right group—a major reason why so many productions seem more earnest than edifying. But art serves the society as well as itself, and avoiding confrontation, joining the group enterprise, and taking part rather than starring are social values intrinsic to the world of ballet no less than to Japanese life as a whole.

For reasons of this sort, as well as middle-class fashion and spiritual discipline, parents are perfectly willing to support lavish recitals that underwrite public ballet productions by their children's teachers. Although Ogawa believes "there is no natural ballet audience outside the biggest cities," many out-of-town parents like to send their children to dance classes because it is considered refined, middle class, and something Tokyo families do.[41] In this way ballet, like oil painting, shingeki, and the orchestra, has become a nationwide phenomenon socially, even if it is not yet fully appreciated artistically.

To raise the level of the art, Hattori and many others think Japan needs a national ballet academy so that gifted young dancers can escape the oppression of senior high-school entrance exams. Students in junior high school face so much pressure to get ready for the tests that few of them can afford to dance more than two or three times a week. A national academy would parallel the high-school system, "allowing students to learn dance and also the history, literature, culture, and music that accompany ballet," says Nishina Tadashi, who notes ruefully that "even the Egyptians are ahead of us now, with a well-rounded ballet academy established with Soviet aid."[42] Men can wait until college, when free time abounds, to take up ballet and still become stars. For reasons of physiology women anywhere must begin dancing at an early age if they are to rise to the top, and potential ballerinas in Japan currently must pick between the studio-only training in private ballet schools and going abroad to London, Moscow, or New York—if they can afford the choice.

As in other countries, most Japanese take up contemporary dance after studying ballet, and correspondingly fewer children and more young adults populate contemporary-dance classes. Today many middleaged housewives are also taking part, according to the critic Ichikawa Miyabi, because "dance is part of the body-culture boom. People everywhere are jogging, doing t'ai-chi, karate, and yoga, and they're also dancing to stay fit." In the biggest cities, learning contemporary dance is just as fashionable among women between fifteen and twenty-five as ballet is among children, and like lessons in any art the training is deemed good for building character among the young. Some Japanese who fear their physiques may be ill-suited for the conventionalized movements of ballet prefer the greater variety of styles offered by contemporary dance. Whatever the motive, the number of pupils has tripled in the last twenty years, and as with the other dance genres nearly all are females.[43]

Students of contemporary dance pay the same monthly fees as in ballet, thirty-five dollars for two ninety-minute classes a week, and they likewise may choose between big dance academies and private lessons from neighborhood teachers, who are even more numerous than ballet instructors. Possibly because contemporary dance in Japan has few works on the scale of grand ballet, the grasp of the companies is weaker and fewer dance schools are directly connected with production groups than in ballet. The largest is the Eguchi Otoya Dance Academy in Osaka, with more than 1,000 pupils, and a half-dozen major schools in Tokyo have several hundred students each. Contemporary-dance people half-jokingly refer to a headmaster system in their art, since pioneers like Ishii Baku, Takada Masao, Hirata Masao, and Watanabe Takashi have conferred stage names on their followers.[44] Ballet too has well-known examples of hereditary succession, notably the Matsuyama and Maki Asami companies. Although the world of contemporary dancers in Japan is more open than ballet, both have been torn by factionalism and neither has much control over defectors who split off to start new academies.

Contemporary dance in Japan takes in everything from kathakali and flamenco to Israeli folk dancing, as well as the main lineages of German and American dance, but much of what is taught to younger pupils and displayed at recitals is still remarkably prettified and dainty. Like students of ballet or classical Japanese dance, contemporary-dance pupils are expected to appear in yearly recitals and pay for the honor. But because they are older than ballet students and less committed to a lifetime of instruction than those in classical dance, the recitalists in contemporary dance are usually spared the tyranny of flowers, strobe flashes, and extravagant honoraria to the teacher. Instead their instructors depend mostly on the income from large classes, often in widely scattered locations, to finance their own stage performances.[45]

Nearly all the lessons in contemporary dance still take place privately, but minute amounts of dance are included in primary-school gym classes, and teachers are free to choose whichever genre they please. Formal dance courses are offered at a few colleges and universities, and graduate training has been available since 1964, but most dance activity is still extracurricular.[46] As with the other arts, the campus is not an important patron of any dance style, either as an employer of instructors or entrepreneur of performances for student audiences.

Nearly all of the twenty main ballet companies and many of the thirty leading performing groups in contemporary dance are based in Tokyo, but ballet is seen more often on the road because of its particular cachet with middle-class families there and because government agencies have funded performances for children, youths, and local arts festivals. Contemporary dance started to become a publicly supported touring enterprise only in the late seventies, even though the cultural agency has long sponsored performances in the biggest cities.[47]

At least two-thirds of all contemporary dance events, and perhaps three-quarters of those in ballet, are student recitals for private audiences. A majority of the performances by professionals open to the public are sponsored by the dancers themselves, as individuals or companies, but a sizeable minority in contemporary dance and a somewhat smaller share in ballet are subsidized by government agencies. Yet dance companies depend relatively less than orchestras or opera groups on public aid. Min'on and Rōon, which used to schedule ballet fairly regularly, still occasionally sponsor performances by Japanese groups, but usually they prefer to book visiting foreign companies. The Tōkyō shinbun is the only regular private backer of contemporary-dance concerts apart from the contemporary-dance association itself. Altogether there were about 750 public performances of contemporary dance in 1980, double the figure just five years earlier, and another 350 or so in ballet. But ballet drew about 60 percent of the nearly 1 million customers who attended public events in the two genres.[48]

The biggest ballet companies have annual budgets of more than $2 million, earning much of their income from their academies. The busiest groups put on a half-dozen different ballets each year, at a cost of $100,000 to $150,000 for each production, and normally perform each work just once or twice because audiences are so small.[b] Only a third of the production expenses are recovered at the box office or through the small patrons' circles that the more important companies maintain. Government subsidies sometimes supplement the receipts, but most of the gap is covered by tuitions and recital fees from the affiliated ballet school.[49] Teaching is so profitable that a relatively large number of ballet companies can afford to put on a handful of performances each, rather than consolidating to form a few groups offering full seasons to the small pool of fans. The Japanese ballet world is so balkanized and uncommunicative that no fewer than three productions of the stale classic *La Bayadère* were staged, by sorry chance, during the 1980-1981 season.

A large company has about forty dancers and brings in others if they are needed for a specific work. It is widely believed that a ballerina must often pay an honorarium to her company if she wishes a star role. The size of the fee, usually estimated at $1,500 to $2,500, cannot be verified, but there is little doubt that the practice is common.[50] Normally only

[b] Critics play a very minor role in the dance world. Shimada Hiroshi of the Japan Ballet Association says they "are usually correspondents assigned to cover ballet by their editors, not critics with a detailed knowledge of dance." He adds that "apparently some dance critics accept gifts of money in exchange for favorable reviews. This is really inevitable in a competitive society. So many young persons want to succeed in the dance world, and some will pay to get ahead." Shimada interview, December 6, 1980.

the male dancers are paid for their performances, and then not very well. For most of the corps, appearing in a production is an extra unpaid duty of teachers at the company's school, as well as a chance to dance in public.

Kasuya Tatsuo forms a company each spring from the teachers at his ballet academy in Tokyo and puts on a single performance of one work. The production usually costs about $30,000, half of it met by ticket sales. Nearly everyone who attends is a pupil of the school or otherwise connected with the performers; virtually no seats are sold through Playguide or to walk-ins on the day of the performance. If his group gets a cultural-agency subvention through the Japan Ballet Association, it can afford to put on a second performance each year in an arts festival or touring program. Advertising and printing costs are so outrageous, Kasuya says, that his company cannot reasonably move beyond its basically private audience to seek a wider public.[51] His group is typical of all but the largest ballet and modern-dance companies, which are essentially part-time clusters of professional teachers who pay, like opera singers, to display their talent.[c]

"We do ballet because we like it," says the former prima Tachikawa Ruriko of Star Dancers Ballet. "If we had a head-master system like classical Japanese dance, we could spend all our time teaching and make a comfortable profit, but we have to do performances for the sake of our art." Her large company hires a top orchestra, rents a big theater, and puts on striking productions of Japanese and foreign works several times a year. About half of the tickets are sold directly by the dancers to their friends and relatives, and many of the rest are bought by current or former pupils at the ballet school.

[c] Ogawa Ayako, who danced extensively in New York, directs a ballet studio in the Koma Stadium in Shinjuku that puts on two public performances a year. Each production costs about $30,000 and loses $7,500 even with crowds of 1,300 per performance. Ogawa is rare among ballet directors in that she pays her dancers fees as high as $250 for each appearance, but in return they must sell as many as fifty tickets to the event or pay for the empty seats themselves. Each production is performed just once since there is no audience for a second showing. Ogawa interview, November 21, 1980.

239

Tachikawa counts on losing $25,000 a year on the public performances, making it up through revenues from teaching.[52]

When choreographers who lack a dance school of their own want to put on a ballet or contemporary-dance work, they often assemble a temporary company of present or former students and a few paid male leads. The contemporary-ballet choreographer Hashiura Isamu offers a single performance of one new work every two years, "because that's all I can afford to put on from my income from teaching." For his production of *Princess Medea* in December 1980, Hashiura brought in perhaps the most skilled premier danseur in the country, Hori Noboru, and counted on the corps of twenty-five to sell thirty tickets each. Even with his mostly volunteer cast, who performed out of loyalty to their teacher and because they wanted the exposure, Hashiura took a heavy loss on the event.[53] Like artists in every genre, he counts on making sacrifices in order to be his own patron.

Ballet audiences often include children whose appreciation of the art is only beginning, and they are overwhelmingly female—even in the case of Star Dancers Ballet, which has more male dancers and fans than most. Although tickets average twenty dollars for performances by one of the top companies, cost is only a minor reason why attendance has stayed relatively small. The Japanese ballet world, says Inumaru Tadashi, "is still a modern form of the headmaster system, although looser," an activity intended mainly for devotees and largely closed to outsiders.[54] Although several million Japanese have received training in ballet technique, there is little public appreciation of it as art and little inclination to watch a performance unless one's teacher is appearing.

The former Bolshoi prima Sulamith Messerer, who has coached Japanese dancers since 1960, praises her pupils for their enthusiasm and discipline. She finds that they have "excellent concentration and musical sense," and she believes their achievements are "amazing considering Japan's lack of a ballet tradition." The only remaining difficulty is that "few Japanese have good bodies for ballet."[55] Hattori Chieko points out another problem: "more than anything else we need a national ballet company. Bringing in foreign coaches and choreographers is far too narrow an approach, since they reach the pupils of just one small company." The proposal has been discussed seriously in the cultural agency, without a decision. A home for a national company could be found in the new national arts complex opening west of Shinjuku in 1986, but the government has expressed no taste for the financial commitment such a step would require. Equally ominous is the hostility among the existing companies, whose complete cooperation would be essential to make the venture work.[56]

Contemporary-dance groups have only recently begun to shed their worst factional rivalries, but they are probably even more riven with artistic disputes than the ballet companies— a healthy omen for the quality of their productions. The contemporary-dance association, now dominated by younger artists, has been exceptionally active in sponsoring performances and contests for newcomers. Since the mid-1970s small companies have sprouted so fast that the association has been unable to channel enough funds from the cultural agency and other public sources to the new groups, forcing them to appear in coffee-shop theaters and other out-of-the-way places. Only the most avant-garde performers lack a financial cushion from teaching, but many of them moonlight in cabaret revues and strip shows. Since the audience for contemporary dance has grown very little while performances have doubled since 1975, the attendance has fragmented because of so many small events.[57]

Some contemporary-dance companies are connected with private dance schools, but all of them consist of a choreographer or teacher and about ten senior pupils, each of whom teaches or does other work on the side. Like most ballet groups, the companies perform sporadically, pay no salaries, and usually retrieve only a third of their performing expenses from ticket sales. Audiences contain almost no one except women under twenty-five, mainly pupils or friends of the dancers.

None of the contemporary-dance groups offers a formal season or maintains a patrons' circle of any size.[58] Like ballet companies and artists who hold one-person shows, they carefully keep mailing lists of prospective customers and religiously circulate questionnaires at their concerts to ferret out new names from each audience.

One of the busiest ensembles is the Akiko Kanda Dance Pantheon, formed in 1969 by the most talented of Japan's many artists who pursue the lyrical tradition of classical modern dance. Members of the company undergo ten years of rigorous training, during which they pay for classes and receive nothing for their appearances in concerts. Currently the group includes sixteen members, five of whom are able to make a living entirely from dance because they teach children in the Tokyo suburbs. The others must find side jobs. Even Kanda herself earns very little from her dance school, because it has only fifty students. "There are three pillars to my work," she says: "choreography, teaching, and dancing. I've been concentrating on dancing and choreography, so I have relatively few students." But she also composes works for the Takarazuka troupe near Osaka and gives master classes there for as many as 4,000 students a year.[59]

The Kanda company offers ten regular productions a year, averaging $50,000 each to put on, and various members give smaller recitals twice a month. Kanda is in the rare position of being able to count on enough ticket revenue to break even for the year, but only because she is famous and "only because I don't pay my dancers—just as I too wasn't paid when I performed with companies in New York." Kanda is unique among Japanese dancers in having drawn outstanding musicians, visual artists, writers, and actors to help with her productions, and in 1981 she opened a new studio where her art can flourish after she retires from the stage. "It's all right for my style to end with me," she says, "so long as some of my ideas stay with my pupils as they develop their own styles."[60] As long as the allure of the classics persists, Kanda's approach is unlikely to perish.

ALL three main forms of dance-art have prospered since the war because of teaching and by now could hardly get by without it. But only contemporary dance has truly flourished artistically as well as financially, quite possibly because it lacks the structured formality of a headmaster system or the institutional security of ballet, with well-established companies attached to businesslike academies. Authority is clear and discipline strict in contemporary-dance troupes no less than in ballet companies or schools of classical Japanese dance. But contemporary groups are organizationally more flexible, far more open to outside ideas, and offer a form of dance with solos and small ensembles that needs no elaborate company system. All of this has helped establish a creative tension that has produced some of the most imaginative and powerful choreography seen anywhere in the 1970s and early 1980s. Yet all three genres of dance in Japan remain fundamentally private arts, watched by audiences that are often more interested in corsages and tutus than in the beauty of movement on the stage.

CHAPTER 9

The Vertical Mosaic

POSING AS a fan carrying a bouquet, the dancer Hanayagi Genshū brushed past guards at the stage entrance, dashed to the dressing rooms, and stabbed Hanayagi Jusuke, head of the dominant school of classical Japanese dance, after a concert one evening in February 1980 at the national theater in Tokyo. Genshū's weapon, concealed in the flowers, inflicted two minor cuts—just enough, she told police, to call attention to her twelve-year campaign to end the headmaster system in the traditional arts. The dancer had been virtually excommunicated by the school after appearing nude onstage in 1968, and ever since she battled the system to no avail.[1]

Like the painting slasher Yamashita nine months later, Genshū shocked the arts world. With her attack on the headmaster, she jolted the establishment that had excluded her for flouting its precepts. Both episodes called attention to the status of artists in contemporary Japanese life, now that society was so prosperous but old-line arts institutions were still so entrenched.[a] Although no responsible artist condoned these acts of violence, each assault symbolized the impatience that churned within the vertical mosaic of the arts as Japan entered the 1980s.

One reason why artists are anxious is that they are paid so poorly, even by the impecunious standards of artists in other countries. Among visual artists there is little evidence except for eloquent personal testimony to verify how skimpy are the

[a] The question is much broader than the arts alone. In a 1978 government poll listing ten major areas of daily life, citizens expressed the greatest satisfaction with the level of health care and the least satisfaction with the degree of social mobility available to them. Japan, Economic Planning Agency, *The Polls on the Preference in National Life—What Are the People Seeking for?* Tokyo, Economic Planning Agency, 1980, p. 29.

earnings from their works, but critics, scholars, dealers, and the artists themselves agree that only the favored 300 have prospered from the booming art market of the seventies. For almost everyone else, art is a labor of love, when side jobs leave time for it.

Performing artists are scarcely better off. According to the prime minister's bureau of statistics and data from a poll of 433 professionals taken in 1979 by the artists' federation Geidankyō, consumer prices rose 70 percent between 1974 and 1979 and the income of all employed persons in Japan increased 53 percent, but for performing artists the gain was only 30 percent, forcing more and more of them to moonlight in unrelated jobs. According to the statistics bureau, the average artist earned $13,600 in 1979, compared with $13,900 for workers as a whole, even though the official statistics exclude many thousands of persons whose income from art is too small for it to be their main occupation.[2] About 38 percent of the artists questioned by Geidankyō said they did not expect to remain performers indefinitely, up from 32 percent in 1974, and almost two-thirds said they would discourage their children from taking up the same profession. The most dissatisfied were those aged twenty-five to twenty-nine, presumably because they were past the idealism of youth but not yet fully launched in their careers.[3]

More of the professionals who answered the survey earned money teaching than performing, whether live or on radio, television, or film. As a rule, the smaller the income, the more dependent the artist was on teaching, whereas the wealthiest performers were those with opportunities in the mass media. Yet even though teaching was the leading source of earnings, many more artists considered themselves stage performers first and teachers second rather than the reverse, reflecting both aspiration and pride. Since unemployment and underemployment are endemic to the performing arts everywhere, it is not surprising that artists in all genres reported having too many idle days. Actors and actresses had the most, because fewer of them teach privately than is true of musicians and dancers.[4]

245

According to the Geidankyō study, the best-paid performing genre in 1979 was theater, including kabuki and all forms of modern drama. Big fees from films and television helped raise the average income for actors and actresses to $22,500, well ahead of nō artists, the next best paid at $18,900. Performers of classical Western music reported earnings of $13,300 that year, whereas specialists in traditional Japanese music had incomes of $10,600. Classical Japanese dancers, at $10,000, and Western-style dancers, at $9,700, were the least well rewarded. The figures are averages, not medians, and reflect small samples in each art form among professionals who were successful enough to belong to the artists' federation. Although there were variables of age and location as well as métier, perhaps the greatest discrepancy was between male performers, who averaged $16,400, and women, at $9,900. On the other hand, the genres most dominated by female artists—hōgaku and dance of all types—reported low individual earnings but high family incomes compared with other art forms.[5]

These statistics are too limited to say very much about the overall economic standing of performing artists, but at least they suggest the relative profitability of each genre and the enormous importance of teaching to the performing arts as a whole. Artists also face much more uncertainty about their incomes from year to year and enjoy far fewer fringe benefits than most professionals in Japan. Some have even mastered the skills of two separate art forms to increase their chances of finding steady jobs, such as dancers who take theater training and join production companies so they can play in musicals.[6] Performers everywhere take financial risks, but artists seem unusually vulnerable in Japan, where so many employees have a predictable package of wages, bonuses, and benefits— and sizeable savings accounts besides.

If society has placed artists in economic distress, it has also fortified them through a spirit of familism and a strong sense of group solidarity, the central pillars of arts patronage in Japan. Rebels like Genshū sometimes challenge its authority, but the hierarchy of very durable social groups is much more important than state aid or private giving as a source of support for artists. To some degree the vertical mosaic of the arts foists an accredited view of culture on each modern genre, from the safe academicism of Nitten and the hard-nosed dramatic realism of shingeki to the classicism of Western music and dance. The many schools of the traditional arts perpetuate an even stricter canon of what constitutes valid expressions of beauty and sentiment in their respective disciplines.

But the main way that hierarchical groups sustain the arts is organizational, not ideological. As the ballet critic Keiko Keene puts it, "the special quality of the dance groups in Japan is their family character,"[7] an observation that applies equally to orchestras, theater companies, associations of painters, and the countless circles of pupils surrounding teachers in each of these arts. Authority in each case is distributed in the pattern of a family, and close emotional bonds as well as instrumental work relationships promote a strong esprit de corps. The headmaster system and its variants in the modern genres form a paradigm for arts organizations of all sizes: just as thousands of student recitals serve as the building blocks for a school of classical Japanese dance, so the local audience association is the central element in the Rōon circuit. Art dealers are clannish and often bar outsiders from holding auctions, jealously guarding their baronies in the same fashion as ballet companies or symphonies. There is a hierarchy both internally within each group and externally among all the organizations in an art form. Galleries and art associations, theater companies and kabuki actors, orchestras and operas, dance groups and department-store museums are all ranked in order of repute, and it is a cause for celebration to move up the ladder a rung.[b]

[b] The Geidankyō survey found that actors and actresses in all forms of drama (except nō) had the highest sense of identity with their groups and that classical Japanese dance and traditional Japanese music performers, who rarely appear as formal companies, had the lowest. Ballet and contemporary dancers, together with performers in the popular entertainments, felt the fiercest competition; nō and bunraku artists felt the least. Nihon Geinō Jit-

Perhaps the most important social group boosting the arts is the family itself. The patronage of millions of middle-class pupils has been the single biggest help in establishing art as a worthy profession since World War Two, through formal schooling but especially through private lessons. Their interest in studying the arts was partly a product of fashion, very much like seeing the latest art show from abroad or hearing the famous recitalist on tour. Yet art served the social system not merely as an index of snobbery but also as a moral exemplar. Many families believed taking lessons helped to build selfhood and inner strength among the young, and the arts became something of a secular church for people of all ages by acting as a source of value in an era of otherwise privatized goals.

The arts and the middle class conferred respectability on each other and profit on promoters who recognized the fact. Proper families retrieved art from the entertainment districts and turned it into a bona fide regimen, emphasizing its merit as a way of study and a path of learning instructive beyond the métier itself. In the same way that official sanction from the government or Nitten brought added prestige to painters and performers, art enshrouded the newspaper companies and department stores with an aura of culture and multiplied their earnings as well. Exhibits and performances soon enjoyed the sanction of embassies and state agencies for the credibility they bestowed, even though other sponsors usually footed the bills. For artists themselves, the route to respectability meant winning acceptance and becoming known, even when the demands of social propriety grated against their artistic dignity and personal pride.

The middle-class fascination with the arts supplied droves of students but very slender audiences during most of the postwar era. Attending an event in the arts was just as much an age-group phenomenon as taking lessons, and both were predominantly female pastimes. Audiences for the arts were

suenka Dantai Kyōgikai, *Geinōjin no seikatsu to ishiki—dainikai geinōjin jittai chōsa hōkokusho*, Tokyo, Nihon Geinō Jitsuenka Dantai Kyōgikai, 1979, p. 26.

drawn from the relatively narrow sector of well-educated persons who could afford to attend, and they were further classified by age and sex for each genre. Traditional arts usually attracted older customers, for example, and university students were in the majority at performances of avant-garde plays and contemporary dance or music. Like licensed merchants in Edo-period castle towns, many arts organizations cultivated defined segments of the overall market to assure themselves of stable patronage, but this noncompetitive approach limited their flexibility as well as their repertoires. Better arts education in the schools will eventually narrow the gap between the clienteles for lessons and performances, and it will doubtless help to overcome the tyranny of the classics as well. But no amount of education will make a real dent in the custom, indeed the necessity, of the artist as self-patron, since art remains immensely gratifying in nonmonetary ways to its practitioners.

Besides middle-class patronage, there was aid from official agencies, foundations, and corporations. Government units at all levels spent $17.9 million on outreach programs in 1980, and private sources contributed another $1 to $2 million for the same purpose. Nearly fifteen times this amount was allocated the same year for erecting new public facilities for the arts throughout the country. The biggest effect of this aid has been to make art of all eras much more accessible to the public. Private audience organizations and performance tours organized by production companies helped to spread the arts still further. Yet Tokyo remains the arts capital of the nation, and much more money will be needed to broaden out-of-town audiences and beef up local museum collections in the future.[c]

Public funds commissioned a great many new works in music, opera, and dance during the 1970s, even though much

---

[c] Umesao Tadao, head of the National Museum of Ethnology, proposed in 1980 that the government create 200 to 300 national cultural centers from existing facilities, anchored by a new national cultural city to be built at the center, to balance the concentration of cultural institutions in Tokyo. *Asahi shinbun*, May 2, 1980.

of the money intended for creative activities ended up erasing deficits in the case of orchestras. But artistic creativity is too intangible, and the aid too limited, for anyone to be certain that support from the government increased the level of innovation in any genre. Much of the most striking new work took place beyond the pale of official sponsorship: in graphics, underground theater, and avant-garde dance. Contemporary music, on the other hand, flourished partly because of commissions funded by the cultural agency, but other creative efforts paid for by the state, especially in opera and ballet, won much less acclaim. Public support for the arts also increased the numbers of exhibitions and performances held throughout the country, but the new money probably did little to improve artists' incomes or reduce unemployment. Instead it enticed still more artists to try the profession—the classic rabbits-and-lettuce principle.

Whether the national government can increase its aid very much in the 1980s is uncertain, since huge tax increases have already been earmarked for other programs like energy and defense. Even though there is little spirit of private philanthropy and big business has benefited the arts thus far mostly as entrepreneur and occasional consumer, the corporate world seems the most promising vein to tap for fresh contributions. Almost all the most financially parlous arts groups have been established only since World War Two, too short a time for the habit of patronage to become routine in a business world that until recently has been preoccupied with expansion and reinvestment. Corporations are likely to offer more support as they come to appreciate art for its inherent worth, not just as entertainment—a lesson already apparent to many of their middle-class shareholders.

No systematic research has yet been done on the economic effects of arts institutions on their home communities in Japan, but only Tokyo and a few other huge cities have large enough concentrations for the impact to be very weighty. Arts administrators generally agree that the tax laws are unfriendly, especially because private giving is discouraged, and they are united in opposing the theater-admission tax. (Since 1975, the government has collected 10 percent on the portion of the ticket price exceeding 3,000 yen for live events and 2,000 yen for movies; kabuki, bunraku, and the visual arts are exempt.) Although the levy brings in only two-hundredths of one percent of national tax revenues, it forces the Imperial Theater alone to collect an additional $1 million from its customers each year, a burden that live performing artists are sure discourages attendance.[8]

The greatest problems facing dance, music, theater, and the visual media in the 1980s are not directly ideological, organizational, or financial but artistic instead—the relative dearth of open competition and scantiness of frank criticism. The headmaster system in the traditional arts, with its priorities of loyalty, longevity, and cash, is merely the most arresting example, although it is true that most schools exist to conserve a tradition rather than to break fresh artistic ground, where candid appraisal may be needed most. Yet even where criticism could best be applied, neither formal schooling in the modern arts nor the recital system in dance and music offers the artist many real critiques, since each minimizes head-to-head rivalry and rewards faithfulness more than imagination.

When the student becomes professional, the situation is much the same. Production companies in all the performing arts freely admit that roles are often assigned out of affective or financial considerations that have little to do with the artist's skill. Museum directors and theater managers equally take a tack of caution, selecting safe works and shirking critically promising but potentially controversial ones. In a middle-class society whose cultural habits are already homogenized by commercialism and the mass media, such a reluctance to take risks further trims the variety of offerings that can compete for audiences. So long as critics accept cakes and muffle their candor, they help to preserve the synthetic hierarchy of values that is good for business but bad for art. Even teaching dulls the competitive appetite for many artists by making them economically secure without having to show their talents in the gallery or onstage.

The habit of avoiding confrontation and criticism is deeply embedded in Japanese social structure and reinforces the group solidarity that undergirds all the arts. Yet as the nation approaches its self-proclaimed age of culture, it seems likely that the arts will serve society best by thriving freely and openly, fulfilling Tachikawa Ruriko's hope that people will turn to art "as they realize material prosperity isn't fully satisfying."[9]

BIBLIOGRAPHIC NOTES

CHAPTER 1 ART FOR SOCIETY'S SAKE

1 The sentence was thirty months in jail. *Japan Times*, November 23, 1980, January 24, 1981, and February 27, 1981; Asahi Shinbunsha, *Asahi nenkan 1981*, Tokyo, Asahi Shinbunsha, 1981, p. 581.

2 Ozawa, quoted in Kimura Eiji, "Nihon no geijutsu josei wa kokkakei ka minkankei ka," *Ongaku geijutsu*, November 1980, p. 52.

3 Figures are for the fiscal year 1980, ending March 31, 1981. Bunkachō, *Bunkachō yosan jimu teiyō, Shōwa 55nen*, Tokyo, Bunkachō, 1980, pp. 22-23. The allocation for modern performing-arts groups was expected to be frozen for fiscal 1981 at its 1980 level. Yoshida Takayoshi interview, December 25, 1980.

4 See Anthony Phillips, "The Arts, Economics and Politics: Four National Perspectives," in Aspen Institute for Humanistic Studies, *The Arts, Economics and Politics: Four National Perspectives*, New York, Aspen Institute for Humanistic Studies, 1975, p. 9; Dick Netzer, *The Subsidized Muse: Public Support of the Arts in the United States*, New York, Cambridge University Press, 1978, pp. 9-12; Alvin Toffler, *The Culture Consumers: A Study of Art and Affluence in America*, Baltimore, Penguin Books, 1965, pp. 15-16.

5 Cesar Graña, *Bohemian versus Bourgeois*, New York, Basic Books, 1964, p. x.

6 Suzanne Langer, "Deceptive Analogies," in James B. Hall and Barry Ubanov, comp., *Modern Culture and the Arts*, New York, McGraw-Hill Book Company, 2nd ed., 1972, p. 25. Cf. Herbert J. Gans, *Popular Culture and High Culture: An Analysis and Evaluation of Taste*, New York, Basic Books, 1974; William P. Malm, "Layers of Music in Japan Since 1945," *The Fourth Kyushu International Cultural Conference: Proceedings*, Fukuoka, Fukuoka UNESCO Association, 1978, pp. D3-1/12.

7 Masui Keiji, ed., *Dēta ongaku Nippon*, Tokyo, Min'on Ongaku Shiryōkan, 1980, p. 81; Segi Shin'ichi, *Shakai no naka no bijutsu*, Tokyo, Tōkyō Shoseki, 1978, p. 162; Kimura Yōichi

interview, December 12, 1980; Haryū Ichirō interview, November 13, 1980.

8 Iino Kiichi interview, December 16, 1980; Bunkachō, *Bunka gyōsei no ayumi*, Tokyo, Bunkachō, 1978, p. 74.

9 Honda Shingo interview, December 15, 1980; Kamiya Shin interview, December 16, 1980; Ikeda Masao interview, November 26, 1980; Yoneda Minoru interview, November 26, 1980.

10 Bunkachō, *Bunka gyōsei no ayumi*, p. 74; Segi, *Shakai*, p. 162.

11 Museum of Modern Art, *The New Japanese Painting and Sculpture*, New York, Museum of Modern Art, 1966, p. 9.

12 Segi, *Shakai*, p. 161.

13 *Japan Times*, January 9, 1981; Bunkachō, *Bunka gyōsei no ayumi*, pp. 95, 138; Segi, *Shakai*, p. 163; Sōrifu Tōkeikyoku, *Nihon tōkei nenkan*, Tokyo, Sōrifu Tōkeikyoku, 1980, p. 614.

14 Masui, ed., *Dēta*, p. 81.

15 Ōkawa Takeo interview, December 4, 1980; Yamashita Fumio, *Atarashii seiji to bunka*, Tokyo, Shin Nihon Shuppansha, 1975, p. 49; Bunkachō, *Bunka gyōsei no ayumi*, p. 83; Takeshi Okochi, "The Theatrical Situation in Tokyo and the Imperial Theatre," conference paper for International Box Office Managers Conference, Atlanta, January 1981, p. 6.

16 Bunkachō, *Bunka gyōsei no ayumi*, p. 85.

17 Thomas G. Moore, *The Economics of the American Theater*, Durham, Duke University Press, 1968, p. 131; Okochi, "Theatrical Situation," p. 6; Okōchi Takeshi interview, November 19, 1980; Kurahashi Takeshi interview, November 12, 1980; Kurabayashi Seiichirō interview, November 11, 1980; Kurabayashi Seiichirō, "Sūji de miru engeki jōkyō no suii," *Teatoro*, January 1978, p. 127; Kurabayashi Seiichirō, "Zuisōteki ni sengo shingeki o kangaeru," part 5, *Teatoro*, July 1979, p. 122; Shingekidan Kyōgikai, *Kaihō*, no. 55, January 1980; Bunkachō, *Bunka gyōsei no ayumi*, p. 86; *Shingeki*, January 1981 and February 1981; Kishi Tetsuo, "Beyond Noh and Kabuki," *Look Japan*, March 10, 1980, p. 6.

18 Iwaki Hiroyuki, "Ongaku kyōiku wa kore de yoi no ka," *Chūō kōron*, May 1969, p. 136. For contemporary music, see Akiyama Kuniharu, *Nihon no sakkyokukatachi*, 2 vols., Tokyo, Ongaku no Tomosha, 1979; Akiyama Kuniharu, "Japan," in John Vinton, ed., *Dictionary of Contemporary Music*, New York, E. P.

Dutton, 1974, pp. 364-367; Akiyama Kuniharu interview, November 7, 1980; Ichiyanagi Toshi interview, November 30, 1980.

19 Masui, ed., *Dēta*, pp. 79, 81-82, 84, 86.

20 Koshimura Sadanao interview, November 5, 1980; Bunkachō, *Bunka gyōsei no ayumi*, p. 76; Nakano Yukio interview, November 21, 1980; Tsunematsu Yukitoshi interview, November 21, 1980.

21 Kawai Shin interview, April 19, 1977.

22 Nihon Ensōka Kyōkai, *Musicians (Including Other Performers) from Foreign Countries into Japan in 1978*, Tokyo, Nihon Ensōka Kyōkai, 1980; Tsunematsu Yukitoshi, "Ongakuka shōgai no sōkessan," *Ongaku geijutsu*, May 1979, p. 45; Bunkachō, *Bunka gyōsei no ayumi*, p. 270; Nakano interview, November 21, 1980; Tsunematsu interview, November 21, 1980.

23 Kawachi Shōzō interview, December 3, 1980; Ōkōchi interview, November 19, 1980; Takeishi Hideo interview, October 29, 1980.

24 Yoshida interview, December 25, 1980; Nakano interview, November 21, 1980; Tsunematsu interview, November 21, 1980; Tsunematsu Yukitoshi, "Nihon no ongaku shakai no genjō to masu medeia to seishōnen mondai," MS, 1979, p. 40.

25 Yoshida interview, December 25, 1980; *Nihon tōkei nenkan*, 1980, p. 615.

26 Ongaku no Tomosha, *Ongaku nenkan 1980*, Tokyo, Ongaku no Tomosha, 1980, p. 588; Tsunematsu, "Nihon no ongaku shakai," p. 41; *Nihon tōkei nenkan*, 1980, p. 433; Japan, Economic Planning Agency, *The Polls on the Preference in National Life—What Are the People Seeking for?* Tokyo, Economic Planning Agency, 1980, p. 103; *Japan Report*, June 1, 1978, p. 6; Masui, ed., *Dēta*, p. 65.

27 Bunkachō, *Bunka gyōsei no ayumi*, pp. 76, 78; Kishibe Shigeo interview, January 26, 1981. The number of public hōgaku performances has remained steady in the 1970s; most are samisen and nagauta.

28 For ballet, Hattori Chieko interview, December 6, 1980; Shimada Hiroshi interview, December 6, 1980; Kasuya Tatsuo interview, October 22, 1980; Dennis Keene interview, November 14, 1980; Zen Nihon Buyō Rengō Buyō Nenkan Iinkai, *Buyō nenkan, IV, 1980*, Tokyo, Zen Nihon Buyō Rengō, 1980, pp. 125-150. For classical Japanese dance, Hinoshita Yoshi-

mitsu interview, December 19, 1980; *Buyō nenkan, IV, 1980,* pp. 91-117; Bunkachō, *Bunka gyōsei no ayumi,* p. 81; Ezaki Tsukasa interview, October 23, 1980. For contemporary dance, Ezaki interview, October 23, 1980; *Buyō nenkan, IV, 1980,* pp. 13-14, 153-201; Bunkachō, *Bunka gyōsei no ayumi,* p. 82; Gendai Buyō Kyōkai, *Nihon gendai buyō nenkan,* Tokyo, Gendai Buyō Kyōkai, 1975, pp. 5-9.

29 *Asahi nenkan 1981,* p. 599; Ezaki interview, February 20, 1981; Kasuya interview, October 22, 1980; Hinoshita interview, December 19, 1980; Bunkachō, *Bunka gyōsei no ayumi,* p. 85; Kanze Hideo interview, *Concerned Theatre Japan,* winter/spring 1971, pp. 14-17.

30 On existentialism, see Walter Kaufmann, ed., *Existentialism from Dostoevsky to Sartre,* Cleveland and New York, Meridian Books, 1956, pp. 11-12, 41-51; on modernism, Hilton Kramer, "Beyond the Avant-garde," *New York Times Magazine,* November 4, 1979, pp. 40-46, 58-62; on postmodernism, Anna Kisselgoff, "Dance View," *New York Times,* December 24, 1978; *Newsweek,* March 26, 1979, pp. 88-91; on performance, Rose Lee Goldberg, *Performance: Live Art, 1909 to the Present,* New York, Harry N. Abrams, Incorporated, 1979, pp. 6-7.

31 NNW Measurement Committee, *Measuring Net National Welfare of Japan,* Tokyo, Economic Council of Japan, 1973, p. 162; *Asahi nenkan 1979,* p. 464; Kurabayashi, "Sūji," p. 118; *Asahi nenkan 1980,* p. 636; *White Paper on Leisure,* 1979, quoted in *Asahi nenkan 1980,* p. 464.

32 Japan, Office of the Prime Minister, Bureau of Statistics, *Statistical Handbook of Japan 1980,* Tokyo, Bureau of Statistics, 1980, p. 137; Masui, ed., *Dēta,* p. 92.

33 Asian Cultural Centre for UNESCO, *Report on Traditional Forms of Culture in Japan,* Tokyo, Asian Cultural Centre for UNESCO, 1975, p. 7.

34 NHK survey, quoted in Masui, ed., *Dēta,* p. 105; Leisure Development Center poll, ibid., p. 100; *Nihon tōkei nenkan,* 1980, p. 626; Bunkachō, *Bunka gyōsei no ayumi,* p. 95; Masui, ed., *Dēta,* p. 96.

35 On the democratization of the arts in the U.S., see Roy McMullen, *Art, Affluence and Alienation: The Fine Arts Today,* New York, Praeger Publishers, 1968, p. 21; Toffler, *Culture Consumers,* p. 41.

36 Tachikawa Ruriko interview, December 8, 1980.

NOTES TO PAGES 18-24

37 Malm, "Layers," p. D3-12.

38 *Asahi nenkan 1975*, p. 694; Shuichi Kato, *Form, Style, Tradition: Reflections on Japanese Art and Society*, trans. by John Bester, Berkeley, University of California Press, 1971, p. 177; *Japan Times*, October 13, 1980 and October 18, 1980; *Asahi nenkan 1980*, pp. 581-583.

39 Cf. Oda Makoto's discussion of the "literature of isolation" in 1975. *Bungei nenkan 1976*, p. 58. See Kato, *Form*, pp. 32-34; Toru Terada, *Japanese Art in World Perspective*, trans. by Thomas Guerin, New York and Tokyo, Weatherhill/Heibonsha, 1976, pp. 27-30.

40 Michishita Kyōko interview, November 19, 1980; Chie Nakane, *Japanese Society*, Berkeley, University of California Press, 1970, p. 118; Mukai Kasue interview, October 27, 1980; Anzai Shigeo interview, October 27, 1980.

41 Etō Shun interview, December 25, 1980; Hase Takao interview, October 14, 1980; Kurosawa, quoted in Jack Kroll, *Newsweek*, October 13, 1980, p. 60.

42 Haryū interview, November 13, 1980.

43 Dennis Keene interview, November 14, 1980; Margaret K. Johnson interview, November 12, 1980; Haryū interview, November 13, 1980; Amaury Saint-Gilles interview, December 6, 1980.

44 Kawashima Takeyoshi, *Ideorogī to shite no kazoku seido*, Tokyo, Iwanami Shoten, 1957, p. 322.

45 Nishiyama Matsunosuke, *Gendai no iemoto*, Tokyo, Kōbundō, 1962, pp. 23, 41, 50; Akiko Kanda interview, November 28, 1980; Kawashima Takeyoshi interview, November 27, 1980; Kumakura Isao, "Iemoto to geinō," seminar paper, Japan Foundation, Tokyo, February 20, 1981; Asian Cultural Centre, *Report*, pp. 66-67; Inumaru Tadashi interview, November 5, 1980. See *Rekishi kōron*, April 1978, for a special issue on the headmaster system.

46 Kawashima, *Ideorogī*, pp. 322-331; Kawashima interview, November 27, 1980; Kumakura, "Iemoto"; Hinoshita interview, December 19, 1980. I have learned much about the headmaster system in classical Japanese dance from conversations with Joyce Malm.

47 Nishiyama Matsunosuke, *Iemoto no kenkyū*, Tokyo, Azekura

257

Shobō, 1959, p. 161; Nishiyama, *Gendai*, pp. 20-27; Kumakura, "Iemoto."

48 Kishibe interview, January 26, 1981; Shibazaki Shirō interview, February 4, 1981; Amano Ryōichi interview, December 22, 1980; Kumakura, "Iemoto."

49 McMullen, *Art*, p. 24; Bunkachō, *Bunka gyōsei chōki sōgō keikaku ni tsuite*, Tokyo, Bunkachō, 1977, p. 3.

50 Phillips, "Arts," p. 8.

51 Yoshimasa Kurabayashi, *Public and Private Expenditure on Cultural Purposes: A Case Study of Performing Arts in Japan*, Tokyo, Institute of Statistical Research, 1979, passim.

52 Quoted in Kimura, "Nihon no geijutsu josei," p. 53.

53 Katō Mikio interview, October 30, 1980.

CHAPTER 2   A POVERTY OF PATRONS

1 *Japan Times*, December 15, 1980 and December 29, 1980.

2 Donald Richie interview, October 6, 1980. See Tanaka Minoru, *Foundations in Japan: Their Legal Provisions and Tax Regulations*, Tokyo, Japan Center for International Exchange, 1975, pp. 1-2; Katō Mikio interview, October 30, 1980.

3 See Langdon Warner, *The Enduring Art of Japan*, Cambridge, Mass., Harvard University Press, 1952, pp. 17-24.

4 See Adolph S. Tomars, *Introduction to the Sociology of Art*, Mexico City, privately published, 1940, pp. 169-172; Peter Burke, *Culture and Society in Renaissance Italy, 1420-1540*, New York, Charles Scribner's Sons, 1972, p. 39.

5 See Burke, *Culture*, p. 112.

6 See Michiaki Kawakita, *Modern Currents in Japanese Art*, trans. by Charles S. Terry, New York and Tokyo, Weatherhill/Heibonsha, 1974, pp. 96, 132-133, 145-146; Ernst Fischer, *The Necessity of Art: A Marxist Approach*, trans. by Anne Bostock, Baltimore, Penguin Books, 1963, pp. 49-62; Adolph S. Tomars, "Class Systems and the Arts," in Werner J. Cahnman and Alvin Boskoff, eds., *Sociology and History: Theory and Research*, New York, The Free Press of Glencoe, 1964, pp. 481-482; Burke, *Culture*, pp. 71-75, 83; Toffler, *Culture Consumers*, pp. 169-170.

7 Shibazaki interview, February 4, 1981; Adachi Kenji interview, October 22, 1980; Hase Takao interview, October 14, 1980.

8   Ohara Shigeo interview, November 20, 1980; Adachi interview, October 22, 1980.

9   Matsushita, quoted in Kimura, "Nihon no geijutsu josei," p. 53; Adachi interview, October 22, 1980; Ōka, quoted in "Nihon no ongaku bunka to dojō," *Ongaku geijutsu*, November 1980, pp. 27-28.

10 Kawashima interview, November 27, 1980; Katō Mikio interview, October 30, 1980; Tanaka, *Foundations*, p. 6; Japan Center for International Exchange, *Philanthropy in Japan*, Tokyo, Japan Center for International Exchange, rev. ed., 1978, p. 18.

11 Tanaka, *Foundations*, pp. 6, 17-18; Koshimura interview, November 5, 1980.

12 Kimura, "Nihon no geijutsu josei," p. 53; Ōfuku Mamoru interview, October 20, 1980.

13 Adachi interview, October 22, 1980; Tachikawa interview, December 8, 1980.

14 Tanaka, *Foundations*, p. 21; Katō Mikio interview, October 30, 1980; Hara Toshio interview, October 28, 1980.

15 Japan Center for International Exchange, *Philanthropy in Japan*, p. 11; Tanaka, *Foundations*, p. 23.

16 Hara interview, October 28, 1980; Bunkachō, *Bunka gyōsei chōki*, p. 27.

17 Japan Center for International Exchange, *Philanthropy in Japan*, p. 7; *"Kigyō no shakai kōken" shiryōshū, 1980*, Tokyo, Sanken, 1980, passim.

18 Ōfuku interview, October 20, 1980; Richie interview, October 6, 1980.

19 Richie interview, October 6, 1980; Matsuki Shōgo interview, October 14, 1980..

20 Haryū Ichirō, *Sengo bijutsu seisuishi*, Tokyo, Tōkyō Shoseki, 1979, pp. 134-136; Hara interview, October 28, 1980.

21 Takeda Michitarō, *Nihon kindai bijutsushi*, Tokyo, Kondō Shuppansha, 1969, p. 152; Hara interview, October 28, 1980; Adachi interview, October 22, 1980; see Laurance P. Roberts, *Roberts' Guide to Japanese Museums*, New York and Tokyo, Kodansha International, 1978.

22 *Asahi nenkan 1967*, p. 739; *Asahi nenkan 1970*, p. 711; Adachi interview, October 22, 1980.

23 Hara interview, October 28, 1980.

24 Japan Center for International Exchange, *Philanthropy in Japan*, p. 74; Kawakita, *Modern Currents*, p. 158; Haryū, *Sengo*, p. 152; Hideo Tomiyama, "Art in Postwar Japan: 1945-1972," in Shuji Takashina, Yoshiaki Tono, and Hideo Tomiyama, eds., *Art in Japan Today*, Tokyo, Japan Foundation, 1974, p. 199.

25 *Asahi nenkan 1973*, p. 705; *Japan Foundation Newsletter*, October-November 1979, p. 8.

26 Fukushima Kikuo interview, October 17, 1980; *Japan Times*, November 23, 1980; Sakisaka Masahisa, "Kigyō to ongaku no kakawariai," *Ongaku geijutsu*, November 1980, p. 62.

27 Matsumae Yoshiaki interview, October 24, 1980; *Sumitomo Corporation News*, no. 21, July 1980, p. 12.

28 *Asahi nenkan 1977*, p. 714; *Sumishō nyūsu*, no. 48, May 1980, p. 8; *Sumitomo Quarterly*, I, 3, August 1980, pp. 11-12; Matsumae interview, October 24, 1980.

29 *Asahi nenkan 1967*, p. 739.

30 Ibid.; *Asahi nenkan 1975*, p. 703. See Roberts, *Roberts' Guide*, and Kawakita, *Modern Currents*, pp. 157-158 for postwar museums.

31 Hara interview, October 28, 1980. See *Bijutsu hyōron*, June 1980, p. 19; *Japan Foundation Newsletter*, February-March 1980, p. 14; *Hara Museum of Contemporary Art*, Tokyo, Hara Museum of Contemporary Art, 1979.

32 Tsutsumi, quoted in Seibu Bijutsukan, *Nihon gendai bijutsu no tenbō*, Tokyo, Seibu Bijutsukan, 1975; Seibu Museum of Art, *Seibu Museum of Art Year in Review*, 1976-1977, Tokyo, Seibu Museum of Art, 1978.

33 *Seibu Museum of Art Year in Review*, 1976-1977 and 1978-1979; Kaneko Kikuo interview, October 13, 1980.

34 Tomiyama, "Art in Postwar Japan," p. 203; Shell Oil Corporation, *Dai24kai Sheru bijutsushōten*, Tokyo, Shell Oil Corporation, 1980; *Asahi nenkan 1972*, p. 708; *Asahi nenkan 1974*, p. 708; *Murex*, no. 14, spring 1980, pp. 1-8, 51-56; "Kigyō no shakai kōken," p. 193.

35 Richie interview, October 6, 1980.

36 "Kigyō no shakai kōken," pp. 50-51, 157, 159, 171, 308, 312; *Japan Foundation Newsletter*, February-March 1980, p. 7.

37 Ikeda interview, November 26, 1980; Johnson interview, No-

vember 12, 1980; Yoshii Chōzō interview, October 14, 1980; *Kiyoharu Geijutsumura*, Tokyo, Yoshii Garō, 1980, pp. 2-4.

38 Sakisaka, "Kigyō to ongaku," p. 62; *Japan Times*, March 9, 1981.

39 Edo Hideo interview, November 6, 1980.

40 Edo interview, November 6, 1980; Edo, quoted in "Nihon no ongaku bunka to dojō," *Ongaku geijutsu*, November 1980, p. 27. Mobile telephones in private cars became available in Japan only in early 1980.

41 *Nihon Kōkyōgaku Shinkō Zaidan nyūsu*, no. 10, June 1980, pp. 1-6; Nihon Kōkyōgaku Shinkō Zaidan, *Nihon Kōkyōgaku Shinkō Zaidan setsuritsu shuisho*, Tokyo, Nihon Kōkyōgaku Shinkō Zaidan, 1973; Nihon Kōkyōgaku Shinkō Zaidan, *Gendai Nihon no ōkesutora ongaku, dai4kai ensōkai*, Tokyo, Nihon Kōkyōgaku Shinkō Zaidan, 1980; *Asahi nenkan 1974*, p. 710; Koshimura interview, November 5, 1980. On Sasakawa, see Keystone Press Agency Japan, *Profile of Ryoichi Sasakawa*, Tokyo, Keystone Press Agency Japan, 1980; *Japan Times*, November 15, 1980; on Cunningham, see *Japan Times*, March 9, 1981.

42 *Nihon Kōkyōgaku Shinkō Zaidan nyūsu*, no. 10, June 1980, pp. 3-5.

43 Koshimura interview, November 5, 1980. See *Nihon Kōkyōgaku Shinkō Zaidan setsuritsu shuisho*.

44 *Nihon Kōkyōgaku Shinkō Zaidan nyūsu*, no. 10, June 1980, p. 6; Nihon Kōkyōgaku Shinkō Zaidan, *Gendai Nihon*.

45 Yoshida interview, December 25, 1980; Nobuya Shikaumi, *Cultural Policy in Japan*, Paris, UNESCO, 1970, p. 26.

46 Machida Yutaka interview, October 29, 1980; Walter Nichols interview, December 1, 1980; Takeishi interview, October 29, 1980.

47 "*Kigyō no shakai kōken*," pp. 26-30, 36-37, 63, 165, 266; Mobil Oil Corporation, *Dai10kai Mōbiru ongakushō (hōgakubumon) jushōsha kimaru*, Tokyo, Mobil Oil Corporation, 1980; Mobil Oil Corporation, *Dai10kai Mōbiru ongakushō (yōgakubumon) jushōsha kimaru*, Tokyo, Mobil Oil Corporation, 1980; *Japan Times*, July 22, 1980, August 10, 1980, and September 12, 1980; Japan Center for International Exchange, *Philanthropy in Japan*, pp. 26-30; *Ongaku nenkan 1980*, p. 1; *Santorī Bunka Zaidan nyūsu*, no. 15, August 11, 1980, pp. 2-

4; Santorī, *Santorī 80nen no ayumi*, Osaka, Santorī, 1979, p. 56; Fukushima interview, October 17, 1980.

48 *"Kigyō no shakai kōken,"* pp. 52, 234.

49 Dan Ikuma interview, December 23, 1980.

50 *"Kigyō no shakai kōken,"* pp. 59, 215-216; Gekidan Shiki, *Gekidan Shiki sōritsu 25 shūnen kinen*, Tokyo, Gekidan Shiki, 1978, pp. 38, 45.

51 Nishina Tadashi interview, October 28, 1980; Nihon Bankoku Hakurankai Kinen Kikin, *Shōwa 55nendo Nihon Bankoku Hakurankai Kinen Kikin jigyō*, Tokyo, Nihon Bankoku Hakurankai Kinen Kikin, 1980, p. 6; Kokusai Butai Geijutsu Shinkō Zaidan, *Daisankai Nihon Sekai Baree Konkūru*, Tokyo, Kokusai Butai Geijutsu Shinkō Zaidan, 1980.

52 *Project Costs for Dance Theatre of Harlem in Japan 1981 (Revised)*, p. 1. See Nippon Bunka Zaidan, *Nippon Bunka Zaidan*, Tokyo, Nippon Bunka Zaidan, 1979; Nippon Cultural Centre, *The Paul Taylor Dance Company 1980*, Tokyo, Nippon Cultural Centre, 1980. I am indebted to Yokoyama Tadashi of the Nippon Cultural Centre for information about its activities. Yokoyama interview, November 13, 1980.

53 Kimura Hideo interview, October 31, 1980. See *International Cultural Newsletter*, I-, 1974-.

54 Dan interview, October 23, 1980; Richie interview, October 6, 1980.

CHAPTER 3 ARTS AND THE STATE

1 Bunkachō, *Bunkachō*, Tokyo, Bunkachō, 1980, p. 1.

2 Bunkachō, *Bunkachō yosan*, pp. 22-25. See Bunkachō, *Bunka gyōsei no ayumi*, pp. 1-4.

3 Bunkachō, *Bunka gyōsei no ayumi*, p. 69. "Education" includes physical education.

4 Kawakita, *Modern Currents*, p. 38; Bunkachō, *Bunka gyōsei chōki*, p. 4.

5 Kyōto Daigaku Bungakubu Kokushi Kenkyūshitsu, *Nihon kindaishi jiten*, Tokyo, Tōyō Keizai Shinpōsha, 1958, pp. 409, 413.

6 See Kawakita, *Modern Currents*, pp. 37-150; Bunkachō, *Bunka gyōsei chōki*, p. 4.

7   Adachi Kenji, *Bunkachō kotohajime*, Tokyo, Tōkyō Shoseki, 1978, pp. 7-8; Shikaumi, *Cultural Policy*, p. 11.

8   Adachi, *Bunkachō*, pp. 6-8; Machida interview, October 29, 1980.

9   Shikaumi, *Cultural Policy*, p. 10; Bunkachō, *Bunka gyōsei chōki*, p. 48; Adachi, *Bunkachō*, p. 10.

10   Bunkachō, *Bunkachō*, p. 6; Machida interview, October 29, 1980; Yoshida interview, December 25, 1980; Adachi, *Bunkachō*, p. 10; Bunkachō, *Bunka gyōsei no ayumi*, p. 61.

11   Adachi interview, October 22, 1980.

12   Bunkachō, *Bunkachō yosan*, pp. 22-25; Bunkachō, *Bunka gyōsei no ayumi*, pp. 62, 69, 111-112; Shikaumi, *Cultural Policy*, p. 36.

13   Budget details in the next five paragraphs are taken from Bunkachō, *Bunkachō yosan*, pp. 22-25; Bunkachō, *Bunka gyōsei no ayumi*, p. 62.

14   Bunkachō, *Bunka gyōsei chōki*, p. 5.

15   Bunkachō, *Bunkachō yosan*, pp. 22-25; Machida interview, October 29, 1980; Yoshida interview, December 25, 1980.

16   *Statistical Handbook of Japan 1980*, p. 135; Bunkachō, *Bunka gyōsei no ayumi*, p. 169; *Nihon tōkei nenkan*, 1980, p. 631; Adachi, *Bunkachō*, pp. 74-76.

17   *Japan Times*, October 16, 1980; Dan interview, December 23, 1980.

18   Bunkachō, *Bunka gyōsei chōki*, pp. 13-21.

19   Faubion Bowers, *Theatre in the East: A Survey of Asian Dance and Drama*, New York, Thomas Nelson & Sons, 1956, pp. 344-345; *Zusetsu*, p. 298; Adachi, *Bunkachō*, p. 121; *Asahi nenkan 1965*, p. 659.

20   *Asahi nenkan 1965*, p. 659; *Asahi nenkan 1968*, p. 729.

21   Statement of purpose, in National Theatre, *National Theatre of Japan*, Tokyo, National Theatre, 1970, p. 12; see also p. 23. *Asahi nenkan 1960*, p. 444; Machida Takako, *Buyō no ayumi hyakunen*, Tokyo, Ofūsha, 1968, p. 799; Shikaumi, *Cultural Policy*, pp. 45-46; Asian Cultural Centre, *Report*, p. 26.

22   Senda Koreya interview, *Concerned Theatre Japan*, summer 1970, p. 68.

23   Kokuritsu Gekijō, *Kokuritsu Gekijō jūnen no ayumi*, Tokyo, Kokuritsu Gekijō, 1976, p. 42; Nihon Engeki Kyōkai, *Engeki*

nenkan '77, Tokyo, Nihon Engeki Kyōkai, 1977, pp. 57-65; Bunkachō, *Bunka gyōsei no ayumi*, p. 217.

24 Ōkōchi interview, November 19, 1980; Asian Cultural Centre, *Report*, pp. 28-29.

25 Ōkawa interview, December 4, 1980; Kokuritsu Gekijō, *Kokuritsu Gekijō jūnen*, p. 42.

26 Adachi, *Bunkachō*, pp. 113-117; *Asahi nenkan 1980*, p. 630.

27 Shikaumi, *Cultural Policy*, p. 22; Bunkachō, *Bunkachō yosan*, pp. 22-25; Machida interview, October 29, 1980.

28 *Zusetsu*, p. 299; Adachi, *Bunkachō*, pp. 117-123; *Asahi nenkan 1979*, p. 630; *Asahi nenkan 1974*, p. 719; Inumaru interview, November 5, 1980; *Japan Times*, February 22, 1981.

29 See J. Thomas Rimer, *Modern Japanese Fiction and Its Traditions: An Introduction*, Princeton, Princeton University Press, 1978, pp. 5-6.

30 Inumaru interview, November 5, 1980; Bunkachō, *Bunka gyōsei no ayumi*, pp. 12, 104; Bunkachō, *Bunkachō*, pp. 9-12.

31 Mukai interview, October 27, 1980; Maki Jun'ichi interview, December 3, 1980; Bunkachō, *Bunka gyōsei chōki*, p. 26.

32 Bunkachō, *Bunkachō*, p. 39; Bunkachō, *Bunka gyōsei no ayumi*, pp. 132-133; Adachi, *Bunkachō*, p. 246.

33 *Asahi nenkan 1967*, p. 724; Adachi, *Bunkachō*, pp. 137-140; Bunkachō, *Bunka gyōsei no ayumi*, pp. 110-111; Bunkachō, *Bunkachō*, p. 12.

34 Bunkachō, *Bunkachō yosan*, pp. 22-25; Bowers, *Theatre*, p. 354; Shikaumi, *Cultural Policy*, pp. 33-34; Adachi, *Bunkachō*, pp. 126-131; Bunkachō, *Bunka gyōsei no ayumi*, pp. 11-12, 105-109.

35 Bunkachō, *Bunka gyōsei no ayumi*, pp. 106-109; *Japan Foundation Newsletter*, February-March 1980, p. 12.

36 Bunkachō, *Bunkachō yosan*, pp. 22-25; Bunkachō, *Bunka gyōsei no ayumi*, pp. 12, 112.

37 Shikaumi, *Cultural Policy*, p. 18; Bunkachō, *Bunkachō*, pp. 33-34; Bunkachō, *Bunka gyōsei no ayumi*, pp. 102-103; Adachi, *Bunkachō*, p. 125.

38 Hattori interview, December 6, 1980; Shimade interview, December 6, 1980; Kimura Yōichi interview, December 12, 1980; Ebara Jun, *Nihon bijutsukai fuhai no kōzō*, Tokyo, Saimaru

Shuppankai, 1978, p. 127; Bunkachō, *Bunka gyōsei chōki*, pp. 25-26.

39 Bunkachō, *Bunka gyōsei no ayumi*, p. 112; Satō Torao, "Bunkachō, Tōkyōto josei no gendai buyō kōen no hensen," in Gendai Buyō Kyōkai, *Nihon gendai buyō nenkan*, Tokyo, Gendai Buyō Kyōkai, 1975, p. 53; Adachi, *Bunkachō*, p. 126; Bunkachō, *Bunkachō yosan*, pp. 22-25.

40 Nihon Ensōka Kyōkai, *Shōwa 45-51nen geijutsu kankei dantai hojokin kōfugaku ichiran*, Tokyo, Nihon Ensōka Kyōkai, n.d. (1978); Bunkachō, *Bunkachō yosan*, pp. 22-25.

41 Nihon Ensōka Kyōkai, *Shōwa*; Machida interview, October 29, 1980; Adachi, *Bunkachō*, p. 113; Sakurai Tsutomu interview, December 2, 1980; Kawachi interview, December 3, 1980.

42 Ogawa Ayako interview, November 21, 1980; Nihon Ensōka Kyōkai, *Shōwa*; Adachi, *Bunkachō*, p. 126.

43 Nihon Ensōka Kyōkai, *Shōwa*; Bunkachō, *Bunkachō yosan*, pp. 22-25; Shingekidan Kyōgikai, *Kaihō*, no. 57, July 1980, pp. 1, 3.

44 Adachi, *Bunkachō*, pp. 60, 124; Ohara interview, November 20, 1980. The Japanese art sent abroad is almost always premodern.

45 Kimura, "Nihon no geijutsu josei," p. 54; Sasaki Yoshihisa, "Bunkachō joseikin no haibun," *Ongaku geijutsu*, October 1980, pp. 32-35; Shibazaki interview, February 4, 1981.

CHAPTER 4   ARTS TO THE PEOPLE

1 Bunkachō, *Bunkachō yosan*, pp. 22-25; Bunkachō, *Bunka gyōsei no ayumi*, pp. 14, 112.

2 Bunkachō, *Bunkachō*, pp. 13-14; Bunkachō, *Bunka gyōsei no ayumi*, p. 131; Bunkachō, *Bunka gyōsei chōki*, pp. 10, 31.

3 Bunkachō, *Bunka gyōsei chōki*, p. 10.

4 Bunkachō, *Bunkachō*, p. 13; Bunkachō, *Bunka gyōsei no ayumi*, pp. 123, 127-128; Asian Cultural Centre, *Report*, p. 31. See Adachi, *Bunkachō*, p. 135; *Asahi nenkan 1968*, p. 729.

5 *Asahi nenkan 1967*, p. 730; Bunkachō, *Bunka gyōsei no ayumi*, pp. 122, 127-128; Bunkachō, *Bunkachō*, p. 13.

6 Gendai Buyō Kyōkai, *Gendai buyō: Bunkachō idō geijutsusai gendai buyō kōen*, Tokyo, Gendai Buyō Kyōkai, 1980, p. 1.

7 Adachi, *Bunkachō*, pp. 135-136; Gendai Buyō Kyōkai, *Gendai buyō*, pp. 1, 14; Bunkachō, *Bunka gyōsei no ayumi*, pp. 124-125; Bunkachō, *Bunkachō*, p. 14.

8 Gendai Buyō Kyōkai, *Gendai buyō*, pp. 1, 14.

9 Shingekidan Kyōgikai, *Kaihō*, no. 57, July 1980, pp. 1, 3; Kurabayashi interview, November 11, 1980.

10 Bunkachō, *Bunka gyōsei no ayumi*, p. 129; Bunkachō, *Bunkachō yosan*, pp. 22-25; Bunkachō, *Bunkachō*, p. 42.

11 Kimura Hideo interview, October 31, 1980.

12 Kawakita, *Modern Currents*, p. 156; *Asahi nenkan 1975*, p. 702; *Japan Times*, January 9, 1981.

13 Roberts, *Roberts' Guide*, passim; Martin Mayer, *Bricks, Mortar and the Performing Arts*, New York, The Twentieth Century Fund, 1970, p. 11; Haryū, *Sengo*, p. 222; *Asahi nenkan 1979*, p. 615; "*Kigyō no shakai kōken*," p. 245; Hara interview, October 28, 1980; *Japan Times*, January 9, 1981.

14 Bunkachō, *Bunkachō*, p. 16; Adachi, *Bunkachō*, pp. 133-134; Bunkachō, *Bunkachō yosan*, pp. 22-25; Bunkachō, *Chihō bunka gyōsei jōkyō chōsa hōkokusho*, Tokyo, Bunkachō, 1980, pp. 126-182.

15 Bunkachō, *Bunkachō yosan*, pp. 22-25; Bunkachō, *Chihō*, pp. 9, 11-12.

16 Projected from figures for 1971-1978 in Bunkachō, *Chihō*, p. 11.

17 Ibid., p. 12; Bunkachō, *Bunkachō yosan*, pp. 22-25.

18 Bunkachō, *Bunkachō yosan*, pp. 22-25; Bunkachō, *Chihō*, pp. 1-4, 82-83, 120; Bunkachō, *Bunka gyōsei no ayumi*, pp. 70-71; Adachi, *Bunkachō*, p. 11.

19 Bunkachō, *Chihō*, pp. 140-145.

20 Yajima Kazuo interview, October 16, 1980; Machida interview, October 29, 1980; *Asahi nenkan 1973*, p. 705; *Bungei nenkan 1976*, pp. 154-155; Tōkyōto Bijutsukan, *Tōkyōto Bijutsukan yōran, Shōwa 54nendo*, Tokyo, Tōkyōto Bijutsukan, 1980, pp. 26-39, 50-51.

21 Iwaki Hiroyuki interview, December 27, 1980; Shikaumi, *Cultural Policy*, p. 45.

22 Masui, ed., *Dēta*, p. 123; Tōkyō Bunka Kaikan, *Yōran 1979*, Tokyo, Tōkyō Bunka Kaikan, 1979, pp. 15-17.

23 Yajima interview, October 16, 1980; Tōkyōto, Kyōikuchō, Shakai Kyōikubu, Bunkaka, *'81 Tomin Geijutsu Fuesuteibaru sanka kōen no gaiyō*, Tokyo, Tōkyōto, 1980, pp. 1-19; *Asahi nenkan 1972*, p. 703; Shingekidan Kyōgikai, *Kaihō*, no. 57, July 1980, p. 2; Tokyo Metropolitan Government, *Education in Tokyo*, Tokyo, Tokyo Metropolitan Government, 1979, pp. 327-328; Tōkyōto, Kyōikuchō, Shakai Kyōikubu, Bunkaka, *'80 Tomin Geijutsu Fuesuteibaru*, Tokyo, Tōkyōto, 1980; Tōkyōto, Kyōikuchō, Shakai Kyōikubu, Bunkaka, *'81 Tomin Geijutsu Fuesuteibaru*, Tokyo, Tōkyōto, 1981.

24 Senda interview, *Concerned Theatre Japan*, summer 1970, p. 69; Ogawa interview, November 21, 1980; Yajima interview, October 16, 1980; Tōkyōto, *'81 Tomin Geijutsu Fuesuteibaru*; Tōkyōto, Kyōikuchō, Shakai Kyōikubu, Bunkaka, *'81 Tomin Geijutsu Fuesuteibaru jigyō naiyō*, Tokyo, Tōkyōto, 1980.

25 Etō interview, December 25, 1980; Itō Takamichi, quoted by Katō Mikio, interview, October 30, 1980; Hara interview, October 28, 1980; Kimura Yōichi interview, December 12, 1980; Ebara, *Nihon bijutsukai*, pp. 77-78.

26 Anzai interview, October 27, 1980.

27 Ebara, *Nihon bijutsukai*, p. 131; Lawrence B. Flood interview, October 22, 1980; Charles H. Walsh, Jr., interview, October 22, 1980; Bunkachō, *Bunka gyōsei no ayumi*, p. 75; National Museum of Modern Art, Tokyo, *National Museum of Modern Art, Tokyo*, Tokyo, National Museum of Modern Art, Tokyo, 1978.

28 Inumaru interview, November 5, 1980; Machida interview, October 29, 1980; Adachi, *Bunkachō*, pp. 105-112; Bunkachō, *Bunka gyōsei*, p. 120.

29 Hase interview, October 14, 1980; Matsuki interview, October 14, 1980.

30 Takeishi interview, October 29, 1980; Komatsu Takeshi interview, October 20, 1980.

31 Bunkachō, *Bunka gyōsei no ayumi*, p. 91; *Asahi nenkan 1979*, p. 622; Takeishi interview, October 29, 1980; Masui, ed., *Dēta*, p. 136.

32 *Ongaku nenkan 1977*, pp. 38-43; *Ongaku nenkan 1980*, p. 37; Takeishi interview, October 29, 1980; Masui, ed., *Dēta*, pp. 152-154.

33 Takasugi Tsuneo interview, October 20, 1980; Saitō Yōichi interview, October 20, 1980; *Asahi nenkan 1977*, p. 713.

34 Ted T. Takaya, ed. and trans., *Modern Japanese Drama: An Anthology*, New York, Columbia University Press, 1979, p. xxvii; *Engeki nenkan '77*, p. 54; Nihon Geinō Jitsuenka Dantai Kyōgikai, *Geinōjin no seikatsu to ishiki—dainikai geinōjin jittai chōsa hōkokusho*, Tokyo, Nihon Geinō Jitsuenka Dantai Kyōgikai, 1979, pp. 3-4; *Japan Times*, October 20, 1980 and October 25, 1980; Takeishi interview, October 29, 1980.

35 Kimura Itaru interview, October 20, 1980; Katō Nobuko interview, October 20, 1980; Netzer, *Subsidized Muse*, pp. 45-46; *New York Times*, February 29, 1980; John S. Harris, *Government Patronage of the Arts in Great Britain*, Chicago, University of Chicago Press, 1970, pp. 6-7.

36 Shikaumi, *Cultural Policy*, p. 12; Bunkachō, *Bunka gyōsei chōki*, p. 36. See annual accounts of international arts activity in *Asahi nenkan*.

37 Kokusai Kōryū Kikin, *Kokusai Kōryū Kikin nenpō, Shōwa 54nendohan*, Tokyo, Kokusai Kōryū Kikin, 1979, p. 9.

38 Japan Foundation, *Annual Report 1978-79*, Tokyo, Japan Foundation, 1979, pp. 30-49, 73-74.

39 Haryū, *Sengo*, p. 223; Haryū interview, November 13, 1980; Ivan P. Hall interview, November 14, 1980; Japan-United States Friendship Commission, *Announcement of Programs 1979-1980*, Washington, D.C., Japan-United States Friendship Commission, 1979, pp. 3-4, 14-17, 23.

40 Nihon Bankoku Hakurankai Kinen Kikin, *Grants Awarded by the JEC Fund*, Tokyo, Nihon Bankoku Hakurankai Kinen Kikin, 1978, 1979; Nihon Bankoku Hakurankai Kinen Kikin, *Shōwa 55nendo Nihon Bankoku Hakurankai Kinen Kikin jigyō*, Tokyo, Nihon Bankoku Hakurankai Kinen Kikin, 1980; Japan Center for International Exchange, *Philanthropy in Japan*, pp. 221-227; Bunkachō, *Bunka gyōsei chōki*, p. 37.

41 Phillips, "Arts," p. 17. See Moore, *Economics*, pp. 123-128; *New York Times*, October 26, 1980.

42 I am indebted to Donald Richie for comments on this point. Richie interview, October 6, 1980. See Phillips, "Arts," pp. 15-16; *Asahi nenkan 1977*, p. 713; *New York Times*, October 26, 1980.

43 Adachi, *Bunkachō*, p. 132; Netzer, *Subsidized Muse*, p. 158;

Frederick Dorian, *Commitment to Culture: Arts Patronage in Europe: Its Significance for America*, Pittsburgh, University of Pittsburgh Press, 1964, pp. 435-436.

44 Bunkachō, *Bunka gyōsei chōki*, p. 5.

45 Adachi interview, October 22, 1980.

CHAPTER 5 THE VISUAL ARTS: SHOW AND SELL

1 Asian Cultural Centre, *Report*, p. 12; Watanuki Fujio interview, November 7, 1980; Haryū interview, November 13, 1980; Kimura Yōichi interview, December 12, 1980; Segi Shin'ichi interview, December 9, 1980.

2 Kawakita, *Modern Currents*, pp. 37-39, 118-119, 149-150; Kramer, "Beyond the Avant-garde," pp. 44-45.

3 Kagesato Tetsurō, "Tayōka to kokusaika—Shōwaki sengo no kaiga," in Hijikata Teiichi, ed., *Nihon kaigakan*, XI, *gendai*, Tokyo, Kōdansha, 1971, p. 158. See *Zusetsu*, p. 345.

4 Takeda, *Bijutsushi*, p. 151. See Hugo Munsterberg, *The Art of Modern Japan*, New York, Hacker Art Books, 1978, p. 36; Kawakita, *Modern Currents*, pp. 84-89, 145-147; *Nihon kindaishi jiten*, pp. 481-482; Kagesato, "Tayōka," p. 160; *Zusetsu*, pp. 339-342.

5 Tanio Nakamura, *Contemporary Japanese-style Painting*, trans. by Mikio Ito, Tokyo, Tokyo International Publishers, Ltd., 1969, p. 12. See ibid., pp. 13-15, 25-26; *Asahi geijutsu nenkan 1977*, Tokyo, Sanpō, 1977, p. 1; *Asahi nenkan 1977*, p. 713; *Asahi nenkan 1978*, p. 615.

6 Kawakita, *Modern Currents*, pp. 115-118, 129, 150; *Zusetsu*, pp. 347-348; *Asahi nenkan 1969*, p. 734.

7 Yoshiaki Tono, "Artists in the Early Sixties," in Shuji Takashina, Yoshiaki Tono, and Hideo Tomiyama, eds., *Art in Japan Today*, Tokyo, Japan Foundation, 1974, pp. 17-19; Munsterberg, *Art of Modern Japan*, pp. 62-63, 70; Haryū, *Sengo*, pp. 147-148; Takeda, *Bijutsushi*, p. 153; Museum of Modern Art, *New*, p. 10; Kawakita Michiaki, ed., *Kindai Nihon no bijutsu*, Tokyo, Shakai Shisōsha, 1964, pp. 183, 197; *Asahi nenkan 1980*, p. 613; *Japan Times*, January 18, 1981.

8 Iino interview, December 16, 1980. See Kawakita, *Modern Currents*, p. 119; *Zusetsu*, pp. 329-335; Munsterberg, *Art of Modern Japan*, pp. 104-108; Shuji Takashina, "Modern Sculpture,"

in Shuji Takashina, Yoshiaki Tono, and Hideo Tomiyama, eds., *Art in Japan Today*, Tokyo, Japan Foundation, 1974, pp. 11-15; *Asahi nenkan 1964*, p. 649; *Asahi nenkan 1970*, pp. 712-713; *Japan Times*, January 18, 1981.

9   Hara interview, October 28, 1980. See Robin Boyd, *Kenzo Tange*, New York, George Braziller, 1962; McMullen, *Art*, p. 172; *Asahi nenkan 1977*, p. 718; Haryū, *Sengo*, p. 205; *New York Times*, December 22, 1978 and January 14, 1979; *Asahi nenkan 1980*, p. 618.

10   Iino interview, December 16, 1980.

11   Etō interview, December 25, 1980; Haryū interview, November 13, 1980. See Aspen Institute, *Arts*, pp. 46-47.

12   Haryū interview, November 13, 1980.

13   Johnson interview, November 12, 1980. See Gaston Petit, *Evolving Techniques in Japanese Woodblock Prints*, New York and Tokyo, Kodansha International, 1977, pp. 14-22; Munsterberg, *Art of Modern Japan*, p. 93; Margaret K. Johnson and Dale K. Hilton, *Japanese Prints Today: Tradition with Innovation*, Tokyo, Shufu no Tomosha, 1980, pp. 66-70.

14   Maki Jun'ichi interview, December 3, 1980. See Museum of Modern Art, *New*, pp. 9-10; *Zusetsu*, p. 344; *Asahi nenkan 1972*, p. 707; Bunkachō, *Bunka gyōsei no ayumi*, pp. 73-74. For Nitten, Narita Kyōichi interview, December 17, 1980.

15   Nihon Geijutsuin, *Nihon Geijutsuinshi*, Tokyo, Nihon Geijutsuin, 1963, p. 4.

16   Statement of purpose, quoted in Nitten, *Nitten yōran Shōwa 54nendo*, Tokyo, Nitten, 1980, p. 12. See Nitten, *Nitten kaigashū 1975-1976*, Tokyo, Nitten, 1977, p. 3; *Asahi nenkan 1960*, p. 451; *Asahi nenkan 1969*, p. 711; *Asahi nenkan 1979*, p. 616.

17   Nitten, *Nitten benran*, Tokyo, Nitten, 1979, pp. 52-58; *Nitten yōran*, pp. 42-47; Nitten, *Daijūnikai Nitten sakuhinshū*, Tokyo, Nitten, 1980, p. 230.

18   Narita interview, December 17, 1980. Income figures are calculated from data in *Nitten benran*, pp. 52-58; *Nitten yōran*, pp. 14, 45-47.

19   Narita interview, December 17, 1980. For Nitten regulations, see *Nitten yōran*, p. 24, and *Nitten benran*, pp. 50-51.

20   Anzai interview, October 27, 1980; Narita interview, December 17, 1980.

21 *Nitten benran*, pp. 50-51; Nitten, *Daijūnikai*, pp. 224, 228.

22 Kimura Yōichi interview, December 12, 1980. Information on the painters from Ikeda interview, November 26, 1980; Haryū interview, November 13, 1980; Maki interview, December 3, 1980; Izeki Masaaki interview, December 12, 1980; Kawashima interview, November 27, 1980; Segi interview, December 9, 1980.

23 For information on informal previews (*shitamikai*), Maki interview, December 3, 1980; Kawashima interview, November 27, 1980; Izeki interview, December 12, 1980; Kimura Yōichi interview, December 12, 1980; Ikeda interview, November 26, 1980; Watanuki interview, November 7, 1980.

24 Haryū interview, November 13, 1980.

25 Segi interview, December 9, 1980. For information on Nitten sales, Kimura Yōichi interview, December 12, 1980; Narita interview, December 17, 1980; Haryū interview, November 13, 1980.

26 Haryū interview, November 13, 1980.

27 Hara interview, October 28, 1980.

28 Saint-Gilles interview, December 6, 1980.

29 Segi, *Shakai*, pp. 145-153, 174. On art in wartime, see Thomas R. H. Havens, *Valley of Darkness: The Japanese People and World War Two*, New York, W. W. Norton & Company, Inc., 1978, pp. 67-68, 202.

30 *Asahi nenkan 1966*, p. 697; Segi interview, December 9, 1980.

31 *Japan Times*, February 22, 1981.

32 John Powers interview, December 3, 1980.

33 Segi interview, December 9, 1980; Yoshii interview, October 14, 1980; Haryū interview, November 13, 1980; Arai Yasuko interview, December 11, 1980; Iino interview, December 16, 1980; Shimanaka Fumio interview, December 17, 1980; Haryū, *Sengo*, pp. 215-217; Segi, *Shakai*, pp. 127, 174, 177, 184-186.

34 Jitsukawa Nobuhiro interview, December 25, 1980; Watanuki interview, November 7, 1980; Segi, *Shakai*, p. 163; Tomars, "Class Systems," pp. 477-478; Haryū, *Sengo*, p. 213.

35 Segi interview, December 9, 1980. For information on the art market, Haryū interview, November 13, 1980; Kawashima interview, November 27, 1980; Hara interview, October 28, 1980;

Kimura Yōichi interview, December 12, 1980; Saint-Gilles interview, December 6, 1980; Takikawa Yoshiko interview, November 27, 1980.

36 Segi interview, December 9, 1980; Saint-Gilles interview, December 6, 1980; Hara interview, October 28, 1980; Tomars, "Class Systems," p. 479; Segi, *Shakai*, pp. 210-220.

37 Mukai interview, October 27, 1980; Saint-Gilles interview, December 6, 1980; Shimanaka interview, December 17, 1980; Kawashima interview, November 27, 1980; Hara interview, October 28, 1980; Johnson interview, November 12, 1980; Tōbi Kenkyūjo, *Tōkyō bijutsu ichibashi*, Tokyo, Tōkyō Bijutsu Kurabu, 1979, p. 695; Segi, *Shakai*, p. 175.

38 Segi interview, December 9, 1980.

39 Hara interview, October 28, 1980; Shimanaka interview, December 17, 1980; Honda interview, December 15, 1980; Anzai interview, October 27, 1980; Yoshii interview, October 14, 1980; Johnson interview, November 12, 1980.

40 Yoshii interview, October 14, 1980; Shimanaka interview, December 17, 1980; Arai interview, December 11, 1980; Jitsukawa interview, December 25, 1980; Saint-Gilles interview, December 6, 1980; Honda interview, December 15, 1980; Kamiya interview, December 16, 1980.

41 Shimanaka interview, December 17, 1980; Johnson interview, November 12, 1980; Frances Blakemore interview, December 27, 1980; Anzai interview, October 27, 1980; Hara interview, October 28, 1980; Saint-Gilles interview, December 6, 1980.

42 Kawashima interview, November 27, 1980; Saint-Gilles interview, December 6, 1980; Segi interview, December 9, 1980.

43 Kimura Yōichi interview, December 12, 1980; Saint-Gilles interview, December 6, 1980; Mukai interview, October 27, 1980; Segi interview, December 9, 1980; Kimura Eiji interview, December 8, 1980.

44 Johnson interview, November 12, 1980; Watanuki interview, November 7, 1980; Haryū interview, November 13, 1980; Honda interview, December 15, 1980; Kamiya interview, December 16, 1980; Arai interview, December 16, 1980; Norman Tolman interview, December 4, 1980; Shimanaka interview, December 17, 1980; Yoneda interview, November 26, 1980; Ikeda interview, November 26, 1980. See *Print Communicator*, 1980, nos. 56-59, 62.

45 Kamiya interview, December 16, 1980; Johnson interview, November 12, 1980. For comments on marketing art, Kimura Yōichi interview, December 12, 1980; Honda interview, December 15, 1980; Arai interview, December 11, 1980; Museum of Modern Art, *New*, p. 10.

46 Johnson interview, November 12, 1980; Takikawa interview, November 27, 1980; Honda interview, December 15, 1980; Kamiya interview, December 16, 1980; Ikeda interview, November 26, 1980. See Mason Griff, "The Recruitment and Socialization of Artists," in Milton C. Albrecht, James H. Barnett, and Mason Griff, eds., *The Sociology of Art and Literature: A Reader*, New York, Praeger Publishers, 2nd ed., 1970, pp. 146-155.

47 Jitsukawa interview, December 25, 1980; Etō interview, December 25, 1980.

48 Tsuji Yutaka interview, December 8, 1980; Mainichi Shinbunsha, *Mainichi shinbun hyakunenshi, 1872-1972*, Tokyo, Mainichi Shinbunsha, 1972, pp. 544, 558-563.

49 Blakemore interview, December 27, 1980; Sakazaki Tarō interview, April 19, 1977; Chiba Kihei interview, May 10, 1977; Yamamoto Noriyuki interview, April 25, 1977; Yomiuri Shinbun Hyakunenshi Henshū Iinkai, *Yomiuri shinbun hyakunenshi*, vol. I, Tokyo, Yomiuri Shinbunsha, 1976, p. 825.

50 Amano interview, December 22, 1980; Yamamoto interview, April 25, 1977; Sakazaki interview, April 19, 1977; Kawai Shin interview, April 19, 1977; Chiba interview, May 10, 1977; *Yomiuri shinbun hyakunenshi*, I, 825; *Mainichi shinbun hyakunenshi*, p. 544.

51 Asano Shōichirō, "Asahi no tenrankai," *Asahijin*, August 1980, pp. 85-89; Sakazaki interview, December 24, 1980; Yamamoto interview, April 25, 1977; Enna Takio interview, December 11, 1980; Kagesato, "Tayōka," p. 158; Haryū, *Sengo*, pp. 143-146; *Asahi nenkan 1955*, p. 505; *Asahi nenkan 1956*, p. 553.

52 Bunkachō, *Bunka gyōsei no ayumi*, pp. 275-284; Enna Takio, *Chinmoku no shishatachi*, Tokyo, Shinchōsha, 1980, p. 162.

53 Enna interview, December 11, 1980; Tsuji interview, December 8, 1980; Amano interview, December 22, 1980.

54 Sakazaki interview, December 24, 1980. See Asano, "Asahi," p. 85.

55 Tsuji interview, December 8, 1980; Amano interview, December 22, 1980; Asano, "Asahi," pp. 82-86.

56 Asano, "Asahi," p. 85; Sakazaki interview, December 24, 1980; Takahashi Chikako interview, December 24, 1980; Asian Cultural Centre, *Report*, p. 15; For data on art shows treating premodern Japanese themes, see annual listings in *Asahi nenkan*.

57 Amano interview, December 22, 1980; Sakazaki interview, April 19, 1977; Kawai interview, April 19, 1977; Takahashi interview, December 24, 1980; Yamamoto interview, April 25, 1977; Chiba interview, May 10, 1977; *Mainichi shinbun hyakunenshi*, pp. 544-556.

58 Tsuji interview, December 8, 1980; Sakazaki interview, December 24, 1980; Takahashi interview, December 24, 1980.

59 Amano interview, December 22, 1980.

60 Chiba Kihei correspondence, December 20, 1980.

61 See Ebara, *Nihon bijutsukai*, pp. 71-72, 74-75.

62 Chiba interview, May 10, 1977; Sakazaki interview, April 19, 1977 and December 24, 1980; Kawai interview, April 19, 1977; Yamamoto interview, April 25, 1977; Takahashi interview, December 24, 1980.

63 Amano interview, December 22, 1980; Sakazaki interview, December 24, 1980.

64 Kaneko interview, October 13, 1980.

65 Amano interview, December 22, 1980.

66 Sakazaki interview, December 24, 1980.

67 *Asahi nenkan 1975*, p. 702; Adachi, *Bunkachō*, pp. 258-259; Sakazaki interview, December 24, 1980; Kaneko interview, October 13, 1980.

68 Katase Keisuke interview, April 21, 1977; *Asahi nenkan 1972*, p. 706; Haryū, *Sengo*, pp. 212-213; Segi, *Shakai*, p. 176.

69 Chiba interview, December 17, 1980; Ebara, *Nihon bijutsukai*, p. 64; Asano, "Asahi," p. 85.

70 Asano, "Asahi," p. 84; Katase interview, April 21, 1977; Kaneko interview, October 13, 1980; Ebara, *Nihon bijutsukai*, pp. 64-65.

71 Kaneko interview, October 13, 1980; *Asahi nenkan 1978*, p. 615.

CHAPTER 6   THEATER: PLAYING SAFE

1   Aoi Yōji interview, October 30, 1980; Kurabayashi interview, November 11, 1980.

2   Aoi interview, October 30, 1980; Machida interview, October 29, 1980; Okochi, "Theatrical Situation," p. 6; Faubion Bowers, *Japanese Theatre*, New York, Hermitage, 1952, p. 217; Shingekidan Kyōgikai, *Kaihō*, no. 55, January 1980.

3   John Allyn, Jr., "The Tsukiji Little Theater and the Beginnings of Modern Theater in Japan," Ph.D. dissertation, University of California, Los Angeles, 1970, p. 92. See J. Thomas Rimer, *Toward a Modern Japanese Theatre: Kishida Kunio*, Princeton, Princeton University Press, 1974, pp. 12-55; Bowers, *Theatre*, pp. 349-350; Earle Ernst, *The Kabuki Theatre*, New York, Oxford University Press, 1956, pp. 251-259; Brian Powell, "Japan's First Modern Theatre—the Tsukiji Shōgekijō and Its Company, 1924-1926," *Monumenta Nipponica*, XXX, 1, spring 1975, pp. 69-85.

4   See David Goodman, "Satoh Makoto and Japanese Underground Theater," seminar paper, Japan-United States Educational Commission, January 30, 1981; Abe Bun'yū and Sugai Yukio, eds., *Rōen undō*, Tokyo, Miraisha, 1970, pp. 9-16; Benito Ortolani, "Shingeki: the Maturing New Drama of Japan," in Joseph Roggendorf, ed., *Studies in Japanese Culture*, Tokyo, Sophia University, 1963, p. 168.

5   Bowers, *Theatre*, p. 352; Ted T. Takaya, ed. and trans., *Modern Japanese Drama: An Anthology*, New York, Columbia University Press, 1979, p. xxii; *Asahi nenkan 1962*, p. 615; Gekidan Haiyūza, *Haiyūzashi, 1965-1973*, Tokyo, Gekidan Haiyūza, 1974, pp. 5-128; Shingekidan Kyōgikai, *Kaihō*, no. 55, January 1980; Ibaraki Tadashi, *Zōho Nihon shingeki shōshi*, Tokyo, Miraisha, 1973, p. 163. On theater censorship during the American occupation of Japan, see Bowers, *Theatre*, p. 351; Ernst, *Kabuki*, pp. 259-266.

6   Ozaki, "Shingeki II," pp. 187-188, 196; Takaya, ed., *Modern Japanese Drama*, pp. xxiii-xxvi; Ibaraki, *Shingeki*, pp. 140-149; Benito Ortolani, "Fukuda Tsuneari: Modernization and Shingeki," in Donald H. Shively, ed., *Tradition and Modernization in Japanese Culture*, Princeton, Princeton University Press, 1971, pp. 470-476; Ortolani, "Shingeki," pp. 170-185; George M. Murphy, " 'Omon Tota': A Folktale Play by Kinoshita Junji," Ph.D. dissertation, University of Washington, Seattle, 1975, pp. v-vii; Eric J. Gangloff, "Introduction," in Junji Kinoshita, *Be-*

tween Gods and Man: A Judgment on War Crimes, trans. by
Eric J. Gangloff, Tokyo, University of Tokyo Press, 1979, pp.
1-2; Bowers, *Theatre,* pp. 357-358; Goodman, "Satoh Makoto."

7   Bowers, *Theatre,* pp. 352, 359-360; *Asahi nenkan 1959,* p. 475;
Asahi nenkan 1960, p. 449; Allyn, "Tsukiji," p. 156; H. Paul
Varley, *Japanese Culture: A Short History,* expanded ed., New
York, Praeger Publishers, 1977, p. 241.

8   Takaya, ed., *Modern Japanese Drama,* p. xxvii. See Ozaki, "Shingeki II," p. 196-199; Ibaraki, *Shingeki,* pp. 156-160.

9   Ibaraki, *Shingeki,* p. 160, 166-167; *Asahi nenkan 1961,* p. 452;
Asahi nenkan 1963, p. 660; *Asahi nenkan 1965,* p. 658; *Zusetsu,* p. 302; *Asahi nenkan 1969,* p. 724; *Asahi nenkan 1970,*
p. 703; Yasuji Toita, *Kabuki: The Popular Theater,* trans. by
Don Kenny, New York and Tokyo, John Weatherhill, Inc. and
Kyoto, Tankosha, 1974, p. 224. The Mishima play was an
adaptation of *Chinsetsu yumiharaizuki* by Takizawa Bakin.

10 Martin Friedman, quoted in Phillips, "Arts," p. 2. On the un-
derground, see Kurabayashi, "Zuisōteki," part 3, *Teatoro,* May
1979, pp. 112-114, and part 4, *Teatoro,* June 1979, p. 121;
Ibaraki, *Shingeki,* pp. 163-167; *Asahi nenkan 1967,* p. 729;
Asahi nenkan 1969, pp. 731-732; *Asahi nenkan 1974,* p. 721;
Asahi nenkan 1979, p. 629.

11 Donald Richie, "Japan's Avant-Garde Theatre," *Japan Foun-
dation Newsletter,* April-May 1979, pp. 1-3; *New York Times,*
April 15, 1979; Goodman, "Satoh Makoto"; Ian Buruma, "How
Traditional is the Avant-Garde?" *Japan Illustrated,* spring 1977,
pp. 2-4; *Concerned Theatre Japan,* October 1969, pp. 8-9; Kishi,
"Beyond Noh and Kabuki," pp. 6-7; Carol Jay Sorgenfrei, "Shuji
Terayama: Avant Garde Dramatist of Japan," Ph.D. disserta-
tion, University of California, Santa Barbara, 1978, p. 72.

12 Yamazaki Masakazu interview, in Yamazaki, *Mask and Sword:
Two Plays for the Contemporary Japanese Theatre,* trans. by
J. Thomas Rimer, New York, Columbia University Press, 1980,
p. 203; A. Horie-Webber, "Modernisation of the Japanese Theatre: The Shingeki Movement," in W. G. Beasley, ed., *Modern
Japan: Aspects of History, Literature and Society,* Berkeley, University of California Press, 1975, p. 152; Gekidan Shiki, *Gekidan Shiki sōritsu 25shūnen kinen,* Tokyo, Gekidan Shiki, 1978,
passim; Aoi interview, October 30, 1980.

13 Nichols interview, December 1, 1980; *Asahi nenkan 1971,* p.

707; *Asahi nenkan 1973*, pp. 717-718, 722; *Asahi nenkan 1974*, p. 721; *Asahi nenkan 1977*, p. 726; *Engeki nenkan '79*, p. 208; *Asahi nenkan 1981*, p. 595.

14 Aoi interview, October 30, 1980; Goodman, "Satoh Makoto"; Akiko Kanda interview, November 28, 1980.

15 Bowers, *Theatre*, p. 217; Machida, *Buyō*, pp. 731-732; Ozaki, "Shingeki II," p. 188. See Moore, *Economics*, pp. 94-96; Jack Poggi, *Theater in America: The Impact of Economic Forces, 1870-1967*, Ithaca, Cornell University Press, 1968, pp. xv-xvi.

16 Machida, *Buyō*, pp. 733, 800-801; Abe and Sugai, eds., *Rōen undō*, p. 141.

17 *Gekidan Shiki*, p. 41; *Asahi nenkan 1974*, p. 719; *Asahi nenkan 1975*, p. 714; *Asahi nenkan 1979*, pp. 629-630; *Asahi nenkan 1980*, p. 628; Ozaki, "Shingeki II," p. 203.

18 *Asahi nenkan 1974*, p. 720; *Asahi nenkan 1979*, p. 630; Okochi, "Theatrical Situation," p. 5; Ōkōchi interview, November 19, 1980; Kurahashi interview, November 12, 1980.

19 Yamabe Yoshihide interview, June 20, 1977; Kurabayashi interview, November 11, 1980; *Zenkoku Rōen nyūsu*, no. 79, June 15, 1980, p. 6; Okochi, "Theatrical Situation," p. 5.

20 Yamabe interview, June 20, 1977; Abe and Sugai, eds., *Rōen undō*, pp. 28-30, 141; Ibaraki, *Shingeki*, p. 150; Senda interview, *Concerned Theatre Japan*, summer 1970, p. 68.

21 "Rōen undō no mondaiten," *Kokumin bunka*, no. 207, February 1977, p. 12.

22 Zen Nihon Amachua Engeki Kyōgikai, *Amateur Theatre in the World*, Yokohama, Zen Nihon Amachua Engeki Kyōgikai, 1975, pp. 91-92; Ōhashi Kiichi and Abe Bun'yū, eds., *Jiritsu engeki undō*, Tokyo, Miraisha, 1975, pp. 6-10, 88-89, 137-141, 306-307; Ibaraki, *Shingeki*, pp. 153-156; *Tōkyō hataraku mono no engekisai*, no. 12, 1974 and no. 13, 1975; *Kokumin bunka*, no. 235, June 1979, p. 7.

23 "Rōen undō," p. 12; Abe and Sugai, eds., *Rōen undō*, p. 142; Yamabe interview, June 20, 1977. See Abe and Sugai, eds., *Rōen undō*, pp. 136-151; Ibaraki, *Shingeki*, p. 151.

24 Kurabayashi, "Zuisōteki," part 5, *Teatoro*, July 1979, p. 122; Abe and Sugai, eds., *Rōen undō*, p. 271; *Asahi nenkan 1962*, p. 616; *Asahi nenkan 1965*, p. 658; *Asahi nenkan 1971*, p. 703; Kurabayashi, "Sūji," p. 128; Yamabe interview, June 20, 1977; *Kokumin bunka*, no. 185, April 1975, pp. 4-16; Hidaka Rokurō,

"Sengo bunka undōshi no susume," *Iwanami kōza Nihon rekishi geppō*, no. 25, May 1977, pp. 3-7; Rimer, *Toward*, p. 281; Ibaraki, *Shingeki*, pp. 151-152; Abe and Sugai, eds., *Rōen undō*, pp. 43-51, 163-168, 196-206, 268-269.

25 "Rōen undō," p. 13; Zenkoku Rōen Kanjikai, *Zenkoku Rōen no jūnen, 1963-1973*, Tokyo, Zenkoku Rōen Renraku Kaigi, 1973, p. 4; Abe and Sugai, eds., *Rōen undō*, pp. 207, 210, 251-252, 270-274.

26 Tanaka Mitsuru interview, April 28, 1977; Abe Bun'yū interview, September 25, 1980; Yamabe interview, June 20, 1977; *Zenkoku Rōen*, pp. 21-23, 29; Abe and Sugai, eds., *Rōen undō*, pp. 275-276; *Zenkoku Rōen nyūsu*, no. 79, June 15, 1980, p. 3.

27 *Asahi nenkan 1971*, p. 703; Abe and Sugai, eds., *Rōen undō*, pp. 211-214, 273-278; Yamashita, *Atarashii*, pp. 163-171; "Rōen undō," pp. 12-14; Kurabayashi, "Sūji," p. 128; Kurabayashi, "Zuisōteki," part 5, *Teatoro*, July 1979, p. 122; *Zenkoku Rōen nyūsu*, no. 79, June 15, 1980, pp. 4-12; Tōkyō Rōen, *Reikai wa anata no ippyō de kimaru!* Tokyo, Tōkyō Rōen, 1980.

28 Ibaraki, *Shingeki*, p. 152; *Asahi nenkan 1964*, p. 640; *Asahi nenkan 1965*, p. 658; Tomin Gekijō, *Tomin Gekijō kaiin no shiori*, Tokyo, Tomin Gekijō, 1980; Tomin Gekijō, *Tomin Gekijō 30nenshi*, Tokyo, Tomin Gekijō, 1976, pp. 1-13, 172-176; *Ongaku nenkan 1977*, pp. 87-89; *Ongaku nenkan 1980*, p. 65; *Tomin Gekijō*, no. 285, March 1977, p. 8; *Tomin Gekijō*, no. 320, February 1980, p. 3.

29 Kurahashi interview, November 12, 1980; Kurabayashi interview, November 11, 1980; Ōkōchi interview, November 19, 1980; Okochi, "Theatrical Situation," pp. 5-6.

30 Tsuno Kaitarō, quoted in *Concerned Theatre Japan*, October 1969, p. 9.

31 Inumaru Tadashi interview, November 5, 1980. See Rimer, *Toward*, pp. 7-11; Ibaraki, *Shingeki*, p. 170; Bowers, *Theatre*, pp. 356-357.

32 *Shingeki*, January 1981 and February 1981; *Gekidan Shiki*, p. 52; Horie-Webber, "Modernisation," pp. 148-149; Shingekidan Kyōgikai, *Kaihō*, no. 55, January 1980; Kurabayashi interview, November 11, 1980; Aoi interview, October 30, 1980.

33 Gekidan Haiyūza, *Haiyūzashi, 1965-1973*, p. 137; *Engeki nenkan '77*, p. 54; Kurabayashi interview, November 11, 1980;

Inumaru interview, November 5, 1980; Aoi interview, October 30, 1980. See Poggi, *Theater*, p. 99.

34 Kurabayashi, "Sūji," p. 127; Kurabayashi interview, November 11, 1980; Aoi interview, October 30, 1980.

35 Kurabayashi, "Zuisōteki," part 3, *Teatoro*, May 1979, p. 110, and part 5, *Teatoro*, July 1979, p. 121; Don Kenny interview, October 8, 1980; Aoi interview, October 30, 1980.

36 Kurabayashi interview, November 11, 1980.

37 Kurabayashi interview, November 11, 1980; Kurahashi interview, November 12, 1980; Kurabayashi, "Zuisōteki," part 5, *Teatoro*, July 1979, pp. 118-119.

38 Kurabayashi, "Zuisōteki," part 4, *Teatoro*, June 1979, p. 123. See Horie-Webber, "Modernisation," pp. 149-151.

39 Kurabayashi, "Zuisōteki," part 3, *Teatoro*, May 1979, pp. 109-110, and part 4, *Teatoro*, June 1979, p. 123; Kurabayashi interview, November 11, 1980; *Bungei nenkan 1976*, p. 142.

40 Kurabayashi interview, November 11, 1980; Machida interview, October 29, 1980; Kurabayashi, "Zuisōteki," part 5, *Teatoro*, July 1979, p. 118.

41 Tanaka interview, April 28, 1977; *Fuorukusubyūne*, no. 133, February 1, 1976.

42 Kurabayashi, "Zuisōteki," part 5, *Teatoro*, July 1979, p. 118; Aoi interview, *New Yorker*, June 9, 1980, pp. 31-32.

43 Kurabayashi interview, November 11, 1980; Machida interview, October 29, 1980; Aoi interview, October 30, 1980; Senda interview, *Concerned Theatre Japan*, summer 1970, p. 68; Horie-Webber, "Modernisation," p. 149; Okochi, "Theatrical Situation," p. 5.

44 Aoi interview, October 30, 1980; Kenny interview, October 8, 1980; Kurabayashi interview, November 11, 1980; *Gekidan Shiki*, p. 35.

45 Ibaraki, *Shingeki*, pp. 149-150; Abe and Sugai, eds., *Rōen undō*, pp. 7, 16-22; Kurabayashi, "Zuisōteki," part 3, *Teatoro*, May 1979, p. 111; Kenny interview, October 8, 1980; Kurabayashi interview, November 11, 1980; Kurahashi interview, November 12, 1980; Aoi interview, October 30, 1980; Machida interview, October 29, 1980.

46 Aoi interview, October 30, 1980.

47 Kurabayashi interview, November 11, 1980; Aoi interview, Oc-

tober 30, 1980; Kenny interview, October 8, 1980; *Gekidan Shiki*, pp. 34-35, 62-63; Kurabayashi, "Zuisōteki," part 5, *Teatoto*, July 1979, pp. 124-125.

48 Inumaru interview, November 5, 1980; Senda interview, *Concerned Theatre Japan*, summer 1970, p. 69; *Engeki nenkan '77*, p. 54; Nihon Geinōjin Jitsuenka Dantai Kyōgikai, *Geinōjin no seikatsu to ishiki—dainikai geinōjin jittai chōsa hōkokusho*, Tokyo, Nihon Geinōjin Jitsuenka Dantai Kyōgikai, 1979, p. 28; Horie-Webber, "Modernisation," p. 149; Aoi interview, October 30, 1980.

49 Kenny interview, October 8, 1980.

50 Goodman, "Satoh Makoto."

51 Kara interview, November 10, 1980.

52 Goodman, "Satoh Makoto." In addition to sources cited in notes 10 and 11, see Ozaki, "Shingeki II," p. 201; *Asahi nenkan 1970*, p. 703; *Asahi nenkan 1975*, 716.

53 Goodman, "Satoh Makoto."

54 Nagai Michio interview, November 7, 1980.

55 Ōkōchi interview, November 19, 1980; Ōkawa interview, December 4, 1980; Diamond Lead Company, Ltd., *Diamond's Japan Business Directory 1979*, Tokyo, Diamond Lead Company, Ltd., 1979, p. 1188; Nobumoto Yasusada interview, January 30, 1981.

56 *Engeki nenkan '78*, p. 35. On postwar kabuki, Ezaki interview, October 23, 1980; Okawa interview, December 4, 1980; Bowers, *Japanese Theatre*, pp. 217-219; Bowers, *Theatre*, pp. 340-342; *Zusetsu*, pp. 303-305; Leonard C. Pronko, "Kabuki Today and Tomorrow," *Comparative Drama*, VI, 2, summer 1972, p. 109; Toita, *Kabuki*, pp. 206-210, 219-222; *Tomin Gekijō 30nenshi*, pp. 8-9.

57 Ezaki interview, October 23, 1980. See Bowers, *Theatre*, p. 356; Toita, *Kabuki*, p. 202; *Engeki nenkan '77*, p. 35.

58 *Asahi nenkan 1979*, p. 630; *Engeki nenkan '77*, pp. 73-79; Ōkawa interview, December 4, 1980; *Zusetsu*, p. 303.

59 Ōkawa interview, December 4, 1980.

60 Ōkawa interview, December 4, 1980.

61 *Asahi nenkan 1981*, p. 594; Okochi, "Theatrical Situation," pp. 2-4; Ōkōchi interview, November 19, 1980; *Asahi nenkan*

1964, p. 646; *Asahi nenkan 1968*, p. 728; *Asahi nenkan 1969*, p. 726; *Engeki nenkan '77*, p. 43.

62 Ōkōchi interview, November 19, 1980; Okochi, "Theatrical Situation," p. 9.

63 Kurahashi interview, November 12, 1980. Theater data from Ōkawa interview, December 4, 1980; Ōkōchi interview, November 19, 1980.

64 Ōkōchi interview, November 19, 1980; Okochi, "Theatrical Situation," p. 6.

65 Ōkōchi interview, November 19, 1980; Okochi, "Theatrical Situation," pp. 10-11.

66 Ōkōchi interview, November 19, 1980; Okochi, "Theatrical Situation," pp. 10-11.

67 Aoi interview, October 30, 1980; Ōkōchi interview, November 19, 1980; Kurahashi interview, November 12, 1980.

68 Senda interview, *Concerned Theatre Japan*, summer 1970, p. 69.

69 *Gekidan Shiki*, p. 23. On Nissei, Kenny interview, October 8, 1980; *Gekidan Shiki*, pp. 19-22; Machida interview, October 29, 1980; Machida, *Buyō*, p. 799; Ibaraki, *Shingeki*, p. 163; Kurabayashi, "Zuisōteki," part 3, *Teatoro*, May 1979, pp. 108-109.

70 *Asahi nenkan 1965*, pp. 659, 661; *Asahi nenkan 1966*, pp. 687-688; *Asahi nenkan 1971*, p. 703; Ibaraki, *Shingeki*, p. 162; *Gekidan Shiki*, p. 31; Kurabayashi, "Zuisōteki," part 4, *Teatoro*, June 1979, pp. 120-121; Kenny interview, October 8, 1980.

71 Kenny interview, October 8, 1980.

72 Ōkōchi interview, November 19, 1980.

CHAPTER 7   MUSIC: CULTIVATED CLIENTELES

1 Tsunematsu interview, November 21, 1980.

2 Ichiyanagi interview, November 30, 1980; Nishiyama, *Gendai*, pp. 1-2; McMullen, *Art*, p. 43.

3 Edward Rothstein, *New York Times Book Review*, July 29, 1979, p. 3; Akiyama interview, November 7, 1980; *Ongaku nenkan 1977*, p. 1; *Asahi nenkan 1981*, pp. 587, 590. See McMullen, *Art*, p. 49.

4 Dan interview, December 23, 1980; Akiyama interview, November 7, 1980; Dan Ikuma and Koizumi Fumio, *Nihon ongaku no saihakken*, Tokyo, Kōdansha, 1976, p. 132; Akiyama, "Japan," pp. 364-365.

5 Akiyama, *Nihon no sakkyokukatachi*, II, 343; Akiyama interview, November 7, 1980; Ichiyanagi interview, November 30, 1980; Akiyama, "Japan," pp. 365-366; Robin J. Heifetz, "Post-World War II Japanese Composition," thesis, University of Illinois, Urbana, 1978, pp. 12, 14, 35, 37, 39, 42, 49, 64; *Asahi nenkan 1963*, p. 668; *Asahi nenkan 1966*, p. 693; *Asahi nenkan 1968*, p. 736; Machida, *Buyō*, p. 797; *Ongaku nenkan 1977*, p. 1.

6 Takemitsu Tōru, quoted in Akiyama, "Japan," p. 365. See Heifetz, "Japanese Composition," pp. 45, 47; *Asahi nenkan 1975*, p. 694.

7 Takemitsu Tōru interview, *New York Times*, February 13, 1981.

8 *Ongaku nenkan 1977*, p. 2. See Akiyama, "Japan," p. 366.

9 Koizumi Fumio, *Nihon no oto*, Tokyo, Seidosha, 1977, p. 36.

10 Takemitsu interview, *New York Times*, February 13, 1981; Ichiyanagi interview, November 30, 1980; Hase interview, October 14, 1980; Akiyama interview, November 7, 1980; Richie interview, October 6, 1980.

11 Dan interview, December 23, 1980; Ichiyanagi interview, November 30, 1980; *Asahi nenkan 1977*, p. 720; Tsunematsu, "Ongakuka shōgai," p. 46; Ōsaka Ongaku Daigaku, *Kansai ongaku bunka shiryō '72*, Osaka, Ōsaka Ongaku Daigaku, 1972, p. 22; Ōsaka Ongaku Daigaku, *Nishi Nihon ongaku bunka shiryō '77*, Osaka, Ōsaka Ongaku Daigaku, 1977, pp. 7-10.

12 Kojima Tomiko, *Nihon no ongaku o kangaeru*, Tokyo, Ongaku no Tomosha, 1976, pp. 133-135; *Asahi nenkan 1973*, p. 710; *Ongaku nenkan 1977*, p. 2.

13 Fukuoka Rōon 20nenshi Henshū Iinkai, *Ongaku no midori o*, Fukuoka, Fukuoka Kinrōsha Ongaku Kyōgikai, 1975, p. 166. See Koizumi, *Nihon no oto*, p. 220; Tōkyō Rōon, *Tōkyō Rōon kiyaku*, Tokyo, Tōkyō Rōon, 1974, p. 3; Zenkoku Rōon Renraku Kaigi, *Rōon undō shōshi*, Tokyo, Zenkoku Rōon Renraku Kaigi, 1968, p. 18.

14 Kojima, *Nihon no ongaku*, pp. 136-138; *Asahi nenkan 1970*, p. 710; *Asahi nenkan 1975*, p. 707; *Asahi nenkan 1977*, p. 722; *Asahi nenkan 1981*, p. 590; *Bungei nenkan 1976*, p. 160.

15 Kishibe interview, January 26, 1981.

16 Nobumoto interview, January 30, 1981; Kishibe interview, January 26, 1981; Inumaru interview, November 5, 1980; *Nihon tōkei nenkan*, 1980, p. 615; Bunkachō, *Bunka gyōsei chōki*, p. 6.

17 Nobumoto interview, January 30, 1981; Nishiyama, *Gendai*, pp. 1-2.

18 Iwaki, "Ongaku kyōiku," p. 134; Malm, "Layers," pp. D3-9/10; Koizumi, *Nihon no oto*, p. 58; Dan and Koizumi, *Nihon ongaku*, pp. 8, 86, 92-93; Asian Cultural Centre, *Report*, p. 45; Nobumoto interview, January 30, 1981.

19 Kishibe interview, January 26, 1981; Bunkachō, *Bunka gyōsei no ayumi*, pp. 76, 78; Kanda interview, November 28, 1980.

20 Kishibe interview, January 26, 1981; Kanda interview, November 28, 1980; Inumaru interview, November 5, 1980.

21 Nobumoto interview, January 30, 1981; Kishibe interview, January 26, 1981; Nishiyama, *Gendai*, p. 31; Asian Cultural Centre, *Report*, pp. 37-39.

22 Nobumoto interview, January 30, 1981; Yoshida interview, December 25, 1980; Kishibe interview, January 26, 1981; Nishiyama, *Gendai*, pp. 1-2.

23 Malm, "Layers," p. D3-11; Dan interview, December 23, 1980.

24 Dan interview, December 23, 1980; Tateda Hitonari, "Tōkei kara mita saikin no ongaku daigaku," *Ongaku geijutsu*, May 1980, p. 34; Nakano interview, November 21, 1980; Tsunematsu interview, November 21, 1980; Masui, ed., *Dēta*, p. 86; Ōsaka Ongaku Daigaku, *Kansai '75*, p. 22.

25 Masui, ed., *Dēta*, pp. 2, 5, 10, 48, 65; Iwaki, "Ongaku kyōiku," p. 142; "*Kigyō no shakai kōken*," p. 198; Bunkachō, *Bunka gyōsei no ayumi*, pp. 78-80; Isaka Hiroshi, "Kurashikku no suitai o sukuu tame ni," *Ongaku geijutsu*, December 1980, p. 19.

26 *Ongaku nenkan 1977*, pp. 17-18; Akiyama interview, November 7, 1980; Kishibe interview, January 26, 1981.

27 Flood interview, October 22, 1980; Dan and Koizumi, *Nihon ongaku*, pp. 12-16; *New York Times*, November 13, 1977.

28 Iwaki interview, December 27, 1980; Iwaki, "Ongaku kyōiku," pp. 136-139.

29   Iwaki, "Ongaku kyōiku," pp. 138-140; Tsunematsu, "Ongakuka shōgai," p. 47.

30   Iwaki, "Ongaku kyōiku," p. 140.

31   Dan interview, December 23, 1980; Iwaki interview, December 27, 1980; Iwaki, "Ongaku kyōiku," pp. 136-143; Nakane, *Japanese Society*, p. 118.

32   See Malm, "Layers," p. D3-5.

33   Fukuoka Rōon, *Ongaku no midori*, p. 11; Zenkoku Rōon, *Rōon undō*, pp. 2, 8; Ozaki, "Shingeki II," pp. 141-142; Malm, "Layers," pp. D3-5/6.

34   Rōon bylaws, in Tōkyō Rōon, *Tōkyō Rōon nyūkai no shiori*, Tokyo, Tōkyō Rōon, 1977, p. 1; Rōon purpose, in *Tōkyō Rōon kiyaku*, p. 1. See Fukuoka Rōon, *Ongaku no midori*, p. 11; Zenkoku Rōon, *Rōon undō*, pp. 1-6.

35   Zenkoku Rōon, *Rōon undō*, p. 14. See also pp. 5-10; *Tōkyō Rōon kiyaku*, p. 3.

36   Zenkoku Rōon, *Rōon undō*, p. 20, quoting a declaration made at a national Rōon convention in November 1967.

37   Zenkoku Kinrōsha Ongaku Kyōgikai Renraku Kaigi, *Ii ongaku o yasuku ōku no hitobito ni*, Tokyo, Zenkoku Kinrōsha Ongaku Kyōgikai Renraku Kaigi, 1974, p. 3; *Asahi nenkan 1968*, p. 737; Yamashita, *Atarashii*, pp. 147-148, 151, 176-177, 181.

38   Zenkoku Kinrōsha, *Ii ongaku*, pp. 63-64; *Ongaku nenkan 1980*, pp. 61-63.

39   Haryū interview, November 13, 1980; *Tōkyō Rōon nyūkai*, p. 2; *Tōkyō Rōon kiyaku*, p. 3; Kurabayashi, "Sūji," p. 125; *Ongaku nenkan 1977*, pp. 83-84; *Ongaku nenkan 1980*, pp. 61-63.

40   Fujiwara Tamon interview, April 26, 1977; Zenkoku Rōon, *Rōon undō*, pp. 11-12; Tōkyō Onkyō, *Tōkyō Onkyō ni tsuite*, Tokyo, Tōkyō Onkyō, 1977, p. 1; Tōkyō Onkyō, *Tōkyō Ongaku Bunka Kyōkai ni tsuite*, Tokyo, Tōkyō Onkyō, 1980, p. 13.

41   *Tōkyō Onkyō ni tsuite*, p. 1.

42   Tōkyō Onkyō, *Tōkyō Ongaku Bunka*, pp. 3-4.

43   *Asahi nenkan 1963*, p. 646; *Asahi nenkan 1966*, p. 693; Tōkyō Onkyō, *Tōkyō Ongaku Bunka*, p. 13.

44   Tōkyō Onkyō, *Tōkyō Ongaku Bunka*, p. 1. See Zenkoku Rōon,

Rōon undō, pp. 10-12; Zenkoku Bunka Dantai Renmei, *Zenkoku Bunka Dantai Renmei (Zenbunren) to Onkyō undō ni tsuite*, Tokyo, Zenkoku Bunka Dantai Renmei, 1980, pp. 1-5; Tōkyō Onkyō, *Tōkyō Ongaku Bunka*, pp. 1-4, 17; *Asahi nenkan 1957*, p. 559; *Asahi nenkan 1959*, p. 483; *Tōkyō Onkyō ni tsuite*, pp. 1-2; Tōkyō Onkyō, *Tōkyō Onkyō nyūkai no shiori*, Tokyo, Tōkyō Onkyō, 1980; "*Kigyō no shakai kōken*," pp. 21, 178.

45 Tōkyō Onkyō, *Tōkyō Ongaku Bunka*, p. 3.

46 *Asahi nenkan 1963*, p. 646; *Asahi nenkan 1965*, p. 664; *Asahi nenkan 1966*, p. 693; *Ongaku nenkan 1977*, p. 89; Minshu Ongaku Kyōkai, *Min'on: '77 Min'on goannai*, Tokyo, Minshu Ongaku Kyōkai, 1977; *Soka Gakkai News*, January 25, 1980, pp. 9-10.

47 Zenkoku Rōon, *Rōon undō*, p. 12; *Ongaku nenkan 1977*, pp. 89-91; *Ongaku nenkan 1980*, p. 64; *Soka Gakkai News*, January 25, 1980, p. 14; Minshu Ongaku Kyōkai, *'81 Min'on sanjo kaiin uketsuke goannai*, Tokyo, Minshu Ongaku Kyōkai, 1980.

48 Minshu Ongaku Kyōkai, *Min'on*; Minshu Ongaku Kyōkai, *'81 Min'on*; Minshu Ongaku Kyōkai, *1980 12gatsu no oshirase*, Tokyo, Minshu Ongaku Kyōkai, 1980; Nishina interview, October 28, 1980. On the musical activities of the Tokyo Citizens' Theater, see *Tomin Gekijō 30nenshi*, pp. 6-7, 10-11; *Asahi nenkan 1959*, p. 481.

49 Koshimura interview, November 5, 1980.

50 For data on types of professional classical Western music performed, Ōsaka Ongaku Daigaku, *Kansai '74*, pp. 29-30; Tsunematsu, "Nihon no ongaku shakai," p. 41. On concert halls, Nihon Ongaku Manējā Kyōkai, *Kurashikku ongaku ensōka sōran*, Tokyo, Nihon Ongaku Manējā Kyōkai, 1979, pp. 70-86. On sponsorship, Ōsaka Ongaku Daigaku, *Kansai '72*, p. 12; Ōsaka Ongaku Daigaku, *Kansai '74*, p. 20. On foreign musicians, Kurabayashi, "Sūji," p. 125; Ōsaka Ongaku Daigaku, *Kansai '74*, p. 12; Yomiuri Shinbunsha, *Yomiuri nenkan 1980*, Tokyo, Yomiuri Shinbunsha, 1980, p. 610. On concerts in Tokyo, Tsunematsu, "Nihon no ongaku shakai," p. 41; *Asahi nenkan 1979*, p. 627. On amateurs, *Asahi nenkan 1979*, p. 627. On total orchestra performances, Nihon Ensōka Kyōkai, *Shinfuonī oke gasshōdan chingin rōdō jōken jittai ichiranhyō*, Tokyo, Nihon Ensōka Kyōkai, 1979; Koshimura interview, November 5, 1980; Hase interview, October 14, 1980; Yajima interview, October 16, 1980; Matsuki interview, October 14, 1980; Nakano in-

terview, November 21, 1980. See Netzer, *Subsidized Muse*, pp. 114-117, on American orchestras.

51 *Asahi nenkan 1969*, p. 729; *Asahi nenkan 1970*, p. 708; *Asahi nenkan 1971*, p. 708; *Asahi nenkan 1979*, p. 627.

52 Ōsaka Ongaku Daigaku, *Kansai '74*, pp. 34-35; see also pp. 32-33. Ōsaka Ongaku Daigaku, *Kansai '72*, pp. 23-24.

53 Yoshida interview, December 25, 1980. See Sakisaka, "Kigyō," p. 60; *Asahi nenkan 1957*, p. 559; *Asahi nenkan 1963*, p. 647; *Japan Times*, September 28, 1980; *Yomiuri Shinbun hyaku-nenshi*, I, 826.

54 Matsuki interview, October 14, 1980; *Asahi nenkan 1962*, p. 621; Sakisaka, "Kigyō," p. 61; *Asahi nenkan 1965*, p. 663; *Asahi nenkan 1973*, p. 708.

55 Kusakabe Yoshihiko, "Ōfuiru ni miru zaikai to no tsunagari," *Ongaku geijutsu*, November 1980, p. 57; *Asahi nenkan 1966*, pp. 566, 692; *Asahi nenkan 1970*, p. 709; *Asahi nenkan 1976*, p. 672; *Tōkyō Rōon kiyaku*, p. 3.

56 Yoshimasa Kurabayashi, *Measurement of Output in Public Supported Services for the International Comparison: A Case of Cultural Activities*, Tokyo, Institute of Economic Research, Hitotsubashi University, 1980, p. 9; Gideon Chagy, *The New Patrons of the Arts*, New York, Harry N. Abrams, Inc., Publishers, 1972, p. 49.

57 Hase interview, October 14, 1980; Komatsu Takeshi interview, October 20, 1980.

58 Matsuki interview, October 14, 1980; Kusakabe, "Ōfuiru," pp. 57-58; Hase interview, October 14, 1980.

59 Yajima interview, October 16, 1980; Koshimura interview, November 5, 1980; Hase interview, October 14, 1980; Matsuki interview, October 14, 1980; Kurabayashi, *Public and Private*, appendix, p. 1; *Tōkyō Fuiruhāmonī Kōkyō Gakudan teiki en-sōkai No. 218*, September 10, 1980. See chapters 3 and 4 for data on the cultural agency.

60 *Ongaku nenkan 1977*, p. 16; Isaka, "Kurashikku," p. 18; Kusakabe, "Ōfuiru," p. 57; Tokyo Metropolitan Government, *Education in Tokyo*, p. 330; Nihon Ensōka Kyōkai, *Tōkyōto Kōkyō Gakudan sōyosan*, Tokyo, Nihon Ensōka Kyōkai, 1980; Yajima interview, October 16, 1980.

61 Nihon Ensōka Kyōkai, *Tōkyōto Kōkyō Gakudan sōyosan*; Kimura Eiji, "Ōkesutora wa ikinokoreru no ka," *Ongaku geijutsu*,

July 1980, p. 27; Kurabayashi, *Public and Private*, pp. 15-17; *Nihon Kōkyōgaku Shinkō Zaidan nyūsu*, no. 10, June 1980, pp. 8-9; New Japan Philharmonic, *New Japan Philharmonic Subscription Concert 1980 Fall Season*, Tokyo, New Japan Philharmonic, 1980; Matsuki interview, October 14, 1980.

62 Tsunematsu interview, November 21, 1980; Nakano interview, November 21, 1980; Akiyama interview, November 7, 1980; *Asahi nenkan 1971*, p. 709; *Asahi nenkan 1972*, p. 703; *Asahi nenkan 1973*, p. 708; Nihon Ensōka Kyōkai, *Subete no ongakuka wa yunion e!* Tokyo, Nihon Ensōka Kyōkai, 1979; Nihon Ensōka Kyōkai, *Shinfuonī oke.*

63 Nakano interview, November 21, 1980; Tsunematsu interview, November 21, 1980; *Ongaku nenkan 1977*, pp. 16-17; Richie interview, October 6, 1980; Nihon Ensōka Kyōkai, *Shinfuonī oke.*

64 Hase interview, October 14, 1980; *Asahi nenkan 1966*, p. 692; *Asahi nenkan 1971*, p. 709; *Asahi nenkan 1980*, p. 619; *Ongaku nenkan 1980*, pp. 2-3.

65 Iwaki interview, December 27, 1980; Iwaki Hiroyuki, *Iwaki ongaku kyōshitsu*, Tokyo, Kōbunsha, 1977, pp. 230-231; Kurabayashi Yoshimasa and Matsuda Yoshirō, "Kurashikku ongaku ensōkai ni okeru chōshū no jitsuzō," *Ongaku geijutsu*, December 1980, pp. 38-41; Kurabayashi, *Public and Private*, pp. 19-32, appendix, pp. 7, 10, 14; Matsuki interview, October 14, 1980; Koshimura interview, November 5, 1980.

66 Kimura Eiji interview, December 8, 1980.

67 Shibata Masashi, *Ongaku to bunka*, Tokyo, Ayumi Shuppan, 1974, p. 167; see also pp. 163-166; Ozaki, "Shingeki II," p. 191; *Asahi nenkan 1959*, p. 481.

68 Nihon Ensōka Kyōkai, *Musicians*; Nakano interview, November 21, 1980; Tsunematsu interview, November 21, 1980.

69 Bunkachō, *Bunka gyōsei no ayumi*, p. 270; Nakano interview, November 21, 1980; Tsunematsu interview, November 21, 1980; Ōsaka Ongaku Daigaku, *Kansai '74*, pp. 15, 21, 24.

70 Nichols interview, December 1, 1980; Nihon Ongaku Manējā Kyōkai, *Kurashikku*, passim; *International Cultural Newsletter*, August 1979-September 1980; *Yomiuri nenkan 1980*, p. 610.

71 Nichols interview, December 1, 1980. See *Ongaku nenkan 1977*, pp. 14-15.

72 *Soka Gakkai News*, January 25, 1980, pp. 12-13; Sakazaki

interview, December 24, 1980; *Asahi nenkan 1960*, p. 453; Nishina interview, October 28, 1980.

73 Ōsaka Ongaku Daigaku, *Nishi Nihon '76*, pp. 73-81; *Asahi nenkan 1978*, p. 622.

74 Kawachi interview, December 3, 1980; Ōkōchi interview, November 19, 1980; Kurahashi interview, November 12, 1980; Mobil Oil Corporation, *Dai10kai Mōbiru ongakushō (yōgakubumon); Asahi nenkan 1981*, p. 587.

CHAPTER 8   DANCE: CONTEMPORARY CLASSICS

1 For details on ballet recitals, Ichikawa Miyabi interview, November 18, 1980; Kasuya interview, October 22, 1980; Dennis Keene interview, November 14, 1980; Ogawa interview, November 21, 1980; Keiko Keene interview, November 29, 1980; Yamano Hakudai, "Nihon no baree chizu wa kore kara dō kawaru ka," *Modan dansu*, no. 13, winter 1974, p. 11.

2 See Machida, *Buyō*, pp. 51-628; Gendai Buyō Kyōkai, *Nihon gendai buyō shiryō, I, 1971*, Tokyo, Gendai Buyō Kyōkai, 1972, pp. 1, 4, 19, 481; *Nihon gendai buyō shiryō, II, 1972*, p. 14.

3 Masakatsu Gunji, *Buyo: The Classical Dance*, trans. by Don Kenny, New York and Tokyo, John Weatherhill, Inc. and Kyoto, Tankosha, 1970, pp. 68-69. See James R. Brandon, "Kabuki Dance: A View from the Outside," ibid., p. 65.

4 Helen Caldwell, *Michio Ito*, Berkeley, University of California Press, 1977; *Nihon gendai buyō shiryō, I, 1971*, pp. 1-5; *Nihon gendai buyō shiryō, II, 1972*, pp. 14-15, 20-21; Machida, *Buyō*, pp. 674-675.

5 *Nihon gendai buyō shiryō, I, 1971*, p. 3; *Nihon gendai buyō shiryō, II, 1972*, p. 18; *Nihon gendai buyō shiryō, III, 1973*, p. 25; Brandon, "Kabuki Dance," p. 6; *Asahi nenkan 1958*, p. 476; *Asahi nenkan 1961*, p. 454; Harold C. Schonberg, *New York Times Book Review*, December 16, 1979, p. 13.

6 Yamano Hakudai, "Baree no gaikyō," *Buyō nenkan, I, 1977*, p. 36; *Asahi nenkan 1979*, p. 632.

7 Dennis Keene interview, November 14, 1980; Yamano, "Baree chizu," pp. 14-15; *Asahi nenkan 1957*, p. 564; *Asahi nenkan 1961*, p. 455; *Asahi nenkan 1964*, p. 644; *Asahi nenkan 1965*, p. 662; *Asahi nenkan 1966*, p. 691; *Asahi nenkan 1970*, p. 704.

8 Donald Richie, in Star Dancers Ballet Company, *Star Dancers Ballet*, Tokyo, Star Dancers Ballet Company, 1980; *Buyō nen-*

kan, IV, 1980, pp. 7-10; *Asahi nenkan 1964*, p. 644; *Asahi nenkan 1966*, p. 691; *Asahi nenkan 1969*, p. 725.

9 Kasuya interview, October 22, 1980; *Asahi nenkan 1980*, p. 632; *Buyō nenkan, IV, 1980*, p. 8.

10 Keiko Keene interview, November 29, 1980; Shimada interview, December 6, 1980; Hattori interview, December 6, 1980; *Asahi nenkan 1979*, p. 632; *Japan Times*, December 20, 1980.

11 Machida, *Buyō*, pp. 719-792; *Nihon gendai buyō nenkan*, 1974, pp. 33-35.

12 Ichikawa interview, November 18, 1980; *Nihon gendai buyō nenkan*, 1975, pp. 7, 155; *Asahi nenkan 1980*, p. 632.

13 Akiko Kanda, "Akiko no modan dansu," part 1, *Modan dansu*, no. 11, autumn 1972, p. 36; part 2, *Modan dansu*, no. 12, summer 1973, pp. 30-32; part 3, *Modan dansu*, no. 13, winter 1974, pp. 45-48; *Nihon gendai buyō nenkan*, 1975, pp. 6-7; Kanda interview, November 28, 1980.

14 Satō Shigeru, "Atsugi Bonjinron," *Modan dansu*, no. 9, summer 1971, pp. 34-37; Horikiri Yoshiko, "Kihyō," *Modan dansu*, no. 15, autumn 1975, pp. 52-53; *Dansu wāku*, no. 16, spring 1976, pp. 7-13; Gendai Buyō Kyōkai, '77 *Tomin Geijutsu Fuesuteibaru gendai buyō kōen*, Tokyo, Gendai Buyō Kyōkai, 1977; *Dansu wāku*, no. 20, spring 1977, pp. 43-44.

15 Kaufmann, ed., *Existentialism*, p. 42; Satō Shigeru, "Mitsu no risaitaru," *Modan dansu*, no. 13, winter 1974, pp. 32-33; *New York Times*, November 29, 1978; Gōda Nario, "Yōbu," *Ongaku nenkan 1977*, pp. 76-77; Horikiri, "Kihyō," pp. 52-53; *Dansu wāku*, no. 16, spring 1976, pp. 12-13.

16 Ichikawa interview, November 18, 1980.

17 Gōda, "Yōbu," pp. 77-78; Richie, "Japan's Avant-Garde," p. 2; *Asahi nenkan 1980*, p. 632.

18 *Nihon gendai buyō nenkan*, 1975, pp. 5-9.

19 Kawashima, *Ideorogī*, pp. 367-369; *Asahi nenkan 1965*, p. 662; *Nihon gendai buyō shiryō, II*, 1972, p. 4; Bunkachō, *Bunka gyōsei no ayumi*, p. 81.

20 *Ongaku nenkan 1977*, pp. 59-61; *Buyō nenkan, IV, 1980*, p. 2.

21 *Buyō nenkan, IV, 1980*, pp. 91-117, 121-122, 202-203.

22 *Japan Times*, January 26, 1981. See *Japan Times*, January 13, 1981.

23 *Asahi nenkan 1981 bekkan*, p. 360; *Japan Times*, January 13, 1981.

24 Inumaru interview, November 5, 1980.

25 Shibazaki interview, February 4, 1981; Nishiyama, *Gendai*, p. 66; Ichikawa interview, November 18, 1980; *Japan Times*, February 14, 1981.

26 Kanze Hideo interview, *Concerned Theatre Japan*, winter/spring 1971, pp. 14-17; Nakane, *Japanese Society*, p. 118; Bunkachō, *Bunka gyōsei no ayumi*, p. 85; Kenny interview, October 8, 1980; Steve Comee interview, October 8, 1980; Inumaru interview, November 5, 1980; Ezaki interview, October 23, 1980.

27 Hinoshita interview, December 19, 1980; Inumaru interview, November 5, 1980; Gunji, *Buyo*, pp. 183-186.

28 Michishita interview, November 19, 1980.

29 Kishibe interview, January 26, 1981; Hinoshita interview, December 19, 1980; Shimada interview, December 6, 1980; Kawashima, *Ideorogī*, p. 344.

30 Kishibe interview, January 26, 1981; Keiko Keene interview, December 3, 1980; Ogawa interview, November 21, 1980.

31 Ogawa interview, November 21, 1980; Shibazaki interview, February 4, 1981; Nobumoto interview, January 30, 1981. Nobumoto notes that tax officials rarely bother one- or two-day recitals.

32 Fujima Tsurutarō interview, December 3, 1980; Keiko Keene interview, December 3, 1980; Nobumoto interview, February 14, 1981.

33 Kawashima, *Ideorogī*, p. 326. On geisha, Liza Crihfield Dalby correspondence, December 29, 1980; Gunji, *Buyo*, p. 181; Hinoshita interview, December 19, 1980.

34 Katō Mikio interview, October 30, 1980; Asian Cultural Centre, *Report*, p. 147; Shibazaki interview, February 4, 1981; Inumaru interview, November 5, 1980; Kumakura, "Iemoto"; Nobumoto interview, January 30, 1981.

35 Ogawa interview, November 21, 1980; Hashiura Isamu interview, December 5, 1980; Shimada interview, December 6, 1980.

36 Ichikawa interview, November 18, 1980.

37 Nishina interview, October 28, 1980; Shimada interview, December 6, 1980.

38 Nihon Geinō Jitsuenka Dantai Kyōgikai, *Geinōjin*, p. 23.

39 Yamano, "Baree chizu," p. 11; Ogawa interview, November 21, 1980; Keiko Keene interview, December 3, 1980. For data on dance pupils, see chapter 1.

40 Hattori interview, December 6, 1980; Dennis Keene interview, November 14, 1980.

41 Ogawa interview, November 21, 1980.

42 Nishina interview, October 28, 1980; Hattori interview, December 6, 1980. I am grateful to Dennis Keene for advice on this point.

43 Ichikawa interview, November 18, 1980; *Nihon gendai buyō shiryō, III, 1973*, p. 102.

44 Ezaki interview, February 20, 1981; Ichikawa interview, November 18, 1980.

45 Ezaki interview, February 20, 1981; Ichikawa interview, November 18, 1980. See Kambayashi, "Modern Dance," p. 45.

46 *Nihon gendai buyō shiryō, III, 1973*, pp. 32-33; Bunkachō, *Bunka gyōsei chōki*, passim; Ezaki interview, October 23, 1980.

47 Kasuya interview, October 22, 1980; Ezaki interview, October 23, 1980; Ogawa interview, November 21, 1980. See Baumol and Bowen, *Performing Arts*, pp. 52-53; Netzer, *Subsidized Muse*, p. 136.

48 *Nihon gendai buyō nenkan*, 1974, p. 106; *Nihon gendai buyō nenkan*, 1975, pp. 8, 110-111; Bunkachō, *Bunka gyōsei no ayumi*, p. 82; Kasuya interview, October 22, 1980; Ezaki interview, October 23, 1980; *Buyō nenkan, IV, 1980*, pp. 125-150, 153-201; *Asahi nenkan 1981*, p. 599.

49 Kasuya interview, October 22, 1980; Yokoyama interview, November 13, 1980; Ogawa interview, November 21, 1980.

50 Ogawa interview, November 21, 1980; Keiko Keene interview, November 29, 1980; Dennis Keene interview, November 14, 1980; Kawachi interview, December 3, 1980; Richie interview, October 6, 1980; Tani Momoko interview, December 2, 1980.

51 Kasuya interview, October 22, 1980.

52 Tachikawa interview, December 8, 1980.

53 Hashiura interview, December 5, 1980; Hori Noboru interview, December 5, 1980.

54 Inumaru interview, November 5, 1980; Tachikawa interview,

December 8, 1980; *Buyō nenkan, IV, 1980,* p. 11; Hattori interview, December 6, 1980; Shimada interview, December 6, 1980.

55 Sulamith Messerer interview, December 2, 1980; Tani interview, December 2, 1980.

56 Hattori interview, December 6, 1980; Dennis Keene interview, November 14, 1980; Sakurai interview, December 2, 1980; *Nihon gendai buyō shiryō, III, 1973,* p. 4.

57 *Nihon gendai buyō nenkan,* 1975, pp. 5-6; *Buyō nenkan, I, 1977,* p. 53; Ezaki interview, October 23, 1980; Ichikawa interview, November 18, 1980.

58 Yokoyama interview, November 13, 1980; Ezaki interview, October 23, 1980; Kasuya interview, October 22, 1980; Ichikawa interview, November 18, 1980.

59 Kanda interview, November 28, 1980.

60 Kanda interviews, November 28, 1980 and January 30, 1981.

CHAPTER 9 THE VERTICAL MOSAIC

1 *Japan Times,* February 23, 1980.

2 Figures from the prime minister's bureau of statistics, quoted in Nihon Geinō Jitsuenka Dantai Kyōgikai, *Geinōjin,* p. 8.

3 Nihon Geinō Jitsuenka Dantai Kyogikai, *Geinōjin,* pp. 8, 14, 16.

4 Ibid., pp. 19, 22-24.

5 Ibid., pp. 28-30. See Tsunematsu, "Ongakuka shōgai," p. 48.

6 Kasuya interview, October 22, 1980; Koshimura interview, November 5, 1980; Richie interview, October 6, 1980.

7 Keiko Keene interview, November 29, 1980.

8 Japan, Ministry of Finance, Tax Bureau, *An Outline of Japanese Taxes, 1979,* Tokyo, Ministry of Finance, 1979, p. 15; Okochi, "Theatrical Situation," pp. 12-13; Bunkachō, *Bunka gyōsei chōki,* p. 27; Tsunematsu, "Ongakuka shōgai," p. 45.

9 Tachikawa interview, December 8, 1980.

SOURCES CITED

INTERVIEWS

Abe Bun'yū, business manager, Tōkyō Kinrōsha Engeki Kyōgikai (Tōkyō Rōen) (April 27, 1977 and September 25, 1980).

Adachi Kenji, director, National Museum of Modern Art, Tokyo; commissioner, Agency for Cultural Affairs, 1972-1975 (October 22, 1980).

Akiyama Kuniharu, poet, composer, music critic (November 7, 1980).

Amano Ryōichi, media study group, *Mainichi* newspapers; director, special projects, including cultural affairs, *Mainichi* newspapers, 1971-1973 (December 22, 1980).

Anzai Shigeo, painter and photographer (October 27, 1980).

Aoi Yōji, playwright, director, translator (October 30, 1980).

Arai Yasuko, owner, Space 31/Arai Planning Gallery (December 11, 1980 and December 16, 1980).

Blakemore, Frances, director, Franell Gallery (December 27, 1980).

Chiba Kihei, director, art exhibitions, cultural promotion department, *Yomiuri* newspapers (May 10, 1977 and December 17, 1980).

Comee, Steve, nō actor (October 8, 1980).

Dan Ikuma, composer (December 23, 1980).

Edo Hideo, chairman, Mitsui Real Estate Development Corporation; chairman, Japan Orchestra Association; chairman, Japan Performance League; chairman, board of trustees, Tōhō Gakuen University (November 6, 1980).

Enna Takio, adviser, cultural affairs, *Asahi* newspapers; director, cultural affairs, *Asahi* newspapers, 1958-1968 (December 11, 1980).

Etō Shun, art critic, professor of art history, Keiō University (December 25, 1980).

Ezaki Tsukasa, secretary-general, Japan Contemporary Ballet and Modern Dance Association (October 23, 1980 and February 20, 1981).

Flood, Lawrence B., director, American Center, Tokyo (October 22, 1980).

Fujima Tsurutarō, classical Japanese dancer (December 3, 1980).

Fujiwara Tamon, head, organization section, Tōkyō Ongaku Bunka Kyōkai (Tōkyō Onkyō) (April 26, 1977).

Fukushima Kikuo, assistant head, public relations department, Suntory (October 17, 1980).

Hall, Ivan P., assistant executive director, Japan-United States Friendship Commission (November 14, 1980).

Hara Toshio, president, Nihon Tochi Sanrin, Ltd.; director, Hara Museum of Contemporary Art (October 28, 1980 and December 3, 1980).

Haryū Ichirō, art critic (November 13, 1980).

Hase Takao, managing director, NHK Symphony Orchestra (October 14, 1980).

Hashiura Isamu, ballet choreographer (December 5, 1980).

Hattori Chieko, president, Japan Ballet Association (December 6, 1980).

Hinoshita Yoshimitsu, business manager, Japan Classical Dance Association (December 19, 1980).

Honda Shingo, print maker, painter (December 15, 1980).

Hori Noboru, ballet dancer (December 5, 1980).

Ichikawa Miyabi, dance critic (November 18, 1980).

Ichiyanagi Toshi, composer (November 30, 1980).

Iino Kiichi, president, Contemporary Sculpture Center (December 16, 1980).

Ikeda Masao, managing director, Shin Nihon Zōkei Co., Ltd. (November 26, 1980).

Inumaru Tadashi, director-general, National Theatre of Japan; commissioner, Agency for Cultural Affairs, 1975-1980 (November 5, 1980).

Iwaki Hiroyuki, life conductor, NHK Symphony Orchestra; music director, Melbourne Symphony (December 27, 1980).

Izeki Masaaki, art critic; head, exhibition section, art department, the Japan Foundation (December 12, 1980).

Jitsukawa Nobuhiro, director, Jiyūgaoka Gallery (December 25, 1980).

Johnson, Margaret K., print maker (November 12, 1980).

Kamiya Shin, print maker (December 16, 1980).

Kanda, Akiko, contemporary dancer and choreographer (November 28, 1980 and January 30, 1981).

Kaneko Kikuo, head, planning department, Seibu Museum of Art (October 13, 1980).

Kara Jūrō, director, Situation Theater (Jōkyō Gekijō, also known as the Red Tent Theater) (November 10, 1980).

Kasuya Tatsuo, director, Kasuya Ballet Company (October 22, 1980).

Katase Keisuke, art exhibition planner, Isetan Co., Ltd. (April 21, 1977).

Katō Mikio, associate managing director, International House of Japan (October 30, 1980).

Katō Nobuko, promotion officer, NHK (October 20, 1980).

Kawachi Shōzō, executive director, Nikikai Opera Foundation (December 3, 1980).

Kawai Shin, assistant director, cultural affairs, *Asahi* newspapers (April 19, 1977).

Kawashima Takeyoshi, lawyer, professor emeritus, Tokyo University (November 27, 1980).

Keene, Dennis, professor of literature, Japan Women's University (November 14, 1980 and November 29, 1980).

Keene, Keiko, ballet critic (November 29, 1980 and December 3, 1980).

Kenny, Don, kyōgen director and actor (October 8, 1980).

Kimura Eiji, music and dance critic (December 8, 1980).

Kimura Hideo, director, International Artists Center (October 31, 1980).

Kimura Itaru, head, promotion division, NHK (October 20, 1980).

Kimura Yōichi, editor-in-chief, *Bijutsu techō* (December 12, 1980).

Kishibe Shigeo, professor emeritus of musicology, Tokyo University (January 26, 1981).

Komatsu Takeshi, manager, NHK Hall (October 20, 1980).

Koshimura Sadanao, manager, Japan Orchestra Association (November 5, 1980).

Kurabayashi Seiichirō, manager, Haiyūza Theater (November 11, 1980).

Kurahashi Takeshi, director, Tsubouchi Memorial Theatre Museum, Waseda University (November 12, 1980).

Machida Yutaka, director, General Arts Corporation; director, Shiki Corporation (October 29, 1980).

Maki Jun'ichi, painter (December 3, 1980).

Matsuki Shōgo, secretary-general, Tokyo Philharmonic Orchestra (October 14, 1980).

Matsumae Yoshiaki, assistant to the general manager, public relations department, Sumitomo Corporation (October 24, 1980).

Messerer, Sulamith, ballet coach (December 2, 1980).

Michishita Kyōko, writer (November 19, 1980).

Mukae Kasue, owner, Galerie Mukai (October 27, 1980).

Nagai Michio, councilor, United Nations University; chief editorial writer, *Asahi* newspapers; minister of education, 1974 (November 7, 1980).

Nakano Yukio, secretary-general, Japan Musicians' Union (November 21, 1980).

Narita Kyōichi, business manager, Nitten (December 17, 1980).

Nichols, Walter, president, Azabu Artists, Inc.; former cultural attaché, U.S. Embassy, Tokyo (December 1, 1980).

Nishina Tadashi, secretary vice-general, International Arts Foundation (October 28, 1980).

Nobumoto Yasusada, president, Akebono Brake Industry Co., Ltd.; librettist in traditional Japanese music (January 30, 1981 and February 14, 1981).

Ōfuku Mamoru, director, Japan Intercultural Communication Society (October 20, 1980).

Ogawa Ayako, director, Ogawa Ayako Ballet Studio (November 21, 1980).

Ohara Shigeo, assistant head, tax bureau, Ministry of Finance (November 20, 1980).

Ōkawa Takeo, chief producer, theater department, Shōchiku Corporation (December 4, 1980).

Ōkōchi Takeshi, manager, Imperial Theater (November 19, 1980).

Ōno Shinji, chief tax examiner, tax bureau, Ministry of Finance (November 20, 1980).

Powers, John, art collector (December 3, 1980).

Richie, Donald, artist, critic, scholar (October 6, 1980).

Saint-Gilles, Amaury, art critic, *Mainichi Daily News* (December 6, 1980).

Saitō Yōichi, arts and sciences program officer, NHK (October 20, 1980).

Sakazaki Tarō, director, cultural affairs, *Asahi* newspapers (April 19, 1977 and December 24, 1980).

Sakuma Etsujirō, assistant executive director, Japan-U.S. Educational Commission (October 16, 1980).

Sakurai Tsutomu, dance critic (December 2, 1980).

Segi Shin'ichi, art critic, president, Joint Art Research Institute (December 9, 1980).

Setsu Iwao, president, Setsu Gatōdō Galleries (December 15, 1980).

Shibazaki Shirō, director, National Theatre of Japan (February 4, 1981).

Shimada Hiroshi, executive managing director, Japan Ballet Association (December 6, 1980).
Shimanaka Fumio, exhibition planner, Tokyo Central Art Gallery (December 17, 1980).

Tachikawa Ruriko, president, Star Dancers Ballet (December 8, 1980).
Takahashi Chikako, assistant to the director, cultural affairs, *Asahi* newspapers (December 24, 1980).
Takasugi Tsuneo, assistant head, arts and sciences program division, NHK (October 20, 1980).
Takeishi Hideo, head, opera and ballet section, music department, NHK (October 29, 1980).
Takemoto Mojitayū, jōruri narrator, Osaka Bunraku Troupe (February 14, 1981).
Takikawa Yoshiko, painter (November 27, 1980).
Tanaka Mitsuru, business manager, Yokohama Theater Research Institute (April 28, 1977).
Tani Momoko, director, Tani Momoko Ballet School (December 2, 1980).
Tolman, Norman, collector and dealer in contemporary Japanese prints (December 4, 1980).
Tsuji Yutaka, managing director, overseas affairs, Asahi Broadcasting Corporation; director, cultural affairs, *Asahi* newspapers, 1968-1976 (December 8, 1980).
Tsunematsu Yukitoshi, vice president, Japan Musicians' Union (November 21, 1980).

Utsumi Makoto, head, tax bureau, Ministry of Finance (November 20, 1980).

Walsh, Charles H., Jr., deputy director, American Center, Tokyo (October 22, 1980).
Watanuki Fujio, president, Contemporary Print Center (November 7, 1980).

Yajima Kazuo, financial officer, culture section, education agency, Tokyo Metropolitan Government (October 16, 1980).
Yamabe Yoshihide, business manager, National Cultural Conference (June 20, 1977).
Yamamoto Noriyuki, director, special projects, including cultural affairs, *Mainichi* newspapers (April 25, 1977).
Yokota Shigeru, manager, contemporary art, Setsu Gatōdō Galleries (December 15, 1980).

297

SOURCES CITED

Yokoyama Tadashi, assistant secretary-general, Nippon Cultural Center (November 13, 1980).
Yoneda Minoru, print maker (November 26, 1980).
Yoshida Takayoshi, managing director, Japan Performance League; former executive director, Yomiuri Japan Symphony Orchestra (December 25, 1980).
Yoshii Chōzō, president, Yoshii Galleries (October 14, 1980).

BIBLIOGRAPHY

Abe Bun'yū and Sugai Yukio, eds. *Rōen undō.* Tokyo, Miraisha, 1970.
Adachi Kenji. *Bunkachō kotohajime.* Tokyo, Tōkyō Shoseki, 1978.
Akiyama Kuniharu. "Japan," in John Vinton, ed., *Dictionary of Contemporary Music*, pp. 364-367. New York, E. P. Dutton, 1974.
————. *Nihon no sakkyokukatachi*, 2 vols. Tokyo, Ongaku no Tomosha, 1979.
Allyn, John, Jr. "The Tsukiji Little Theater and the Beginnings of Modern Theater in Japan." Ph.D. dissertation, University of California, Los Angeles, 1970.
Asahi Evening News.
Asahi geijutsu nenkan. Tokyo, Sanpō, annual.
Asahi shinbun.
Asahi Shinbunsha. *Asahi nenkan.* Tokyo, Asahi Shinbunsha, annual.
Asano Shōichirō. "Asahi no tenrankai." *Asahijin*, August 1980, pp. 82-89.
Asian Cultural Centre for UNESCO. *Report on Traditional Forms of Culture in Japan.* Tokyo, Asian Cultural Centre for UNESCO, 1975.
Aspen Institute for Humanistic Studies. *The Arts, Economics and Politics: Four National Perspectives.* New York, Aspen Institute for Humanistic Studies, 1975.

Baumol, William J. and William G. Bowen. *Performing Arts: The Economic Dilemma.* Boston, M.I.T. Press, 1968.
Bijutsu hyōron.
Bowers, Faubion. *Japanese Theatre.* New York, Hermitage, 1952.
————. *Theatre in the East: A Survey of Asian Dance and Drama.* New York, Thomas Nelson & Sons, 1956.
Boyd, Robin. *Kenzo Tange.* New York, George Braziller, 1962.
————. *New Directions in Japanese Architecture.* New York, George Braziller, 1968.
Brandon, James R. "Kabuki Dance: A View from the Outside," in

Masakatsu Gunji, *Buyo: The Classical Dance*, trans. by Don Kenny, pp. 3-16, 65-66. New York and Tokyo, John Weatherhill, Inc. and Kyoto, Tankosha, 1970.

Brustein, Robert. "Can the Show Go On?" *New York Times Magazine*, July 10, 1977, pp. 9-11, 54-59.

Bungei nenkan. Tokyo, Bungei Nenkan, annual.

Bunkachō. *Bunka gyōsei chōki sōgō keikaku ni tsuite.* Tokyo, Bunkachō, 1977.

———. *Bunka gyōsei no ayumi.* Tokyo, Bunkachō, 1978.

———. *Bunkachō yosan jimu teiyō, Shōwa 55nen.* Tokyo, Bunkachō, 1980.

———. *Chihō bunka gyōsei jōkyō chōsa hōkokusho.* Tokyo, Bunkachō, 1980.

Burke, Peter. *Culture and Society in Renaissance Italy, 1420-1540.* New York, Charles Scribner's Sons, 1972.

Buruma, Ian. "How Traditional is the Avant-Garde?" *Japan Illustrated*, spring 1977, pp. 2-13.

Buyō nenkan. See Zen Nihon Buyō Rengō.

Caldwell, Helen. *Michio Ito.* Berkeley, University of California Press, 1977.

Chagy, Gideon. *The New Patrons of the Arts.* New York, Harry N. Abrams, Inc., Publishers, 1972.

Chiba Kihei. Correspondence, December 20, 1980.

Concerned Theatre Japan.

Dalby, Liza Crihfield. Correspondence, December 29, 1980.

Dan Ikuma and Koizumi Fumio. *Nihon ongaku no saihakken.* Tokyo, Kōdansha, 1976.

Dansu wāku.

Diamond Lead Company, Ltd. *Diamond's Japan Business Directory 1979.* Tokyo, Diamond Lead Company, Ltd., 1979.

Dorian, Frederick. *Commitment to Culture: Arts Patronage in Europe: Its Significance for America.* Pittsburgh, University of Pittsburgh Press, 1964.

Ebara Jun. *Nihon bijutsukai fuhai no kōzō.* Tokyo, Saimaru Shuppankai, 1978.

Engeki nenkan. See Nihon Engeki Kyōkai.

Enna Takio. *Chinmoku no shishatachi.* Tokyo, Shinchōsha, 1980.

Ernst, Earle. *The Kabuki Theatre.* New York, Oxford University Press, 1956.

Fischer, Ernst. *The Necessity of Art: A Marxist Approach*, trans. by Anne Bostock. Baltimore, Penguin Books, 1963.
Fukuoka Rōon 20nenshi Henshū Iinkai. *Ongaku no midori o*. Fukuoka, Fukuoka Kinrōsha Ongaku Kyōgikai, 1975. *Fuorukusubyūne*.

Gangloff, Eric J. "Introduction," in Junji Kinoshita, *Between Gods and Man: A Judgment on War Crimes*, trans. by Eric J. Gangloff, pp. 1-2. Tokyo, University of Tokyo Press, 1975.
Gans, Herbert J. *Popular Culture and High Culture: An Analysis and Evaluation of Taste*. New York, Basic Books, 1974.
Gekidan Haiyūza. *Haiyūzashi, 1965-1973*. Tokyo, Gekidan Haiyūza, 1974.
Gekidan Shiki. *Gekidan Shiki sōritsu 25shūnen kinen*. Tokyo, Gekidan Shiki, 1978.
Gendai Buyō Kyōkai. *Gendai buyō: Bunkachō idō geijutsusai gendai buyō kōen*. Tokyo, Gendai Buyō Kyōkai, 1980.
——. *'77 Tomin Geijutsu Fuesuteibaru gendai buyō kōen*. Tokyo, Gendai Buyō Kyōkai, 1977.
——. *Nihon gendai buyō nenkan*, 2 vols. Tokyo, Gendai Buyō Kyōkai, 1975-1976.
——. *Nihon gendai buyō shiryō*, 3 vols. Tokyo Gendai Buyō Kyōkai, 1972-1974.
Gōda Nario. "Yōbu," in Ongaku no Tomosha, *Ongaku nenkan 1977*, pp. 72-82. Tokyo, Ongaku no Tomosha, 1977.
Goldberg, Rose Lee. *Performance: Live Art, 1909 to the Present*. New York, Harry N. Abrams, Incorporated, 1979.
Goodman, David. "Satoh Makoto and Japanese Underground Theater." Seminar paper, Japan-United States Educational Commission, Tokyo, January 30, 1981.
Graña, Cesar. *Bohemian versus Bourgeois*. New York, Basic Books, 1964.
Griff, Mason. "The Recruitment and Socialization of Artists," in Milton C. Albrecht, James H. Barnett, and Mason Griff, eds., *The Sociology of Art and Literature: A Reader*, pp. 145-158. New York, Praeger Publishers, 2nd ed., 1970.
Gunji, Masakatsu. *Buyo: The Classical Dance*, trans. by Don Kenny. New York and Tokyo, John Weatherhill, Inc. and Kyoto, Tankosha, 1970.

Hara Museum of Contemporary Art. Tokyo, Hara Museum of Contemporary Art, 1979.
Harris, John S. *Government Patronage of the Arts in Great Britain*. Chicago, University of Chicago Press, 1970.

Haryū Ichirō. *Sengo bijutsu seisuishi*, Tokyo, Tōkyō Shoseki, 1979.
Havens, Thomas R. H. *Valley of Darkness: The Japanese People and World War Two*. New York, W. W. Norton & Company, Inc., 1978.
Heifetz, Robin J. "Post-World War II Japanese Composition." Thesis, University of Illinois, Urbana, 1978.
Hidaka Rokurō. "Sengo bunka undōshi no susume." *Iwanami kōza Nihon rekishi geppō*, 25, May 1977, pp. 3-7.
Horie-Webber, A. "Modernisation of the Japanese Theatre: The Shingeki Movement," in W. G. Beasley, ed., *Modern Japan: Aspects of History, Literature and Society*, pp. 147-165. Berkeley, University of California Press, 1975.
Horikiri Yoshiko. "Kihyō." *Modan dansu*, no. 15, autumn 1975, pp. 52-53.

Ibaraki Tadashi. *Zōho Nihon shingeki shōshi*. Tokyo, Miraisha, 1973.
International Cultural Newsletter.
Isaka Hiroshi. "Kurashikku no suitai o sukuu tame ni." *Ongaku geijutsu*, December 1980, pp. 18-19.
Iwaki Hiroyuki. *Iwaki ongaku kyōshitsu*. Tokyo, Kōbunsha, 1977.
———. "Kokuhakuteki chōshūron." *Chūō kōron*, October 1970, pp. 218-235.
———. "Ongaku kyōiku wa kore de yoi no ka." *Chūō kōron*, May 1969, pp. 134-149.

Japan, Economic Planning Agency. *The Polls on the Preference in National Life—What Are the People Seeking for?* Tokyo, Economic Planning Agency, 1980.
Japan, Ministry of Finance. *Tax Bureau, an Outline of Japanese Taxes, 1979*. Tokyo, Ministry of Finance, 1979.
Japan, Office of the Prime Minister, Bureau of Statistics. *Statistical Handbook of Japan*. Tokyo, Bureau of Statistics, annual.
Japan Center for International Exchange. *Philanthropy in Japan*. Tokyo, Japan Center for International Exchange, rev. ed., 1978.
Japan External Trade Organization. *Towards a Working Knowledge of Japan: An Overall View*. Tokyo, JETRO, 1977.
Japan Foundation. *Annual Report 1978-79*. Tokyo, Japan Foundation, 1979.
Japan Foundation Newsletter.
Japan Report.
Japan-United States Friendship Commission. *Announcement of Programs 1979-1980*. Washington, D.C., Japan-United States Friendship Commission, 1979.

301

SOURCES CITED

Johnson, Margaret K. and Dale K. Hilton. *Japanese Prints Today: Tradition with Innovation.* Tokyo, Shufu no Tomosha, 1980.

Kagesato Tetsurō. "Tayōka to kokusaika—Shōwaki sengo no kaiga," in Hijikata Teiichi, ed., *Nihon kaigakan,* XI, *gendai,* pp. 158-160. Tokyo, Kōdansha, 1971.

Kambayashi, Sumio. "Modern Dance in Japan." *Impulse,* 1965, pp. 29-47.

Kanda, Akiko. "Akiko no modan dansu." Part 1, *Modan dansu,* no. 11, autumn 1972, pp. 36-40; part 2, *Modan dansu,* no. 12, summer 1973, pp. 30-32; part 3, *Modan dansu,* no. 13, winter 1974, pp. 45-49.

Kato, Shuichi. *Form, Style, Tradition: Reflections on Japanese Art and Society,* trans. by John Bester. Berkeley, University of California Press, 1971.

Kaufmann, Walter, ed. *existentialism from Dostoevsky to Sartre.* Cleveland and New York, Meridian Books, 1956.

Kawakita Michiaki, ed. *Kindai Nihon no bijutsu.* Tokyo, Shakai Shisōsha, 1964.

———. *Modern Currents in Japanese Art,* trans. by Charles S. Terry. New York and Tokyo, Weatherhill/Heibonsha, 1974.

Kawashima Takeyoshi. *Ideorogī to shite no kazoku seido.* Tokyo, Iwanami Shoten, 1957.

Kawazoe, Noboru. *Contemporary Japanese Architecture,* trans. by David Griffith. Tokyo, Kokusai Kōryū Kikin, 2nd ed., 1973.

Keystone Press Agency Japan. *Profile of Ryoichi Sasakawa.* Tokyo, Keystone Press Agency Japan, 1980.

"*Kigyō no shakai kōken*" *shiryōshū, 1980.* Tokyo, Sanken, 1980.

Kimura Eiji. "Nihon no geijutsu josei wa kokkakei ka minkankei ka." *Ongaku geijutsu,* November 1980, pp. 52-55.

———. "Ōkesutora wa ikinokoreru no ka." *Ongaku geijutsu,* July 1980, pp. 26-29.

Kishi Tetsuo. "Beyond Noh and Kabuki." *Look Japan,* March 10, 1980, pp. 6-7.

Kisselgoff, Anna. "Dance View." *New York Times,* December 24, 1978.

Kiyoharu Geijutsumura. Tokyo, Yoshii Garō, 1980.

Koizumi Fumio. *Nihon no oto.* Tokyo, Seidosha, 1977.

Kojima Tomiko. *Nihon no ongaku o kangaeru.* Tokyo, Ongaku no Tomosha, 1976.

Kokumin bunka.

Kokuritsu Gekijō. *Kokuritsu Gekijō jūnen no ayumi.* Tokyo, Kokuritsu Gekijō, 1976.

Kokusai Butai Geijutsu Shinkō Zaidan. *Dansankai Nihon Sekai Baree Konkūru.* Tokyo, Kokusai Butai Geijutsu Shinkō Zaidan, 1980.

Kokusai Kōryū Kikin. *Kokusai Kōryū Kikin nenpō, Shōwa 54nendohan.* Tokyo, Kokusai Kōryū Kikin, 1979.

Kramer, Hilton. "Beyond the Avant-garde." *New York Times Magazine,* November 4, 1979, pp. 40-46, 58-62.

Kumakura Isao. "Iemoto to geinō." Seminar paper, Japan Foundation, Tokyo, February 20, 1981.

Kurabayashi Seiichirō. "Sūji de miru engeki jōkyō no suii." *Teatoro,* January 1978, pp. 118-134.

———. "Zuisōteki ni sengo shingeki o kangaeru." Part 1, *Teatoro,* March 1979, pp. 158-166; part 2, *Teatoro,* April 1979, pp. 106-115; part 3, *Teatoro, May 1979,* pp. 107-115; part 4, *Teatoro,* June 1979, pp. 120-128; part 5, *Teatoro,* July 1979, pp. 118-127.

Kurabayashi, Yoshimasa. *Measurement of Output in Public Supported Services for the International Comparison: A Case of Cultural Activities.* Tokyo, Institute of Economic Research, Hitotsubashi University, 1980.

———. *Public and Private Expenditure on Cultural Purposes: A Case Study of Performing Arts in Japan.* Tokyo, Institute of Statistical Research, 1979.

———and Matsuda Yoshirō. "Kurashikku ongaku ensōkai ni okeru chōshū no jitsuzō." *Ongaku geijutsu,* December 1980, pp. 38-41.

Kusakabe Yoshihiko. "Ōfuiru ni miru zaikai to no tsunagari." *Ongaku geijutsu,* November 1980, pp. 56-59.

Kyōto Daigaku Bungakubu Kokushi Kenkyūshitsu. *Nihon kindaishi jiten.* Tokyo, Tōyō Keizai Shinpōsha, 1958.

Langer, Suzanne. "Deceptive Analogies," in James B. Hall and Barry Ubanov, comp., *Modern Culture and the Arts,* pp. 22-31. New York, McGraw-Hill Book Company, 2nd ed., 1972.

Lyle, Cynthia. *Dancers on Dancing.* New York, Drake Publishers, Inc., 1977.

Machida Takako. *Buyō no ayumi hyakunen.* Tokyo, Ōfūsha, 1968.

Mainichi Shinbunsha. *Mainichi shinbun hyakunenshi, 1872-1972.* Tokyo, Mainichi Shinbunsha, 1972.

Malm, William P. "Layers of Music in Japan Since 1945," *The Fourth Kyushu International Cultural Conference: Proceedings,* pp. D3-1/12. Fukuoka, Fukuoka UNESCO Association, 1978.

Masui Keiji, ed. *Dēta ongaku Nippon.* Tokyo, Min'on Ongaku Shiryōkan, 1980.

Mayer, Martin. *Bricks, Mortar and the Performing Arts.* New York, The Twentieth Century Fund, 1970.

McMullen, Roy. *Art, Affluence and Alienation: The Fine Arts Today.* New York, Praeger Publishers, 1968.

Meyer, Karl E. *The Art Museum: Power, Money, Ethics.* New York, William Morrow and Company, 1979.

Minshu Ongaku Kyōkai. *'81 Min'on sanjo kaiin uketsuke goannai.* Tokyo, Minshu Ongaku Kyōkai, 1980.

————. *Min'on: '77 Min'on goannai.* Tokyo, Minshu Ongaku Kyōkai, 1977.

————. *1980 12gatsu no oshirase.* Tokyo, Minshu Ongaku Kyōkai, 1980.

Mobil Oil Corporation. *Dai10kai Mōbiru ongakushō (hōgakubumon) jushōsha kimaru.* Tokyo, Mobil Oil Corporation, 1980.

————. *Dai10kai Mōbiru ongakushō (yōgakubumon) jushōsha kimaru.* Tokyo, Mobil Oil Corporation, 1980.

Monbushō. *Zatsubun dai26go.* Tokyo, Monbushō, 1979.

Moore, Thomas G. *The Economics of the American Theater.* Durham, Duke University Press, 1968.

Munsterberg, Hugo. *The Art of Modern Japan.* New York, Hacker Art Books, 1978.

Murex.

Murphy, George M. " 'Omon Tota': A Folktale by Kinoshita Junji." Ph.D. dissertation, University of Washington, Seattle, 1975.

Museum of Modern Art. *The New Japanese Painting and Sculpture.* New York, Museum of Modern Art, 1966.

Nakamura, Tanio. *Contemporary Japanese-style Painting,* trans. by Mikio Ito, Tokyo. Tokyo International Publishers, Ltd., 1969.

Nakane, Chie. *Japanese Society.* Berkeley, University of California Press, 1970.

Nakanishi Saburō. "Chihō bunka gyōsei—Shigaken no baai," in Bunkachō, *Nihon bunka kōza,* III, pp. 169-199. Tokyo, Gyōsei, 1979.

National Museum of Modern Art, Tokyo. *National Museum of Modern Art, Tokyo.* Tokyo, National Museum of Modern Art, Tokyo, 1978.

National Theatre. *National Theatre of Japan.* Tokyo, National Theatre, 1970.

Netzer, Dick. *The Subsidized Muse: Public Support of the Arts in the United States.* New York, Cambridge University Press, 1978.

New Japan Philharmonic. *New Japan Philharmonic Subscription Concert 1980 Fall Season.* Tokyo, New Japan Philharmonic, 1980.

New London Day.
New York Times.
New Yorker.
Newsweek.
Nihon Bankoku Hakurankai Kinen Kikin. *Grants Awarded by the JEC Fund.* Tokyo, Nihon Bankoku Hakurankai Kinen Kikin, 1979.
———. *Shōwa 55nendo Nihon Bankoku Hakurankai Kinen Kikin jigyō.* Tokyo, Nihon Bankoku Hakurankai Kinen Kikin, 1980.
Nihon Engeki Kyōkai. *Engeki nenkan.* Tokyo, Nihon Engeki Kyōkai, annual.
Nihon Ensōka Kyōkai. *Musicians (Including Other Performers) from Foreign Countries into Japan in 1978.* Tokyo, Nihon Ensōka Kyōkai, 1980.
———. *Shinfuonī oke gasshōdan chingin rōdō jōken jittai ichiran-hyō.* Tokyo, Nihon Ensōka Kyōkai, 1979.
———. *Shōwa 45-51nen geijutsu kankei dantai hojokin kōfugaku ichiran.* Tokyo, Nihon Ensōka Kyōkai, n.d. (1978).
———. *Subete no ongakuka wa yunion e!* Tokyo, Nihon Ensōka Kyōkai, 1979.
———. *Tōkyōto Kōkyō Gakudan sōyosan.* Tokyo, Nihon Ensōka Kyōkai, 1980.
Nihon Geijutsuin. *Nihon Geijutsuinshi.* Tokyo, Nihon Geijutsuin, 1963.
Nihon Geinō Jitsuenka Dantai Kyōgikai. *Geinōjin no seikatsu to ishiki—dainikai geinōjin jittai chōsa hōkokusho.* Tokyo, Nihon Geinō Jitsuenka Dantai Kyōgikai, 1979.
Nihon gendai buyō nenkan. See Gendai Buyō Kyōkai.
Nihon gendai buyō shiryō. See Gendai Buyō Kyōkai.
Nihon Hanga Kyōkai. *Dai48kai Nihon Hanga Kyōkaiten.* Tokyo, Nihon Hanga Kyōkai, 1980.
Nihon kindaishi jiten. See Kyōto Daigaku.
Nihon Kōkyōgaku Shinkō Zaidan. *Gendai Nihon no ōkesutora ongaku, dai4kai ensōkai.* Tokyo, Nihon Kōkyōgaku Shinkō Zaidan, 1980.
———. *Nihon Kōkyōgaku Shinkō Zaidan setsuritsu shuisho.* Tokyo, Nihon Kōkyōgaku Shinkō Zaidan, 1973.
Nihon Kōkyōgaku Shinkō Zaidan nyūsu.
"Nihon no ongaku bunka to dojō." *Ongaku geijutsu,* November 1980, pp. 26-37.
Nihon Ongaku Manējā Kyōkai. *Kurashikku ongaku ensōka sōran.* Tokyo, Nihon Ongaku Manējā Kyōkai, 1979.
Nihon tōkei nenkan. See Sōrifu Tōkeikyoku.

Nippon Bunka Zaidan. *Nippon Bunka Zaidan.* Tokyo, Nippon Bunka Zaidan, 1979.
Nippon Cultural Centre. *The Paul Taylor Dance Company 1980.* Tokyo, Nippon Cultural Centre, 1980.
Nishiyama Matsunosuke. *Gendai no iemoto.* Tokyo, Kōbundō, 1962.
―――. *Iemoto no kenkyū.* Tokyo, Azekura Shobō, 1959.
Nitten. *Daijūnikai Nitten sakuhinshū.* Tokyo, Nitten, 1980.
―――. *Nitten benran.* Tokyo, Nitten, 1979.
―――. *Nitten kaigashū 1975-1976.* Tokyo, Nitten, 1977.
―――. *Nitten yōran Shōwa 54nendo.* Tokyo, Nitten, 1980.
NNW Measurement Committee. *Measuring Net National Welfare of Japan.* Tokyo, Economic Council of Japan, 1973.

Ōhashi Kiichi and Abe Bun'yū, eds. *Jiritsu engeki undō.* Tokyo, Miraisha, 1975.
Okochi, Takeshi. "The Theatrical Situation in Tokyo and the Imperial Theatre." Conference paper for International Box Office Managers Conference, Atlanta, January 1981.
Ongaku no Tomosha. *Ongaku nenkan.* Tokyo, Ongaku no Tomosha, annual.
Ortolani, Benito. "Fukuda Tsuneari: Modernization and Shingeki," in Donald H. Shively, ed., *Tradition and Modernization in Japanese Culture,* pp. 463-499. Princeton, Princeton University Press, 1971.
―――. "Shingeki: the Maturing New Drama of Japan," in Joseph Roggendorf, ed., *Studies in Japanese Culture,* pp. 163-186. Tokyo, Sophia University, 1963.
Ōsaka Ongaku Daigaku. *Kansai ongaku bunka shiryō,* 4 vols. Osaka, Ōsaka Ongaku Daigaku, 1972-1975.
―――. *Nishi Nihon ongaku bunka shiryō.* Osaka, Ōsaka Ongaku Daigaku, annual.
Ozaki Hirotsugu. "Shingeki II," in Tsugami Tadashi et al., eds., *Engekiron kōza,* 1, *engekishi, Nihonhen,* pp. 157-208. Kyoto, Sekibunsha, 1976.

Palsson, Roland. "Cultural Policy for an Open Society," in Stephen A. Greyser, ed., *Cultural Policy and Arts Administration,* pp. 6-30. Cambridge, Mass., Harvard Summer School Institute in Arts Administration, Harvard University Press, 1973.
Petit, Gaston. *Evolving Techniques in Japanese Woodblock Prints.* New York and Tokyo, Kodansha International, 1977.
Phillips, Anthony. "The Arts, Economics and Politics: Four National Perspectives," in Aspen Institute for Humanistic Studies, *The*

Arts, Economics and Politics: Four National Perspectives, pp. 1-22. New York, Aspen Institute for Humanistic Studies, 1975.

Poggi, Jack. *Theater in America: The Impact of Economic Forces, 1870-1967.* Ithaca, Cornell University Press, 1968.

Powell, Brian. "Japan's First Modern Theatre—the Tsukiji Shōgekijō and Its Company, 1924-1926." *Monumenta Nipponica,* XXX, 1, spring 1975, pp. 69-85.

Print Communicator.

Project Costs for Dance Theatre of Harlem in Japan 1981 (Revised).

Pronko, Leonard C. "Kabuki Today and Tomorrow." *Comparative Drama,* VI, 2, summer 1972, pp. 103-114.

Rekishi kōron.

Richie, Donald. "Japan's Avant-Garde Theatre." *Japan Foundation Newsletter,* April-May 1979, pp. 1-4.

Rimer, J. Thomas. *Modern Japanese Fiction and Its Traditions: An Introduction.* Princeton, Princeton University Press, 1978.

———. *Toward a Modern Japanese Theatre: Kishida Kunio.* Princeton, Princeton University Press, 1974.

Roberts, Laurance P. *Roberts' Guide to Japanese Museums.* New York and Tokyo, Kodansha International, 1978.

"Rōen undō no mondaiten." *Kokumin bunka,* no. 207, February 1977, pp. 12-15.

Rothstein, Edward. *New York Times Book Review,* July 29, 1979, p. 3.

Sakisaka Masahisa. "Kigyō to ongaku no kakawariai." *Ongaku geijutsu,* November 1980, pp. 60-63.

Santorī. *Santorī 80nen no ayumi.* Osaka, Santorī, 1979.

Santorī Bunka Zaidan nyūsu.

Sasaki Yoshihisa. "Bunkachō joseikin no haibun." *Ongaku geijutsu,* October 1980, pp. 32-35.

Satō Shigeru. "Atsugi Bonjinron." *Modan dansu,* no. 9, summer 1971, pp. 33-37.

———. "Mitsu no risaitaru." *Modan dansu,* no. 13, winter 1974, pp. 32-33.

Satō Torao. "Bunkachō Tōkyōto josei no gendai buyō kōen no hensen," in Gendai Buyō Kyōkai, *Nihon gendai buyō nenkan,* pp. 53-55. Tokyo, Gendai Buyō Kyōkai, 1975.

Schonberg, Harold C. *New York Times Book Review,* December 16, 1979, p. 13.

Segi Shin'ichi. *Shakai no naka no bijutsu.* Tokyo, Tōkyō Shoseki, 1978.

Seibu Bijutsukan. *Nihon gendai bijutsu no tenbō.* Tokyo, Seibu Bijutsukan, 1975.

307

Seibu Museum of Art. *Seibu Museum of Art Year in Review,* 1976-1977 and 1978-1979. Tokyo, Seibu Museum of Art, 1978 and 1980.

Shell Oil Corporation. *Dai24kai Sheru bijutsushō sakuhin kōbo.* Tokyo, Shell Oil Corporation, 1980.

———. *Dai24kai Sheru bijutsushōten.* Tokyo, Shell Oil Corporation, 1980.

Shibata Masashi. *Ongaku to bunka.* Tokyo, Ayumi Shuppan, 1974.

Shikaumi, Nobuya. *Cultural Policy in Japan.* Paris, UNESCO, 1970.

Shingeki.

Shingekidan Kyōgikai. *Kaihō.* Tokyo, Shingekidan Kyōgikai, monthly.

Soka Gakkai News.

Sorgenfrei, Carol Jay. "Shuji Terayama: Avant Garde Dramatist of Japan." Ph.D. dissertation, University of California, Santa Barbara, 1978.

Sōrifu Tōkeikyoku. *Nihon tōkei nenkan.* Tokyo, Sōrifu Tōkeikyoku, annual.

Star Dancers Ballet Company. *Star Dancers Ballet.* Tokyo, Star Dancers Ballet Company, 1980.

Statistical Handbook of Japan. See Japan, Office of the Prime Minister.

Sumishō nyūsu.

Sumitomo Corporation News.

Sumitomo Quarterly.

Takashina, Shuji. "Modern Sculpture," in Shuji Takashina, Yoshiaki Tono, and Hideo Tomiyama, eds., *Art in Japan Today,* pp. 11-15. Tokyo, Japan Foundation, 1974.

Takaya, Ted T., ed. and trans. *Modern Japanese Drama: An Anthology.* New York, Columbia University Press, 1979.

Takeda Michitarō. *Nihon kindai bijutsushi.* Tokyo, Kondō Shuppansha, 1969.

Tanaka Minoru. *Foundations in Japan: Their Legal Provisions and Tax Regulations.* Tokyo, Japan Center for International Exchange, 1975.

Tateda Hitonari. "Tōkei kara mita saikin no ongaku daigaku." *Ongaku geijutsu,* May 1980, pp. 34-39.

Terada, Toru. *Japanese Art in World Perspective,* trans. by Thomas Guerin. New York and Tokyo, Weatherhill/Heibonsha, 1976.

Time.

Tōbi Kenkyūjo. *Tōkyō bijutsu ichibashi.* Tokyo, Tōkyō Bijutsu Kurabu, 1979.

Toffler, Alvin. *The Culture Consumers: A Study of Art and Affluence in America.* Baltimore, Penguin Books, 1965.

Toita, Yasuji. *Kabuki: The Popular Theater*, trans. by Don Kenny. New York and Tokyo, John Weatherhill, Inc. and Kyoto, Tankosha, 1974.

Tōkyō Bunka Kaikan. *Yōran 1979*. Tokyo, Tōkyō Bunka Kaikan, 1979.

Tōkyō Fuiruhāmonī Kōkyō Gakudan teiki ensōkai No. 218, September 10, 1980.

Tōkyō hataraku mono no engekisai, annual.

Tōkyō Kokuritsu Kindai Bijutsukan. *Tōkyō Kokuritsu Kindai Bijutsukan yōran*. Tokyo, Tōkyō Kokuritsu Kindai Bijutsukan, 1977.

Tokyo Metropolitan Government. *Education in Tokyo*. Tokyo, Tokyo Metropolitan Government, 1979.

Tōkyō Onkyō. *Tōkyō Ongaku Bunka Kyōkai ni tsuite*. Tokyo, Tōkyō Onkyō, 1980.

————. *Tōkyō Onkyō ni tsuite*. Tokyo, Tōkyō Onkyō, 1977.

————. *Tōkyō Onkyō nyūkai no shiori*. Tokyo, Tōkyō Onkyō, 1980.

Tōkyō Rōen. *Reikai wa anata no ippyō de kimaru!* Tokyo, Tōkyō Rōen, 1980.

Tōkyō Rōon. *Tōkyō Rōon kiyaku*. Tokyo, Tōkyō Rōon, 1974.

————. *Tōkyō Rōon nyūkai no shiori*. Tokyo, Tōkyō Rōon, 1977.

Tōkyōto, Kyōikuchō, Shakai Kyōikubu, Bunkaka. *'80 Tomin Geijutsu Fuesuteibaru*. Tokyo, Tōkyōto, 1980.

————. *'81 Tomin Geijutsu Fuesuteibaru*. Tokyo, Tōkyōto, 1981.

————. *'81 Tomin Geijutsu Fuesuteibaru jigyō naiyō*. Tokyo, Tōkyōto, 1980.

————. *'81 Tomin Geijutsu Fuesuteibaru sanka kōen no gaiyō*. Tokyo, Tōkyōto, 1980.

Tōkyōto Bijutsukan. *Tōkyōto Bijutsukan yōran, Shōwa 54nendo*. Tokyo, Tōkyōto Bijutsukan, 1980.

Tomars, Adolph S. "Class Systems and the Arts," in Werner J. Cahnman and Alvin Boskoff, eds., *Sociology and History: Theory and Research*, pp. 472-483. New York, The Free Press of Glencoe, 1964.

————. *Introduction to the Sociology of Art*. Mexico City, privately published, 1940.

Tomin Gekijō. *Tomin Gekijō Kaiin no shiori*. Tokyo, Tomin Gekijō, 1980.

————. *Tomin Gekijō 30nenshi*. Tokyo, Tomin Gekijō, 1976.

Tomin Gekijō.

Tomiyama, Hideo. "Art in Postwar Japan: 1945-1972," in Shuji Takashina, Yoshiaki Tono, and Hideo Tomiyama, eds., *Art in Japan Today*, pp. 197-208. Tokyo, Japan Foundation, 1974.

Tono, Yoshiaki. "Artists in the Early Sixties," in Shuji Takashina,

309

Yoshiaki Tono, and Hideo Tomiyama, eds., *Art in Japan Today*, pp. 16-21. Tokyo, Japan Foundation, 1974.

Tsunematsu Yukitoshi. "Nihon no ongaku shakai no genjō to masu medeia to seishōnen mondai." *MS*, 1979.

———. "Ongakuka shōgai no sōkessan." *Ongaku geijutsu*, May 1979, pp. 44-49.

Varley, H. Paul. *Japanese Culture: A Short History*. New York, Praeger Publishers, expanded ed., 1977.

Warner, Langdon. *The Enduring Art of Japan*. Cambridge, Mass., Harvard University Press, 1952.

Yamano Hakudai. "Baree no gaikyō," in Zen Nihon Buyō Rengō Buyō Nenkan Iinkai, *Buyō nenkan*, I, 1977, pp. 36-40. Tokyo, Zen Nihon Buyō Rengō, 1977.

———. "Nihon no baree chizu wa kore kara dō kawaru ka." *Modan dansu*, no. 13, winter 1974, pp. 11-16.

Yamashita Fumio. *Atarashii seiji to bunka*. Tokyo, Shin Nihon Shuppansha, 1975.

Yamazaki, Masakazu. *Mask and Sword: Two Plays for the Contemporary Japanese Theatre*, trans. by J. Thomas Rimer. New York, Columbia University Press, 1980.

Yomiuri Shinbun Hyakunenshi Henshū Iinkai. *Yomiuri shinbun hyakunenshi*, 2 vols. Tokyo, Yomiuri Shinbunsha, 1976.

Yomiuri Shinbunsha. *Yomiuri nenkan*. Tokyo, Yomiuri Shinbunsha, annual.

Zen Nihon Amachua Engeki Kyōgikai. *Amateur Theatre in the World*. Yokohama, Zen Nihon Amachua Engeki Kyōgikai, 1975.

Zen Nihon Buyō Rengō Buyō Nenkan Iinkai. *Buyō nenkan*. Tokyo, Zen Nihon Buyō Rengō, annual.

Zenkoku Bunka Dantai Renmei. *Zenkoku Bunka Dantai Renmei (Zenbunren) to Onkyō undō ni tsuite*. Tokyo, Zenkoku Bunka Dantei Renmei, 1980.

Zenkoku Kinrōsha Ongaku Kyōgikai Renraku Kaigi. *Ii ongaku o yasuku ōku no hitobito ni*. Tokyo, Zenkoku Kinrōsha Ongaku Kyōgikai Renraku Kaigi, 1974.

Zenkoku Rōen Kanjikai. *Zenkoku Rōen no jūnen, 1963-1973*. Tokyo, Zenkoku Rōen Renraku Kaigi, 1973.

Zenkoku Rōen nyūsu.

Zenkoku Rōon Renraku Kaigi. *Rōon undō shōshi*. Tokyo, Zenkoku Rōon Renraku Kaigi, 1968.

Zusetsu Nihon bunkashi taikei, XIII, *gendai*. Tokyo, Shōgakukan, 1968.

INDEX

BY THE SAME AUTHOR

Nishi Amane and Modern Japanese Thought,
Princeton University Press, 1970

Farm and Nation in Modern Japan:
Agrarian Nationalism, 1870-1940,
Princeton University Press, 1974

Valley of Darkness: The Japanese People and World War Two,
W. W. Norton & Company, Inc., 1978

The Historical Encyclopedia of World War II (coauthor),
Facts-on-File Publications, 1980

Library of Congress Cataloging in Publication Data

Havens, Thomas R. H.
  Artist and patron in postwar Japan.

  Includes bibliographical references and
index.
  1. Art patronage—Japan.   2. Arts, Japanese.
3. Arts—Japan.   I. Title.
NX705.5.J3H38   700′.7952   82-47598
ISBN 0-691-05363-4   AACR2